Broadman Comments, 1991-92

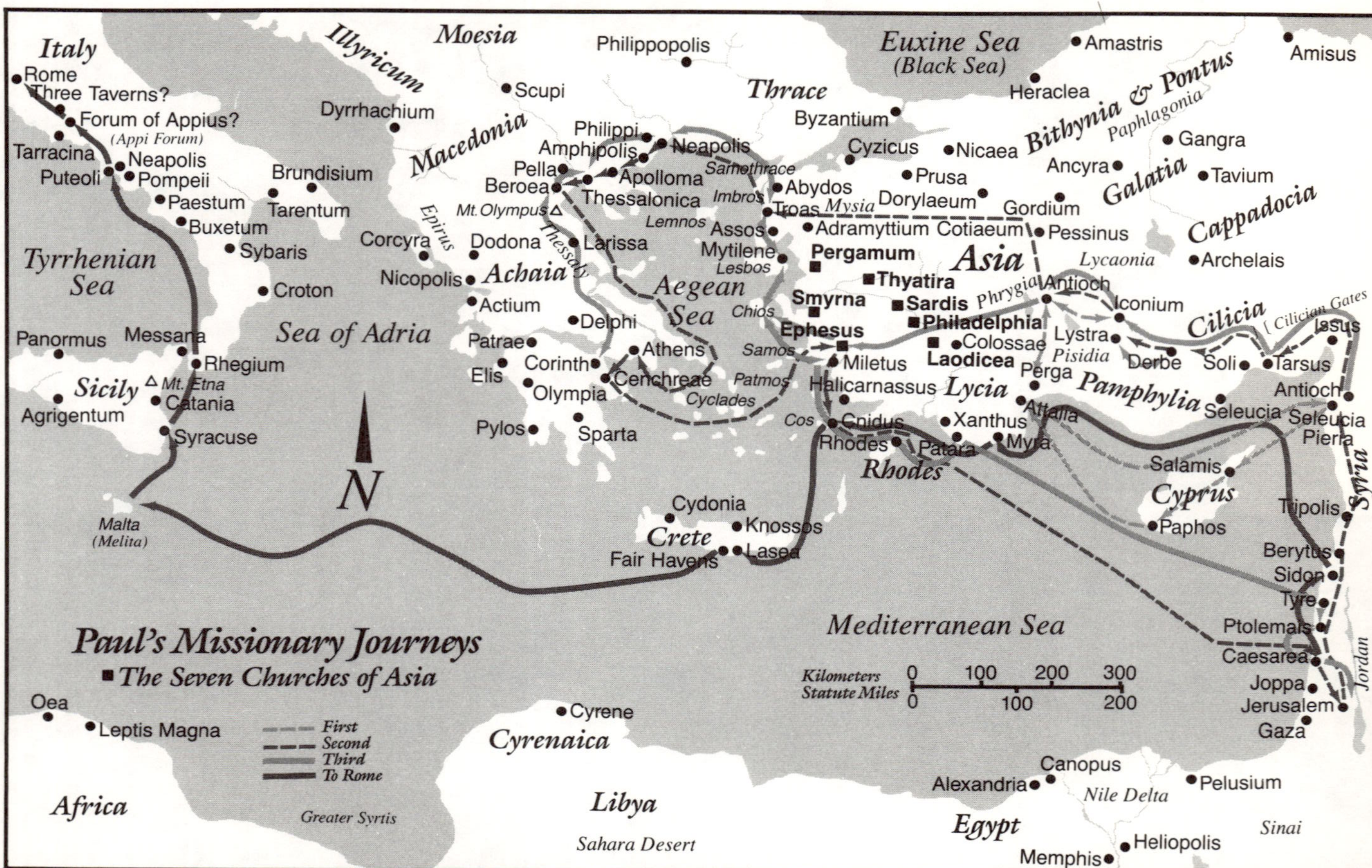
Paul's Missionary Journeys
■ The Seven Churches of Asia
First
Second
Third
To Rome
Kilometers 0 100 200 300
Statute Miles 0 100 200
N
Italy
Rome
Three Taverns?
Forum of Appius?
(Appi Forum)
Tarracina
Neapolis
Puteoli
Pompeii
Paestum
Buxetum
Brundisium
Tarentum
Sybaris
Croton
Tyrrhenian Sea
Messana
Rhegium
Panormus
Sicily
Mt. Etna
Catania
Agrigentum
Syracuse
Malta
(Melita)
Sea of Adria
Illyricum
Moesia
Dyrrhachium
Scupi
Macedonia
Epirus
Corcyra
Nicopolis
Actium
Dodona
Achaia
Philippopolis
Philippi
Amphipolis
Neapolis
Pella
Apolloma
Beroea
Thessalonica
Mt. Olympus
Thessaly
Larissa
Delphi
Patrae
Corinth
Elis
Olympia
Pylos
Sparta
Athens
Cenchreae
Cyclades
Aegean Sea
Samothrace
Imbros
Lemnos
Lesbos
Chios
Samos
Patmos
Cos
Thrace
Byzantium
Euxine Sea
(Black Sea)
Heraclea
Amastris
Amisus
Bithynia & Pontus
Paphlagonia
Gangra
Cyzicus
Nicaea
Ancyra
Galatia
Tavium
Abydos
Prusa
Troas
Mysia
Dorylaeum
Gordium
Cappadocia
Assos
Adramyttium
Cotiaeum
Pessinus
Mytilene
Pergamum
Asia
Lycaonia
Archelais
Thyatira
Smyrna
Sardis
Phrygia
Antioch
Iconium
Cilicia
Cilician Gates
Ephesus
Philadelphia
Colossae
Lystra
Issus
Miletus
Laodicea
Pisidia
Derbe
Soli
Tarsus
Halicarnassus
Lycia
Perga
Pamphylia
Antioch
Seleucia
Seleucia
Pieria
Cnidus
Xanthus
Attalia
Rhodes
Patara
Myra
Rhodes
Salamis
Cyprus
Paphos
Syria
Tripolis
Berytus
Sidon
Tyre
Ptolemais
Caesarea
Joppa
Jerusalem
Gaza
Jordan
Cydonia
Crete
Knossos
Fair Havens
Lasea
Mediterranean Sea
Oea
Leptis Magna
Africa
Greater Syrtis
Cyrene
Cyrenaica
Libya
Sahara Desert
Alexandria
Canopus
Nile Delta
Pelusium
Egypt
Memphis
Heliopolis
Sinai

Broadman Comments

1991-92

on
THE INTERNATIONAL
BIBLE LESSONS

for
Christian Teaching

CONVENTION UNIFORM SERIES

by
Donald F. Ackland
Brian L. Harbour
Polly Cooper

BROADMAN PRESS
NASHVILLE, TENNESSEE

4215-87
ISBN: 08054-1587-4

Dewey Decimal Classification: 268.61
Subject Heading: SUNDAY SCHOOL LESSONS—COMMENTARIES

Library of Congress Catalog Card Number: 45-437
Printed in the United States of America

Abbreviations and Translations

GNB	From the *Good News Bible,* the Bible in Today's English Version. Old Testament: Copyright © American Bible Society 1976; New Testament: Copyright © American Bible Society 1966, 1971, 1976. Used by permission.
KJV	*King James Version*
NASB	From the *New American Standard Bible.* © The Lockman Foundation, 1960, 1962, 1963, 1968, 1971, 1972, 1973, 1975, 1977. Used by permission.
NIV	From the Holy Bible, *New International Version,* copyright © 1973, 1978, 1984 by International Bible Society. Used by permission.
NRSV	From the *New Revised Standard Version Bible* copyright © 1989, by the Division of Christian Education of the National Council of Churches of Christ in the United States of America, and used by permission.
RSV	From the *Revised Standard Version of the Bible* copyright 1946, 1952, © 1971, 1973 by the National Council of the Churches of Christ in the U.S.A., and used by permission.
TLB	Verses marked TLB are taken from *The Living Bible.* Copyright © Tyndale House Publishers, Wheaton, Illinois, 1971. Used by permission.

Foreword

This is your opportunity to become more acquainted with Paul, the great missionary to the Gentiles. It would also be a great time to read the Book of Acts at one sitting. To do so would give you a look at the early church from Jesus' ascension to Paul's imprisonment in Rome. This reading could give you a new appreciation for the powerful work of the Holy Spirit in the life of the early church. The theme is "From the Damascus Road to Rome."

From December through February you will get an introduction to the "Songs and Prayers of the Bible." This is not a well-known subject among Christians. Perhaps it will be a time of growth for you.

In March and April, you will have eight lessons from the Gospel of Mark. Set yourself a goal to read straight through Mark before studying these lessons. Entitled "The Strong Son of God," these eight lessons show Jesus as a person of action. You will thrill again to see how Jesus brought the full redemptive power of God to bear on humanity's sin.

Beginning the last Sunday of April and going through May, you will study 1 and 2 Peter as they relate to "God's People in the World." The focus is a believing church living the resurrection life in a sinful and hurtful world.

In June and most of July, the little-known prophets Obadiah, Jonah, Nahum, Habakkuk, and Zephaniah will be studied under the theme, "God's Judgment and Mercy." Although little known, the messages of these prophets are still needed today.

This year of Bible study concludes with a study of 1 and 2 Timothy and Titus. "Guidelines for Ministry" will give you an opportunity to translate guidelines for ministry given to Timothy and Titus into useful daily ministries today.

What an opportunity for growth! From the well-known Paul to the little-known prophets, from the well-known Gospel of Mark to the little-known songs and prayers of the Bible, there is room for new knowledge, new understanding, and new ministry. Study of the Word of God can do all of that—and more.

May God bless the writers of these materials that make up *Broadman Comments*. May He also bless you who use these materials to grow in the knowledge of the Lord in order to minister to a dying world.

Contents

September, October, November 1991

From the Damascus Road to Rome

Aids from BROADMAN for Studying and Teaching

Books:
The Heart of the New Testament, H. I. Hester
The Book of Acts, Frank Stagg
The Broadman Bible Commentary, Volume 10
Layman's Bible Book Commentary, Volume 19

INTRODUCTION

The apostle Paul was fortunate in having a friend to record his story. Although Luke's purpose in the Book of Acts was more than biographical, from its ninth chapter onward it does unfold the remarkable story of how an enemy of Christ and His gospel became their greatest messenger. We shall study this story in four units.

"Chosen by God" (Unit I) has a strong evangelistic emphasis as it deals with Paul's conversion and his early witnessing.

"Emerging Leader" (Unit II) introduces us to the apostle's first recorded sermon. In two following lessons we will consider difficulties and dangers in missionary work, both from outside and within the Christian fellowship.

"Traveling Preacher" (Unit III) contains four lessons in which the trials and triumphs of Christ's messenger are vividly portrayed. Reaching out beyond Asia Minor, Paul visited great Gentile centers such as Philippi and Athens.

"Destination: Rome" (Unit IV) takes us to the end of Luke's story as Paul is falsely accused and arrested, and he appeals to Rome for justice. His detention in Rome proved to be a victory for the gospel.

September 1

A Chosen Instrument of God

Basic Passages: Acts 7:54—8:3; 9:1-22

Focal Passage: Acts 9:1-16

The story of Christianity contains many heroes. They are men and women whose contribution to the cause of Christ provides, at the human level, an explanation for its amazing progress from a small, persecuted group in Jerusalem to a worldwide fellowship of great diversity and influence. Foremost among these stands a man named Paul, originally known as Saul of Tarsus. We have no formal biography of this man, and there are gaps in our knowledge about his life; but this lack is more than compensated by the abundance of material in the New Testament that relates to his ministry as Christ's apostle to the Gentiles. A record of his conversion and subsequent journeys throughout the Roman world in the task of founding churches is found in Acts, a book written by Luke the physician, Paul's friend and companion. Acts is followed by thirteen letters written by the apostle, chiefly to those churches, in which the writer himself is clearly mirrored and his teaching explained and elaborated. Our studies this quarter focus on Acts and its developing story of this giant in the faith.

Study Aim: *To reacquaint us with the evidence in Saul's story of the power of the risen Christ to transform lives*

STUDYING THE BIBLE

At first, the Christian church in Jerusalem was thoroughly Jewish. But it contained two parties, described in Acts 6:1 as "Grecians" and "Hebrews." The former, also known as "Hellenists," were Greek-speaking Jews, many of them natives of countries outside Palestine. The "Hebrews" were Palestinians by birth and residence, firmly committed to the traditions of race and religion, although accepting Jesus as the Messiah. Among the Hellenists was Stephen, one of the seven chosen to "serve tables" (Acts 6:1-8). He proved to be the first Christian activist whose understanding of the teaching of our Lord brought him into conflict with other Jews. He was stoned to death as a blasphemer, a grim event that introduces us to a young man "whose name was Saul" who is described as "consenting unto his death" (7:58).

I. Saul the Persecutor (Acts 7:54—8:3)

The statement just quoted has raised the question as to whether Saul was a member of the Sanhedrin, the ruling body of the Jews, described as "the council" in 6:15. Had this been so, one would expect him to have mentioned it in a passage like Philippians 3:4-6. Probably we should read no more into it than that Saul gave his assent to the execution of Stephen, which he demonstrated by minding the clothes of those who cast the stones (7:58). Our knowledge of Saul's background is limited to a few statements, such as that just quoted from Philippians and Acts 21:39; 22:3. When, after the death of Stephen, a campaign of persecution against other Christians was launched, Saul committed himself fully to this endeavor. Hellenist Christians were at first the chief target, the phrase "except the apostles" (8:1) indicating that the core of the Jerusalem church was not affected. It continued to adhere to many traditional Jewish practices, including attendance at the Temple, and thus had "favor with all the people" (2:47). This, of course, was to change; but for the time, Hellenists were considered extremists, and they were scattered widely by persecution. Saul's earliest efforts were against those of this group who remained in Jerusalem and its environs.

II. The Road to Damascus (Acts 9:1-2)

Luke interrupted his story of Saul of Tarsus to tell about another member of the seven (6:1-7) whose Greek name, Philip, suggests that he too was a Hellenistic Jew. Philip was one of many who fled Jerusalem to escape the persecution in which Saul was now engaged (8:3-4). He took refuge in a city of Samaria and there "preached Christ" (v. 5) and performed miracles. This witness bore results. After leaving Samaria, Philip encountered "a man of Ethiopia" (v. 27) and led him to the Lord. This early spirit of evangelism was reaching out and breaking down boundaries. But the adversary was also at work, and Saul was his willing tool.

> **1 And Saul, yet breathing out threatenings and slaughter against the disciples of the Lord, went unto the high priest,**
>
> **2 And desired of him letters to Damascus to the synagogues, that if he found any of this way, whether they were men or women, he might bring them bound unto Jerusalem.**

The authority of the high priest extended beyond Jerusalem to synagogues in foreign countries. Saul took advantage of this provision, recognized and approved by the Romans, to request letters to synagogues in Damascus that would secure the extradition of Christians who had fled Jerusalem and taken up residence there. The description of Christianity as "the Way" ("any who belonged to the Way," v. 2, NRSV) introduces an early term used by believers for their movement, which they considered a way of life.

III. A Transforming Experience (Acts 9:3-9)

The crisis in Saul's life that changed him from a persecutor of Christians to a preacher of the gospel and founder of churches took place as he journeyed to Damascus. There he was confronted by the risen and glorified Christ. The experience was so real that he would later challenge others with the question: "Have I not seen Jesus Christ our Lord?" (1 Cor. 9:1). Later in the same epistle, having listed the appearances of the resurrected Son of God, Paul added, "last of all he was seen of me also" (15:8).

3 And as he journeyed, he came near Damascus: and suddenly there shined round about him a light from heaven:

4 And he fell to the earth, and heard a voice saying unto him, Saul, Saul, why persecutest thou me?

5 And he said, Who art thou, Lord? And the Lord said, I am Jesus whom thou persecutest: it is hard for thee to kick against the pricks.

6 And he trembling and astonished said, Lord, what wilt thou have me to do? And the Lord said unto him, Arise, and go into the city, and it shall be told thee what thou must do.

7 And the men which journeyed with him stood speechless, hearing a voice, but seeing no man.

8 And Saul arose from the earth; and when his eyes were opened, he saw no man: but they led him by the hand, and brought him into Damascus.

9 And he was three days without sight, and neither did eat nor drink.

This was more than a vision. It was an encounter. The incident is so clearly described, and its result so amazing, that little comment is called for beyond the clarification of a couple of points. An ox, in service on farmland, would be controlled and directed by a goad ("pricks," v. 5). The more the animal resisted, the more pain it would suffer from the sharp point. Saul was resisting pricks of conscience, probably since witnessing the martyrdom of Stephen. The apparent conflict between verse 7 and 22:9, "they heard not the voice of him that spake to me," is removed by assuming that Saul's companions heard the sound of a voice without recognizing words.

IV. The Mission of Ananias (Acts 9:10-16)

During his three days of sightless fasting, Saul experienced "a vision" of a man coming to him and restoring his sight (v. 12). That "vision" came true. God spoke to Ananias, a member of the Jewish Christian community in Damascus, telling him to go to "the street which is called Straight" (still in existence) and find Saul. Ananias was at first reluctant. He knew of Saul's purpose in journeying to the Syrian city. But God did not yield to the objection.

10 And there was a certain disciple at Damascus, named Ananias; and to him said the Lord in a vision, Ananias. And he said, Behold, I am here, Lord.

11 And the Lord said unto him, Arise, and go into the street which is called Straight, and inquire in the house of Judas for one called Saul, of Tarsus: for, behold, he prayeth,

12 And hath seen in a vision a man named Ananias coming in, and putting his hand on him, that he might receive his sight.

13 Then Ananias answered, Lord, I have heard by many of this man, how much evil he hath done to thy saints at Jerusalem:

14 And here he hath authority from the chief priests to bind all that call on thy name.

15 But the Lord said unto him, Go thy way: for he is a chosen vessel unto me, to bear my name before the Gentiles, and kings, and the children of Israel:

16 For I will show him how great things he must suffer for my name's sake.

Saul later described Ananias as "a devout man according to the law, having a good report of all the Jews" (22:12). Although Ananias has no continuing place in the Bible story, he is to be honored for risking his life to minister to the man who was to become Paul the apostle. He faithfully conveyed God's message to Saul, greeted him as a brother, and healed his blindness so that "something like scales" (v. 18, NRSV) fell from his eyes. Presumably, Ananias also baptized him (v. 18). Saul the persecutor thus became "a chosen vessel" with a new outlook. His major mission would be to Gentiles, although he would never fail to minister to his own people, as opportunity came.

V. Saul Begins to Witness (Acts 9:19-22)

Saul had left Jerusalem with high priestly authority to make prisoners of Christians found in the synagogues of Damascus (v. 2). As Christ's newly ordained apostle, he lost no time going to those same synagogues to witness to Christ as "the Son of God" (v. 20). By using this term, Paul affirmed the title that had been made the ground of accusation before Pilate (John 19:7), an affirmation that would be at the heart of his future preaching (Rom. 1:4).

APPLYING THE LESSON

Learning from those who suffer.—Howard Snyder and Daniel Runyon, in their book *Foresight* that highlights ten major trends dramatically affecting the future of Christians and the church, suggest that one of the major trends affecting the church in the world today is the move from Communist China to Christian China. Through much suffering and persecution, the Christian church in China is emerging with amazing strength. These two authors suggest seven lessons we can learn from the Chinese experience: the sovereignty of God in His world, the indestructibility of the body of Christ, the unshakable foundation of the Word of God, the purification that comes through suffering, the importance of prayer, the effectiveness of lay witness, and the impact of Christian love on community life.[1]

Most of those same lessons are apparent in the story of the persecution and oppression of the early church as it is described in the Book of Acts. The martyrdom of Stephen became the seedbed of growth in the life of the church.

Giving a witness for Christ.—Jim Elliot, martyred missionary to the Aucas in South America, once described missionaries as "a bunch of nobodies trying to exalt a Somebody." No better description can be found of these first Christians, men like Stephen and Philip and later Paul and Barnabas. They didn't have the Roman Road of salvation or the Four Spiritual Laws or Continued Witness Training or Evangelism Explosion. They were simply "a bunch of nobodies trying to exalt a Somebody."

Names for Christians.—Paul Powell points out that the Scriptures give five names to Christians: "believers, for their faith; brethren, for their love; disciples, for their knowledge; servants, for their work; and saints, for their holiness."[2] Before they were known by those names, Christians were known simply as followers of the Way.

Proof of the power of Christ.—Many years ago a famous Methodist preacher in London, Hugh Price Hughes, was a bold and controversial figure who attracted enemies as well as admirers. Once, a prominent agnostic challenged Reverend Hughes to a public debate. Hughes said he would accept, on one condition. Each speaker must bring to the platform as exhibits a score of persons whose lives had been changed for the better by their respective philosophies. The challenge went by default, for the agnostic never showed up, and the debate was never held.

Throughout his ministry, Paul pointed to the change in his life as the proof of the power of Christ (see particularly Acts 22; 26). When Paul's enemies in the church at Corinth asked for letters of recommendation to confirm the authenticity of his ministry, Paul told them that they were his living letters of recommendation (2 Cor. 3:2). Their changed lives were proof of the power of Christ that was manifest through the life and ministry of Paul.

The power of influence.—John Henry Jowett (1864-1923), was one of the greatest of the English Congregationalist preachers. His fame spread as he pastored the Carr's Lane Chapel in Birmingham, England, the Fifth Avenue Presbyterian Church in New York City, and the Westminster Chapel in London. He delivered the Yale Lectures on preaching in 1912, and, even today, he is still being quoted from the pulpits of America.

His biographer tells of a brief encounter with an anonymous man which set the direction of John Henry Jowett's life. As a young man, he was sitting in the Mechanics' Institute newsroom, poring over a book. An elderly gentleman, whom he had never seen before and never saw again, paused and looked over Jowett's shoulder to see what the boy was reading so attentively. Then, touching Jowett gently on the back, he said, "My boy, you must make your way to the university." He passed out of the room and out of Jowett's life, but the words rang in the boy's ears and became the motivation that sent him to the university and, eventually, to worldwide fame as a preacher of the gospel. In the same way, Ananias touched the life of Paul for just a brief moment, but his influence became the motivation that sent Paul out into the world and, eventually, to worldwide fame as a missionary for Jesus Christ.[3]

TEACHING THE CLASS

Main Idea: God's power to save extends to all people regardless of attitudes toward Him.

Suggested Teaching Aim: Learners will renew their belief that God can and will save people who rebel against Him.

Introduce the Bible Study

Use information from the introduction for an overview of the study for this quarter. State that the first unit presents an evangelistic emphasis.

Write *Paul* on the chalkboard. Invite learners to state any facts they can recall about Paul. Use information from the introduction to today's lesson about Paul and his work.

Ask: Who is the least likely candidate that you can think of to receive Christ as Savior? Elicit response. Continue with this rhetorical question: Who among your own acquaintances seems the least likely candidate for God to save? Allow a brief time for learners to consider the question.

State that Paul is one who would fit into that category. Continue: the study of Paul's conversion is designed to help us renew our belief that God can and will save persons regardless of current attitudes toward Him. Invite learners to turn to Acts 9.

Search for Biblical Truth

Use information from the introductory paragraphs of *Studying the Bible* to describe the church in these early days. Continue with the information about Saul of Tarsus. State that these facts now bring us to a very dramatic moment in Paul's life.

Write this outline on the chalkboard to guide the Bible searching:

A rebel against God (Acts 9:1-2)
A transforming experience (Acts 9:3-9)
A reluctant helper (Acts 9:10-16)
A flaming witness (Acts 9:19-22)

Share the information titled "Learning from those who suffer" (*Applying the Lesson*). State that out of a similar climate came the conversion of a man who would be used of God to shape the Christian world.

Call on someone to read Acts 9:1-2 aloud while otherss listen for words that describe Saul. Call for response. Ask: Would you consider this man a likely candidate for God to save? How would you describe his attitude toward God? Do you know anyone with similar attitudes?

Invite learners to discover how God dealt with these rebellious attitudes in Acts 9:3-9 as they read the verses silently. Call for response. Share the information titled "Proof of the power of Christ" (*Applying the Lesson*). Note that a transformed life is proof of the power of Christ in our lives today.

Call attention to the third line of the outline. Invite learners to read Acts 9:10-16 to learn about the role of the reluctant helper.Call for response. Share the story titled "The power of influence" (*Applying the Lesson*).

A Teaching Outline

1. Introduce study for the quarter and unit.
2. Identify "least likely" candidates for God to save.
3. Study the story of Paul's conversion, a least likely candidate.
4. Consider ways God might choose to bring the learners' least likely candidates to Himself.
5. Praise God that His power to save extends to all people.

Call on someone to read Acts 9:19-22 aloud to learn of the flaming witness. Ask: How could such a rebellious man become such a committed follower?

Give the Truth a Personal Focus

Suggest learners recall the "least likely" candidates they thought of as the study began. Direct them to think a moment about ways God might choose to bring those persons to Himself. Call for response.

Encourage learners to consider the love and grace of God that would bring such unlikely candidates to salvation. Express praise to

Him in prayer that His power to save extends to all people regardless of their attitudes toward Him.

---

1. Howard A. Snyder and Daniel V. Runyon, *Foresight* (Nashville: Thomas Nelson, 1986), 55-56.
2. Paul W. Powell, *The Nuts and Bolts of Church Growth* (Nashville: Broadman Press, 1982), 77.
3. Arthur Porritt, *John Henry Jowett* (George H. Doran Co., 1924), 11.

September 8

Barnabas and Saul

Basic Passages: Acts 9:26-30; 11:19-30; 12:25

Focal Passages: Acts 9:26-30; 11:19-26,29-30

In the matter of Bible biography, we are naturally inclined to make distinctions between major and minor characters. In Luke's historic narrative, the Book of Acts, Paul (formerly Saul) overshadows others such as Ananias, Barnabas, Mark, and Silas. There can be no objection to this so long as the service rendered by the lesser personalities is not minimized. As we have already realized, the contribution of the great apostle to the Gentiles was made possible by the performance of persons who appear, and then quickly disappear, from the stage of New Testament history. Barnabas is an outstanding example of this. Less than halfway through the record, his name is dropped (15:36-41), but the rest of the story would not have been possible apart from the relationship that developed between him and Saul. Barnabas reminds us that we do not need to have our names carved in granite to play our part in the ongoing redemptive program of Christ and His gospel.

Study Aim: *To encourage us to use what gifts we have, including that of friendship, to further the cause of Christ*

STUDYING THE BIBLE

The name of Barnabas appears early in the Acts narrative (4:36-37). When the young Christian community in Jerusalem was struggling with poverty, a Jew born in Cyprus, named Joseph, sold a piece of land that he owned and gave the proceeds to the common fund. He was nicknamed Barnabas, meaning either son of exhortation or consolation, in recognition of his friendly, generous spirit. The nature of the property is in doubt, but it could have been a burial lot.

I. Damascus to Jerusalem (Acts 9:26-30)

The immediate preceding verses tell how Saul escaped enemies by fleeing Damascus. He was let down the wall of the city in a basket and made his way back to Jerusalem, a hardly less dangerous place for him than Damascus. He needed a friend and found one in Barnabas.

> **26 And when Saul was come to Jerusalem, he assayed to join himself to the disciples: but they were all afraid of him, and believed not that he was a disciple.**
>
> **27 But Barnabas took him, and brought him to the apostles, and declared unto them how he had seen the Lord in the way, and that he had spoken to him, and how he had preached boldly at Damascus in the name of Jesus.**
>
> **28 And he was with them coming in and going out at Jerusalem.**
>
> **29 And he spake boldly in the name of the Lord Jesus, and disputed against the Grecians: but they went about to slay him.**
>
> **30 Which when the brethren knew, they brought him down to Caesarea, and sent him forth to Tarsus.**

1. A friend in need (vv. 26-28).—In Jerusalem, Saul found himself without a friend. His old associates regarded him as a traitor. Members of the church suspected him of posing as a convert in order to infiltrate their ranks and accuse them to their enemies. Fortunately, Barnabas came to his rescue. Barnabas was able to attest to the genuineness of Saul's claim, telling how he had "seen the Lord in the way" and immediately began to preach Christ in Damascus. Barnabas's testimony was believed, and Saul was able to move freely, "coming in and going out," among the believers.

2. Conflict and escape (vv. 29-30).—Saul appears to have taken the place of Stephen in witnessing to Greek-speaking Jews (Hellenists). The same group that had attacked Stephen (6:9-14) now turned their anger against Saul. Local Christians, now persuaded of Saul's genuineness, whisked him away, first to the coastal city of Caesarea, and then to his hometown of Tarsus. This thousand-year-old city of Cilicia had been made an outpost of Rome nearly one hundred years before. Its citizens were honored as Romans (16:37; 22:25) and enjoyed appropriate privileges. Tarsus also was renowned as a center of learning, hence Saul's famous understatement when he described himself as "a citizen of no mean city" (21:39). During the years that he remained in Tarsus, Paul engaged in a work of evangelism, a report of which reached the churches of Judea, "That he which persecuted us in times past now preacheth the faith which once he destroyed" (Gal. 1:23).

II. Great Events in Antioch (Acts 11:19-26)

While Saul was witnessing to his home folks, big things were happening in which he would play a major part. The scattering of believers, for which his persecuting zeal had been responsible, resulted in the preaching of the gospel in places as far apart as Phoenicia (modern Lebanon), Cyprus, and Syrian Antioch. At first, this preaching was confined to Jewish audiences, to which Jesus would be presented as the promised Messiah. But in Antioch, a broadening of mission began as some courageous souls included Gentiles in their evangelism. The fields were white unto harvest, and there was a great ingathering as a result.

> **19 Now they which were scattered abroad upon the persecution that arose about Stephen travelled as far as Phenice, and Cyprus, and Antioch, preaching the word to none but unto the Jews only.**
>
> **20 And some of them were men of Cyprus and Cyrene, which, when they were come to Antioch, spake unto the Grecians, preaching the Lord Jesus.**
>
> **21 And the hand of the Lord was with them: and a great number believed, and turned unto the Lord.**
>
> **22 Then tidings of these things came unto the ears of the church which was in Jerusalem: and they sent forth Barnabas, that he should go as far as Antioch.**
>
> **23 Who, when he came, and had seen the grace of God, was glad, and exhorted them all, that with purpose of heart they would cleave unto the Lord.**
>
> **24 For he was a good man, and full of the Holy Ghost and of faith: and much people was added unto the Lord.**
>
> **25 Then departed Barnabas to Tarsus, for to seek Saul:**
>
> **26 And when he had found him, he brought him unto Antioch. And it came to pass, that a whole year they assembled themselves with the church, and taught much people. And the disciples were called Christians first in Antioch.**

1. Mission of inquiry (vv. 22-24).—This enlargement of the church to include Gentiles must have been disturbing news to the apostles in Jerusalem. But they had been earlier prepared for this development when they sent two of their number to investigate Philip's activities in Samaria (8:14). This time, they made a wise choice in assigning the Antioch visit to Barnabas who immediately recognized that the Spirit of God was at work. He began to teach the new converts as he "exhorted them . . . that . . . they would cleave unto the Lord." Antioch, famous as the third largest city in the world, was a center of heathen worship steeped in sexual excesses. Young Christians needed encouragement, which Barnabas provided, to stand strong against temptation and in loyalty to their new master, the Lord Jesus.

2. Colleagues in ministry (vv. 25-26).—The task in Antioch soon outgrew Barnabas's ability to handle it alone. He began to look around for a helper, and his thoughts turned to Saul. We could assume that he had learned of the latter's evangelistic activities in Tarsus and felt him to be the man to respond to the challenge of Antioch. The words "seek" (v. 25) and "found" (v. 26) are strong enough in the Greek to indicate a demanding search. Had Paul been disowned by his family and, therefore, was not to be located in his parents' home? Whether or not this was the case, Barnabas sought until he found Saul, and he took Saul back with him to Antioch, where the two labored together for a year. The Antioch church so magnified the name of Christ that "the disciples were called Christians."

III. Return to Jerusalem (Acts 11:27-30)

The New Testament refers several times to prophets, people who had special revelations from God that they communicated to others. One such person, named Agabus, visited Antioch and foretold a great famine, which actually took place during the reign of Claudius Caesar (A.D. 41-54).

> **29 Then the disciples, every man according to his ability, determined to send relief unto the brethren which dwelt in Judea:**
> **30 Which also they did, and sent it to the elders by the hands of Barnabas and Saul.**

The gospel that had brought such joy to many in Antioch had its origin in Jerusalem. Gentile converts, therefore, felt a debt of gratitude toward the Jerusalem church. They dipped into their pockets to show that gratitude in a practical way and sent the collection by their two eminent leaders, Barnabas and Saul. Thus Saul was involved in a cause that would engage him in the years to come. He promoted "the collection for the saints" (1 Cor. 16:1) in the churches he founded, thus creating a bond between the mother church, which was Jewish, and the Gentile churches of the New Testament world. Raymond Bryan Brown wrote: "In four letters Paul mentions an offering to be taken among the churches he established and to be sent to the poor Christians in Jerusalem . . . Probably the various pressures on the impoverished Christians in Jerusalem made their need of financial assistance acute. . . . The offering was an excellent way to demonstrate the unity of the church."[1] As our passage shows, this fund, that was maintained throughout the apostle's ministry, had its beginning in the response of the Christians of Antioch to an urgent need brought on by famine.

V. Back Again to Antioch (Acts 12:25)

Luke's narrative reminds us that while the gospel was having successes in one area, it was suffering setbacks in others. Acts 12 begins, "Now about that time Herod the king stretched forth his hands to vex certain of the church." James, brother of the apostle John, was put to the sword. Peter was imprisoned and would probably have suffered the same fate had he not been delivered from prison. These severe actions were taken because Herod "saw it pleased the Jews" (v. 3). Thus those who had stoned Stephen found an ally in Herod Agrippa I. But while that king died a miserable death (vv. 20-23), the record of Luke reads, "The word of God grew and multiplied" (v. 24). Future growth of the Christian movement would outpace anything yet experienced, and it was to have its beginnings in Antioch, to which city Barnabas and Saul returned after their visit of mercy to Jerusalem. They took with them a young man, John Mark, to whom reference will be made in our next lesson. For now, tribute must be paid to Barnabas, soon to disappear from Luke's story. Barnabas was the man who helped to launch the great ministry of the apostle to the Gentiles, known first as Saul, but more readily recognized as Paul.

APPLYING THE LESSON

Every little bit helps.—I read an anonymous piece once that went something like this: "There was a man named Little. Mr. Little was married to a woman whose name was Mrs. Little. Mr. and Mrs. Little had seven little Littles. They lived in a little town where Mr. Little taught in a little school for which he received a little salary. One day somebody asked Mr. Little how he and Mrs. Little and the seven little Littles got along on such a little salary, and he said, 'Every little bit helps!' "

That is a beautiful statement about the Christian church. Billy Sunday once said, "It is amazing God is doing as well as He is with the crowd He has to work with." Yet, God has always used "little" people to carry out His kingdom work, because every little bit helps.

The importance of friends.—William Barclay, Scottish preacher and popular expositor of Scripture, explained in his autobiography one of the keys to his productive life. Barclay told of an encounter of Socrates with a simple old man. Socrates asked the old man for what he was most thankful. The old man answered, "That being such as I am I have had the friends I have had." Barclay then concluded, "And as I look back that is exactly how I feel."[2]

The name that stands out as the most prominent name in the New Testament, apart from that of the Master Himself, is the name Paul. However, we cannot understand him without understanding his friends.

Passing it on.—Someone has referred to the gospel as "hot-potato news." If someone tosses a hot potato to us, we don't hold it for long. We pass it on. We don't discuss its relative merits. We pass it on. We don't stick it into our pockets. We pass it on. That's the way it is with the gospel. The gospel is not something to hear and keep. It is something to hear and repeat. We have to pass it on. Paul is a good illustration of this truth. After having received the good news, he immediately began to pass it on.

Hard to get in.—Dwight Moody filled an aristocratic church with a pew full of boys and girls from the street. It so disturbed the sophisticated members of the church that when Moody was presented for membership in the church, the board suggested that he think it over and pray about it for a month. The next month Moody came before the board again. "Did you follow our suggestions?" they asked him. "I certainly did," Moody replied. "And what did the Lord say?" Moody answered, "He told me not to feel bad about it because He has been trying to get into this church Himself for the last twenty-five years!"

We often have a hard time accepting those who are not "our kind." This was also a problem in the early church. The Jewish Christians were suspicious of the Gentile Christians because they were not their "kind."

What God promises.—Tim Hansel in his book *Holy Sweat* says that God promises us four things: peace, power, purpose . . . and trouble.[3] Preachers today focus more on the first three in the list than on the last one. However, both the proclamations of the Bible and the characters of the Bible confirm the truth of the fourth word in the list. God does not isolate us from problems. Rather, He provides the strength and endurance to prevail over our problems.

Paul provides an excellent example of this truth. No one was stronger in his faith than the apostle Paul. Yet, he explained in 2 Corinthians 12:7 that he had a thorn in the flesh from which God would not deliver him. He prayed for God to remove the thorn so he could more fully serve Him. God responded, "I'm going to leave the thorn so you can more fully serve Me" (author's paraphrase).

Paul learned two lessons in the midst of his trouble. First, he learned that God's grace is sufficient. No matter what happened, God's grace went deeper than his problem. Second, he learned the true secret of spiritual power. Spiritual power comes not from us but from God. In our weakness, we can more fully experience the strength of God.

These first Christians experienced trouble. However, they endured in the midst of this trouble; and God used their troubles to deepen their faith and to spread the good news of Christ.

TEACHING THE CLASS

Main Idea: God uses the gifts and abilities of all types of people to bring men and women to Himself.

Suggested Teaching Aim: Learners will dedicate their gifts and abilities to be used by God to bring people to Himself.

Introduce the Bible Study

Write the name *Annie Sullivan* on the chalkboard. Ask: How many know who this person was? Ask for a show of hands. Write *Helen Keller* on the board. Ask learners to raise their hands if they know the identity of this person. (Annie Sullivan was Helen Keller's teacher.) Continue: Why do more of us recognize the name Helen Keller than Annie Sullivan? Elicit response.

Write the word *Star* beside Helen Keller. Write the words *Support Role* beside Annie Sullivan. Ask: Which is more important? Give time for response.

A Teaching Outline

1. Focus on "stars" and "supporting" roles.
2. Discover how God used a person in a supporting role to bring people to Himself.
3. Identify personal gifts and abilities that may be used by God to bring people to Himself.
4. Dedicate selves to being used of God to bring people to Himself.

State that just as has been illustrated with these two historical figures, God's work needs and uses both stars and supporting figures. Write the names *Barnabas* and *Paul* on the chalkboard. Note that God used the abilities of both of these men to bring people to Himself. One was a star. The other occupied a more supporting role.

Note that the purpose of the study for today is to lead each of us to recognize and dedicate our abilities for God's use in bringing people to Himself whether we function in a star role or a support role. Draw a circle around the name *Barnabas* and the words *support role.* State that today's study will focus on Barnabas and this function. Invite learners to open their Bibles to Acts 9.

Search for Biblical Truth

Call on three learners who have previously agreed to read these passages of Scripture aloud: Acts 9:26-30; Acts 11:19-26; and Acts 11:27-30. Direct learners to listen to discover some activities that filled the life of Barnabas. When the reading is finished, call for response. Share historical information from *Studying the Bible.* In noting the reservation of the church at Jerusalem to take Paul in, use the story titled "Hard to get in" (*Applying the Lesson*).

Direct learners to work with those sitting near them to review the

Scripture passages and to list the personal gifts, abilities, and characteristics of Barnabas. After several minutes for study, invite learners to share their conclusions. Write them on the chalkboard. Responses should be similar to the following: Honest, daring, (9:27, Barnabas risked befriending Saul. He spoke honestly of Paul's experience.) teaching, rejoicing (11:23), full of Holy Ghost, great faith (11:24), supporting (11:26, Barnabas brought Saul presumably because he was a "star."), trustworthy, and caring (11:29-30). Ask learners to explain reasons for their choices. Explain reasons for the above choices by using the Scriptures.

Give the Truth a Personal Focus

Share the story titled "Every little bit helps" (*Applying the Lesson*). State that each of us has something that will help in the work of God whether it qualifies us as stars or puts us in support roles.

Direct learners to write their name on paper you have provided for them. Continue by asking them to privately list their own gifts, abilities, and characteristics. After allowing several minutes for thoughtful reflection, state that these are those things learners have that may be offered to the Lord for His use. Note that this is exactly what Barnabas did. He did not ask for special abilities. He simply used who he was and what he was to help bring people to God. Share the comments titled "What God promises" (*Applying the Lesson*).

Conclude with the story titled "Passing it on" (*Applying the Lesson*). Invite learners to dedicate themselves to being used of God to tell others about Him.

---

1. Raymond Bryan Brown, "1 Corinthians" in *The Broadman Bible Commentary,* vol. 10 (Nashville: Broadman Press, 1970), 394.
2. William Barclay, *A Spiritual Autobiography* (Grand Rapids: Wm. B. Eerdmans Publishing Co., 1975), 14-15.
3. Tim Hansel, *Holy Sweat* (Waco: Word Books, 1987), 42.

September 15

A Sermon at Antioch of Pisidia

Basic Passages: Acts 13:1-3,13-52

Focal Passage: Acts 13:26-39

A number of towns in the United States are named Antioch. In Luke's story of the spread of the gospel there are two: Antioch in Syria and Antioch in Pisidia. This lesson will trace the outreach of the Christian message from one to the other. The record occupies the whole of Acts 13, too long a chapter for us to study in detail but too important for us to pass over its early verses without comment. While our printed passage is concerned with the message delivered, in this case to a largely Jewish audience, the chapter as a whole reveals the pattern of the campaign. After being commissioned by the Antioch (Syria) church, Barnabas took Saul to Cyprus, his native country (4:36) and, therefore, his "Jerusalem" (1:8). From there they journeyed to Asia Minor, which was to be the scene of so much of the apostle Paul's ministry. Jewish synagogues were still their primary choice for witnessing. But in Pisidian Antioch, hostility compelled Paul's exclamation, "Lo, we turn to the Gentiles" (v. 46). The Master's plan for "the uttermost part of the earth" (1:8) was being realized.

Study Aim: *To renew commitment to the gospel of the crucified and risen Christ as the message of salvation to Jew and Gentile*

STUDYING THE BIBLE

We have already made use of the name *Paul,* replacing Saul. In the Bible record, this change occurs in 13:13. The reference to Sergius Paulus (v. 7) has led some to assume that the apostle adopted this man's name. But it was not unusual for a person to have two names, in this case Saul (Jewish) and Paul (Roman). In view of the apostle's Gentile mission, the change was appropriate.

I. The Church in Syrian Antioch (Acts 13:1-3)

Here we are introduced to a local church, independent of Jerusalem, functioning under the leadership of the Holy Spirit, and engaging in pioneering missionary activity. The list of "prophets and teachers" is fascinating. Added to Barnabas and Saul are an African ("Niger" means "black") and an aristocrat who was raised in the court of the Herods. This church felt itself called to surrender its two principal leaders to the work of missions. The membership committed themselves to the support of the two by laying hands on them, not as a means of communicating power or authority, but as an expression of fellowship.

II. Barnabas's Home Territory (Acts 13:4-13)

Though the church commissioned the two missionaries, Luke was careful to point out that the real authority behind this was the Holy Spirit. So frequent are this writer's references to the Holy Spirit that some have proposed that his book should be named *The Acts of the Holy Spirit.* But, as Stagg says, "Certainly in Acts we have the account of something effected by the Holy Spirit—something which could not have been effected apart from the Holy Spirit. But Luke's concern surely was with that which was accomplished and not with the Spirit himself."[1] The immediate destination was Cyprus, a large island in the eastern Mediterranean of continuing importance to this day. John Mark accompanied the two senior men. He was son to Mary, in whose home Jerusalem Christians assembled (12:11-12), and a kinsman to Barnabas (Col. 4:10). Why Mark so soon left the missionary party (Acts 13:13) we are not told, though Paul regarded his defection serious enough to disqualify him from later service (15:38). The two men were subsequently reconciled (Philem. 24).

III. Ministry in Another Antioch (Acts 13:14-25)

When the Scripture says that "Paul and his company loosed from Paphos" (v. 13), it means that they took a ship from the island of Cyprus and sailed in a northerly direction for the mainland of Asia Minor (see map). They traveled inland as far as Perga, where John Mark left the party, and apparently nothing of note occurred. The next significant stop was at Antioch in Pisidia, a city that straddled the boundary between Phrygia and Pisidia. This Antioch was strategically situated on a lofty plateau and had been designated a Roman colony. It had a large Jewish population, and its synagogue became the scene of Paul's first recorded sermon. After the customary two readings from the Old Testament, Paul and Barnabas were invited to speak. On a second visit, Barnabas participated in the discussion (v. 46), but at this time, reference is made only to Paul's response. His congregation was mixed and consisted of "Men of Israel" (true Jews) and "ye that fear God" (Gentiles, known as God-fearers, who were drawn to the Jewish faith). Paul began his message with a brief review of the early history of the Jews, from the exodus to the appointment of David as king (vv. 17-22). Claim was then made that a descendant of David, "a Savior, Jesus," had come in fulfillment of divine promise and had been so proclaimed by John the Baptist, who called his listeners to repentance (vv. 23-25).

IV. Preaching Christ Crucified (Acts 13:26-37)

In these verses Luke has provided a sample of Paul's preaching to Jews and Jewish sympathizers. Before non-Jewish audiences he modified this message, but even before the sages of Athens he called for repentance (17:30). The crucified, risen Savior held the forefront in all Paul's preaching.

26 Men and brethren, children of the stock of Abraham, and whosoever among you feareth God, to you is the word of this salvation sent.

27 For they that dwell at Jerusalem, and their rulers, because they knew him not, nor yet the voices of the prophets which are read every sabbath day, they have fulfilled them in condemning him.

28 And though they found no cause of death in him, yet desired they Pilate that he should be slain.

29 And when they had fulfilled all that was written of him, they took him down from the tree, and laid him in a sepulcher.

30 But God raised him from the dead:

31 And he was seen many days of them which came up with him from Galilee to Jerusalem, who are his witnesses unto the people.

32 And we declare unto you glad tidings, how that the promise which was made unto the fathers,

33 God hath fulfilled the same unto us their children, in that he hath raised up Jesus again; as it is also written in the second psalm, Thou art my Son, this day have I begotten thee.

34 And as concerning that he raised him up from the dead, now no more to return to corruption, he said on this wise, I will give you the sure mercies of David.

35 Wherefore he saith also in another psalm, Thou shalt not suffer thine Holy One to see corruption.

36 For David, after he had served his own generation by the will of God, fell on sleep, and was laid unto his fathers, and saw corruption:

37 But he, whom God raised again, saw no corruption.

1. Sentence of death (vv. 26-29).—Recognizing the two groups in his congregation (vv. 16,26), Paul announced "the word of this salvation." In fulfillment of Old Testament prophecy, the Jerusalem leadership, in collaboration with Pilate, had condemned Jesus to death, "though they found no cause of death in him" (v. 28). Not for any fault that could be found in Him, Jesus died on "the tree," a description of the cross that echoed Deuteronomy 21:22-23. As in other references to our Lord's substitutionary death, Paul affirmed His burial, knowing that some in his audience accepted the false report that Jesus did not die but only swooned. Paul never avoided the offense of the cross, but he made a basic truth in all his preaching that the salvation God offers was made possible by the death of His Son: the guiltless for the guilty.

2. Resurrection to life (vv. 30-31).—The crucified and buried Christ was raised from the dead. This was Paul's bold claim, which he supported by telling of many witnesses of His resurrection. We should recognize that Luke's record of this sermon probably abbreviated what Paul said, so that he may have gone on to name himself as a witness (1 Cor. 15:8). Whether so or not, we know from other sources that the resurrection of our Lord was a major emphasis in all apostolic preaching.

3. Glad tidings (vv. 32-37).—The resurrection was Paul's "glad tidings," for what God had promised He had fulfilled. He quoted Psalms 2:7; 16:10; and Isaiah 55:3; and he argued that since David was long-time dead and buried, these passages had to be understood as referring not to him but to his descendant: Jesus of Nazareth, Messiah of His people.

V. Casting the Gospel Net (Acts 13:38-52)

Making a direct application of his message by addressing his hearers as "men and brethren" (v. 38), Paul issued an invitation and a warning. His invitation was to both forgiveness and justification, thus dealing with our sinfulness and our inability to help ourselves. He had once depended on the Mosaic law to give him acceptance before God. But after his conversion Paul lived to proclaim the good news that "what the law could not do, in that it was weak through the flesh, God sending his own Son in the likeness of sinful flesh, and for sin, condemned sin in the flesh: That the righteousness of the law might be fulfilled in us, who walk not after the flesh, but after the Spirit" (Rom. 8:3-4).

> **38 Be it known unto you therefore, men and brethren, that through this man is preached unto you the forgiveness of sins:**
> **39 And by him all that believe are justified from all things, from which ye could not be justified by the law of Moses.**

An invitation given is not necessarily an invitation accepted. Paul knew the disposition of human nature to postpone response, or reject truth outrightly. So, using more Old Testament quotations (Hab. 1:5;

Isa. 29:14), he spoke seriously of the consequences of despising the "glad tidings" he brought. His words made a deep impression on many of his hearers, Jews and "religious proselytes" alike (v. 43), the reference being not this time to God-fearers but to Gentiles who had fully embraced the Jewish faith and submitted to its rituals. Thus, in a Jewish synagogue, a great victory could be recorded for the gospel. But, as verses 44-52 show, another faction was at work and showed its hand the following Sabbath. So great was the hostility that Paul and Barnabas exclaimed, "Seeing ye put it from you, and judge yourselves unworthy of everlasting life, lo, we turn to the Gentiles" (v. 46). A great Gentile ingathering had begun (v. 48).

APPLYING THE LESSON

Let someone else do it.—Little Carla met the preacher as she came out of the drugstore in a little country town. She was eating an ice cream cone. The preacher said, "Carla, why didn't you give that money to missions?" Carla responded, "I've figured out a better way. I buy ice cream cones, and let the druggist give the money to missions!"

That's the approach many take to missions. Let someone else do it. Not the Christians at Antioch. They wanted to be personally involved, so they commissioned Paul and Barnabas to go out with the message of the gospel. They were directly involved in missions.

No power without God's power.—Every time a little boy in my church sees me he asks, "When are you going to preach about Samson?" Samson, the strong man, is one of children's favorite Bible characters. Yet the most intriguing part of Samson's story did not revolve around his strength but around his weakness. Delilah was determined to discern the secret of Samson's power. Three times she had begged Samson for his secret, and three times he had given her a false answer. Each time the Philistines would try to capture Samson, and each time he overpowered them with his strength. However, the fourth time Delilah approached him, he told her about his hair. He had made a vow to God not to have his hair cut. While he was asleep, she cut his locks. When the Philistines jumped on him, Samson thought he would overpower them as he had before. This time, however, his strength was gone, and he was captured. What happened? The biblical writer explained: "He did not know that the Lord had left him" (Judg. 16:20, NRSV). Samson was not powerful because of his own physical strength. He was powerful because of the strength of God within him, and he had no power without God's power.

Samson's experience is a picture of what often happens to us. We try to fight our battles in our own strength. Consequently, we are doomed to failure. Like Samson, we have no power without God's power.

Likewise, these first missionaries from Antioch went out in the power of the Holy Spirit, for they knew that they had no power without God's power.

Pointing to Jesus.—Vance Havner used to tell the story of two boats that passed each other on the Mississippi River one day. An old black man, who worked on one of the boats, said to a passenger, "Look, there's the captain. Years ago, we were going along like this when I fell overboard, and the captain rescued me. Ever since then I just love to point him out!"[2]

These first disciples had been rescued from their sin by Jesus Christ. He was their Savior. That's why their preaching centered on Him. Since He saved them, they just loved to point Him out!

The cross.—The preaching of the first Christians centered on the cross where Jesus died for our sins. What does the cross mean? To some it is simply a religious ornament to be worn around the neck. To the architect, the cross is a symbol used to adorn a church. To the skeptic, the cross is a superstition that needs to be discarded. To the Jews, Paul said, the cross was something to avoid. To the Gentiles, the cross was something to ridicule. Paul concluded, "But unto them which are called, both Jews and Greeks, Christ the power of God, and the wisdom of God" (1 Cor. 1:24).

Unwillingness to choose.—I ran across an interesting new term the other day: *catmatic.* What does it mean? It is the opposite of *dogmatic.* Dogmatic people are those who have opinions about everything and are always expressing those opinions. Catmatic persons are those who pussyfoot around! They can't make a decision. They are wishy-washy about everything.

In reality, even the catmatic person makes decisions. The failure to make a decision is a decision. This is particularly true in relationship to the gospel message. When a person hears the gospel, he or she has to make a choice. If one does not say yes to the gospel, he or she says no. A decision not to decide is a decision nevertheless.

TEACHING THE CLASS

Main Idea: Belief in Christ as Savior brings the salvation that the law of Moses could not bring.

Suggested Teaching Aim: Learners will determine what should be included in telling the unsaved about Jesus and decide to share that message.

Introduce the Bible Study

Write the unit title "Emerging Leader" on the chalkboard. State that in this unit we will see Paul begin his work and will experience with him some of the difficulties and dangers from both outside and within the Christian community.

Ask: If you were in Paul's shoes just beginning your mission to tell others about salvation through Jesus Christ, what would you include in the message? Elicit response. State that the Scripture for today's study begins with Paul's first recorded sermon. One purpose of this study is to discover what Paul said to his unsaved audience. A second purpose is to discover what we need to include when we discuss reliance on Christ for salvation with the unsaved around us. Invite learners to turn to Acts 13.

Search for Biblical Truth

Use the information from *Studying the Bible* to present the background experiences described in Acts 13:1-25 that lead up to Paul's first recorded sermon. Point out that the Christians at Antioch did not turn away from their responsibility to share the gospel. Therefore, they commissioned Paul and Barnabas to go for them. Share the information titled "Let someone else do it" (*Applying the Lesson*).

A Teaching Outline

1. Consider what needs to be told to an unsaved person.
2. Discover what Paul told the unsaved audience in his first sermon.
3. Decide what needs to be included in sharing Jesus with lost persons today.
4. Decide to share this information about Jesus with someone who is unsaved.

Call on a learner who has previously agreed to read aloud this first recorded sermon (Acts 13:26-39) from a modern speech translation. Direct other learners to listen to discover the bottom line of Paul's sermon. When the reading is finished, call for response. The response should indicate the bottom line was that only Jesus Christ can save and that He can do what the law of Moses could not do.

With this bottom line established, invite learners to discover what Paul included in his sermon to these unsaved hearers. Proceed through the Scripture passage verse by verse determining what has been included. Note response on the chalkboard. The following is an example of conclusions that may be drawn:

1. This message is for you (v. 26).
2. Jesus was crucified just as the Scripture said He would be (vv. 27-29).
3. Jesus rose from the grave (v. 30-37).
4. Jesus can forgive your sins and justify you before God (vv. 38-39).

Give the Truth a Personal Focus

Ask: If you were going to tell someone who is lost about Jesus, what would you include in your conversation? Elicit response that suggests the information found in Paul's sermon is vital to understanding salvation through Christ. Share the comments titled "Pointing to Jesus" (*Applying the Lesson*).

Ask: Would you be willing to share that information with someone who does not know the saving grace of Jesus? Note that it may be as difficult for us as it was for Paul, but there is a source for empowerment for the responsibility. Share the remarks found in "No power without God's power" (*Applying the Lesson*).

Conclude the study with a time of commitment to the joy of sharing this information about Jesus with someone who is unsaved.

1. Frank Stagg, *The Book of Acts* (Nashville: Broadman Press, 1955), 5-6.
2. Vance Havner, *The Best of Vance Havner* (Grand Rapids: Baker Book House, 1980), 43.

September 22

A Healing in Lystra

Basic Passage: Acts 14

Focal Passage: Acts 14:8-18

The man whose story we are studying is correctly known as the apostle to the Gentiles. This does not mean that he abandoned his own people, the Jews. He remained true to the words of his divine commission, "He is a chosen vessel unto me, to bear my name before the Gentiles, and kings, and the children of Israel" (Acts 9:15). Under the leadership of the Holy Spirit, Paul would break through the boundaries that separated people of different races as he declared a gospel that was for all people. He called that gospel "the power of God unto salvation to everyone that believeth; to the Jew first, and also to the Greek" (Rom. 1:16). So long as he was permitted, Paul took his message first to the synagogues. Only intense opposition drove him from them. Increasingly, his audiences were Gentiles; but it still remained true, "Brethren, my heart's desire and prayer to God for Israel is, that they might be saved" (Rom. 10:1). Witness to the Jews should be a priority for Christians today.

Study Aim: *To recognize the adaptability of the gospel to persons of differing backgrounds and persuasions*

STUDYING THE BIBLE

Acts 14 contains a description of a great missionary journey that took Paul and Barnabas back to their base: Antioch in Syria. There they had an exciting story to tell of their Christian witness before contrasted groups, with equally contrasted results. Through it all, the gospel proved its power to save, though not without cost to the messengers.

I. A Work of Healing (Acts 14:8-10)

Patience and persistence were two impressive qualities displayed by Paul and Barnabas. After rough treatment in the synagogue in Pisidian Antioch, they traveled on to Iconium where they "went both together into the synagogue" (v. 1), only to meet with fresh opposition. "Long time therefore abode they speaking boldly in the Lord" (v. 3) until violence was threatened against their persons (v. 5). This threat of violence caused them to leave for another field of service: Lystra. "And there they preached the gospel" (v. 7).

> **8 And there sat a certain man at Lystra, impotent in his feet, being a cripple from his mother's womb, who never had walked:**
> **9 The same heard Paul speak: who steadfastly beholding him, and perceiving that he had faith to be healed,**
> **10 Said with a loud voice, Stand upright on thy feet. And he leaped and walked.**

God worked a miracle through Paul on a listener whose physical disability is carefully described (v. 8). From a human viewpoint, the man was a helpless case. But the power in Paul's message excited a belief in this crippled man that healing was possible. The apostle recognized this and responded with a spoken command to get to his feet, regardless of his condition. The man's faith was evident in his quick response. He jumped up and began to walk.

II. Pagan Reaction (Acts 14:11-13)

The native people of those parts reacted instantaneously to the miracle. In their own dialect, not intelligible to Paul or Barnabas, they hailed these two visitors as gods, probably recalling a local legend about a visitation from Zeus (Jupiter) and Hermes (Mercury).

11 And when the people saw what Paul had done, they lifted up their voices, saying in the speech of Lycaonia, The gods are come down to us in the likeness of men.
12 And they called Barnabas, Jupiter; and Paul, Mercurius, because he was the chief speaker.
13 Then the priest of Jupiter, which was before their city, brought oxen and garlands unto the gates, and would have done sacrifice with the people.

Jupiter was the chief among Greek gods, and Mercurius (Mercury) was their messenger. The bestowment of these names suggests that Barnabas was the more physically impressive of the two men. The natives, convinced that they had two divine visitors, made preparation to honor them with appropriate worship. A temple of Jupiter, located near the city gates, was the natural place for this. Garlands were put around the necks of animals that were to be sacrificed.

III. Appropriate Preaching (Acts 14:14-18)

Though the apostles could not understand what the people were saying, they quickly reacted to their actions. Nothing could be more abhorrent to them than to be treated as gods. The depth of their concern was displayed by the tearing of their clothes, a traditional method for expressing profound grief.

14 Which when the apostles, Barnabas and Paul, heard of, they rent their clothes, and ran in among the people, crying out,
15 And saying, Sirs, why do ye these things? We also are men of like passions with you, and preach unto you that ye should turn from these vanities unto the living God, which made heaven, and earth, and the sea, and all things that are therein:
16 Who in times past suffered all nations to walk in their own ways.
17 Nevertheless he left not himself without witness, in that he did good, and gave us rain from heaven, and fruitful seasons, filling our hearts with food and gladness.
18 And with these sayings scarce restrained they the people, that they had not done sacrifice unto them.

This is doubtless a brief summary of what the apostles said. We have another speech to a pagan audience in 17:22-31 recorded at greater length. There is an interesting and informing contrast between these messages and that given in a synagogue in Antioch in Pisidia (13:14-41). Old Testament history was a major emphasis there. In Lystra and Athens the more basic note of God as Creator and Provider was prominent, with studied insistence that idolaters needed to "turn from these vanities unto the living God" (v. 15). Those who have not received the gospel are held responsible for their failure to recognize and respond to the witness of nature to the greatness and goodness of God. See also Romans 1:18-21. God exercised patience toward those who lacked the gospel, withholding His judgments. That situation changed with the coming of the gospel that places all its hearers under the responsibility of acceptance or rejection. The impression given by verse 18 is that there was no response of belief in Jesus on the part of the people of Lystra, only a hard-won restraint from carrying out their intentions of sacrificing to Paul and Barnabas. However, a reference to disciples in verse 22 indicates that some were won, even from this pagan group, to faith in Christ as Savior.

IV. Violence Unheeded (Acts 14:19-28)

Although our printed passage ends with verse 18, our background material includes the whole of chapter 14. We need to include all of it in our study to gain an adequate view of the courage and endurance of Christ's two messengers.

1. Paul stoned (vv. 19-20).—Persistence is a quality that can be used for good or bad. It is to be commended in Paul and Barnabas but deplored in their enemies, who followed them to Lystra, from Antioch and Iconium. The Jews found ready listeners to their charges against the apostles among people whose superstitious enthusiasm had been raised to a high point, only to have cold water thrown over it by the protesting Christian missionaries. In a mood of deep frustration, they turned against those whom they had so recently hailed as benefactors. Paul was stoned and presumed dead. The memory of this ordeal stayed with the apostle for long years: "once was I stoned" (2 Cor. 11:25). Did he die, or was he knocked unconscious? Of this we cannot be sure, but the record indicates that both his enemies and friends regarded him as dead. Either Paul was unconscious or God was not finished with His apostle to the Gentiles.

2. A peaceful visit? (v. 21).—From Lystra, Paul and Barnabas proceeded to Derbe, twenty miles away. After the disorder and violence previously experienced, it seems that Derbe provided a contrast. No opposition is mentioned; yet a clear reference to converts is made: "when they had preached . . . and had taught many" (v. 21). If Derbe provided only encouragement, the apostles needed that, and God gave it to them.

3. Return trip (vv. 21-26).—Perhaps this respite motivated Paul and Barnabas to retrace their steps and to visit centers where they had been recently mistreated. G. Campbell Morgan says that, from Derbe, "The great eastern road ran through the passes of the Taurus range of mountains straight to Tarsus, from whence Paul and his company could have taken ship, and crossed quickly over to Seleucia, and so would have arrived in Antioch in Syria."[1] (See map.) That would have been a speedy and safe route. But they chose the more dangerous road in order to minister to the groups of new Christians in Lystra, Iconium, Antioch in Pisidia, and Perga. Among these they taught, organized, and prayed. Their gospel was not one of cheap grace, but of hardship accepted and endured for Christ's sake (v. 22). Leadership was recognized and assigned, and intercession offered (v. 23). In all his dealings with young churches, Paul consistently emphasized the importance of mutual intercession.

4. Reporting to home base (vv. 27-28).—Paul and Barnabas had been away for nearly a year. Their starting point had been Antioch in Syria where they were commissioned by the church. To that church they returned to report on work accomplished under the leadership of the Holy Spirit and the blessing of God. Since this was mainly a Gentile church, its members would be anxious to hear "how he had opened the door of faith unto the Gentiles" (v. 27). A pattern was being provided for modern missions through which, supported by home churches, men and women go forth into the world with the message of the gospel. Report on progress made is brought to those home churches by the printed word and missionary speakers.

APPLYING THE LESSON

He wouldn't give up.—Don Williams was his name, and he simply would not give up on his dream. From the time he was eight years old, Don Williams was determined to be a Disney cartoonist. During four years in the Navy and a stint as a bank teller in Springfield, Massachusetts, Don never lost sight of the dream. His first vacation from the bank was a trip to Disneyland. For the next ten years he rotated his vacations between Disney World and Disneyland. At the age of forty, he was drawing Disney characters and displaying them locally while still working at the bank. A friend sent copies of Don's work to Walt Disney's son-in-law. Two months later, Don had an interview with a Disney executive. The executive was interested, but Disney was not hiring then. "Maybe someday," the executive said. A year and a half later Don left his job and moved to Orlando, hoping something would open up. Two months later he was offered a temporary job at the Magic Kingdom doing chalk portraits of guests in the park. Six weeks later, he was called to the art department. They offered him a thirty-day trial job as a cartoonist. At the end of the thirtieth day, no one said anything. So on the following Monday, Don came back to his job. Three years later he was promoted to senior artist. And in 1987, Don Williams, who would not give up on his dream, was named Disney senior illustrator.[2]

The key to Don Williams's achievement as a Disney cartoonist was his persistence. Likewise, the key to Paul's achievement as a missionary of the gospel was his persistence. He simply would not quit. Persecution stimulated him instead of stopping him. Opposition energized him instead of discouraging him. Closed doors motivated him to look for other open doors. God called Paul to preach the gospel, and he simply would not give up.

Was it a miracle?—A doctor on a visit to the Vatican astonished the nuns and other bystanders by climbing out of a wheelchair after being blessed by the Pope. Was it a miracle? Not really. The man was Dr. Jan Lavric, an able-bodied doctor from England who went to Rome with a group of disabled people. He sat down in the wheelchair because it was the only seat left in the Vatican's audience. A Swiss guard unexpectedly began wheeling him forward. The doctor tried to stop him, but the guard said, "Don't exert yourself." After the Pope blessed him, and he was wheeled away by the guard, Dr. Lavric stood up and folded the chair and carried it off.

That was not a miracle, only a misunderstanding. But the Bible is filled with stories of true life miracles when the power of God brought a physical transformation. When we remember that God created this majestic universe in which we live and He by His power keeps it going, should we be surprised that He has the power to cause physical healing?

He did not fear the face of man.—John Knox, 1514-1572, was a key figure in the Protestant Reformation. Both England and Scotland were greatly impacted by his preaching and his personal efforts. The reason for Knox's impact was his courage. At his death, the newly elected regent of the church said about John Knox, "There lies he who never feared the face of man."[3]

That statement could have been made about Paul. Once Paul met Christ on the Damascus road and was captured by the fear of God, he never feared the face of man.

Definition of fellowship.—What is fellowship? We often talk about it and claim we have it, but what is fellowship? One little boy defined fellowship as "two fellows in a ship." That's a pretty good definition because when two fellows are in a ship together, they go up together and down together. They are together! That's what fellowship is.

Perhaps an even better definition of fellowship is "linking-thinking." Fellowship seems to link our thoughts and actions with others of like mind. Linking-thinking or two fellows in a ship—both accurately picture the meaning of *fellowship.*

The word *fellowship* is not used in this week's lesson, but the experience of fellowship is clearly pictured. Paul's return to the churches he had founded, his words of encouragement, and the intercession of these Christians for one another—all of these were manifestations of fellowship.

TEACHING THE CLASS

Main Idea: The gospel is a powerful persuasion to persons of diverse backgrounds and experiences.

Suggested Teaching Aim: Learners will discuss ways to present the gospel effectively to persons of diverse backgrounds and persuasions in their own community.

Introduce the Bible Study

Share the comments titled "Definition of fellowship" (*Applying the Lesson*). State that the church is ideally a fellowship. Note that it is made up of persons of diverse backgrounds and persuasions who have come to think the same way about Jesus Christ. Ask: What are some of the diverse characteristics of persons in our fellowship? Elicit responses that include such things as race, educational level, social status, and economic status. Continue by asking: What differences are there in our community that might not be represented in our church fellowship? Elicit response.

State that the study for today demonstrates the gospel is effective among persons with diverse backgrounds and persuasions. The purpose of the study is to help us to identify ways to present this gospel effectively to persons of different backgrounds. Invite learners to turn in their Bibles to Acts 14.

Search for Biblical Truth

Share the comment titled "Was it a miracle?" (*Applying the Lesson*). Explain that such a misunderstanding was not the case when Paul began sharing the gospel in Lystra. Call on a learner to read Acts 14:8-10. Ask: What was it that healed this man? Would you expect faith in a man from this kind of background? Why or why not?

A Teaching Outline

1. Identify diverseness in the local church and community.
2. Discover how the gospel touched persons of diverse backgrounds when Paul presented it.
3. Decide on characteristics of this situation that made Paul's presentation effective.
4. Discuss ways to present the gospel effectively to diverse groups in learners' community.

State that there was immediate reaction to the miracle among the local people. Call on a learner to read Acts 14:11-13 while others listen to discover the reaction. Call for response. Ask: Was this reaction desirable or undesirable? Elicit response. Continue by asking: What kind of backgrounds does this incident imply existed among the people of Lystra? (They worshiped the gods Jupiter and Mercury and believed in earthly manifestations of those gods.)

Call on a learner to read Acts 14:14-18 to discover how Paul and Barnabas reacted. Note that even in this instance Paul was faithful to present the truth of God. Ask: What was included in his message to these persons of varied backgrounds? Responses should include ideas like these: God is living today as He did in the past; we are only people who witness about Him.

Note the emphasis by Paul on God as Creator and Provider. This appealed to the citizens of Lystra and helped them to understand Paul's message.

Use information from *Studying the Bible* to summarize events recorded in the remainder of Acts 14.

Give the Truth a Personal Focus

Share the comments titled "He wouldn't give up" (*Applying the Lesson*). State that witnesses for Christ today need not give up because the gospel is effective regardless of the backgrounds of persons who hear it. Ask: What are some effective ways to present the witness of Christ to persons of varied persuasions in our own community? Elicit response that demonstrates understanding and caring for the variety of people to whom the church should reach for Christ.

---

1. G. Campbell Morgan, *The Acts of the Apostles* (New York: Fleming H. Revell, 1924), 346.
2. Jerry Dahmen, *I Love Life* (Nashville: Broadman Press, 1989), 126-131.
3. Roland Q. Leavell, *Evangelism: Christ Imperative Commission*, rev. (Nashville: Broadman Press, 1979), 78.

September 29

A Conference in Jerusalem

Basic Passage: Acts 15:1-35

Focal Passage: Acts 15:1-12

The history of the Christian church abounds in crises and conferences as well-meaning people strove for truth as they understood it. None had greater consequences for the cause of Christ and His gospel than those recorded in Acts 15. At issue was what the apostle Paul was to call "the liberty wherewith Christ hath made us free" (Gal. 5:1). The very nature of the gospel was at stake. Had Paul and his associates in the Antioch church not resisted, Christianity might have become a Jewish sect and would have lost its influence in the Gentile world. By taking a firm stand, these early church leaders preserved the doctrine of salvation by grace, through faith alone, and left the way open for the message to be taken into all the world. Subtle influences are always at work seeking to add a human contribution to the divine work of redemption. Therefore, a constant need exists to reaffirm and defend the truth that "by grace are ye saved through faith; and that not of yourselves: it is the gift of God: Not of works, lest any man should boast" (Eph. 2:8-9).

Study Aim: *To understand and subscribe to the biblical truth that we are not saved by works of the law but by grace through faith*

STUDYING THE BIBLE

Things were going so well for the cause of the gospel in Syrian Antioch that some kind of adversarial action was to be expected. This came in the form of Old Testament legalism, introduced from outside. Only firm resistance on the part of Paul and others prevented serious division in the early churches.

I. Controversy in Antioch (Acts 15:1-3)

A great Gentile ingathering brought the church in Syrian Antioch into existence (11:20-21). Barnabas was sent from Jerusalem to investigate this development, and, in characteristic fashion, he "was glad, and exhorted them all, that with purpose of heart they would cleave unto the Lord" (v. 23). The work prospered to the degree that

Barnabas sought a colleague and found him in Saul of Tarsus (vv. 25-26. The teaching of these men persuaded the new believers of their responsibility to share the gospel with others, and so missions were born (13:1-4). In our last two lessons we have seen how the preaching of Paul and Barnabas, to both Jews and Gentiles, produced a harvest of converts, howbeit not without hardship for the messengers. They returned to Antioch only to be confronted by a controversy that threatened the future of their ministry.

> **1 And certain men which came down from Judea taught the brethren, and said, Except ye be circumcised after the manner of Moses, ye cannot be saved.**
>
> **2 When therefore Paul and Barnabas had no small dissension and disputation with them, they determined that Paul and Barnabas, and certain other of them, should go up to Jerusalem unto the apostles and elders about this question.**
>
> **3 And being brought on their way by the church, they passed through Phenice and Samaria, declaring the conversion of the Gentiles: and they caused great joy unto all the brethren.**

The circumstances in which "certain men . . . from Judea" visited Antioch is not stated. They may have come as representatives of the Jerusalem church or have done so independently. They probably belonged to "the sect of the Pharisees" (v. 5); and, though professed believers in Jesus as the Messiah, they were still bound to observance of Old Testament ritual laws. Controversy arose when the Jerusalem Jews insisted that Gentile believers must submit to these laws and that they could not be saved without doing so. In other words, they must become Jewish proselytes before admission to church membership. As might be expected, Paul and Barnabas led the protest against this attempted imposition of legalism. They recognized that if this was not curbed, there could be a rupture of fellowship between the Jerusalem and Antioch churches. Therefore, they decided to go to Jerusalem and bring the matter to the attention of the leadership. It should be noted that they were under no compulsion to do this, but they made the journey in the interests of Christian unity and harmony.

II. Conference in Jerusalem (Acts 15:4-6)

A friendly reception is suggested by verse 4. After all, the Jerusalem church had previously given approval to the ministry of Philip in Samaria (8:14-17) and to the Gentile ingathering in Antioch (11:22-23). Obviously, this approval was not total, but it gave reason to hope for a tolerant attitude toward Gentile believers. Paul and Barnabas were given opportunity to speak freely about "all things that God had done with them" (15:4).

4 And when they were come to Jerusalem, they were received of the church, and of the apostles and elders, and they declared all things that God had done with them.

5 But there rose up certain of the sect of the Pharisees which believed, saying, That it was needful to circumcise them, and to command them to keep the law of Moses.

6 And the apostles and elders came together for to consider of this matter.

Opposition came from a group within the Jerusalem church that was allied with the party of the Pharisees. The Pharisee movement began after the return from Babylonian exile with the purpose of calling Israel back to the observance of the Mosaic law. This had much to commend it, but the purpose was pursued with such bigoted zeal that Pharisees were constantly in conflict with our Lord, specially on Sabbath observance. Pharisees believed in the resurrection of the dead; therefore, they were more open to the Christian message than some others. After accepting Christ as Messiah and Savior, however, they continued to practice traditional Jewish rituals, such as circumcision, and they insisted that Gentile converts should do the same. From time to time in church history, there have been those who would make Old Testament laws obligatory for believers.

III. Testimony from Apostles (Acts 15:7-12)

This unfortunate controversy was disruptive of Christian fellowship. It threatened to maintain the separation between Jews and Gentiles that, carrying over into dietary laws, made common meals impossible, including the observance of the Lord's Supper. At one time, Peter yielded to the pressure of the Judaizers (as they came to be called). He "withdrew and separated himself" although he had previously eaten with Gentile Christians (Gal. 2:11-12). But this was a temporary lapse, and at the Jerusalem meeting Peter stood forth boldly in testimony to the truths he had learned in his dealings with Cornelius (Acts 10).

7 And when there had been much disputing, Peter rose up, and said unto them, Men and brethren, ye know how that a good while ago God made choice among us, that the Gentiles by my mouth should hear the word of the gospel, and believe.

8 And God, which knoweth the hearts, bare them witness, giving them the Holy Ghost, even as he did unto us;

9 And put no difference between us and them, purifying their hearts by faith.

10 Now therefore why tempt ye God, to put a yoke upon the neck of the disciples, which neither our fathers nor we were able to bear?

11 But we believe that through the grace of the Lord Jesus Christ we shall be saved, even as they.

12 Then all the multitude kept silence, and gave audience to Barnabas and Paul, declaring what miracles and wonders God had wrought among the Gentiles by them.

After the Cornelius incident, Peter was called upon to give account for his departure from racial discrimination by fellowshipping with Gentiles. He was able then to silence his critics and win approval so that they "held their peace, and glorified God, saying, Then hath God also to the Gentiles granted repentance unto life" (11:18). But old prejudices die hard, so Peter retold the story of Cornelius and his household who had been saved, not by the observance of laws, but "through the grace of the Lord Jesus Christ." Since grace was the great theme of Paul's preaching and teaching, we may be sure that when Barnabas and he were called on to speak, Paul enlarged on this subject. The two men told of the gospel victories they had seen in the Gentile world. Paul's contribution would have been specially impressive, because he had once been "an Hebrew of the Hebrews; as touching the law, a Pharisee" (Phil. 3:5). However, through confrontation with the living Christ, Paul became the ardent messenger of a gospel that had at its heart this truth: "A man is not justified by the works of the law, but by the faith of Jesus Christ . . . for by the works of the law shall no flesh be justified" (Gal. 2:16).

IV. Conclusions Reached (Acts 15:13-21)

A new voice was now heard, that of James, brother of our Lord. With the rest of the family, James had opposed the ministry of Jesus (Matt. 12:46), but he had been won to faith in Christ by His postresurrection appearance to James personally (1 Cor. 15:7). Thereafter, he became a leader in the Jerusalem church, and we are indebted to James for the epistle that bears his name. He began his speech by endorsing what Peter had said.

1. Old Testament quote (vv. 15-18).—James's quotation from Amos 9:11-12 was taken from the Septuagint, the Greek version of the Old Testament, which was the Bible of our Lord and His contemporaries. It anticipated the time when God would "build again the tabernacle of David," the church, that would include believing Jews and Gentiles. These together would constitute "a people for his name" (v. 14). Hence, attempts to impose circumcision and other rituals on Gentiles must be abandoned. The terms for salvation were the same for all persons, regardless of race.

2. Recommendations (vv. 19-21).—This basic principle, however, had to be considered in light of the need for agreeable fellowship between Jews and Gentiles. Gentile Christians should be willing to consider the scruples of at least some of their Jewish brethren in the faith. They should avoid eating food that had been offered to idols (1 Cor. 8). They should be careful to observe God's moral laws, a necessary injunction for all Christians, but particularly for those with pagan backgrounds and environments. Jewish dietary laws should also be respected. Some think "from blood" (v. 20) refers to murder. But the greater probability is that it refers to eating kosher food, certainly when Jewish believers were present. Verse 21 appears to have been a reminder to some of the more rigid brethren that Gentiles had opportunity to become acquainted with the law of Moses since it was read in the synagogues every Sabbath.

APPLYING THE LESSON

Can't escape from trouble.—A Wyoming cattleman rode into a clearing and saw a mad bull after a cowboy who had fallen off his horse. With head down and nostrils snorting, the bull charged. The cowboy dived into a hole in the ground as the bull plunged across the hole. Suddenly, the cowboy leaped out of the hole, and the bull came back madder than ever. The cowboy dived into the hole again, only to spring out as soon as the bull passed by. The cattleman watched the cowboy do this several times. Finally, he shouted, "Cowboy, why don't you just stay in the hole?" Leaping out again, the cowboy responded, "Because there's a bear in that hole!"

That's the way things were in the early church. They went from one problem to another. Yet, in each case, through the power of God, these first Christians were able to transform adversity into advancement.

The reality of criticism.—A young preacher stood up to preach his first sermon in his new church. Being rather nervous, he misquoted the Scripture. He said, "I will take for my text the words, 'They fed five men with five thousand loaves of bread and two thousand fishes.' " One of the critical members said with a volume that all could hear: "That's no miracle. I could do that myself." The next week the young preacher announced the same text again. This time he got it right. He said, "They fed five thousand men on five loaves of bread and two fishes." He waited for a moment and then, leaning over the pulpit, he looked at the member who had criticized him the previous week. "Mr. Smith," he asked, "Could you do that, too?" "Of course I could," Mr. Smith replied, "And how would you do it?" said the preacher. Mr. Smith said, "With what was left over from last Sunday!" That's about like some of the criticism we have to face.

Criticism is not a new thing. The early Christians had their critics as well. When the gospel was spread to the Gentiles and many of them responded in faith, all of the early Christians did not rejoice. Some raised questions about the genuineness of the Gentile Christians' experiences.

There's just something about you.—I've heard a story in several different forms. One of the versions pictures a man who had just gone through a terrible time in his life. His business failed, and he declared bankruptcy. With the loss of his money came the loss of many people he thought were his friends. His wife became disillusioned and threatened to divorce him. He couldn't make the payments on his mortgage, so he was going to lose his house. Then, as he went out looking for a new job, he had a wreck. While waiting for the ambulance to arrive, this man looked toward heaven and cried, "God, why me?" A voice from heaven responded, "To be perfectly honest with you, Sam, there is just something about you that ticks Me off!"

That is not a true picture of God, of course. God is not turned off by our sins. He is not affected by the color of our skins. He is neither impressed by our wealth nor disgusted by our poverty. Whatever our race, whatever our condition, whatever our past, and whatever our weaknesses, the Bible declares that God loves us.

The first Christians struggled continually to understand that simple truth: God's love is not determined by us but by Him. God does not love us because we are lovable. He loves because it is His nature to love.

Responsibility.—The businessman was interviewing a prospective worker. After asking him a few questions, he concluded by saying: "The bottom line is this. I need someone who is responsible." The young man jumped up and said, "Then, I'm your man. In my other job, whenever something went wrong, everyone always said I was responsible."

Responsibility is one of the forgotten words in Christian living today. We like to talk about our rights, about what is coming to us, and about our liberty in Christ. We often forget that our liberty stops at the point of another person's need. Our personal rights are limited by our responsibilities to others. The final decision of the Jerusalem Council called for responsible Christian living.

TEACHING THE CLASS

Main Idea: Salvation is available by grace through faith and not through works.

Suggested Teaching Aim: Learners will recommit themselves to a firm stand on salvation by grace.

Introduce Bible Study

Share the comments titled "Can't escape from trouble" (*Applying the Lesson*). Note that solving problems has always been a part of what the church had to work through. Today's study focuses on one of the problems that continues in discussion even today.

Write this question on the chalkboard: What must a person do to be saved? Ask: If you asked ten people gathered in ten different churches that question, what answers would you get? Wait for their response.

Continue by asking: Why is there a difference among the answers that would be given? .

Note again that this is one of the issues with which the early church grappled. The purpose of today's study is to help us to be able to clearly state our beliefs about how a person is saved and to recommit ourselves to a firm stand on salvation by grace.

Search for Biblical Truth

Invite learners to open their Bibles to Acts 15. Share information about the church at Antioch from the introductory paragraphs of *Studying the Bible.*

Call on a learner to read Acts 15:1-3 aloud while others listen to discover what action was decided on to bring this issue to resolution. Call for response.

Call on someone to read Acts 15:4-5 aloud while others listen to learn how Paul and Barnabas were received in Jerusalem. Call for response. Call attention to verse 5. Ask: If you asked these Pharisees what someone had to do to be saved, what would they have said? (Note that these were Pharisees who believed in Jesus. Their answer would have been to accept Jesus as Savior, be circumcised, and keep the law of Moses.)

A Teaching Outline

1. Focus on the variety of beliefs about salvation.
2. Discover the strong stand taken by some of the early leaders on salvation by grace through faith.
3. Discuss how and why learners would take a strong stand on salvation by grace through faith.
4. Recommit selves to maintaining a firm stand on salvation by grace through faith.

Note that Peter was among the group at Jerusalem, and after listening to the discussion, he began a persuasive argument. Invite learners to listen to his explanation of how to be saved. Call on someone to read Acts 15:7-12 aloud. When the reading is finished, ask: How would Peter answer the question about how a person can be saved? Elicit response. Continue by asking: Was salvation by grace through faith for Gentiles only? Note verse 11.

Share information from *Studying the Bible* about the content of verses 13-21. Share the comments titled "The reality of criticism" (*Applying the Lesson*).

Give the Truth a Personal Focus

Ask: Suppose you were among that group that was asked what a person must do to be saved, what would you say? Wait for their response. Establish the validity of salvation by grace through faith. Continue by asking: Would you be willing to stand firmly on this position when other church members vigorously disagreed with you? Why or why not? Establish through the discussion that a bold stand on this position is necessary because it is the foundation stone of the Christian faith. It is worth disagreeing over. It is worth standing for.

Share the comments titled "Responsibility" from *Applying the Lesson.* Invite learners to recommit themselves to maintaining a firm stand on salvation by grace through faith. Conclude with a prayer of commitment.

October 6

A Call from Macedonia

Basic Passage: Acts 15:36—16:24

Focal Passages: Acts 16:9-12,16-23

Increase in the number of Christian congregations is often due to what are known as church splits. A membership becomes divided on some issue, and one group leaves the fellowship to form a new church. While this is not the ideal way of multiplying churches (the planned establishment of missions is better), the Lord often overrules an exhibition of human weakness to open up new fields of work and witness. It was so with Paul and Barnabas. These previously good friends had a disagreement about a third party: John Mark (Acts 15:36-41). Barnabas, who was related to the young man (Col. 4:10), wanted to take him along on a new missionary journey. But Paul considered John Mark unreliable since he had once defaulted (Acts 13:13). It was inevitable that Barnabas should stand by his kinsman, apart from which, his very nature made him sympathetic toward the younger man. Luke, who recorded the incident, made no effort to attribute blame, and we should not do so either. But the consequence was two missionary groups instead of one. Paul was later reconciled to Mark (Philem. 23-24; 2 Tim. 4:11).

Study Aim: *To seek and respond to the leadership of the Holy Spirit, as did Paul*

STUDYING THE BIBLE

Luke, the author of Acts, placed special emphasis on the work of the Holy Spirit. Malcolm Tolbert points out that there are seventeen references to the Holy Spirit in Luke's Gospel and fifty-seven in Acts.[1] The apostle Paul's sensitivity to the leadership of the Spirit is stated in Acts 16:6-8. In two distinct situations he changed his plans as the result of the Spirit's intervention. How the Holy Spirit communicated with Paul is not stated. Perhaps through inner persuasion or the words of others. But by his ready response, the apostle was led into a new field of ministry that was to bear rich fruit.

I. A Cry for Help (Acts 16:9-12)

Directed away from other places by the Spirit's influence, Paul arrived in Troas, a port on the Aegean Sea (see map), that enjoyed the status of a Roman colony. There, on the docks, many races mingled; and Paul must have been impressed by people he saw, people who had never heard the gospel. The impression may have led to the night vision: one of these strangers, a man of Macedonia, was heard pleading, "Come over . . . and help us." The response was immediate, for Paul recognized this as a commission from God to open up new territories. We should exercise caution in saying that thus Europe was made a mission field for the first time. For one thing, Europe as a continent did not exist then. For another, there is evidence that Christianity was introduced to Rome before this.

9 And a vision appeared to Paul in the night; There stood a man of Macedonia, and prayed him, saying, Come over into Macedonia, and help us.

10 And after he had seen the vision, immediately we endeavored to go into Macedonia, assuredly gathering that the Lord had called us for to preach the gospel unto them.

11 Therefore loosing from Troas, we came with a straight course to Samothracia, and the next day to Neapolis;

12 And from thence to Philippi, which is the chief city of that part of Macedonia, and a colony: and we were in that city abiding certain days.

An important feature of this passage is the introduction of the pronoun *we,* indicating that at this point the writer of Acts, none other than Luke, joined the missionary group. Since Luke was a physician (Col. 4:14), some have suggested that he may have gone along to minister to an ailing Paul. In the providence of God, Luke was to become the chronicler of Paul's missionary activities, able to record as an eyewitness many of his words and deeds.

II. A Distinguished Convert (Acts 16:13-15)

Though omitted from the print passages, these verses belong to the larger lesson and should not be overlooked. Evidently, the Jewish population of Philippi was small. Ten males were required to constitute a synagogue, and since these were not available, a group of godly women, both Jews and Gentiles, met on the banks of the Gangites River for worship. At this period, many Gentiles, disillusioned by paganism, turned toward the Jewish faith without, however, converting to Judaism. These Gentiles were known as God-fearers. Lydia was one of these. She traded in a purple dye, for which her native city of Thyatira was famous. As Paul preached Jesus, her heart was moved; she accepted Him as Savior and was baptized, as were members of her household. There is no authority here for infant baptism. On making this profession of faith, Lydia invited the missionaries to be guests in her home.

III. A Woman Liberated (Acts 16:16-18)

What is told about Lydia gives the impression of a woman of substance and status. Luke, whose sympathies were always with the disadvantaged, drew a sharp contrast in the "damsel possessed with a spirit of divination" (v. 16). She was a fortune-teller, and more, since her words were considered to be inspired by a pagan power, "a spirit of Python" (Luke's actual statement in the Greek). In her frenzied state, she followed the Christian missionaries around the city. Although her testimony was true, it came from a polluted source and was unacceptable to Paul, who commanded the evil spirit to come out of the girl. The exorcism resulted in the loss of her powers. This enraged her owners who had profited from her activities.

16 And it came to pass, as we went to prayer, a certain damsel possessed with a spirit of divination met us, which brought her masters much gain by soothsaying:

17 The same followed Paul and us, and cried, saying, These men are the servants of the most high God, which show unto us the way of salvation.

18 And this did she many days. But Paul, being grieved, turned

and said to the spirit, I command thee in the name of Jesus Christ to come out of her. And he came out the same hour.

The devil has two approaches in his campaign against Christianity: antagonism and association. We think of him mainly as an adversary of truth. But sometimes he attains his ends by posing as a friend. When Satan started using Scripture in our Lord's temptation in the wilderness, Jesus' reaction was strong and unmistakable, "Get thee hence, Satan" (Matt. 4:10). People are being seduced today by heretical movements that claim biblical authority and use biblical language. Paul silenced unwelcome testimony in Philippi by casting out the evil spirit. At the same time, he was the benefactor of the afflicted girl, though he made enemies as a consequence. For the first time, Paul faced civic opposition that was not instigated by Jewish enemies but was completely pagan in origin.

IV. Accusation and Prison (Acts 16:19-24)

The issue was not doctrinal but financial. Paul's action had deprived some citizens of Philippi of ill-gotten gains, money made by the exploitation of a slave girl. Not for the first or last time, business interests began to organize against the truth that offers salvation to all who believe.

19 And when her masters saw that the hope of their gains was gone, they caught Paul and Silas, and drew them into the marketplace unto the rulers,

20 And brought them to the magistrates, saying, These men, being Jews, do exceedingly trouble our city,

21 And teach customs, which are not lawful for us to receive, neither to observe, being Romans.

22 And the multitude rose up together against them: and the magistrates rent off their clothes, and commanded to beat them.

23 And when they had laid many stripes upon them, they cast them into prison, charging the jailor to keep them safely.

1. Racial animosity (v. 20).—Four people were in the apostolic party: Paul, Silas, Luke, and Timothy. Silas, also known as Silvanus, was one of the Christian leaders in Jerusalem. After the conference in that city, he was sent with Barnabas and Paul to Antioch to convey its decisions to the church there (15:27). After the disagreement between Paul and Barnabas, Silas was selected by Paul as his companion in service (v. 40). The violence in Philippi was directed against Paul and Silas not only because they were leaders of the Christian missionaries, but probably because they also could be easily identified as Jews. Luke, on the other hand, was a Gentile, and Timothy partly Gentile.

So racial animosities figured in what happened. The contemptuous reference to the two men as "being Jews" revealed the evil of anti-Semitism that continues to afflict society.

2. Racial pride (v. 21).—Philippi was a Roman colony administered by two magistrates (praetors) before whom Paul and Silas were dragged. No mention was made of the financial issue, which was the true cause of the attack on the apostles; rather, appeal was made to racial pride. Laws existed against the propagation of new religions among Roman citizens, and these were cited. Actually, Christianity was tolerated at this time under the Roman system as a branch of Judaism. But patriotism has too often been used as an excuse for intolerance and oppression. The ruse succeeded in Philippi.

3. Rough justice (vv. 22-23).—Apparently there were no appropriate judicial proceedings, no opportunity for Paul and Silas to defend themselves, no witnesses in their behalf. The owners of the slave girl carried sufficient clout in Philippi to secure the immediate sentencing of the two missionaries. After Roman custom, the two magistrates were accompanied by lictors, officials whose sign of office was a bundle of rods—often with an axe inserted among them. These rods were used to beat Paul and Silas, after their clothes were torn from their backs. Since we are dealing with a Roman situation, the phrase "rent off their clothes" must refer to the prisoners and not to their judges. The two Christian messengers were then thrown into prison and subjected to further painful indignities (v. 24). We must leave the story there, resuming it next week. But we do well to remind ourselves that we have been observing the beginnings of a Christian movement in Philippi that was to blossom into a church having the tenderest relationships with Paul. (See his Epistle to the Philippians.)

APPLYING THE LESSON

Problems turned into possibilities.—One of my favorite stories tells of a lady who decided to save some money by hanging the wallpaper in her bedroom. She bought the paper, set aside the day, and began to do her work. However, nothing went right. As soon as she put some paper up, it would begin to fall off. At one point, several of the strips fell off at the same time and lapped over her head. She cried out in anguish for her husband. When he came into the room, he laughed at the sight. Then, he grabbed his camera and took a picture. Later, she sent the picture to a contest and won first prize. With the prize money, she paid someone to come hang her wallpaper!

That's making the most out of an unpleasant situation. That is God's specialty. God has a way of transforming tragedies into triumphs. He did this in the early church, following the split of Barnabas and Paul. Instead of dividing the church, this split simply multiplied their mission teams. God turned a problem into a possibility.

God's guidance.—In reference to the experience of Paul discussed in our text, W. E. Sangster (1900-1960), famous minister of Westminster Central Hall in London, said, "The steps of a good man are ordered by the Lord. Also the stops of a good man are ordered by the Lord. Paul planned well, prayed, and wanted God's guidance. When he wanted to go to Bithynia, God said no. Then a call came from Macedonia. God vindicates himself in the experiences of life when we follow His will."[2]

The steps and stops of good people are ordered by God. What a beautiful description of the guidance God gives through His Holy Spirit!

Acting like a lady.— To say that someone is "acting like a lady" is usually a compliment. It is interesting to note, for example, that the New Testament never tells of any woman who opposed Jesus. Many men lined up in opposition to Jesus. Many men accused Jesus unjustly. Many men plotted to kill Him. But no record is given of any woman who opposed Jesus. Lydia is a good example of those women of the Bible and of history who followed Jesus.

Suffering for Christ.—Charles Allen, famous Methodist preacher, quoted from a book now out of print written by Dr. W. M. Clow. In that book, Dr. Clow distinguished between a burden, a thorn, and a cross. He said that a burden is the normal load which life lays upon every person, the daily responsibilities and work of life. A thorn, he said, is an affliction that some must bear. It may be a handicap, an illness, a disappointment, or a deep sorrow. A cross is a voluntary denial of ourselves in order to carry the load for Jesus. The difference, Dr. Clow concluded, is that burdens and thorns are thrust upon us. Only volunteers carry crosses.[3]

Paul and Silas had all three. They suffered as a part of their daily work for the Lord. They also had afflictions that came as a result of their work for Christ. This was not something they had to do, however. They voluntarily accepted these things as crosses to bear.

The right stuff.—A Swede was urged by friends to give up the idea of returning to India as a missionary because it was so hot there. "Man," his friend said, "it is one hundred twenty degrees in the shade!" "Vell," said the Swede, "ve don't always have to stay in the shade, do ve?"

That was the spirit of Paul and Silas. In every city, they faced opposition. Yet they faced their opposition with a spirit of optimism and faith, knowing that those whom God calls, He also provides for.

TEACHING THE LESSON

Main Idea: The Holy Spirit directs believers for the purpose of bringing glory to God.

Suggested Teaching Aim: Learners will seek and respond to the leadership of the Holy Spirit in their lives.

Introduce the Bible Study

Share the comments titled "God's guidance" (*Applying the Lesson*). Ask rhetorically: Do you believe that God directs the steps and stops of people today? How does He give direction in the life of believers today? Does He direct you in things you do in your life? Allow several minutes for learners to consider these questions thoughtfully.

State that the Scripture for today gives information about an experience Paul had in which God gave direction for his life. Invite learners to turn in their Bible to Acts 16 to learn about Paul's experience.

Search for Biblical Truth

Display the following outline of Acts 16 to guide the study. As each point is presented, use information from *Studying the Bible* to inform and clarify.

Following Directions from God

1. A Cry for Help (Acts 16:9-12)
2. The Conversion of Lydia (Acts 16:13-15)
3. The Liberation of a Young Woman (Acts 16:16-18)
4. The Result of Following God's Direction (Acts 16:19-23)

Invite learners to read Acts 16:9-12 silently to learn of a time when God gave directions to Paul. Call on a learner to describe the situation. Ask: How did God speak to Paul? Use information from *Studying the Bible* to clarify.

Note the introduction of "we" in the text. Use information from *Studying the Bible* to clarify. Share the comment titled "Problems turned into possibilities" (*Applying the Lesson*).

A Teaching Outline

1. Discuss how the Holy Spirit gives direction to believers.
2. Discover Paul's experience with the direction of the Spirit.
3. Discover the outcome of Paul's following the leadership of God.
4. Decide how to personally seek the leadership of the Spirit.
5. Commit to responding to the Spirit of God.

Invite learners to read Acts 16:13-15 silently to learn of the conversion of Lydia. Share the comments titled "Acting like a lady" (*Applying the Lesson*).

Share information from *Studying the Bible* titled "A Woman Liberated." Direct learners to read silently this incident from Acts 16:16-18.

Ask: What kind of reward would most of us expect for following the directions of God in our lives? State that the final section of the Scripture passage tells us of the results in this situation, and it is not what most of us would expect or want. Direct learners to read Acts 16:19-24 to themselves to discover these results. Share information from *Studying the Bible.* Share the comments titled "Suffering for Christ" (*Applying the Lesson*).

Give the Truth a Personal Focus

State that the purpose of today's study is to help us to learn to seek and respond to the leadership of God in our own lives. Ask: How would you expect God to give direction to believers for their lives today? Wait for response. Encourage learners to be as specific as possible.

Continue by asking: Is it appropriate to seek the leadership of God for your life, or do you wait for Him to intervene to show you? If it is appropriate to seek His leadership, how is this done? How can you know if it is God or some other source, like your own personal desire? Elicit response and discussion.

Ask: Why did God give Paul specific directions? (To bring glory to Himself and to promote the spread of His message.) Continue: Why would God give direction in your life? In what ways do we seek God's direction for other purposes? Elicit response. Note that believers often seek the direction of God in promoting their own causes and personal welfare. Recall the results in Paul's life of following God's directions.

Share the comments titled "The right stuff" (*Applying the Lesson*). Invite learners to commit themselves to seeking and responding to the direction of God through His Holy Spirit.

---

1. Malcolm O. Tolbert, "Luke" in *The Broadman Bible Commentary,* vol. 9 (Nashville: Broadman Press, 1970), 12.
2. Pulpit Digest, September-October, 1979, 78.
3. Charles Allen, *Prayer Changes Things* (Old Tappan: Fleming H. Revell, 1964), 77.

October 13

A Song at Midnight

Basic Passage: Acts 16:25-40

Focal Passage: Acts 16:25-39

In the use of Sunday School curriculum, every opportunity should be taken to present the basics of the Christian gospel. Some lessons lend themselves more readily to this than others. Today we have a lesson that lends itself freely to this purpose. In our journey through Acts, we have come upon several examples of the power of the gospel to change lives, beginning, of course, with the apostle Paul. There are general statements, such as, "As many as were ordained to eternal life believed" (13:48). The witness borne in Philippi provided the contrasted cases of a Gentile businesswoman, Lydia, and a Roman jailer. We have no clear statement on the "damsel possessed with a spirit of divination" (16:16), and we can only hope that she found her place in the believing community that became the Philippian church. But no doubt exists about the jailer, whose story provides a step-by-step example of what it means to accept the Lord Jesus Christ as Savior.

Study Aim: *To lead persons to accept the Lord Jesus who is able to save all who come to Him in faith*

STUDYING THE BIBLE

One of the more frequently quoted verses of the New Testament is Philippians 1:3, "I thank my God upon every remembrance of you." The church thus generously saluted by Paul had its beginnings in the incidents we are now studying. From a small beginning it was to grow into a fellowship of believers that exceeded expectations in the support it gave to Paul as he continued his missionary journeys (2 Cor. 8:1-5; Phil. 4:14-16). We are, therefore, studying events that played a significant part in the spread of the gospel in those early years.

I. Praises in Prison (Acts 16:25-26)

The hardship and hurt inflicted on Paul and Silas are described in verse 24. According to Ramsay, an authority on Paul, the "inner prison" was "a small cell, which had no window and no opening, except into the outer and larger prison."[1] The stocks were wooden contrivances that forced the legs apart and caused considerable pain. In spite of this physical misery, the two men engaged in the worship of God through song, probably psalms. Thus even in confinement they bore witness, for "the prisoners heard them."

25 And at midnight Paul and Silas prayed, and sang praises unto God: and the prisoners heard them.

26 And suddenly there was a great earthquake, so that the foundations of the prison were shaken: and immediately all the doors were opened, and everyone's bands were loosed.

Earthquakes were not uncommon in these parts. If, as has been suggested, the prison was built into the side of a hill, it would have been shaken sufficiently to loosen doors and cause chains that restrained prisoners to fall from their wall sockets. Other prisoners appear to have been petrified by the event so that they made no attempt to escape (v. 28).

II. A Jailer's Fears (Acts 16:27-30)

How should we think of this jailer? Rackham suggests, "He was no mere turn-key, but the governor of the prison,—probably of the rank of a centurion, like Cornelius at Caesarea."[2] That he had a private home in the prison area would seem to bear this out, as would his authority over others: "he called for a light" (v. 29).

27 And the keeper of the prison awaking out of his sleep, and seeing the prison doors open, he drew out his sword, and would have killed himself, supposing that the prisoners had been fled.

28 But Paul cried with a loud voice, saying, Do thyself no harm: for we are all here.

29 Then he called for a light, and sprang in, and came trembling, and fell down before Paul and Silas,

30 And brought them out, and said, Sirs, what must I do to be saved?

A Roman jailer was responsible with his life for his prisoners. His false assumption, therefore, that the earthquake had caused the escape of the prison population led him to contemplate suicide rather than face the judgment of his superiors. Only Paul's loud cry prevented him from taking this course. Overwhelmed by the complexity of the situation, the jailer rushed trembling into the presence of the Christian missionaries. Two men whom he had done his utmost to confine safely had taken care of a chaotic condition and were more in charge of it than he was. What did he mean by "Sirs, what must I do to be saved?" Somehow he had become acquainted with the message of

Paul and Silas, perhaps through the cry of the possessed girl, "These men are the servants of the most high God, which show unto us the way of salvation" (v. 17). This is certain: he asked the right question, the question all guilty sinners must ask if they are to find the way into God's forgiveness.

III. The Gospel Presented (Acts 16:31-34)

Before Lydia accepted Christ, she had listened to Paul's teaching (vv. 13-14). She was already a God-fearer, that is, a person who had turned from paganism to the truths of Judaism. Her heart was to this extent prepared for the message of the gospel. But the case of the jailer was different. He was, however, acquainted with the concept of lordship. Caesar was his lord, and the challenge presented to him was to come under another lordship, that of Jesus the Savior.

> **31 And they said, Believe on the Lord Jesus Christ, and thou shalt be saved, and thy house.**
> **32 And they spake unto him the word of the Lord, and to all that were in his house.**
> **33 And he took them the same hour of the night, and washed their stripes; and was baptized, he and all his, straightway.**
> **34 And when he had brought them into his house, he set meat before them, and rejoiced, believing in God with all his house.**

1. Needed instruction (v. 32).—The essential message of that day is in verse 31. But this was not all that Paul and Silas said to the jailer and his household, which probably consisted not only of family but also of subordinates. The two missionaries must have made clear the meaning of "believe," and told the "old, old story of Jesus and His love." A foundation was provided for faith, and the lordship of Christ was explained in terms of obligation and obedience.

2. Faith's evidence (vv. 33-34).—Currently there is a debate in some Christian circles as to whether salvation is received by faith in Jesus alone or by faith in Him plus submission to His lordship. The gospel presented to the jailer may not have spelled this out, but by his actions this man showed response to the biblical challenge, "Show me thy faith without thy works, and I will show thee my faith by my works" (Jas. 2:18). He attended to the physical needs of his recent prisoners by cleansing their wounds and feeding them at his own table. He also made public profession of his faith by being baptized "and all his, straightway." Members of his family, and others in his household, were saved on the same terms as he, so that the last we hear of this unlikely convert is that he was "believing in God with all his house." We can suppose that this group of persons became active members in the Philippian church, and that in later years they helped repay their debt to Paul by their generous gifts for his support.

IV. Citizenship Claimed (Acts 16:35-40)

The question has been asked: Why did not Paul and his companion claim their citizenship rights before being beaten and imprisoned? We cannot answer with certainty, but it appears that they had no opportunity. The rough justice administered to them, amid the shouting of an excited mob, made no provision for a defense or for a statement of any kind. They were condemned as "being Jews" (v. 20); no thought was given to the possibility of their being Roman citizens, and no way was left open for them to make this claim for themselves. The dangers of mob action continue to be demonstrated in many parts of the world.

35 And when it was day, the magistrates sent the sergeants, saying, Let those men go.

36 And the keeper of the prison told this saying to Paul, The magistrates have sent to let you go: now therefore depart, and go in peace.

37 But Paul said unto them, They have beaten us openly uncondemned, being Romans, and have cast us into prison; and now do they thrust us out privily? nay verily; but let them come themselves and fetch us out.

38 And the sergeants told these words unto the magistrates: and they feared, when they heard that they were Romans.

39 And they came and besought them, and brought them out, and desired them to depart out of the city.

1. Morning release (vv. 35-36).—The apparent thought of the Philippian magistrates had been that a night in jail would teach these preachers to get out of the city and never return. So, with the dawn of a new day, they sent the lictors to tell them good-bye. But these men were in for a shock.

2. Rights affirmed (vv. 37-39).—We learn from Acts 22:28 that Paul was born with the status of a Roman citizen. His father must have received this honor, which was granted under a variety of circumstances. A Roman citizen could not be punished without trial and must not be exposed to degrading penalties such as beating, although Paul suffered this painful indignity three times (2 Cor. 11:25). We do not know how a citizen gave proof of his status, but probably it was by something comparable to a modern passport. The honor was coveted by many so that we find a "chief captain" saying, "With a great sum obtained I this freedom" (Acts 22:28).

3. Fellowship enjoyed (v. 40).—Realizing their mistake, the magistrates came personally to the jailer's home to ask Paul and Silas to leave Philippi. But the missionaries were in no hurry. Before departing, they went to the home of Lydia where a growing number of believers assembled to bid them Godspeed. A relationship was developing that would mean much to Paul and the cause he represented in the years ahead.

APPLYING THE LESSON

Do you talk about being saved?—In my last church, I received a phone call from a young lady who had recently gone through a religious experience. She was looking for a church to join where she could profess her newfound faith and grow in it. The question she asked me was this: "Does your church still talk about being saved?" I assured her we did. We must, for that is the heart of what we are up to. The reason Jesus came is to seek and save the lost. The reason He established the church is to be a lighthouse to those who are in darkness. All around us people are asking the question raised by the Philippian jailer: "What must I do to be saved?" We must be ready and willing to give them the answer.

The influence of a Christian life.—Dionysius had been a pagan scholar and became a Christian. Later he served as bishop of Alexandria in the mid-third century A.D. Dionysius described the different reactions of Christians during a plague. He wrote: "Most of our brethren did not spare themselves and held together in the closest love of their neighbors. They were not afraid to visit the sick, to look after them and to take care of them for Christ's sake, and to die joyfully with them. But the heathen did exactly the opposite. They cast out any who began to be sick, deserted those who were dearest to them, threw the sick and half-dead into the streets, and left the dead unburied." Someone later made this comment about the words of Dionysius: "When the life of the Christian group is recognizably different from the life of the world outside, then no tricks are needed to attract people."[3]

Paul and Silas clearly reacted to their imprisonment in a recognizably different way. Instead of moaning, they were singing. Instead of cursing God, they were praising God. That recognizable difference is what led the jailer to turn to them and ask, "What must I do to be saved?"

Believe.—What does it mean to believe? Our English word *believe* comes via Old and Middle English from the root word *Leubh*. This word means "to care" or "to desire." In Old and Middle English, the prefix *be* carries the idea of "entirely" or "overwhelming." To believe in God, therefore, means to love God entirely or overwhelmingly.[4]

Faith and works.—What is the connection between faith and works? A lady responded to her pastor, "I think that getting to heaven is like rowing a boat. One oar is faith, and the other is works. If you use both, you get there. If you use only one, you go around in circles." The pastor replied, "There is only one thing wrong with your illustration. Nobody is going to heaven in a rowboat!"

The New Testament clearly declares that we are not saved by our works. Ephesians 2:8-9 says, "For by grace you have been saved through faith; and that not of yourselves, it is the gift of God; not as a result of works, that no one should boast" (NASB). Yet, the New Testament just as clearly declares that works are the result of and evidence of true faith. Paul continued in Ephesians 2:10 to say, "For we are His workmanship, created in Christ Jesus for good works" (NASB). Faith and works go together.

No retreat.—In one of Napoleon's battles, things were not going well for his troops. Napoleon thought it would be better to retreat from the field of battle and try again the next day. He said to the drummer boy, "Beat a retreat." The drummer looked at the general and said, "Sir, you never taught me how to beat a retreat. I only know how to beat a charge." Napoleon was inspired by the boy's answer and said, "All right, then beat a charge."

How many times do we retreat as Christians when we ought to charge. We usually opt for the comfort zone rather than facing a challenge. How different was the apostle Paul. After being beaten and treated roughly by the authorities, we would probably beat a retreat when freedom was offered. Not Paul. He refused to leave until they apologized to him!

Why did he do that? I don't think he did this because of his own personal pride. He did this to establish some credibility for the Christian movement. He wanted the Roman officials to know that someone with Roman citizenship was a vital part of the Christian movement.

TEACHING THE CLASS

Main Idea: Witnessing includes praising God, sharing Jesus, and keeping the message in the public eye.

Suggested Teaching Aim: Learners will determine ways they can emulate the witnessing of Paul and Silas in their daily life.

Introduce the Bible Study

Ask: What was happening when you first began to think about accepting Jesus? Elicit response. Continue by asking: What is the most unusual way of telling someone about Jesus that you have heard about? Listen for response.

State that the study for today focuses on an unusual witnessing moment. Share the comments titled "Do you talk about being saved?" (*Applying the Lesson*). State that it is necessary to talk about being saved to be a witness for Jesus Christ. Note that there are other ways that witness to the saving and changing power of Jesus Christ. Share the comments titled "The influence of a Christian life" (*Applying the Lesson*).

Invite learners to open their Bibles to Acts 16. State that the purpose for studying this incident in the life of Paul is to help us to decide how to be effective witnesses in our own daily experience.

Search for Biblical Truth

Share information from *Studying the Bible* about the conditions under which Paul and Silas were living in the prison. Invite attention to the Scripture to discover what these two believers did to witness in these circumstances.

Consider using the following approach for Scripture study. If the method is not considered appropriate for your group, use the outline to guide the Bible reading and discussion.

A Teaching Outline

1. Focus on ways of witnessing.
2. Discover the witness approaches of Paul and Silas.
3. Determine ways men and women of the nineties can witness best.
4. Decide specific ways to witness to persons around us this week.

Direct learners to work with those sitting near them. Provide paper and pencil. Give the following instructions. Study the witnessing experience of Paul and Silas found in Acts 16:25-39. Prepare a funny paper type drawing to illustrate what happened. This would consist of frames or boxes depicting different scenes that tell the story. Encourage learners to be creative in illustrating the events. After a period of study and work, invite learners to pass their finished product around the room for review by other learners.

As an alternative to this approach, write the following outline on the chalkboard. Use it for reading and discussing Acts 16:25-39.

A Song at Midnight

1. Praises in Prison (Acts 16:25-26).
2. A Jailer's Fears (Acts 16:27-30).
3. The Gospel Presented (Acts 16:31-34).
4. Citizenship Claimed (Acts 16:35-39).

When learners have searched the Scripture, ask: What did Paul and Silas include in their witnessing from the jail? Response should include praise for God, information about Jesus, and praise so that others would hear it. Write these elements on the chalkboard. Share the comments titled "Believe" and "Faith and works" (*Applying the Lesson*) to clarify the information about Jesus that Paul and Silas shared.

Give the Truth a Personal Focus

Ask: If singing songs from a prison cell doesn't fit into your life pattern today, what is it we need to be doing in the 1990s that will focus the attention of men and women on Jesus? Elicit response. Encourage learners to be creative in thinking about ways to witness today. Continue by asking: What should be included in the message today to make it more effective with today's hearers? Elicit response.

Share the comments titled "No retreat" (*Applying the Lesson*). Lead learners to decide specific ways they will witness to those around them this week.

---

1. William M. Ramsay, *Saint Paul the Traveller* (Grand Rapids: Baker, 1949), 221-22.
2. R. B. Rackham, *The Acts of the Apostles* (London: Methuen, 1953) 288.
3. Nelson Price, *Servants, Not Celebrities* (Nashville: Broadman Press, 1989), 119-120.
4. J. Moulton Thomas, *Prayer Power* (Waco: Word, 1976), 37.

October 20

A Proclamation in Athens

Basic Passage: Acts 17

Focal Passage: Acts 17:22-34

A major emphasis of this lesson is clearly intended to be on Paul's speech before the distinguished Athenian assembly that met at the Areopagus (Mars' Hill). The speech differed widely from others delivered by the apostle, for example, his first recorded message given in the synagogue at Pisidian Antioch (13:14-43). There he was addressing Jews whose attention he sought by rehearsing details of their national history, leading up to the announcement that God had provided for "Israel a Savior, Jesus" (v. 23). In Athens he was speaking to Greeks and to intellectuals. Paul's approach was therefore different as he sought to persuade his listeners that they should worship God the Creator and not idols. His conclusion made reference to Jesus and His resurrection. Those who present the gospel have always needed to make it apply to their audience and to do this without diluting or distorting its basic truths. We have the same responsibility to make truth appealing and understandable to our contemporaries. The task is not easy, but the Holy Spirit's help is available.

Study Aim: *To learn how to speak to persons about God and the gospel in ways that recognize the needs and receptivity of hearers*

STUDYING THE BIBLE

The whole of Acts 17 merits our attention if we are to get a true picture of Paul's missionary strategies and methods. One of his basic principles was to take the gospel to large centers of population, a sort of "trickle down" policy that would get the message ultimately to all surrounding communities. Thessalonica, Berea, and Athens feature in our chapter.

I. Cities in Contrast (Acts 17:1-15)

After Philippi came Thessalonica "where was a synagogue of the Jews" (v. 1). We take note that, regardless of the discouragement expressed in 13:46, the apostle continued to go to the Jews first. Also, his message concerned the Christ (Messiah) who "suffered," was "risen again from the dead; and that this Jesus, whom I preach unto you, is Christ" (17:3).

1. Violence in Thessalonica (vv. 1-9).—The response to this preaching was impressive. Jews, "devout Greeks" (God-fearers), and "chief women" were among the converts. But opposition was organized and strong. The missionaries were described as "these that have turned the world upside down" (v. 6) in a court appearance that threatened Jason and other new believers. Local Christians felt that Paul and Silas should leave the city. However, the New Testament contains two epistles addressed to the church there.

2. Nobility in Berea (vv. 10-15).—A synagogue in Berea was the next stop whose attenders were described as "more noble than those in Thessalonica" (v. 11). They listened to what Paul had to say and checked his statements in the Old Testament Scriptures. This went on daily. Not surprisingly, this openness resulted in many decisions for Christ. We have the name of one of the converts in 20:4. But the troublemakers in Thessalonica followed the missionaries to Berea, making necessary their departure for Athens. Silas and Timothy were left behind for a brief period.

II. Idolatry in Athens (Acts 17:16-21)

Paul was understandably tired and intended to rest in Athens as he waited for Timothy and Silas to catch up with him. But what he saw quickly moved him to action. Athens was honored in the Roman Empire as the artistic and intellectual center of the world. It excelled in sculpture, literature, and oratory. Yet it was given over to idolatry.

1. Paul's reaction (vv. 16-17).—Resuming his usual practice, the apostle started in the Jewish synagogue where, once again, his audience included "devout persons," Gentiles who were attracted to the Hebrew faith. But, perhaps for the first time, he also made a direct approach to a pagan audience that gathered "in the market daily" (v. 17). This was the civic center of Athens, known as the Agora, where public business was conducted.

2. Philosophers perplexed (vv. 18-21).—Two major philosophical groups in Athens were the Stoics and Epicureans, both with their good points but falling far short of the gospel. Neither believed in an afterlife, so that Paul's preaching on the risen Christ was an offense to them. They called Paul a "babbler," a derisive term that can be rendered "seed-picker," that is, a person of no real wisdom who picks up pieces of knowledge here and there. But they were interested enough to invite the apostle to the Areopagus, a traditional center for learned discussion. Verse 21 aptly describes the fascination of new ideas for many Athenians.

III. Revealing the Unknown (Acts 17:22-31)

Athens presented a strangely contradictory condition. This center of learning—some have described it as a "university town"—was also steeped in idolatry. Its many shrines and images gave it fame. The Parthenon, for example, considered the finest example of Doric architecture, was erected in honor of the patron goddess of the city. One of its two rooms housed an immense statue in gold and ivory of this goddess, known either as Athena or Minerva. But all this devotion to pagan deities still left the Athenians wondering whether they had overlooked one, hence the shrine inscribed: "To the Unknown God."

22 Then Paul stood in the midst of Mars' hill, and said, Ye men of Athens, I perceive that in all things ye are too superstitious.

23 For as I passed by, and beheld your devotions, I found an altar with this inscription, TO THE UNKNOWN GOD. Whom therefore ye ignorantly worship, him declare I unto you.

24 God that made the world and all things therein, seeing that he is Lord of heaven and earth, dwelleth not in temples made with hands;

25 Neither is worshiped with men's hands, as though he needed anything, seeing he giveth to all life and breath, and all things;

26 And hath made of one blood all nations of men for to dwell on all the face of the earth, and hath determined the times before appointed, and the bounds of their habitation;

27 That they should seek the Lord, if haply they might feel after him, and find him, though he be not far from everyone of us:

28 For in him we live, and move, and have our being; as certain also of your own poets have said, For we are also his offspring.
29 Forasmuch then as we are the offspring of God, we ought not to think that the Godhead is like unto gold, or silver, or stone, graven by art and man's device.
30 And the times of this ignorance God winked at; but now commandeth all men everywhere to repent:
31 Because he hath appointed a day, in the which he will judge the world in righteousness by that man whom he hath ordained; whereof he hath given assurance unto all men, in that he hath raised him from the dead.

1. The true God (vv. 22-23).—The NRSV has Paul describing his listeners as "extremely religious," and makes the concluding statement of verse 23 read, "What therefore you worship as unknown, this I proclaim to you." These alternatives take the harshness out of the apostle's introduction, which even so remains a frank description of the prevailing idolatry. Paul then proceeded to talk about the true God, unknown and unrecognized among the shrines and idols that abounded in Athens.

2. Pointers to truth (vv. 24-29).—The true God is the Creator of all things who cannot be contained in any earthly temple or worshiped as though He had need of our contributions. He, on the contrary, is the Giver, making us dependent on Him for "life and breath, and all things." Moreover, He is the Creator of "all nations," who furnished living space and the means for maintaining life. This He did to cause humankind to seek after Him so that they might not remain ignorant of Him. Such ignorance, in fact, is inexcusable since "in him we live, and move, and have our being" (v. 28). Paul then displayed his breadth of knowledge by quoting Greek poets in support of his statements. As the offspring of God, that is, the products of His hands, we should not presume to worship Him through images our hands have made.

3. God's Man proclaimed (vv. 30-31).—Paul had reached the point where he needed to introduce the theme of all his preaching: the Lord Jesus Christ. He acknowledged that God had allowed centuries to pass by in which His only revelation to the Gentile world was through nature and providence. But this had changed; and the change centered in "that man whom he hath ordained" (v. 31), none other than "the Son of man." as Jesus described Himself when talking to His fellow countrymen. Paul had called for repentance (v. 30). Now he spoke of judgment that would be administered through Him whom God had raised from the dead (v. 31).

IV. Mockery and Belief (Acts 17:32-34)

This reference to resurrection divided Paul's listeners, some mocking the idea, others showing a desire to hear more. We may suppose that we have an abbreviated version of what Paul said for he would not have spoken of our Lord's resurrection without mention of the circumstances of His death. But it was the idea of resurrection that brought adverse reaction, specially we may suppose, from the Epicureans who believed at death personality ceased to exist.[1]

32 And when they heard of the resurrection of the dead, some mocked: and others said, We will hear thee again of this matter.
33 So Paul departed from among them.
34 Howbeit certain men clave unto him, and believed: among the which was Dionysius the Areopagite, and a woman named Damaris, and others with them.

Did Paul later regret the nature of his speech in Athens? Some think that this is the implication of his statement to the Corinthians, "For I determined not to know any thing among you, save Jesus Christ, and him crucified" (1 Cor. 2:2). But it can be argued that Paul was contrasting his preaching with "the wisdom of the wise" (1:17-31) that prevailed in Corinth. Certainly his preaching in Athens was not fruitless, for among the converts was a member of the learned group that he addressed and others beside.

APPLYING THE LESSON

First one who really explained it.—A pastor in Virginia shared this story. He made friends with a 78-year-old husband of one of his church members. After helping the man to be comfortable with him, the pastor used the Bible to show the man how to be a Christian. The gospel was explained simply by the pastor. The man nodded that he understood. After praying a prayer of repentance, the man was saved. The entire family rejoiced. Following his baptism, the pastor asked the man why he had taken so long to become a Christian. He replied, "You are the first one to witness to me in my life. You are the first one who really explained it." There are many people in our communities and world who are waiting for someone to *really explain it.*

Hunger for the Word of God.—The manager of a bookstore in a Southern city was invited to bring a devotional message to a group of workers at a Christian agency in the same city. On her way to her speaking engagement, she dropped her Bible without knowing it. When she reached her destination, she did not have it. This was a special Bible that she used for her personal study, so she was quite upset. Retracing her steps, she searched for the Bible but could not find it. Several months later a big, burly policeman approached the counter in the bookstore, and the manager was at the counter. The policeman asked her if he could buy a Bible like the one he held in his hand. Immediately, she recognized it as her lost Bible. She told him that a similar Bible had been lost and asked him where he got it. He explained, "Pete down at the service station on the corner found it in the gutter. I stop there every night. Me and Pete have been reading it, and I want one."

Hearts are hungry for the Word of God. Such is the case all over the world today, and such was the case in Berea where Paul visited on his mission trip. Daily they listened to the preaching of Paul and studied God's Word.

Always knew about God.—Helen Keller achieved worldwide fame because of the way in which she overcame her physical handicaps. The secret of her life was her faith. She told Phillips Brooks, the great Boston preacher, "I always knew about God. I didn't know what he was called until I learned the word."[2]

That is a good description of the Athenians whom Paul addressed in our lesson for this week. They knew about God, but they didn't know who God really was until they heard His name in the preaching of Paul.

God only is great.—At the funeral of Louis XIV the great cathedral was packed with mourners paying final tribute to the king whom they all considered great. The room was dark except for one lone candle on the casket of the king. Jean Massillon—a leading preacher of his day who had often preached before Louis XIV and who after the king's death became bishop of Clermont—stood to address the congregation gathered to honor their greatly beloved king. As he rose, he reached from the pulpit and snuffed out the one candle that had been put there to symbolize the greatness of the king. Then, from the darkness, came just four words: "God only is great!"

That was the thrust of Paul's message to the Athenians. They believed in many gods. Paul proclaimed that only the God revealed in Jesus Christ is the real God. Only He is great and worthy of our worship.

TEACHING THE CLASS

Main Idea: Witnessing is more effective when the needs and receptivity of hearers are considered.

Suggested Teaching Aim: Learners will identify some ways to speak to the needs and increase receptivity of persons to whom they witness.

Introduce the Bible Study

Share the comments titled "First one who really explained it" (*Applying the Lesson*). Explain the importance of being able to communicate the message about Jesus in a way that it will be heard. Ask: Why would people you know be willing to listen to the gospel? Responses should suggest that people listen when what they are hearing addresses some need they feel.

State that the study for today shows Paul tapping into the interests and needs of his audience so that they would hear the message of Jesus. Invite learners to open their Bibles to Acts 17.

Search for Biblical Truth

Write Philippi, Thessalonica, Berea, and Athens on the chalkboard. Share information from *Studying the Bible* about Paul's experience in each one of these cities. Emphasize that the difference in the hearers made it necessary to consider how the gospel should be presented in each city.

A Teaching Outline

1. Consider why persons would be willing to hear the gospel.
2. Discover how Paul spoke to the needs of his hearers.
3. Identify needs of today's hearers.
4. Determine ways to speak to the needs of today's hearers and thereby increase receptivity to the gospel message.

State that the Scripture for today tells us what Paul said when he brought witness to people who lived in Athens. Call on a learner who has agreed to present a dramatic reading of Paul's sermon on Mars' Hill. The sermon is found in Acts 17:22-31 and should be read from a modern translation. Invite learners to listen to the sermon and try to determine how Paul addressed the needs of his hearers. When the reading is finished, call for response.

Needs learners might identify as existing among the Athenian hearers are superstitious concerns, making sure all bases were covered, and knowing about God and how to please Him. Identify verses from the passage that indicate these needs.

Share the comments titled "Hunger for the Word of God" (*Applying the Lesson*). Ask: What evidence do you see around you, if any, that people have a felt need to know the Word of God? Elicit response.

Share the comments titled "Always knew about God" (*Applying the Lesson*). Ask: Do people today have a sense of God even though they may not know Him? How would you be able to use that sense of God to increase their receptivity to the message of Jesus? Wait for response.

Ask: What response would you expect from the Athenians to this message from Paul? Call on a learner to read Acts 17:32-34 while others listen to learn how the listeners responded. Call for response.

Give the Truth a Personal Focus

Direct learners to work with those sitting near them to develop a list of needs of persons living in our world. After several minutes, call for response. List responses on the chalkboard. Answers might include needs for meaning in life, love, family stability, appropriate self-esteem, and assurance about life after death.

Continue by asking: Are people always able to identify their needs? How can a witness help persons become aware of their own needs? Make certain that these points are included in the responses: (1) People are not always aware of their needs. (2) Much like the Athenians, they may feel a need but not know what to name it. (3) Paul pointed to behaviors of the Athenians to try to make them aware of their needs. A similar approach may be useful in today's witnessing.

Ask: In what way would helping people become aware of their needs increase receptivity to the gospel? Elicit response. Help learners to determine ways that they can address the needs of people around them with the message of the love of God in Jesus Christ.

---

1. Stagg, *Acts*, 180-81.
2. Catherine Owens Peare, *The Helen Keller Story* (New York: Thomas Y. Crowell, Co., 1959), 42.

October 27

Disciples in Ephesus

Basic Passage: Acts 18:1—19:20

Focal Passage: Acts 18:24—19:6

Around persons of renown invariably gather less-known individuals who contribute to the success of their mission. So it was with Paul. In the narrative of Acts we have already met Luke, its writer, Barnabas, John Mark, Timothy, and Silas, all of whom played important parts in the work to which the apostle had committed his life. Three other names are added to this list in today's lesson passage: Aquila, Priscilla, and Apollos. There might also be added the name Crispus (18:8), who as "chief ruler of the synagogue" must have contributed greatly to the cause of the gospel in Corinth. Without these, and others like them, the apostle's mission would not have met with the success recorded in Acts and further indicated in Paul's epistles. Human beings have a tendency to assign responsibility to conspicuous leaders and forget that those who support their cause have personal obligations to contribute what they can to its success. In the church of Jesus Christ there is abundant opportunity for persons of every level of competency to lend their help to attain the goal of bringing the lost to salvation.

Study Aim: *To respond with personal commitment to the example of men and women who were Paul's colleagues in ministry*

STUDYING THE BIBLE

No biblical record exists of a church being started in Athens. In another very different kind of city, Corinth, not more than fifty miles away, Paul not only established a church but began a correspondence that has enriched the New Testament with two epistles (a third was probably written, but lost). Corinth was a center of government and trade, and it was notorious throughout the ancient world for its loose morals. It became, for Paul, a focal point for intense evangelism that lasted over eighteen months (18:11).

I. The Apostle's Travels (Acts 18:1-17)

Paul's stay in Corinth was marked by serious disturbance. His ministry in the local synagogue was ended by open opposition, so he moved his meetings next door, in the home of a God-fearer (Gentile adherent to Judaism) whose name was Justus (v. 7). Many were won to faith in Christ in that home, including Crispus.

1. Favorable verdict (vv. 12-17).—The opposing Jewish element in the city took their case to the Roman proconsul charging the apostle with breaking the law. This official interpreted this as meaning Jewish law, ruled the case outside his jurisdiction, and "drove them from the judgment seat" (v. 16).

2. Aquila and Priscilla (vv. 1-3,18).—When the apostle finally left Corinth, he went in the company of a couple introduced in verses 1-3. Aquila and Priscilla, husband and wife, were tentmakers or leather workers, a trade in which Paul had been trained after Jewish custom. They had been forced to leave Rome because of an edict of the Emperor Claudius, and they had set up business in Corinth. A strong friendship was forged between these two and the apostle so that he lived with them and worked at their craft. Thus he helped to support himself while preaching the gospel. In Romans 16:3-4, Paul greeted Aquila and Priscilla as those "who risked their necks for my life"

(NRSV), an act of heroic devotion about which we have no further information.

II. Ephesus and Elsewhere (Acts 18:19-23)

The reference to Paul's vow (v. 18) seems to be related to his visit to Jerusalem (v. 21), but it is not explained. There was no inconsistency in this vow of Paul. Although now a Christian, Paul remained a Jew to whom traditional practices, when not in conflict with his new faith, were important. Hebrew Christians today do not surrender their Jewishness when making a profession of faith in the Messiah. Cenchrea was a port that served Corinth (see map).

1. Paul in Ephesus (vv. 19-21).—The apostle's first visit to this great city was brief because of his desire to be in Jerusalem for one of the feasts. But it was a contact to be renewed and to become significant for Paul's total ministry. The statement concerning Aquila and Priscilla that Paul "left them there" (v. 19) fits the belief that this worthy couple remained in Ephesus a number of years, until conditions permitted their return to Rome, where Romans 16:3-4 places them. They were to render valuable service while in Ephesus, which was the capital of the province of Asia and had a large Jewish population. In the synagogue there Paul was given a good reception, and although he left the city to go to Jerusalem, he promised to return (v. 21).

2. Strengthening the churches (vv. 22-23).—Paul traveled by ship from Ephesus to Caesarea, a considerable voyage, and then by land to Antioch (Syria) where he and Barnabas had been commissioned. To check a map (see map) is to realize the extent of these journeys and the cost in physical strength to the apostle. Still following land routes, he went on to visit churches in Galatia and Phrygia, "strengthening all the disciples" (v. 23). This splendid missionary knew the importance of undergirding the converts so that they stood firm against pagan pressures.

III. Apollos the Eloquent (Acts 18:24-28)

During the apostle's absence from Ephesus, an important person arrived in that city. His name was Apollos, his birthplace Alexandria, an Egyptian city renowned throughout the world for its learning. Alexandria was home to a large colony of Jews who were instrumental in producing the Septuagint, the Greek version of the Old Testament, over two centuries before Christ. How Christianity reached Alexandria is not definitely known, but Jews from Egypt were among those who heard the gospel from Peter's lips on the Day of Pentecost (Acts 2:10).

24 And a certain Jew named Apollos, born at Alexandria, an eloquent man, and mighty in the scriptures, came to Ephesus.
25 This man was instructed in the way of the Lord; and being fervent in the spirit, he spake and taught diligently the things of the Lord, knowing only the baptism of John.
26 And he began to speak boldly in the synagogue: whom when Aquila and Priscilla had heard, they took him unto them, and expounded unto him the way of God more perfectly.
27 And when he was disposed to pass into Achaia, the brethren wrote, exhorting the disciples to receive him: who, when he was come, helped them much which had believed through grace:
28 For he mightily convinced the Jews, and that publicly, showing by the scriptures that Jesus was Christ.

1. His deficiency (vv. 24-25).—High tribute is paid to Apollos as a preacher. Evidently he knew the basics about the Lord Jesus and presented these fervently. But he lacked understanding of Christian baptism, knowing only the baptism of John. The distinction made between the two baptisms is important. John preached repentance and baptized people on confession of their sin. But, by his own statement (Matt. 3:11), he anticipated both a greater Baptizer and a greater baptism. This could only be fully revealed after the death and resurrection of our Lord because Christian baptism portrays Jesus' death and resurrection and applies them spiritually to the experience of the believer (Rom. 6:1-11). How Apollos, with all his learning, missed this truth is not explained; but that he did is a warning against accepting preaching merely because it is attractively packaged. Preaching should be judged by its faithfulness to the teachings of the Bible.

2. Help in a home (v. 26).—Aquila and Priscilla heard Apollos in the synagogue at Ephesus and quickly recognized his shortcoming. They did not engage in public criticism of him, however, but they took steps to help him do better. We have a marvelous picture of the tentmakers taking Apollos home and there, in private, disclosing to him those deeper truths about baptism of which he was not informed. Apollos displayed a gracious spirit by accepting instruction from this source. Christians need to learn to avoid public criticism of people and help them in private.

3. On to Corinth (vv. 27-28).—Paul's first Corinthian letter lets us know that the place in Achaia to which Apollos was invited was Corinth (see also Acts 19:1). There his influence was such as to secure him a following that threatened the church with division. Paul recorded the facts without any suggestion of criticism (1 Cor. 3). In fact, other references show appreciation of Apollos and his ministry (16:12; Titus

3:13). Some attribute the Epistle to the Hebrews to Apollos, and although this is open to question there can be no doubt that he stood tall among early church leaders.

IV. Corrective Teaching (Acts 19:1-6)

These verses, following immediately upon the story of Apollos, lend support to the supposition that the twelve people (v. 7) whose understanding of baptism was at fault had been instructed by Apollos. But this is not necessarily so. The influence of John the Baptist lasted long after his death and penetrated into far away parts of the world. In fact, there is a sect in the Middle East to this day that claims the Baptist as its founder. So these twelve may have gathered their ideas from some other source than Apollos.

1 And it came to pass, that, while Apollos was at Corinth, Paul having passed through the upper coasts came to Ephesus: and finding certain disciples,

2 He said unto them, Have ye received the Holy Ghost since ye believed? And they said unto him, We have not so much as heard whether there be any Holy Ghost.

3 And he said unto them, Unto what then were ye baptized? And they said, Unto John's baptism.

4 Then said Paul, John verily baptized with the baptism of repentance, saying unto the people, that they should believe on him which should come after him, that is, on Christ Jesus.

5 When they heard this, they were baptized in the name of the Lord Jesus.

6 And when Paul had laid his hands upon them, the Holy Ghost came on them; and they spake with tongues, and prophesied.

Another translation of verse 2 has the twelve saying, "Nay, we did not so much as hear whether the Holy Spirit was given" (ASV). This ignorance was remedied, and the twelve readily submitted to Christian baptism in the name of the crucified and risen Savior. Evidence of their possession of the Holy Spirit paralleled that of 10:44-48, although in that case the evidence preceded baptism, indicating that the grace of God does not operate by fixed patterns. "The wind blows where it chooses, . . . So it is with everyone who is born of the Spirit" (John 3:8, NRSV).

APPLYING THE LESSON

It takes an orchestra.—Halford E. Luccock (1885-1960), gifted professor of preaching at Yale Divinity School for half a century, once said, "No one can whistle a symphony. It takes an orchestra to play it." That is true of a symphony. It is also true of the church. No one person can do the work of the church. It takes a group of people working in cooperation with each other. This is true today, and it was true in the early days of the church. This week's lesson focuses on some who worked with Paul.

Friendly people make friends.—A psychologist once asked a group of college students to jot down, in thirty seconds, the initials of the people within a certain group they disliked. Some of the students taking the test could think of only one person. Others listed as many as fourteen. The researchers had the full names of the ones in the study and could make comparisons on the basis of the initials. The study revealed that those who disliked the largest number of people were themselves the most widely disliked. Apparently, their attitude toward others determined the others' attitude toward them.

Perhaps that's why Paul had so many friends, because he liked people. He had a special knack for making friends, a special gift for encouraging others.

Falling asleep too soon.—The mother put her little girl to bed and went into the den to clean up. She heard her little girl cry and went back into the bedroom to see what had happened. The little girl was on the floor, crying. "What happened?" the mother asked. The little girl responded, "I guess I just fell asleep too close to where I got in."

That happens to a lot of Christians. They are born into the family of God but they never grow in their understanding of the faith because they fall asleep too close to where they got in. Paul was aware of that danger, so he left Aquila and Priscilla as teachers in Ephesus to instruct and encourage the new Christians there.

Not surprised but unprepared.—I heard someone say once, "You can claim to be surprised once; after that, you're unprepared." Louis Pasteur (1822-1895) once said, "Chance favors a prepared mind." Both were saying basically the same thing: success or failure is determined to a large degree by our preparation. Those who are prepared for the tasks of life will usually succeed in them. Those who are unprepared for the tasks of life will usually fail.

This is also true in the Christian life. Every day we face challenges and opportunities. Christians who are prepared will successfully face these challenges and will fruitfully develop these opportunities. Christians who are unprepared will crumble in the face of the challenges and will waste their opportunities.

How does a Christian prepare himself or herself for these challenges and opportunities? The key is to practice the Christian disciplines of prayer, meditation, and study.

Misunderstanding.—A photographer from *Life* magazine was assigned to cover the great fires of Yellowstone National Park. When he got there, he discovered the smoke was so dense he could not get any pictures from the ground level. He asked if he could rent a plane and get some aerial shots. His request was approved, and arrangements were made. He was told to go to the nearby airport, and a plane would be waiting for him. He found a plane warming up by the gate, so he said, "Let's go!" as he jumped into the plane. The pilot swung the little plane into the wind and within minutes they were in the air. "Fly over the park," the photographer said. "Make two or three low-level passes." "Why?" the pilot asked. "Because I'm going to take some pictures.

I'm a photographer, and photographers take pictures." The pilot was silent for a moment. "You mean," he finally asked, "you're not the instructor?"

We all misunderstand things at times, but most of our misunderstandings are not as dangerous as the misunderstanding by that would-be pilot. Believing the wrong thing is equally as dangerous because wrong beliefs lead to wrong consequences. That's why the wrong beliefs of the disciples at Ephesus had to be corrected.

TEACHING THE CLASS

Main Idea: God uses persons of varying abilities and prominence to teach and witness to others.

Suggested Teaching Aim: Learners will decide to use whatever abilities they have to minister to others regardless of the level of their prominence.

Introduce the Bible Study

Direct learners to write down what they think they do best among all the tasks they have to do. Call for response. Emphasize the variety and differences.

A Teaching Outline

1. Focus on differences in abilities among believers.
2. Discover the importance of persons of lesser prominence in spreading the gospel of Christ.
3. Consider personal abilities that can support the more prominent witnesses.
4. Commit personal abilities to support the spread of the gospel.

Continue by asking: Which of these skills gets the greatest attention? Invite honest sharing of responses. Ask: Does the attention given to one ability over another make it more valuable? Why or why not? Share the comments titled "It takes an orchestra" (*Applying the Lesson*). State that the study for today will show us how God used persons of varying abilities and prominence to teach and witness to others. Invite learners to open their Bibles to Acts 18.

Search for Biblical Truth

Use information from the introduction of *Studying the Bible* to identify persons of varying abilities and prominence who surrounded Paul. Write the names on the chalkboard. Share brief information about each person.

Circle the names *Apollos, Aquila,* and *Priscilla.* State that today's study focuses on incidents that involve these persons.

Because this incident is less well known and the historical facts somewhat vague, share information from *Studying the Bible* about the passage before the Scripture is read aloud. When the events have been explained, call on a learner to read Acts 18:24-28 aloud.

Note that Apollos is also mentioned in the next section of Scripture to be considered. Call on a learner to read Acts 19:1-6 aloud while others listen to prepare to tell what happened at Ephesus. When the reading is finished, share information from the paragraph titled "Corrective Teaching" (*Studying the Bible*). Share the comments titled "Misunderstanding" (*Applying the Lesson*). Note that regardless of the source of the previous information, Paul led those at Ephesus to accept Jesus as Savior.

Point out that although Apollos, Priscilla, and Aquila do not share the prominence of Paul, their abilities were equally used of God. Paul acknowledged their contribution to the spread of the gospel.

Direct learners to review the Scripture passage to consider the personal abilities and characteristics of these three people. Invite them to discuss their conclusions with those sitting near them. After several minutes, call for response. List responses on the chalkboard.

Give the Truth a Personal Focus

Continue by asking: What personal abilities do you have that could be used in supporting the work of more prominent persons as they spread the gospel? Suggest that learners list privately what they believe their personal abilities to be. They may include understanding of correct doctrine, supportive attitudes, speaking ability, and giving. Encourage learners to see whatever abilities they have as abilities that can be used of God.

Share the comments titled "Not surprised but unprepared" (*Applying the Lesson*). Invite learners to commit whatever abilities they have to the support of spreading the gospel of Jesus Christ.

November 3

A Sad Farewell

Basic Passage: Acts 20

Focal Passage: Acts 20:17-31

The city of Ephesus had an important place in Paul's missionary strategy. Located in the Roman province of Asia, Ephesus was the most populous city in the area and its foremost trading center. It was the place from which the whole province could be most effectively reached and, in fact, was reached with the gospel. At the same time, it offered the challenge of a powerful center of paganism. The principal shrine in Ephesus was the temple of Artemis (Diana), which housed the multibreasted image that was said to have fallen from heaven (19:35). This temple was one of the seven wonders of the ancient world, four times as large as the Parthenon in Athens. Paul's ministry in Ephesus extended from two to three years (19:10; 20:31). Our printed lesson passage, which deals with Paul's farewell speech to leaders of the Ephesian church, needs the support of these and other facts that we may understand the strength of the relationship that existed between the apostle and these people.

Study Aim: *To measure the standard of our faithfulness in service by the devotion of Paul and his expectation of church leaders*

STUDYING THE BIBLE

The Roman province of Asia (see map), not to be confused with modern Asia, or Asia Minor, had been Paul's longtime goal for evangelism. Acts 16:6 reveals his desire to go there, and although temporarily prevented, he fulfilled his purpose as recorded in 18:18-19. That visit, however, was brief, compelling the apostle to say, like a modern American general, "I will return" (v. 21). This he did after a trip that included Jerusalem and Antioch (19:1).

I. Paul's Ties to Ephesus

The incident of the twelve men who had knowledge only of John's baptism is followed by significant information on Paul's activities in Ephesus (19:8-14). Brief note is taken of the following.

1. The Jew first (v. 8).—Even in this largely Gentile city, the apostle continued his policy of evangelizing his fellow Jews. For three months he visited a synagogue where his theme was the kingdom of God. For most Jews this meant their restoration as a nation, but Paul proclaimed a new society of redeemed persons drawn from all nations.

2. Separation compelled (vv. 9-10).—Opposition to his message forced the apostle to move out of the synagogue into "the school of one Tyrannus." This was probably a lecture hall that Tyrannus owned or used for his own teaching. There Paul stayed for two years during which time his message penetrated throughout the province. There is evidence that others aided Paul in spreading the gospel and through their concerted efforts the churches named in Revelation 2—3 were founded—Smyrna, Pergamos, Thyatira, Sardis, Philadelphia, and Laodicea.

3. Paganism challenged (vv. 11-12).—Magic was practiced widely by adherents of paganism, and this magic was answered by miracles of healing and exorcism. The result is given in verses 18-20 where heathen practitioners burned valuable books on the occult and embraced the faith Paul proclaimed.

4. Riot over Diana (vv. 21-41).—But this success for the gospel produced a new form of opposition. Ephesian businessmen, who made and sold souvenirs of Diana's temple, created a disturbance that became a dangerous riot. But for the intervention of "the townclerk" (v. 35), things could have gone badly for Paul and his company.

II. Destination Jerusalem (Acts 20:1-16)

This mob action put an end to Paul's ministry in Ephesus. But we need to remember that he had spent the best part of three years there and had laid a firm foundation for the future. It was not his policy to remain as permanent pastor of the churches he founded but to hand the leadership over to local believers. He had earlier intimated his plans for the future. He would visit the churches in Macedonia and Achaia, proceed to Jerusalem, after which, he said, "I must also see Rome" (19:21). Luke did not tell us that the apostle's purpose in going to Jerusalem was to deliver gifts from Gentile churches for the relief of poverty there.

1. Death threat (v. 3).—The strenuous and risky nature of Paul's travels is revealed in this chapter, which crowds a heap of experiences into a brief statement. After ministering to churches in Macedonia, he proceeded to Greece where he stayed three months, presumably in Corinth. From there he planned to sail direct to Syria and so on to Jerusalem. But knowledge of a plot against his life, presumably to kill him at sea, changed his plans so that he decided to go back into Macedonia and sail from there. Reference to a map (see map) will show the arduous nature of these travels, some part made on foot, other by ship.

2. Bypassing Ephesus (vv. 13-16).—Paul's original purpose had been to reach Jerusalem in time for the Passover, but delays compelled him to settle for Pentecost, fifty days later. To achieve this meant accepting a limited schedule, excluding Ephesus from his travel plans. The nearest port at which his ship would stop was Miletus, some thirty miles from Ephesus. Again we should be impressed by the physical demands of the journey.

III. Summons to Ephesian Elders (Acts 20:17-27)

This somewhat detailed review of events provides background to Paul's speech to the elders who traveled from Ephesus to meet him at Miletus. He would deal with the price he had paid, and must yet pay, to be a faithful minister of the gospel.

17 And from Miletus he sent to Ephesus, and called the elders of the church.

18 And when they were come to him, he said unto them, Ye know, from the first day that I came into Asia, after what manner I have been with you at all seasons,

19 Serving the Lord with all humility of mind, and with many tears, and temptations, which befell me by the lying in wait of the Jews:

20 And how I kept back nothing that was profitable unto you, but have showed you, and have taught you publicly, and from house to house,

21 Testifying both to the Jews, and also to the Greeks, repentance toward God, and faith toward our Lord Jesus Christ.

22 And now, behold, I go bound in the spirit unto Jerusalem, not knowing the things that shall befall me there:

23 Save that the Holy Ghost witnesseth in every city, saying that bonds and afflictions abide me.

24 But none of these things move me, neither count I my life dear unto myself, so that I might finish my course with joy, and the ministry, which I have received of the Lord Jesus, to testify the gospel of the grace of God.

25 And now, behold, I know that ye all, among whom I have gone preaching the kingdom of God, shall see my face no more.

26 Wherefore I take you to record this day, that I am pure from the blood of all men.

27 For I have not shunned to declare unto you all the counsel of God.

1. Ministry reviewed (vv. 17-21).—The recurring pronoun "we" (vv. 13-16) indicates that Luke was with Paul at this time. We have, therefore, Luke's personal recollections of what the apostle said to the Ephesian leaders, his only recorded speech addressed to Christians. Because Paul was about to challenge these church elders with their responsibilities, he began by reminding them of his own self-denying conduct as the messenger of Christ to them. Our previous review of events recorded in preceding chapters helps to fill in details of Paul's dedicated service and its cost in terms of opposition and arduous travel. His reference to teaching "from house to house" (v. 20) is interesting. This may have been family visitation although churches that met in homes were common then (Rom. 16:5).

2. Grim prospect (vv. 22-27).—Paul was going to Jerusalem with the knowledge that affliction awaited him there. Although he would be the bearer of gifts from Gentile churches, he would meet with a hostile reception. Again and again he was reminded of this by prophetic utterance (21:4,11), but he was not deterred from his purpose, even by the thought of death (20:24).

IV. A Painful Good-bye (Acts 20:28-38)

The apostle clearly believed that he was seeing his Ephesian friends for the last time (v. 25). He solemnly charged them to be faithful to their task and warned them of future developments within the church that could undermine the work of the gospel.

> **28 Take heed therefore unto yourselves, and to all the flock, over the which the Holy Ghost hath made you overseers, to feed the church of God, which he hath purchased with his own blood.**
> **29 For I know this, that after my departing shall grievous wolves enter in among you, not sparing the flock.**
> **30 Also of your own selves shall men arise, speaking perverse things, to draw away disciples after them.**
> **31 Therefore watch, and remember, that by the space of three years I ceased not to warn everyone night and day with tears.**

These elders must be careful of their own behavior as they ministered to others. An inconsistent messenger can neutralize the good that is in his message. The phrase "which he hath purchased with his own blood" (v. 28) is better rendered: "by means of the blood of his own," that is, the blood of His Son, Jesus our Lord. Watchfulness over the flock must be a major concern because of the threat of false teachers, "grievous wolves," from the outside and perverse influences within the church itself. That these dangers became realities is evident from Revelation 2:1-2. But, however difficult and demanding the task, adequate spiritual resources were available (v. 32). Self-sacrifice would be involved as Paul himself had experienced when he labored at tentmaking to support himself and his associates in ministry. Verse 35 includes words from our Lord Himself, not recorded in the Gospels, which apply to all who engage in His service, "It is more blessed to give than to receive."

APPLYING THE LESSON

A bridge of friendship.—Palmer Ofuoku, a distinguished preacher in Nigeria, told of how he became a Christian. His family was not Christian. However, they placed him in a mission school to obtain a quality education. Palmer attended the school many years but remained a follower of his traditional religion. He met many missionaries over those years, and although he learned from them, he was not influenced by them to become a Christian. One year a new missionary came to the school who became involved in the lives of the Nigerians. He brought a new quality of relationships and eventually led Palmer to the Lord. Palmer later explained, "He built a bridge of friendship to me, and Jesus walked across."

That is a good definition of "friendship evangelism": we build a bridge of friendship to the lost so that Jesus can walk across that bridge and into their hearts. Paul practiced friendship evangelism in Ephesus, and consequently, many people were led to Jesus Christ.

Envy.—Envy has been defined as our unhappiness at someone else's happiness. To check to see if you have envy, think about how you would react to these two situations. Suppose you were with a friend, and he received a phone call informing him that his father had just died. How would you respond? Most of us would respond with sympathy and support. But suppose you were with a friend, and she received a phone call informing her that a rich uncle had just died, leaving her five million dollars. How would you respond to that? Outwardly, you would probably express joy at her great fortune. But how would you really feel? Would you say, "Can you believe it? Good things always happen to her. She doesn't deserve it!" How would you respond?

The religious leaders of Ephesus observed the things that were happening to people around them. Instead of rejoicing with them, they became envious because they were losing influence and financial support. They were unhappy at the other people's happiness. Consequently, they created a riot in which they sought to destroy these Christian intruders who were causing the problems.

Sacrificing for the kingdom.—Early in the nineteenth century, Frederick William III of Prussia was in financial trouble. He was running out of funds needed to carry out his expensive wars. He wanted to make a great nation of the Prussian people. He could not give in or give up. But he needed more money. He finally decided to approach the women of Prussia. He asked them to bring their gold and silver jewelry to be melted down and made into money to finance the battles. In exchange for each gold or silver ornament, the king gave a bronze or iron decoration. Each decoration bore the inscription: "I gave gold for iron, 1813." The response was overwhelming. The women valued the decorations more than the jewelry itself because the decorations were symbols of their sacrifices for their nation.

No advancement has ever been made in God's kingdom without sacrifices by His people. In a letter to Corinth, Paul summarized in detail the suffering he endured for Christ (2 Cor. 11:23-29). In his address to the Ephesians in our text, Paul also alluded to that suffering.

The results of faithfulness.—An old minister in Scotland was nearing the end of a long ministry in an obscure church field. He was disappointed that he had not been able to accomplish more for the Lord. He was discouraged because he had not won more to the Lord. He was telling his discouraging tale to Ralph Sockman (1889-1970), a well-known pastor who had achieved everything this minister felt he had missed. The distinguished minister listened until the old man had finished. Then he said, "Do you remember a young woman who used to worship in your church some twenty years ago?" When Sockman described the woman, the old minister said, "Yes, I remember her. She came for quite a while, but never joined the church." The famous pastor continued, "That young woman had a younger brother who was rapidly becoming a drunkard. She would come home from church and talk to him about your sermons until finally she changed his habits. I was that young man."

Paul encouraged the Ephesian leaders to remain faithful because of the influence they would have over others.

TEACHING THE CLASS

Main Idea: Watchfulness both without and within oneself to continuing service to God.

Suggested Teaching Aim: Learners will be able to explain the watchfulness that is required of them as they continue in service.

Introduce the Bible Study

Share information from the introductory paragraphs of *Studying the Bible.* Note that at this point in his experience Paul had a grave concern about the work that he had done with the Ephesians. Read Acts 20:29-30 aloud from a modern translation. Point out that Paul believed there would be threats to the gospel he had taught.

Write *caution, danger,* on the chalkboard. Ask: What are the threats to the teaching of the gospel in today's world? Are they more or less than in Paul's day? Are they different or the same? List threats mentioned on the chalkboard.

Add lack of contact with nonbelievers to the list of threats. Ask: To what extent is this a threat in our community? Share the comments titled "A bridge of friendship" (*Applying the Lesson*).

State that the purpose of the study for today is to raise our awareness of the need for watchfulness in our own lives and in our church body. Invite learners to turn in their Bibles to Acts 20.

Search for Biblical Truth

Share information from *Studying the Bible* that provides background for Paul's speech to the elders who traveled from Ephesus to meet him at Miletus. Conclude by reading Acts 20:17.

A Teaching Outline

1. Consider threats to the teaching of the gospel in today's world.
2. Discover Paul's concerns about the continued witness of the Ephesian believers.
3. Identify threats to the witness and service in the local body of believers.
4. Explain the watchfulness that is required.

Call on a learner who has previously agreed to read Paul's speech to the Ephesians from Acts 20:18-31. Plan with the learner before the class session to have the speech read in a dramatic way from a modern translation of the Bible. Direct other learners to listen to identify some of the feelings Paul had as he spoke these words of farewell. When the reading is finished, call for response. List responses on the chalkboard. They may include reflection, concern, sadness, determination, and the need to warn.

Ask: What was the greatest concern (vv. 29-30) Paul had for the believers at Ephesus? Response should include these concerns: (1) that persons outside the fellowship of these believers would come in with false teachings and lead them astray, and (2) that some within the congregation would draw them away from true teachings.

Continue by asking: What precaution did Paul give against this happening? (See v. 31, watch and remember). Continue: What were they to watch for? What were these believers to remember? Elicit response. Share the comments titled "Envy" (*Applying the Lesson*).

Give the Truth a Personal Focus

Ask rhetorically: Are there threats to the well-being of churches today? Would you agree that threats come from the same sources as in Paul's day, both from without and from within? Continue by directing learners to privately list the specific threats to their local congregation from both outside and inside. After several minutes for consideration, share the conclusions as it is appropriate. (This should not be a time of attack on anyone or any program, but it should be an awareness-raising activity.)

Ask: What was Paul's admonition to the church at Ephesus when they faced threats? (To maintain watchfulness.) Continue by asking: What does watchfulness mean for us with the threats to our own church? What should we be doing? How should we be thinking? Encourage thoughtful response.

November 10

Arrested and Accused

Basic Passages: Acts 21:17-40; 22:25—23:11

Focal Passages: Acts 21:26-33,37-39a

The word *Jerusalem* has frequently occurred in recent lessons. No place in the biblical world is more familiar to us than this. The apostle Paul's story, so far as his friend Luke's record is concerned, began in that city (Acts 7:58; 8:1). It was from Jerusalem that Paul set out for Damascus, a journey that was to transform his life. To Jerusalem he returned in hope of resolving a controversy that was dividing the Gentile church in Antioch (15:1-6). That visit marked the beginning of hostilities toward Paul that would eventually lead to imprisonment and death. But this tragic prospect could not keep him away from Jerusalem where, in addition to enemies, he had many friends. There were also Jewish Christians whose poverty moved Gentile churches to generous giving for their relief. Paul was the bearer of these gifts, which he carried on his final visit, recorded in our study passages. From this point on, Jerusalem drops out of the New Testament record. In a few years, the city would be destroyed by the Romans.

Study Aim: *To identify with persons, past and present, whose faithfulness, in spite of hardship, has preserved witness to Christ*

STUDYING THE BIBLE

An unusually long Scripture selection challenges us to produce a connected review of events in Jerusalem. We shall see how another city, Rome, assumed increasing significance for the apostle as the strategic center for Christianity shifted from the Jewish to the Gentile world.

I. Reception in Jerusalem (Acts 21:17-25)

A strong warning that going to Jerusalem would endanger Paul's life was given him in Caesarea, by "a certain prophet, named Agabus" (vv. 10-11). But the apostle replied that he was "ready . . . to die at Jerusalem for the name of the Lord Jesus" (v. 13). As already mentioned, Luke made only brief reference to a major purpose for this visit (24:17), but we know from such passages as Romans 15:25-26 that Paul carried the offering from the Gentile churches.

1. Cordial welcome (vv. 17-19).—James, brother of our Lord, had become acknowledged leader of the church in Jerusalem, a function he exercised with the help of an unstated number of elders. These all extended a warm welcome to Paul and his companions, who included Luke (note the "we" in verse 17). To this friendly group the apostle rehearsed the story of his Gentile ministry.

2. Suggested appeasement (vv. 20-25).—This happy occasion was marred by the announcement of opposition to Paul from believing Jews who were "zealous of the law" (v. 20)—that is, they believed that, although Christians, they should continue to observe the Mosaic law. These people were spreading the report that Paul advised converted Jews living among Gentiles to abandon all traditional rituals, a report, of course, that had some truth in it. But James and his company recommended that while in Jerusalem Paul show his esteem for ancient laws by joining four men who were fulfilling a vow and paying their expenses.

II. Incitement to Violence (Acts 21:26-33)

This scheme miscarried, causing some to suggest that Paul made a mistake by this concession to legalism. We would need to read the apostle's mind at this time to have an answer. He was doing no more than following his declared principle of being "all things to all men" that he "might by all means save some" (1 Cor. 9:22).

> **26 Then Paul took the men, and the next day purifying himself with them entered into the temple, to signify the accomplishment of the days of purification, until that an offering should be offered for everyone of them.**

27 And when the seven days were almost ended, the Jews which were of Asia, when they saw him in the temple, stirred up all the people, and laid hands on him,

28 Crying out, Men of Israel, help: This is the man, that teacheth all men everywhere against the people, and the law, and this place: and further brought Greeks also into the temple, and hath polluted this holy place.

29 (For they had seen before with him in the city Trophimus an Ephesian, whom they supposed that Paul had brought into the temple.)

30 And all the city was moved, and the people ran together: and they took Paul, and drew him out of the temple: and forthwith the doors were shut.

31 And as they went about to kill him, tidings came unto the chief captain of the band, that all Jerusalem was in an uproar.

32 Who immediately took soldiers and centurions, and ran down unto them: and when they saw the chief captain and the soldiers, they left beating of Paul.

33 Then the chief captain came near, and took him, and commanded him to be bound with two chains; and demanded who he was, and what he had done.

1. Accusations made (vv. 26-30).—The attack on Paul shifted from persons within the church to enemies outside. Jews from all parts of the world were in Jerusalem for the celebration of Pentecost, among them persons who had caused him trouble in Ephesus (20:3,19). Among the apostle's companions in Jerusalem was an Ephesian named Trophimus. The groundless charge was made that Paul had taken this Gentile into forbidden areas of the temple. Racial and religious feelings ran high at feast times, and a quickly gathering crowd seized Paul, cast him out of the temple, and intended to kill him.

2. Roman intervention (vv. 31-33).—Overlooking the temple area, Herod the Great had built the Fortress of Antonia, garrisoned by Roman soldiers and with two flights of steps that led into the outer court of the temple. Its purpose was to break up disturbances in quick time. The officer in charge, being informed of the riot against Paul, despatched probably more than two hundred men, since centurions are mentioned, each commanding one hundred. Paul was assumed to be the cause of the disturbance; thus he was arrested and put in chains.

III. Paul Under Arrest (Acts 21:34-40)

An ugly scene now became uglier. Those who had purposed to kill Paul were not to be thwarted. Even the soldiers could not hold them back; therefore, to save his life, they carried him bodily up the stairs that led to their headquarters.

37 And as Paul was to be led into the castle, he said unto the chief captain, May I speak unto thee? Who said, Canst thou speak Greek?

38 Art not thou that Egyptian, which before these days madest an uproar, and leddest out into the wilderness four thousand men that were murderers?

39 But Paul said, I am a man which am a Jew of Tarsus, a city in Cilicia, a citizen of no mean city: and, I beseech thee, suffer me to speak unto the people.

1. Mistaken identity (vv. 34-38).—According to the Jewish historian Josephus, three years before the events we are studying, an Egyptian arrived in Jerusalem, claiming to be a prophet. He led a crowd of followers to the Mount of Olives where, according to him, they would witness the collapse of the walls of the city, providing opportunity to overcome the Roman garrison. But word reached Roman authorities who moved in, killed some, and made prisoners of others. The Egyptian escaped; so the captain now assumed he had reappeared and been set upon by outraged Jews.

2. Stairway speech (vv. 39-40).—Paul exploded the Roman's false conclusion when he asked, in perfect Greek, "May I speak unto thee?" (v. 37). No Egyptian adventurer this, but a man of culture who, in response to further questioning, claimed to be "a Jew of Tarsus, . . . a citizen of no mean city." Whether this statement carried an implication of Roman citizenship we cannot be sure, although the apostle would later make plain this claim (22:25-28). In any case, the chief of the temple guard was sufficiently impressed to allow the apostle to address the unruly crowd. While Paul's Greek surprised the Roman officer, his Aramaic (for so we should probably understand the reference to "the Hebrew tongue"), silenced the mob. No summary of his speech is needed here since it largely paralleled Paul's statement before Agrippa to be studied next week.

IV. Destination Rome (Acts 22:25—23:11)

Toward the conclusion of his speech, Paul told of his visit to Jerusalem following his conversion on the Damascus road (9:26-30). While in Damascus, he had a message from God to get out because what he had to say would not be accepted. Paul was reticent to go, but the divine warning persisted since God had a mission for him among Gentiles. It was this word that set the match to the fuse.

1. Scourging avoided (22:25-30).—Paul's audience exploded with wrath when he mentioned Gentiles. He had affirmed his Jewishness (v. 3), told of his conversion and commission (vv. 14-15), and then outraged his listeners by speaking of Jewish rejection and Gentile acceptance. He was rescued by the chief captain who, still convinced that he had a criminal in his hands, ordered scourging to extract the truth. The centurion assigned to this task hurried back to his superior officer when Paul claimed to be a Roman. We do not know how Paul substantiated this claim. Perhaps he carried papers to this effect. In any case, the chief captain was persuaded and revealed that he had bought Roman citizenship, to which the apostle replied, "But I was free born" (v. 28). Evidently Paul's father was a Roman citizen, though under what circumstances we do not know.

2. Word from God (23:11).—Our basic Scripture selection continues to 23:11, thus including Paul's appearance before the Jewish Sanhedrin. This appearance led to further disorders that threatened the apostle's life, causing the chief captain to give him protection in the Fortress of Antonia. There God spoke to him: "Be of good cheer, Paul: for as thou hast testified of me in Jerusalem, so must thou bear witness also at Rome." The apostle's expressed purpose (19:21) was to be realized in unexpected ways.

APPLYING THE LESSON

Giving without love.—A church collected clothes to send for overseas relief. Many of the things were of good quality and were in good shape. But many of the clothes given were hardly worth sending. They were ragged and torn and needed mending. The saddest thing of all was that some people had cut all the buttons off the clothing they had given.

When it comes to giving, some people stop at nothing! How selfish we are with the manifold blessings God has given to us. Not so with the Christians in Macedonia who contributed to the offering that Paul brought to the poor Christians in Palestine. Paul described their spirit in 2 Corinthians 8:1-2: "Now, brethren, we wish to make known to you the grace of God which has been given in the churches of Macedonia, that in a great ordeal of affliction their abundance of joy and their deep poverty overflowed in the wealth of their liberality" (NASB).

Casting the first stone.—A cartoon showed the minister at the door following the morning worship service. He was being greeted by one of the members who said, "It seems to me you cast the first stone several times in there, Reverend."

How easy it is to cast the first stone. Some bad may exist in any situation and in any person. If we are looking for it, we can find it.

Paul, dedicated Christian that he was, was not perfect. He had faults and imperfections. Throughout Paul's ministry he was hounded by those who, focusing only on his faults and imperfections, were ready to criticize.

It didn't work.—The little boy watched his big sister as she put on her makeup. He saw her array of creams and powders. "What is all that stuff?" he asked his sister. She replied, "If it's any of your business, this is what I put on my face to make me look pretty." He watched without another word until she finished at which point he made the comment, Well, it didn't work."

A lot of things don't work. Our best laid plans often fall apart. Our best intentions are often not rewarded in kind. Paul had that experience in our text. A plan to appease his critics actually fueled the fire of criticism. Paul tried to alleviate the problem, but it didn't work.

Three kinds of angry.—Patrick Morley in his book *The Man in the Mirror* describes three kinds of angry men: Freddie Flash, Cary Control, and Gary Grudge. Freddie Flash is a person with a short fuse. He gets mad quickly, and it happens all the time. Cary Control is a person who simmers and simmers until, finally, something sets him off, and he just explodes. Gary Grudge never has an outburst of anger at all. Instead, he holds his anger in. He spends his energy trying to plot revenge on his enemies.[1]

Luke did not describe the ones in Jerusalem who became angry at Paul. Perhaps Freddie Flash, Cary Control, and Gary Grudge were all represented in the crowd.

God-confidence.—Confidence comes in two varieties: God-confidence and self-confidence. Self-confidence was illustrated in the life of world conqueror Alexander the Great. Alexander lead his army against a powerful foe whose men greatly outnumbered his own. Consequently, his army was pessimistic about the outcome. When Alexander unloaded his men and equipment on enemy shores, he issued an order for all the ships to be burned. As their means of retreat slowly sank in flames behind them, Alexander said to his troops: "None of us can leave this place unless we are victorious. When we go home, we are going home in their ships!" That is self-confidence.

Paul illustrated God-confidence. He never said, "I can do this," or, "I am able to accomplish that." Paul's confidence was based on God. As he said to the Corinthians, "Not that we are adequate in ourselves to consider anything as coming from ourselves, but our adequacy is from God" (2 Cor. 3:5, NASB).

TEACHING THE CLASS

Main Idea: Witnesses for Christ do not always avoid conflict and hardship.

Suggested Teaching Aim: Learners will decide to accept conflict and hardship, if necessary, to be continuing witnesses for Christ.

Introduce the Bible Study

Share this life situation.

Bill has lived on the same block with Jim and Mary for five years. Their children frequently play together. Bill visits with Jim as they do their weekend lawn mowing. In one of these conversations, Bill talks with Jim about his relationship with Jesus.

Ask: What kind of response to his witnessing might Bill expect from Jim? Listen to the response.

Share this life situation followed by the same questions.

Joyce has worked in the same office with Lucille for almost five years. They frequently talk about their families and activities at lunch or break time. Joyce has learned that Lucille is a member of a church but has had no association with the church since she was a child. Joyce feels impressed to talk with Lucille about a personal relationship with Christ. What response might Joyce expect from Lucille?

State that the study for today focuses on some of the response to the witnessing of Paul. Invite learners to turn in their Bibles to Acts 21.

Search for Biblical Truth

Use information from *Studying the Bible* to set the stage for the incidents for study. Call on a learner to read Acts 21:26-33 aloud while others listen to learn what happened at this point. When the reading is finished, call for response.

Clarify the details of the incident with questions like these: Who were these Jews who stirred up the people against Paul? Why were they so angry? What were their plans for Paul when they threw him out of the temple? What prevented these plans from being carried out? What response to Paul's witness of Jesus is evident here?

A Teaching Outline

1. Discuss responses that witnesses for Christ can expect today.
2. Discover the response of some to the witness of Paul.
3. Identify conflict and hardship learners have experienced as a result of witnessing for Christ.
4. Decide to accept whatever conflict and hardship is necessary to be a continuing witness for Christ.

Note that Paul was now being taken chained to prison. Direct learners to read Acts 21:37-39 silently to see what Paul did in the midst of these circumstances. Call for response. Share some of the comments from *Applying the Lesson* to illustrate the kinds of situations in which Paul found himself.

Use information from the final paragraphs of *Studying the Bible* to describe Paul's speech and the events that followed. Ask: When Paul began to tell people about Jesus, do you think he would have expected a response like this? Why or why not?

Give the Truth a Personal Focus

Ask learners to recall the life situations given as the study began. Ask: What extreme response might follow the witness of John and Joyce? Ask learners for examples of the kind of conflict or hardship that witnesses today may experience. Examples may include social exclusion, gossip about them, affected job opportunities, and hostility.

Ask: Why would anyone want to tell others about Jesus if this is the response? Wait for response. Share the comments titled "God-confidence" (*Applying the Lesson*). Ask: Would you be willing to accept conflict and hardship if it is necessary to be a continuing witness for Christ? Allow a moment of silence for learners to consider their response. Close the study with a moment of prayer asking for commitment to telling others about Jesus regularly regardless of the response.

---

1. Patrick M. Morley, *The Man in the Mirror* (Brentwood, Tenn.: Wolgemuth and Hyatt, 1989), 215.

November 17

Before Agrippa

Basic Passage: Acts 25:13—26:32

Focal Passages: Acts 26:1-8,22-23,27-29

Paul was detained in Caesarea for two years (24:27) while Roman officials hesitated over what to do with him. This important coastal city is not to be confused with Caesarea Philippi, situated inland, north of Galilee. The Caesarea that became the scene of events we are studying was the object of great Roman pride because of the artificial harbor built there and other structures of great beauty. Continuing archaeological discoveries confirm the engineering skills of the builders and the splendor that existed in Paul's day, when Caesarea was the Roman capital of Palestine. How Paul occupied his time in Caesarea is a subject of debate. Some think that certain of his epistles were written there, but of this we cannot be sure. Luke, who remained with

Paul as his companion (note the "we" in 27:1) probably used the time to good advantage, gathering materials for his Gospel. He would certainly have had opportunity to interview persons who "from the beginning were eyewitnesses" of the life of our Lord (Luke 1:2). We may certainly believe that these two years were used to the advantage of the cause of Christ.

Study Aim: *To recognize the overruling sovereignty of God in hardships that befall His people*

STUDYING THE BIBLE

How the apostle got to Caesarea is too important and interesting a story to be passed over without reference, however brief. So we pick up our narrative where we left it last week.

I. Jerusalem to Caesarea

Recent world events have revealed, again and again, the extremes to which people will go in the name of religion. While strong convictions are allowable, when those convictions are expressed in acts of terrorism they cease to have spiritual validity. The hostility shown to Paul by those who disagreed with him is a case in point.

1. Death plot (23:12-24).—Forty men pledged not to eat or drink until they had killed Paul. A nephew of the apostle disclosed this plot. When the Roman tribune in charge of Paul (his name was Claudius Lysias, see v. 26) learned of it, he decided that Jerusalem was too dangerous for his prisoner and accordingly despatched him to the governor in Caesarea.

2. Vacillating Felix (24:1-27).—This man had been a slave in the household of the mother of the Roman emperor Claudius. He was the only freedman to be appointed to a governorship, and it was said of him that he had the power of a king and the heart of a slave. His wife was Drusilla, a Jewess (24:24), which may account for his interest in Paul's case. But after listening to testimony for and against, he made no decision, and Paul remained in custody.

3. Enter Festus (25:1-12).—We know little of this man who succeeded Felix. On appointment, Festus wanted to transfer Paul's case back to Jerusalem. But Paul knew that this could only mean trouble for him. So he exercised a right of Roman citizenship and asked to have his case heard before Caesar.

II. Visit from Agrippa (Acts 25:13-27)

Now we can turn our attention to our basic Scripture passage. Festus was in a quandary. The subtleties of Paul's case were baffling to him. To his rescue came Herod Agrippa II, ruler of a small area northeast of Palestine. He had strong ties to Judaism both by birth and office because Rome had given him charge over the high priest's vestments, virtually giving him the power of appointment to this sacred office. On the negative side, his relationship to Bernice, who passed as his wife, was a scandal throughout the Roman world. She was his sister.

1. Interest shown (vv. 13-22).—Agrippa's reputation as an authority on Judaism encouraged Festus to tell him about Paul. He said he had resisted efforts of the Jewish leaders to have judgment passed against Paul. Instead, he had invited the apostle's accusers to Caesarea to state their case. To his surprise, so he said, the issues were about "certain questions against him of their own superstition," or, "their own" religion, issues that centered in a person known as Jesus, "which was dead, whom Paul affirmed to be alive" (v. 19). Agrippa had probably heard about Jesus, hence his expressed desire to "hear the man myself" (v. 22).

2. The governor's dilemma (vv. 23-27).—Festus had a motive in telling Agrippa about Paul. He could not send the apostle to Rome without an adequate statement of the charges leveled against him. But he was baffled to know what to say and hoped that Agrippa would come to his help after he had interviewed Paul.

III. An Apostle Faces a King (Acts 26:1-32)

This was not a trial, and Agrippa did not function as a judge. As already stated, Festus had two purposes in arranging this audience: to compliment Agrippa for his knowledge of Judaism and to provide himself with an intelligent statement to send, with Paul, to Rome. The situation was dramatic: the king in "great pomp" (25:23) and Christ's apostle in chains (26:29).

1 Then Agrippa said unto Paul, Thou art permitted to speak for thyself. Then Paul stretched forth the hand, and answered for himself:

2 I think myself happy, king Agrippa, because I shall answer for myself this day before thee touching all the things whereof I am accused of the Jews:

3 Especially because I know thee to be expert in all customs and questions which are among the Jews: wherefore I beseech thee to hear me patiently.

4 My manner of life from my youth, which was at the first among mine own nation at Jerusalem, know all the Jews;

5 Which knew me from the beginning, if they would testify, that after the most straitest sect of our religion I lived a Pharisee.

6 And now I stand and am judged for the hope of the promise made of God unto our fathers:

7 Unto which promise our twelve tribes, instantly serving God day and night, hope to come. For which hope's sake, king Agrippa, I am accused of the Jews.

8 Why should it be thought a thing incredible with you, that God should raise the dead?

1. Courteous salute (vv. 1-3).—Paul recognized the significance of the occasion. Here he was, an apostle of Christ, condemned by his fellow Jews, given opportunity to state his case before a Herod, in this instance a Herod who could be considered an expert in Jewish matters. In "stretched forth the hand" (v. 1), we have the touch of an eyewitness, Luke.

2. Paul's background (vv. 4-7).—His early allegiance had been to the sect of the Pharisees, a strict brotherhood dedicated to the observance of the Mosaic law. As a Jew, Paul shared with all others the messianic hope that rested on divine promises concerning the coming of a great deliverer. Surprisingly, he had been accused by Jews for his beliefs about this very matter. Note "twelve tribes" (v. 7). Paul knew nothing of ten lost tribes!

3. The real issue (v. 8).—We can probably assume that what we have in these verses is a condensation of Paul's speech. He indicated the messianic hope had been fulfilled in a person (the Lord Jesus) who, though put to death, had risen from the dead. Pharisees believed in resurrection, but they rejected it in the case of Jesus, who to Paul was the Christ.

4. Conversion experience (vv. 9-21).—At one time, Paul went on to say, he had been prominent among those who were opposed to Jesus Christ and engaged in persecution of His followers. In fact, it was while pursuing this purpose that he was confronted by Christ Himself (lesson for Sept. 1). Given a commission by the risen Lord, to Jew and Gentile alike, "to open their eyes, and to turn them from darkness to light, and from the power of Satan unto God" (v. 18), Paul had devoted his life to this ministry. For no other reason, he had been arrested in the temple by those who went about to kill him (v. 21). In two verses, Paul proceeded to summarize the teaching that had produced such enmity.

22 Having therefore obtained help of God, I continue unto this day, witnessing both to small and great, saying none other things than those which the prophets and Moses did say should come:

23 That Christ should suffer, and that he should be the first that should rise from the dead, and should show light unto the people, and to the Gentiles.

5. Paul's teaching (vv. 22-23).—Again we probably have considerable condensation. As he did in his epistles, we may suppose Paul cited Old Testament Scriptures that supported the truths of a suffering Savior, raised from the dead, and proclaimed to Jew and Gentile alike. These, however, were truths totally unacceptable to his contemporaries who saw their messiah as a national deliverer, denied that Jesus rose from the dead, and were affronted by the thought that Gentiles were included in God's redemptive purposes.

6. Dramatic dialogue (vv. 24-32).—As a listener to what Paul said, Festus was more and more out of his depth. To his unenlightened mind, all this talk was gibberish, hence his rude interruption, "You are out of your mind, Paul! Too much learning is driving you insane!" (v. 24, NRSV). The apostle politely repudiated this charge, and addressing Agrippa, said:

> **27 King Agrippa, believest thou the prophets? I know that thou believest.**
>
> **28 Then Agrippa said unto Paul, Almost thou persuadest me to be a Christian.**
>
> **29 And Paul said, I would to God, that not only thou, but also all that hear me this day, were both almost, and altogether such as I am, except these bonds.**

Although it hurts to abandon popular interpretations, we should understand Agrippa's words in verse 28 as the exclamation of an embarrassed man. Paul had him in a corner, and he was not about to endorse his position on Moses and the prophets, certainly not in front of Festus. So he turned the subject aside by accusing Paul of attempting to make a Christian out of him. The occasion was not lost by the apostle, however, who replied with a fervent wish that Agrippa, and all present, might be what he was—a follower of the risen Christ.

APPLYING THE LESSON

Dealing with enemies.—George Bernard Shaw and Sir Winston Churchill were notable enemies. They looked for opportunities to dig at each other. On one occasion, Shaw telegraphed Winston Churchill: "Have reserved two tickets for my first night. Come and bring a friend, if you have one." Churchill answered back, "Impossible to come the first night. Will come to second night, if you have one!" That kind of sparring between enemies is harmless. Often, however, dislike turns into hatred and hatred turns ugly.

Such was the case with Paul's enemies in Jerusalem. They went beyond dislike to hatred, and they went beyond harmless sparring to a desire to kill Paul.

Things aren't always as they seem.—Before the Civil War was over and victory was obtained for the United States, President Lincoln was asked to deliver a dedicatory address for a national cemetery where thousands had been slain. Many officials did not expect the president to appear. His speech was only a minor part of the program. A major address was given by someone else. The president spoke briefly from notes he had jotted on an envelope. The response to his address was minimal. One newspaper reported about his speech, "We pass over the silly remarks of the president . . . willing that the veil of oblivion shall be dropped over them that they shall no more be respected or thought of." Another paper said, "The cheek of every American must tingle with shame as he reads the silly, flat, and dish-watery utterances of the man who has to be pointed out to intelligent foreigners as the president of the United States." What was this address criticized by the press and literally ignored by those who heard it? It was the most quoted and most revered speech ever given by any president. The place was Gettysburg, and the speech was the Gettysburg address. Things aren't always what they seem.[1]

That evaluation could be given of the confrontation between Paul and Agrippa in our text. Agrippa was a king, and Paul seemed to be a nobody. Yet two thousand years later we look back at that event, not concerned with what Agrippa said but eternally concerned about what Paul said. We know that it was not Paul before Agrippa but Agrippa before Paul. Things aren't always as they seem.

All the speaker could talk about was Jesus.—Martin Niemoeller was a German Christian leader who spent several years in a Nazi prison camp because of his resistance to Hitler. In the early 1960s, Niemoeller came to America on a speaking tour. Knowing of his traumatic experiences under Hitler, two newspaper reporters went to hear him, expecting to hear some exciting adventures. After listening to Dr. Niemoeller preach about Christ, they left the church disappointed. One said to the other, "Six years in a Nazi prison camp, and all he has to talk about is Jesus Christ." After six years in a Nazi prison camp, Niemoeller knew the only thing worth talking about was Jesus.

Paul was motivated by that same spirit. He always began where the people in his audience were. He wanted to relate his message to them. But the heart of his message was always the same. As he said to the Corinthians, "For we do not preach ourselves but Christ Jesus as Lord, and ourselves as your bond-servants for Jesus' sake" (2 Cor. 4:5, NASB).

A matter of choice.—Dr. Pierce Harris, pastor of First Methodist Church in Atlanta, Georgia, at the time, was a guest speaker at the state penitentiary. He was introduced by one of the inmates, who said, "Two boys lived in the same neighborhood. They went to the same school. They even went to the same church. One of those boys decided he would be smart. He rebelled and quit going to church. He did the things he should not have done. The other boy continued down the path of doing the right things. Those two boys are grown men now, and both are here today. The boy who continued down the right path is the great minister who will speak to us today. The boy who decided to be smart and rebelled is the prisoner who is introducing the preacher." The difference was the choice each boy made. Paul challenged Agrippa to make a choice about Christ, which he refused to do.

TEACHING THE CLASS

Main Idea: Opportunity to witness about Jesus comes in varying circumstances.

Suggested Teaching Aim: Learners will accept that whatever life brings to them can be used as a platform for witnessing.

Introduce the Bible Study

Remind learners that last week the discussion was about witnessing and responses we might expect from our witness. Ask: Under what circumstances would you most prefer to tell someone about Jesus? Elicit response from learners.

State that the study for today is set in perhaps one of the least desirable circumstances for witnessing. Remind learners of the arrest of Paul studied last Sunday. State that today we learn about Paul standing before his accusers as a prisoner and his being able to give a witness about Jesus. Invite learners to open their Bibles to Acts 26.

Search for Biblical Truth

Share the comments titled "Dealing with enemies" (*Applying the Lesson*). Use the information from *Studying the Bible* to provide a background for Paul's speech before King Agrippa. Display the following outline to guide the Scripture study.

An Apostle Faces a King

A. A courteous salute (Acts 26:1-3).
B. Personal background (Acts 26:4-7).
C. The real issue (Acts 26:8).
D. Conversion experience (Acts 26:9-21).
E. Important teaching (Acts 26:22-23).
F. Dramatic dialogue (Acts 26:24-32).

Share the comments titled "Things aren't always as they seem" (*Applying the Lesson*). Call attention to the title of the outline.

Ask: How did Paul show courtesy to King Agrippa in verses 1-3? Call for response.

Direct learners to read verses 4-7 to themselves and be prepared to give some of Paul's background. Call for response.

Call on someone to read verse 8 aloud. Note that in Paul's mind Jesus' resurrection is the real issue. Contrast Paul's view with the view of the Pharisees who believed in the resurrection but denied that Jesus had been raised from the dead. This was unacceptable to Paul because He believed Jesus to be the Messiah.

Invite learners to scan verses 9-21 in their Bibles to learn of Paul's conversion. Recall the study on September 1.

A Teaching Outline

1. Discuss desirable circumstances for witnessing.
2. Discover an unusual circumstance in which Paul gave witness of Jesus.
3. Identify difficult circumstances in personal lives that make witnessing difficult.
4. Indicate acceptance that witnessing will be a part of all circumstances of learners' lives.

Note that Paul presented the entire gospel in two verses as he concluded the testimony of his conversion. Call on a learner to read verses 22-23 aloud.

Call attention to the title for verses 24-32. Prearrange with four learners to read this passage aloud with three persons reading the words of Paul, Festus, and Agrippa. The fourth person should read the narrative. Call on these persons to read this dialogue in a dramatic manner.

Give the Truth a Personal Focus

Ask: What circumstance can you imagine in which it would be as difficult to talk about Jesus as these circumstances? Continue by inviting learners to name the most difficult or unusual circumstances in their lives for talking about Jesus? After their response, share the information from the comments titled "All the speaker could talk about was Jesus" (*Applying the Lesson*).

Note that witnessing can be a part of any circumstance in our lives. Invite learners to decide this moment to accept witnessing as a part of all circumstances of their lives.

---

1. C. W. Bess, "Time Will Tell," *Pulpit Digest* (May-June 1986): 24-25.

November 24

Paul in Rome

Basic Passage: Acts 27—28

Focal Passage: Acts 28:21-31

This quarter's lessons have been about the apostle Paul and his ministry. They began with his conversion on the Damascus road and conclude with his arrival in Rome, where he proclaimed the gospel "with all confidence, no man forbidding him" (28:31), or, "with all boldness and without hindrance" (NRSV). What kind of man was this who, in spite of constant opposition, propagated the Christian message from Jerusalem to Rome? In spite of such self-deprecating statements as we find in 1 Corinthians 2:3 and 2 Corinthians 10:10 (though the latter was what his enemies said about him), Paul appears in Scripture as a man of strong personality, and nowhere more than in the closing chapters of Acts. We see him preaching before a Roman governor until "Felix trembled" (Acts 24:25). His testimony before Agrippa was so persuasive that this king said, "This man might have been set at liberty, if he had not appealed unto Caesar" (26:32). On the voyage to Rome, the captain, crew, and a centurion eventually yielded to Paul's authority. And the final picture is of a man who, though a prisoner, went about his mission "unhindered" (NASB). The explanation came from Paul: "I can do all things through Christ which strengtheneth me" (Phil. 4:13).

Study Aim: *To claim for ourselves the secret of Paul's steadfastness and success in mission*

STUDYING THE BIBLE

The last two chapters of Acts are outstanding in literary excellence. Luke's account of a storm at sea aboard a ship of the first century A.D. is widely saluted for its graphic details. In spite of this lesson's intended focus on Paul in Rome, we would not wish to miss some reference to the adventurous journey to that city.

I. Journey to Rome (Acts 27:1-44)

The pronoun "we" (v. 1) indicates that Luke accompanied Paul on this voyage, together with Aristarchus (19:29) of Thessalonica.

Whether Paul had to pay his expenses, we do not know; but undoubtedly his companions would pay for themselves, or Paul for them. This raises the interesting question of Paul's resources. Some authorities think that the apostle had come into some family money.

1. Counsel disregarded (vv. 1-12).—The ship hugged the coast as far as Myra (see map). There transfer was made to a grain ship from Alexandria, Egypt, which proceeded to a port called Fair Havens in Crete. Dangerous sailing weather was ahead, and Paul warned against leaving that safe harbor, but he was disregarded. The fact that he was listened to at all indicates the esteem in which he was held.

2. Shipwreck and escape (vv. 13-44).—Sailing into the open sea, the Egyptian vessel was soon in the grasp of a fierce northeaster. Fascinating details are provided of efforts made to outride the storm. As danger increased, Paul's confidence in God gave him standing so that his advice now prevailed. After a terrible buffeting of the vessel, all escaped to safety on the island of Malta.

II. The Final Stages (Acts 28:1-16)

A man on his way to Rome for trial became the benefactor of all who sailed with him and of the people of the island of Malta (Melita, v. 1) on whose shores the ship was wrecked.

1. Memories of Malta (vv. 1-10).—Though dubbed "barbarians" (v. 4) because they did not speak Greek, the people of Malta befriended the water-soaked visitors by lighting a fire. Paul joined with others in gathering fuel, and so came in contact with a snake. When no bad consequences resulted, the apostle was hailed as a god (v. 6). After he healed the father of a local dignitary, people flocked to the scene for healing, an activity in which Luke may have joined as a doctor. There was a generous response (v. 10).

2. Rome at last (vv. 11-16).—The shipwrecked group remained on Malta for three months. When at last they again took ship, they reached Italy at Puteoli, on the Bay of Naples. There the apostle was greeted by "brethren," that is, fellow Christians. We know nothing about the establishment of a church there, but we are reminded that others besides Paul were active in spreading the gospel. So forward along the famous Appian Way where the party was met by other Christians "whom when Paul saw, he thanked God, and took courage" (v. 15). Having arrived in Rome, the apostle was allowed to live in his own house with one soldier to guard him. Again he had expenses, which apparently he was able to meet.

III. Rome's Jewish Community (Acts 28:17-29)

The Jewish community was large, had roots going back for two hundred years, and contained both orthodox and liberal elements, liberal in the sense of being lax in the observance of some Mosaic laws.[1] Perhaps it was representatives of the latter who met with Paul since they acknowledged no close contact with Jerusalem. We must assume that the apostle sought a conference with these people because the charge against him originated in Jerusalem, and it was to be expected that when his case came to trial Jerusalem Jews would be present to support their charges. He affirmed his lack of guilt and explained why he had appealed to Caesar. As in his statement before Agrippa, he claimed that it was "for the hope of Israel" (v. 20) that he was a prisoner. Perhaps to his surprise, the response was a denial of knowledge about Paul's case.

21 And they said unto him, We neither received letters out of Judea concerning thee, neither any of the brethren that came showed or spake any harm of thee.

22 But we desire to hear of thee what thou thinkest: for as concerning this sect, we know that everywhere it is spoken against.

23 And when they had appointed him a day, there came many to him into his lodging; to whom he expounded and testified the kingdom of God, persuading them concerning Jesus, both out of the law of Moses, and out of the prophets, from morning till evening.

24 And some believed the things which were spoken, and some believed not.

25 And when they agreed not among themselves, they departed, after that Paul had spoken one word, Well spake the Holy Ghost by Isaiah the prophet unto our fathers,

26 Saying, Go unto this people, and say, Hearing ye shall hear, and shall not understand; and seeing ye shall see, and not perceive:

27 For the heart of this people is waxed gross, and their ears are dull of hearing, and their eyes have they closed; lest they should see with their eyes, and hear with their ears, and understand with their heart, and should be converted, and I should heal them.

28 Be it known therefore unto you, that the salvation of God is sent unto the Gentiles, and that they will hear it.

29 And when he had said these words, the Jews departed, and had great reasoning among themselves.

1. The Scriptures and Jesus (vv. 22-24).—F. F. Bruce thinks that these Jews were "anxious not to be associated with the prosecution of a Roman citizen who had secured a favorable hearing from Festus and Agrippa and was now to be heard by the emperor."[2] This may also explain their professed ignorance of Christianity (v. 22). But they were open-minded enough to want to hear Paul speak for himself. The fact that they met in "his lodging" would indicate spaciousness and again suggest that the apostle had the means to live comfortably, not that comfort was his aim but rather adequacy for receiving guests to whom he might unfold his message (v. 30). This he did to the assembled Jews, taking them through the Old Testament Scriptures to prove that Jesus was the promised Messiah.

2. Mixed reception (vv. 25-29).—As might be expected, Paul's audience was divided in response to his message. Some believed, not only the apostle's words but the Savior of whom he spoke. Others disbelieved, and to these Paul addressed an Old Testament passage used by our Lord to reprove those who rejected Him during His days on earth. These words are from Isaiah 6:9-10, quoted in this case from the Greek Septuagint that makes clear their meaning—that is, the blame is with those who close their ears, eyes, and hearts to the gospel. As a consequence, others would be given the opportunity to hear and respond, namely, the Gentiles. The apostle added, from experience and in anticipation, "they will hear it."

IV. Two Years Well Used (Acts 28:30-31)

Luke has been criticized for ending Acts so abruptly. But he should be complimented for a dramatic conclusion by which his purpose in writing Acts was fulfilled. "How could one improve on this dramatic and climactic summary of the issues with which he—and Christianity—was most concerned: the self-exclusion of the Jews because of the Gentile inclusion and the Gospel boldly preached—unhindered!"[3]

> **30 And Paul dwelt two whole years in his own hired house, and received all that came in unto him,**
>
> **31 Preaching the kingdom of God, and teaching those things which concern the Lord Jesus Christ, with all confidence, no man forbidding him.**

1. A rented house (v. 30).—There are three statements of significance here. (1) The reference to two years implies an end to his detention after that time. Although some differ, there is strong opinion that he was released and resumed his missionary travels, even going as far as Spain. (2) Paul lived in a rented house to which he was confined. An alternative reading is: "at his own expense" (NRSV). Did he resume tentmaking as a source of income? (3) He was free to receive visitors and made good use of this privilege.

2. An unhindered ministry (v. 31).—Among those who visited him was a runaway slave named Onesimus, who is the subject of the Letter to Philemon, written from Rome. Besides this personal letter, the apostle also wrote his epistles to the Ephesians, Philippians, and Colossians. So he turned his imprisonment to good account. There is no knowing how many people heard about "the kingdom of God" and "the Lord Jesus Christ" from his lips. If, at the end of two years, Paul was given his liberty, this was temporary. We know from 2 Timothy that he was returned to Rome for further imprisonment and eventual martyrdom. He could truthfully claim, "I have fought a good fight, I have finished my course, I have kept the faith" (2 Tim. 4:7).

APPLYING THE LESSON

The strongest man on earth.—Who holds the title for strongest man in the world? Those familiar with the Bible might suggest Samson as a candidate for that title. However, in recent days, Paul Anderson has claimed to be the strongest man in the world. Another candidate from the past was Louis Cyr. He stood only five feet, ten inches, but he weighed 300 pounds and sported a sixty-inch chest. He could lift a full barrel of cement with one arm. He could push a freight car on the railroad tracks up an incline. He lifted a platform holding eighteen men with an aggregate weight of 4,300 pounds. He lifted a weight of 588 pounds off the floor—with one finger. And on December 20, 1891, before a crowd of 10,000 people, Louis Cyr was fitted with a special harness with two draft horses hitched up to each side of him. He stood with both feet planted wide and his arms on his chest. Helpers urged the horses to pull, but the four horses together, two pulling in each direction, could not dislodge Louis' arms from his chest nor cause him to lose his footing.[4] Perhaps he really was the strongest man in the world.

I believe one of the strongest men in the world was the apostle Paul. Not physical strength but spiritual strength was his specialty. He possessed this incredible spiritual strength not because of who he was but because of whose he was. He was a man possessed by the Spirit of God. That was the source of Paul's power. This power of God enabled Paul to stand firm in the midst of severe opposition.

The key is fellowship.—Lyle Schaller is one of the church growth experts today. His numerous books have presented helpful clues to building a church in today's world. In one of his books, Schaller distinguished between the small and large church in this way: "For those interested in church growth the obvious conclusion is the larger the size of the congregation, the more likely the quality and depth of the worship experience will be the primary reason why first-time visitors return. The smaller the church, the more likely the inclusionary or exclusionary character of the fellowship will be the number one factor in determining whether first-time visitors return.[5]

I understand what he is saying, but I think we need to take the subject a step further and say that without a sense of fellowship, a person will not stay long at a church, even if the church has dynamic worship services. One may return because of the worship, but the key to one's staying in that church is the inclusionary attitude of the people which can be expressed in the word *fellowship.*

Even in the early days of the church, fellowship was the key. Everywhere Paul went, he discovered others with whom he shared a commitment to Christ. Because of that common commitment, Paul experienced fellowship with people he had never met before.

Looking for opportunities.—Many of us complain that we do not have any opportunities to serve the Lord while the truth is that we don't think we have opportunities because we are not looking for them. One man suggested we miss our opportunities because they are dressed in overalls and look like work. One of the secrets of Paul's success is that he was alert to the opportunities God gave to him. Whether in prison or free, whether in Jerusalem or Rome, whether standing before a responsive crowd or a hostile one, Paul was alert to his opportunities and ready to speak a good word on behalf of his Lord. Our problem is not that we don't have opportunities but that we are not willing to take advantage of the opportunities we have.

Everywhere evangelism.—We use different words today to describe our evangelistic task. Perhaps the best expression would simply be "everywhere evangelism." In Acts 8:4 (TLB), the Bible says that the early Christians "went everywhere preaching the Good News about Jesus." This concept of "everywhere evangelism" is rooted in the Great Commission recorded in the closing verses of Matthew's Gospel. We are not just to go out to witness. We are to witness as we go. We are not just to witness on special outreach visits from the church. We are to witness every day to everyone we meet in the regular traffic patterns of our lives.

TEACHING THE CLASS

Main Idea: Strength and courage to give the gospel is always adequate through the power of Christ.

Suggested Teaching Aim: Learners will seek and accept the power of Christ to maintain a constant, persistent witness of Him.

Introduce the Bible Study

Share the information titled "The strongest man on earth" (*Applying the Lesson*). Ask rhetorically: How is your spiritual strength? Would you be considered a ninety-pound weakling spiritually?

Continue by asking: Where did Paul get the courage to witness in all the circumstances in which he found himself? Elicit response. Again ask rhetorically: Is it possible that you could get the strength and courage that you need from the same source?

State that today's study is the last to focus on Paul, and we find him talking about Jesus. Invite learners to turn in their Bibles to Acts 28.

Search for Biblical Truth

Review the quarter's study with the summary found in the introductory paragraphs for *Studying the Bible.* Display the following outline of Acts 27 and 28 to provide information about the journey to Rome.

A Final Journey—A Final Witness

1. A troublesome sea (Acts 27:1-12).
2. Shipwreck and escape (Acts 27:13-44).
3. Memories of Malta (Acts 28:1-10).
4. Rome at last (Acts 28:11-16).
5. Rome's Jewish community (Acts 28:17-29).
6. Two years well used (Acts 28:30-31).

Invite learners to scan the Scripture passages as information related to the first four points from *Studying the Bible* is shared. Emphasize the respect with which Paul was treated despite the fact that he was a prisoner. Share the drama of the events by telling about them in a compelling manner.

Share information about Rome's Jewish community from *Studying the Bible.* Share the comments titled "The key is fellowship" (*Applying the Lesson*).

Note that the Jews assembled in Paul's residence suggest he must have been in house arrest, and these claimed ignorance of his teachings. Call on a learner to read Acts 28:21-22 aloud.

A Teaching Outline

1. Consider the need for strength and courage to witness.
2. Discover the effects of the strength and courage of Paul.
3. Determine the source of Paul's strength in witnessing.
4. Seek the power of Christ to maintain a constant, persistent witness of Him.

Read from a modern translation the explanation of his teachings that Paul gave to the Jews when the appointed day came (Acts 28:22-28). Ask: How would you expect the Jewish community to respond? Elicit response. Call on a learner to read Acts 28:29 aloud. Ask: What do you suppose they talked about as they reasoned among themselves?

Give the Truth a Personal Focus

Remind learners again that Paul continued to witness anytime anywhere. Share the comments titled "Looking for opportunities" (*Applying the Lesson*). Ask again: Where did Paul get the courage and strength to continue this witness in all circumstances? Remind learners of a line written by Paul from a prison cell: Philippians 4:13. Call on a learner to read the verse aloud.

Share the comments titled "Everywhere evangelism" (*Applying the Lesson*). Invite learners to seek and accept the power of Christ to maintain this constant and persistent witness about Jesus. Close with a time of meditation and prayer.

---

1. Paul Johnson, *A History of the Jews* (New York: Harper, 1987), 132.
2. F. F. Bruce, *The Book of Acts* (Grand Rapids: Eerdmans, 1954), 530-31.
3. Stagg, *Acts*, 263.
4. Richard B. Manchester, *Incredible Facts* (New York: Galahad Books, 1985), 228.
5. Lyle E. Schaller, *44 Ways to Increase Church Attendance* (Nashville: Abingdon Press, 1988), 22.

December 1991, January, February 1992

Songs and Prayers of the Bible

Aids from BROADMAN for Studying and Teaching

Books:
The Broadman Bible Commentary, Volumes 1,2,3,4,5,8,9,11,12
Layman's Bible Book Commentary, Volumes 2,4,5,8,9,10,15,17,18,22,24

The religion of Israel had a strong musical expression. A New Testament apostle exhorted believers to engage in "psalms and hymns and spiritual songs, singing and making melody in your heart to the Lord" (Eph. 5:19). This quarter's lessons provide opportunity to renew acquaintance with songs of the Bible, together with some selected prayers.

Unit I is entitled "Songs From Ancient Israel" and includes songs from the Old Testament, and, for the celebration of Christmas, the *Magnificat*, Mary's outburst of joy over the knowledge that she was to be the mother of the Savior.

Unit II reviews "Songs From Festive Occasions," using the Book of Psalms, the Song of Solomon, and a song of rebuke from the prophet Isaiah.

Unit III takes us into the New Testament with an emphasis on its teaching on prayer. What may be an early Christian hymn is found in Paul's writings, and the series concludes with two songs of the redeemed of God in heaven. In all, a quarter to put a song in our hearts.

December 1

Song of Moses

Basic Passage: Exodus 14:19—15:21

Focal Passages: Exodus 15:1-10,13

Many national songs are born in times of crisis. Francis Scott Key's *The Star-Spangled Banner* is one. If it breathes a warlike atmosphere with its references to "bombs bursting in air" and "the battle's confusion," this is readily understood. Our country had been fighting for what it regarded as its rights, and victory was gained through conflict. The memory of violent events that led to the triumph of justice and laid foundations for prosperity and peace need not imply approval of that violence. Bible history, that focuses on the nation Israel, contains many scenes of violence. These are recorded and recalled, not necessarily with endorsement of the tragic loss of human life that was entailed, but to trace the sovereign acts of God whereby He gave protection to, and carried out promises made to, His chosen people. Where human folly resisted those divine purposes, tragedy was the inevitable result. The enemies of Israel perished, and the people of God greeted their future with a song in their hearts.

Study Aim: *To consider divine interventions that give reason to praise God in song*

STUDYING THE BIBLE

Moses' song is inseparable from the events that inspired it. These must occupy much of our study time. Our basic passage provides substantial material about those events that accompanied the release of the Hebrew people from a probable four hundred years of bondage in Egypt. "Exodus is to the Old Testament as the Gospels are to the New Testament. Both proclaim the redemptive activity of God . . . Each anchors the revelation of God firmly to history."[1]

I. The Historic Record (Ex. 14:19-31)

From the start, we need to keep in mind the words of 15:13, "Thou in thy mercy hast led forth the people which thou hast redeemed."

The destruction of Pharaoh's army in the Red Sea was the tragic consequence of persistent endeavor to resist the purposes of God. To effect the release of His people it was necessary to break that resistance, which survived the ten plagues (chapters 7—12) and sought to reenslave the Hebrews after they had made their escape.

1. Cloud and fire (vv. 19-20).—The term "angel of God" indicates the presence of Yahweh with His people as their true leader. He revealed that presence in a pillar of cloud by day and of light by night (v. 20), the former to hide them from their enemies and the latter to illuminate their way. Both cloud and fire are symbolic of the divine presence (19:18).

2. Safety and destruction (vv. 21-31).—Moses' stretched out hand, the Lord, and a strong east wind worked together to bring about Israel's deliverance from the army of Pharaoh. The Lord controlled the east wind. He recruited Moses as His human instrument. And so "the waters were divided" (v. 21). The Red Sea (literally, "sea of reeds") parted to furnish a pathway to safety for God's people and then returned to normal depth to engulf the pursuing Egyptians. As a consequence, "the people feared the Lord, and believed the Lord, and his servant Moses" (v. 31).

II. Praise Given to God (Ex. 15:1-3)

Moses led the people in a song of deliverance after they assembled on the far side of the Red Sea. The song they sang is attributed to Moses, who is also named author of Psalm 90, a composition rich in such statements as, "Lord, thou hast been our dwelling place in all generations" (v. 1); "a thousand years in thy sight are but as yesterday when it is past" (v. 4); and "So teach us to number our days, that we may apply our hearts unto wisdom" (v. 12). The intellectual stature of Moses is clear. He was songster, psalmist, and prophet (Deut. 18:15; 34:10), the final claim being important for our interpretation of Exodus 15.

> **1 Then sang Moses and the children of Israel this song unto the Lord, and spake, saying, I will sing unto the Lord, for he hath triumphed gloriously: the horse and his rider hath he thrown into the sea.**
>
> **2 The Lord is my strength and song, and he is become my salvation: he is my God, and I will prepare him an habitation; my father's God, and I will exalt him.**
>
> **3 The Lord is a man of war: the Lord is his name.**

There are two emphases in these verses. First, what happened at the Red Sea was a triumph for God Himself. Pharaoh, a worshiper of strange gods, had long shown contempt for God by keeping His people in slavery and defying His commands to let them go. After demonstrating great patience, up to the point where an attempt was made to return the Israelites to slavery, God vindicated His name at the crossing of the sea. Second, what He did was for the "salvation" of His people who made the occasion an opportunity to "exalt him" (v. 2). How much greater reason have we!

III. Deliverance in Retrospect (Ex. 15:4-12)

By describing the destruction of the Egyptians in a song, memory of the event was preserved in the popular mind. Edersheim states that sections of this song were made part of Sabbath morning services in the temple.[2] In his review of God's dealings with Israel, Joshua referred specifically to events at the Red Sea (Josh. 24:6-7). Mention is also made in Psalms 106:7-12 and 136:13-15. In the New Testament are references in Acts 7:36; 1 Corinthians 10:1-4; and Hebrews 11:29. For Israel, what happened at the Red Sea was an integral part of God's redemptive activity whereby a race of slaves was brought out of captivity, saved from their enemies, and established as His covenant people.

4 Pharaoh's chariots and his host hath he cast into the sea: his chosen captains also are drowned in the Red Sea.

5 The depths have covered them: they sank into the bottom as a stone.

6 Thy right hand, O Lord, is become glorious in power: thy right hand, O Lord, hath dashed in pieces the enemy.

7 And in the greatness of thine excellency thou hast overthrown them that rose up against thee: thou sendest forth thy wrath, which consumed them as stubble.

8 And with the blast of thy nostrils the waters were gathered together, the floods stood upright as an heap, and the depths were congealed in the heart of the sea.

9 The enemy said, I will pursue, I will overtake, I will divide the spoil; my lust shall be satisfied upon them; I will draw my sword, my hand shall destroy them.

10 Thou didst blow with thy wind, the sea covered them: they sank as lead in the mighty waters.

Did Pharaoh die with his army? Psalm 136:15 could be taken to say so, and Exodus 14:6-7 describes him as making preparation for the pursuit. But this is the last reference to Pharaoh personally in the ongoing record, and Moses' song contains no mention of his death. So we cannot say for sure. The cream of Pharaoh's army was undoubtedly destroyed including his "chosen chariots . . . and captains," or his "picked chariots . . . with officers" (v. 7, NRSV). The question of verse 11, "Who is like unto thee, O Lord, among the gods?" is a reminder that, from the beginning, the contest pitted the innumerable gods of Egypt against the God of the Hebrews, the only true God. Hence, Moses' song focuses on the vindication of God's honor rather than on the benefits brought to Israel by the overthrow of their enemies. Tribute is paid to God's "right hand," which had become "glorious in power," that is, in the sight of others (v. 6). By His powerful intervention on behalf of His people and against His and their foes, God had displayed "the greatness of your majesty" (v. 7, NRSV). The impact of this would be felt by other nations, as following verses show.

IV. Divine Purpose at Work (Ex. 15:13-19)

Behind what happened at the Red Sea were promises given to ancestors of the people who passed over on dry land. The basic promise given to Abraham, in response to his obedience, contained reference to "a land that I will show thee" (Gen. 12:1). Egypt was not that land but just a stopping point along the way. The children of Abraham had to be liberated from their bondage in Egypt and set free to journey toward that Promised Land that God had in mind as the home of His people. Did the promises still hold? The answer is found in a word translated "mercy," elsewhere "steadfast love" (v. 13, NRSV). This is the Hebrew word *chesed*, sometimes rendered "lovingkindness." Actually, *chesed* is a covenant word and affirms the dependability of God's promises. What He pledges to His covenant people, He will carry out.

> **13 Thou in thy mercy hast led forth the people which thou hast redeemed: thou hast guided them in thy strength unto thy holy habitation.**

1. Fear among nations (vv. 14-16).—Having looked back and commemorated past deliverance, Moses' song now looks forward to coming events. After a long sojourn in the wilderness, the people Israel would begin the conquest of Canaan, or "Palestina" as it is called here (v. 14). The word *Palestine* has close links with "Philistina" and describes the territory that would eventually become the home of the Hebrews. Its inhabitants, and those of neighboring nations (Edom and Moab, v. 15), would learn of the destruction of Pharaoh's hosts and be filled with fear.

2. Settlement in Canaan (v. 17).—So the way would be opened up for possession of the land by God's people. The words "mountain" and "Sanctuary" suggest anticipation of the time when Jerusalem and its temple would be at the center of national life. However, authorities suggest that the land as a whole is intended, not any particular site. Either way, the song looked forward to the time when God's territorial purposes for His people would be fulfilled.

V. Song of Miriam (Ex. 15:20-21)

The song of Moses caught fire in the heart of his sister, Miriam. This is one of the great merits of songs and singing, that they spread their enthusiasm as more and more join in. Miriam set the example, and "all the women" followed, singing and dancing to express their overflowing gratitude to God for His deliverance. Women have special reasons to be glad when enemies are subdued and a prospect of better times is ahead. But this particular woman, Miriam, had her own personal reason, for it was she who saved her baby brother when he was discovered by Pharaoh's daughter (2:4,7-8).

APPLYING THE LESSON

A God who stays.—Among the native people of the Congo region of Central Africa, their myths describe a god who went away. The women of the area used a long pole and wooden tub to break the hulls off the grain in order to make food. According to one of the myths, one of the women lifted her pole too high and struck the god in the face. He asked her to stop. When she refused, the god became angry and left. According to another of the myths, in ancient days when the sky was much lower than it is now, the people kept wiping their dirty hands on the sky. God became disgusted and left. In both of these ancient stories, the focus is on a god who became angry with human disobedience, and because of that anger He left them in their sorry condition.

In the biblical narrative of history, we see another picture of God. God did become angry with the disobedience of human beings. God did become disgusted with the sins of Pharaoh and his people. He did become concerned that the Hebrews were in bondage. However, God did not leave. Instead, He became involved in history to bring about humanity's redemption. God is not one who leaves us in our problems. Instead, He is one who redeems us from our problems. He does not abandon us. He rescues us.

Doxology in my heart.—Vance Havner referred to a time in his earlier days when he said, "I didn't have much theology in my head, but I had a lot of doxology in my heart." Actually, it doesn't have to be either/or. We can have a lot of theology in our heads and at the same time have a lot of doxology in our hearts. In fact, the most powerful Christian is one who has both and keeps them in proper balance in his or her life.

Havner's phrase could describe the Hebrews at the point of their deliverance from Israel. They did not understand much about God at that point. That would come later, with the giving of the Ten Commandments and the expansion of the law. What they knew at this point was that God was sovereign over the "gods" of Egypt and that He was a God who delivers. Consequently, they had a lot of doxology in their hearts.

Only a real God can win victory.—William Barclay told of a legend concerning Abraham and his father, Terah, who manufactured idols to sell. One day, Abraham was left in charge of the shop. When people came in to buy an idol, Abraham asked them how old they were. They would answer, "Fifty or sixty years old." Abraham would respond, "How tragic for a man of such an age to adore an idol made in one day!" When a woman brought in a dish of meat for the gods, Abraham took a stick and smashed all the idols except one. He set the stick in that idol's hand. When Terah returned, he was angry about all the smashed idols. Abraham explained, "This woman brought a dish of meat for your gods. They all wanted to have it, so they fought. The strongest of your idols knocked the heads off the rest, lest they should eat it all." Terah responded, "That is impossible for these idols are made of wood and stone." Abraham replied, "Let thine own ear hear what thine own mouth has spoken!"[3]

The point of the legend is clear: Only a real God can win the victory for His people. That's what the Hebrews discovered. Their God was real and powerful and sovereign. He could thus win victory over the idols of the Egyptians that were made of wood and stone.

He gave up too soon.—After surviving fifty-five hours adrift off the coast of South Carolina, Robert Louis Watson slipped off a life raft into the ocean about one hour before the raft was spotted by the Coast Guard. His partner, Greg Palmer, was willing to hold on a little longer. Consequently, Palmer was saved by a coast guard helicopter that took him to a Charleston hospital. Like so many people, the first man gave up too soon.

The Hebrews could have easily given up in their bondage in Egypt. They could have lost hope and refused to follow Moses out of Egypt. If they had lost hope, they would have lost their opportunity for God to lead them to their land of promise.

TEACHING THE CLASS

Main Idea: God works in the lives of His people in ways that can be praised in song.

Suggested Teaching Aim: Learners will consider events in their lives for which they can praise God in song.

Introduce the Bible Study

Ask: Do you think that you should be able to sing more hymns and spiritual songs or quote more verses of the Scripture? Elicit response. State that our faith as well as the faith of Israel has always had a strong musical expression. Note that the lessons for this quarter provide opportunity to renew acquaintance with songs of the Bible. Note that some selected prayers will also be included. Use information from *Studying the Bible* to comment about the three units of the quarter.

Share the story titled "Doxology in my heart" (*Applying the Lesson*). State that we like Israel can sing praise to God for events that have occurred in our lives. Note that when the Bible searching is finished, learners will be asked to consider events in their own lives for which they can praise God in song.

Search for Biblical Truth

Invite learners to open their Bibles to Exodus 15. Use information from *Studying the Bible* to review the circumstances from which this song of Moses grew. Display the headings for Exodus 14:19-31 found in *Studying the Bible.* Use them as an outline to present the background.

A Teaching Outline

1. Introduce the study for the quarter, the first unit, and the study for today.
2. Review the background from which the song in Exodus 15 grew.
3. Read together the song of Moses praising God for what He did in these events.
4. Emphasize the value of bolstering our faith in the future with God through using Moses' model.
5. Identify personal events for which learners can praise God in song.
6. Review songs from hymnals and discuss their personal meaning to learners.

Share information about Moses found in the paragraph titled "Praise Given to God" in *Studying the Bible.* Call on a learner to read Exodus 15:1-13 aloud while other learners listen to consider Moses' skill as a songster.

Share the story titled "A God who stays" (*Applying the Lesson*). Use information from *Studying the Bible* to comment on the events about which Moses was singing.

Share the comments titled "Only a real God can win victory" (*Applying the Lesson*). Note further that while events of the past can bring rejoicing, there is continued need for faith to walk into the future. Share the comments titled "He gave up too soon" (*Applying the Lesson*).

Invite learners to review Exodus 15:14-17. Ask: What turn does Moses' song take at this point? Note again the necessity of faith for the future as well as praise for the past.

Call attention to Exodus 15:20-21. Ask: How did Moses' song affect those around him? Share information from *Studying the Bible* about Miriam.

Give the Truth a Personal Focus

Provide learners notepaper and pencil. Direct them to spend several minutes reviewing events of their lives and privately to list those for which they would like to especially praise God. When the time is finished, invite any learners who wish to do so to share some of their thoughts.

Note that learners may not be as much of a songster as Moses, but they might wish to write out some expressions of that praise either in class or in a personal time of devotion.

Provide hymnbooks for learners to review. Call on a few to read a favorite hymn. Ask: Is there an element of praise in the hymn? For what do the words praise our God? Encourage learners to plan to be aware of the effect of songs used in worship services.

---

1. Roy L. Honeycutt, "Exodus" in *The Broadman Bible Commentary*, vol. 1, rev. ed. (Nashville: Broadman Press, 1973), 289.
2. A. Edersheim, *Bible History*, vol. 2 (Grand Rapids: Wm. B. Eerdmans Publishing Co., 1949), 88.
3. William Barclay, *The Letter to the Hebrews* (Philadelphia: The Westminster Press, 1955), 162.

December 8

Song of Deborah and Barak

Basic Passage: Judges 4:4—5:31

Focal Passage: Judges 5:1-11

The reference to Miriam, sister to Moses, at the conclusion of last week's lesson prepares us for the appearance in the Bible narrative of another woman: Deborah. She is described as "a prophetess" (v. 4), which means that she was a messenger from God, and she was obviously a poet. The authorship of chapter 5 has been traditionally ascribed to her and appears to be confirmed by verse 7. Scholars pay high tribute to the quality of this poem that is one of the most ancient pieces of Hebrew verse to come down to us. We should not be discouraged by any difficulties we may have in understanding some of its statements. Do we not have problems with Shakespeare's plays, that are only four hundred years old? The song of Deborah goes back to the twelfth century B.C. Fortunately, our understanding of the song is helped by the prose account, in chapter 4, of the battle it describes.

Study Aim: *To recognize and honor women who have been used of God in the furtherance of His redemptive purposes*

STUDYING THE BIBLE

All Old Testament studies need to be made in the realization that a full understanding of the nature and ways of God awaited the coming of His Son, the Lord Jesus Christ. The song of Deborah, magnificent as it is as a piece of ancient literature, does not breathe the spirit of the New Testament. But it does illustrate the activity of God in history and the praise that is due to Him for deliverances granted to His people.

I. Honor Given to God (Judg. 5:1-3)

In our previous lesson, we majored on the historic account that inspired Moses' song, rather than on the song itself. This time we will attempt to blend the two, using the content of chapter 4 to help our understanding of chapter 5. The opening lines of the song consist of praises to God.

> **1 Then sang Deborah and Barak the son of Abinoam on that day, saying,**
>
> **2 Praise ye the Lord for the avenging of Israel, when the people willingly offered themselves.**
>
> **3 Hear, O ye kings; give ear, O ye princes; I, even I, will sing unto the Lord; I will sing praise to the Lord God of Israel.**

Deborah was the prophetess and songster while Barak was the military leader in a final phase of the conquest of Canaan. Barak's reputation as a national deliverer is recognized in Hebrews 11:32. We find Deborah also named as a judge (4:4-5). The people brought their causes to her "under the palm tree of Deborah," apparently a recognized location for her to hold court. Her praise to God is mingled with a warning to kings and princes who should take notice of the fate of Canaanites for their oppression of the Israelites.

II. Advance from Sinai (Judg. 5:4-5)

Looking back over Israel's history, Deborah recalled the significant happenings at Sinai and Seir (Edom). In Moses' blessing of the tribes, set in poetic form, is a similar statement, "The Lord came from Sinai, and rose up from Seir" (Deut. 33:2). The forty years of wilderness wandering are passed over in silence. Eric Rust said that Deborah was "endeavouring to convey the truth that the God who is fighting for his people is the God who showed himself specially and savingly to them in the manifestation on Sinai's height."[1] Omitting the wilderness disaster, God's establishment of a covenant relationship with His people at Sinai was connected to the fulfillment of His purposes for them as they advanced through Edom on their way to Canaan.

> **4 Lord, when thou wentest out of Seir, when thou marchedst out of the field of Edom, the earth trembled, and the heavens dropped, the clouds also dropped water.**
>
> **5 The mountains melted from before the Lord, even that Sinai from before the Lord God of Israel.**

According to Numbers 20:14-21, the king of Edom refused to allow passage through his kingdom for the Hebrews. But his refusal did not stop their progress that brought them to the conquest of Jericho and thus into Canaan. Probably Deborah's brief reference to these things was intended mainly for the consumption of the kings and princes (v. 3) who might attempt to intervene in the war that was then brewing.

III. Plight of Israel (Judg. 5:6-8)

Still reviewing recent history, Deborah came to the time of the Judges, to which, of course, she belonged. Shamgar was the third of these leaders whom God raised up for the deliverance of His people. He was preceded by Othniel (3:9) and Ehud (3:15). Shamgar's record is briefly given in 3:31.

> **6 In the days of Shamgar the son of Anath, in the days of Jael, the highways were unoccupied, and the travelers walked through byways.**
>
> **7 The inhabitants of the villages ceased, they ceased in Israel, until that I Deborah arose, that I arose a mother in Israel.**
>
> **8 They chose new gods; then was war in the gates: was there a shield or spear seen among forty thousand in Israel?**

1. Cause and effect.—The triumphant tone of verses 4-5 now gives place to a description of the sorry condition of the people for whom God had such great purposes. Highways used for transportation and trade were deserted. Those who traveled used obscure routes rather than risk the open road. Whole communities were closed down, and a potential army of 40,000 men were without weapons. A brief explanation is given, "They chose new gods" (v. 8). Israel allowed itself to be seduced into idolatry by its pagan neighbors. The monotonous statement appears throughout the Book of Judges, "And the children of Israel did evil in the sight of the Lord" (2:11), with this equally monotonous consequence, the Lord "sold them into the hands of their enemies round about, so that they could not any longer stand before their enemies" (2:14).

2. Parallel passage (4:1-4).—In Deborah's time, God again chastised His people by Jabin, king of Canaan, whose military leader was Sisera. He "reigned in Hazor," to the north of the Sea of Galilee. His strength was indicated by his "nine hundred chariots of iron," instruments of war that were not possessed by the Israelites. Not surprisingly, "he mightily oppressed the children of Israel," who cried to God for help. In His patience and mercy, the Lord responded by raising up another leader, this time a woman, Deborah.

IV. Preparation for War (Judg. 5:9-18)

This is one of the more difficult passages. Such a translation as the *Good News Bible* may help our understanding. Verses 9-11 are probably an offering of praise (1) to the "peasantry in Israel" (v. 11, NRSV) for rallying to the defense of their country and (2) to God ("Bless ye the Lord," v. 9) as the real giver of victory.

9 My heart is toward the governors of Israel, that offered themselves willingly among the people. Bless ye the Lord.

10 Speak, ye that ride on white asses, ye that sit in judgment, and walk by the way.

11 They that are delivered from the noise of archers in the places of drawing water, there shall they rehearse the righteous acts of the Lord, even the righteous acts toward the inhabitants of his villages in Israel: then shall the people of the Lord go down to the gates.

1. Praise and blame.—The songster invites others to join in this offering of praise, rich and poor alike, "you who ride on white donkeys," and "you who walk by the way" (v. 10, NRSV). But while there is praise for some, there is blame for others, for not all responded to the call to arms. Among those tribes commended are Ephraim, Benjamin, Zebulun, Naphtali, and Issachar. They inhabited that part of Canaan mainly involved in the Canaanite attacks, that is, the north. Other tribes were censured for withholding their support: Gilead (Gad), Dan, and Asher.

2. Parallel passage (4:5-10).—The prose account majors on the relationship of Deborah and Barak, who is named in 5:12. Speaking for God, this woman commanded Barak to position an army at Mount Tabor. To engage this army, Sisera would have to cross the open plain of Esdraelon and the stream Kidron. Barak insisted that Deborah accompany him, apparently putting more confidence in her than in the Lord. Deborah agreed to go, but she told Barak that little credit would accrue to him for the forthcoming victory. Credit would go to a woman, presumably a reference to Jael (vv. 18-24).

V. Battle of Kishon (Judg. 5:19-23)

The battle site is stated as "by the waters of Megiddo" (v. 19), another name for the Brook Kidron. Secular history confirms that a fierce storm caused the waters to swell and overwhelm the forces of the Canaanites. In poetic style, the song states that "the stars in their courses fought against Sisera" (v. 20), an acknowledgment that forces of nature aided the defeat of the enemy.

A parallel passage, 4:13-17, contains no reference to the storm, unless we may understand Deborah's question, "Is not the Lord gone out before thee?" (v. 14) as suggestive of divine intervention on the part of His people. Barak's attack was successful so that the Canaanite commander, Sisera, fled on foot.

VI. Death of Sisera (Judg. 5:24-27)

Sisera took refuge in the tent of "Jael the wife of Heber the Kenite" (4:17); see reference in 1:16. The Kenites were a tribe closely related to Israel, and some became part of the tribe of Judah. A portion of the tribe had settled in the north and had become on friendly terms with the Canaanites led by Jabin. Sisera supposed that he would be safe in this tent, but he was sadly mistaken. Jael apparently sided with the Israelites, and, while Sisera slept, she took his life in a violent way (see 5:24-27). Though Jael was hailed as a deliverer by her contemporaries, we recognize the conflict between this incident and the teaching of the New Testament.

APPLYING THE LESSON

You'll see the flag.—Nineteen-year-old Jerry did not know what was ahead of him when he shipped out to Iwo Jima. The attempt to retake the island was one fraught with much danger and accomplished with much loss of life. The enemy was entrenched in strategic positions. As Jerry and the other American soldiers landed on the beach, every inch of the beach was covered with rifle and machine gun fire. He tried to find refuge in a foxhole on the beach. The heat of the day was replaced by bitter cold in the night. The date was February 21, 1945. Jerry was trying to find safety in a crater formed by an exploding artillery shell. At the same time he was fighting against an enemy he couldn't even see. The shelling kept him awake all night. The morning dawned with rain and fog. Already, Jerry had given up hope of coming off the island alive. Of the fourteen men in his rifle section, only six of them remained. When his hope was at the lowest point, his corporal crawled up next to him and said, "We've gaining on them, you know." Jerry responded, "How do you know that?" The corporal replied, "I have it on good authority. Tomorrow you'll see our boys on top of that hill. We're going to make it. You'll see the flag tomorrow."

The hill to which the corporal referred was the top of Mount Suribachi, the highest point of the island. To have the flag up there would mean that the Americans had gained the highest point and would soon be able to win the victory. Two days later it happened. The American flag was raised on that hill, the Americans rallied, and the victory was won. For the rest of his life, those five words were words of hope to Jerry: "Hang in there, Jerry. You'll see the flag tomorrow."[2]

The people of Israel looked back to a special hill called Sinai where God made covenant with His people. That covenant agreement served the same purpose as did the flag for the soldiers on Iwo Jima. Sinai was a reminder that God was a sovereign God who won victory over His enemies and made a covenant with His people, a covenant that contained promises that would inevitably be fulfilled. Consequently, no matter how bad the situation seemed, they knew that God's promises would be kept and God's provisions would be given.

When we let go of God.—A little girl and her grandfather were visiting a zoo in Washington, D.C. He held her hand tightly as they walked through the zoo, watching at a distance the beautiful but dangerous animals. Finally, she pulled her hand away from her grandfather saying, "I like to hold my own hand, Grandfather." When he took his eye off her for an instant, the little girl crawled under the guardrail that kept people a safe distance from the lion's cage. Before anyone could get to her, the lion had pulled the little girl into the cage with him and mauled the girl to death.

Like this little girl, the Hebrew people continually said to God, "God, we want to hold our own hand." Walking independently of God, the Hebrews took a pathway of disobedience that led eventually to destruction at the hands of first one enemy and then another.

Your sins will find you out.—Many people sow their wild oats and then go to church on Sunday and pray for crop failure. However, certain consequences accompany our sins from which we cannot escape. Our sins will find us out.

The story of Haman and Mordecai, told in the Book of Esther, beautifully illustrates this truth. Haman, leading advisor to King Ahasuerus of the Medes and the Persians, developed an intense hatred for Mordecai. He made plans to kill Mordecai. He even constructed a gallows on which to hang Mordecai. However, the tables turned on him. King Ahasuerus discovered while reading the book of records that Mordecai had saved his life and he had never rewarded him. At the banquet in which Haman expected to be honored, Mordecai was honored instead. When Esther revealed the plot of Haman to destroy herself and the other Jewish people in the kingdom, King Ahasuerus ordered Haman to be hanged on the gallows he had prepared for Mordecai.

In a similar way, Sisera fled from the battlefield thinking he could escape the consequences of his opposition to God's people. Instead, he found Jael who took his life. Inevitably, we must face the consequences of our sins.

TEACHING THE CLASS

Main Idea: God will redeem His people when they willingly give themselves to Him.

Suggested Teaching Aim: Learners will willingly offer themselves to God in response to His desire to redeem them.

Introduce the Bible Study

Recall that the unit of study is titled "Songs From Ancient Israel." State that the song for study today is a song of a woman who led ancient Israel, Deborah. Use information from the introduction preceding *Studying the Bible* to provide brief information about her.

Write the main idea for this lesson on the chalkboard and note that the statement is the theme of the words of Deborah's song. Share comments from the first paragraphs of *Studying the Bible* to prepare learners for these words.

Note that throughout history God has been working to redeem His people and that He continues this work today. Invite learners to open their Bibles to Judges 5 for the song of Deborah, which is about this work.

Search for Biblical Truth

Display the following outline on the chalkboard to guide the Scripture searching.

Song of Deborah and Barak

1. Honor Given to God (Judg. 5:1-3)
2. Advance from Sinai (Judg. 5:4-5)

3. Plight of Israel	(Judg. 5:6-8)
*Parallel Passage	(Judg. 4:1-4)
4. Preparation for War	(Judg. 5:9-18)
*Parallel Passage	(Judg. 4:5-10)
5. Battle of Kishon	(Judg. 5:19-23)
*Parallel Passage	(Judg. 4:13-17)
6. Death of Sisera	(Judg. 5:24-27)

Note that this outline covers the larger passage of Scripture for today and that only parts of it can be studied in depth. The complete outline shows the progression and the correlation with Judges 4.

A Teaching Outline

1. Focus on God's redemptive work throughout history.
2. Discover from Deborah's song how God worked to redeem people who lived in her era.
3. Discuss how God is at work today to redeem people and to call them back to Him.
4. Commit themselves to God in response to His desire to redeem them.

Share information from *Studying the Bible* related to verses 1-3. Identify both Deborah and Barak. Call on learners to read Judges 5:1-3 aloud. Ask: What theme for the song is stated in the first sentence? (See v. 2.)

Share the story titled "You'll see the flag" (*Applying the Lesson*). Emphasize the importance of Sinai to the nation of Israel.

Share information from *Studying the Bible* related to Judges 5:4-5. When finished, call on a learner to read the verses aloud.

Share information from *Studying the Bible* related to Judges 5:6-8. Identify Shamgar, Othniel, and Ehud. Remind learners of the familiar phrase: "Every man did that which was right in his own eyes." Share the story titled "When we let go of God" (*Applying the Lesson*). Call on a learner to read Judges 5:6-8 aloud.

Call attention to the parallel passage. Share information from *Studying the Bible.*

Share information from *Studying the Bible* about Judges 5:9-18. Have the passage read aloud. Call attention to the parallel passage. Share related information.

Share the story titled "Your sins will find you out" (*Applying the Lesson*). Provide background information from *Studying the Bible* on Judges 5:19-23. Have the passage read aloud. Call attention to the parallel passage sharing comments from *Studying the Bible.*

Call attention to the last point on the outline. Share information from *Studying the Bible.* Have the passage read aloud.

Give the Truth a Personal Focus

Ask: Is it easier to see God at work in past events or in our present world? Elicit response. Continue: In what ways does God continue to be at work to redeem people in our day? Answers might include the work of the Holy Spirit, the widespread use of media, and continued demonstration of His love and grace.

Conclude by asking: In what ways is God at work to bring you closer to Himself? What are the conditions for God doing this redemptive work? (Review Judges 5:2.) Invite and encourage commitment by learners to respond to God's desire to bring them closer to Himself.

---

1. Eric Rust, *Layman's Bible Commentary,* vol. 6 (Richmond: John Knox, 1961), 29.
2. Gary Smalley and John Trent, *The Language of Love* (Pomona: Focus on the Family Publishing, 1988), 87-88.

December 15

David's Lament for Saul and Jonathan

Basic Passage: 2 Samuel 1

Focal Passage: 2 Samuel 1:17-27

How to handle grief is a much-discussed subject these days. In books, newspaper articles, seminars, and counseling sessions people are being told of the importance of giving expression to grief and that suppression can be dangerous. One of several facets of today's lesson is how David reacted to the news of the deaths of Saul and Jonathan. There is something remarkable in the tribute he paid to Saul, who had been his enemy. But the sorrow he showed over the loss of Jonathan comes nearer to our own feelings (expressed or suppressed) when a friend or family member is taken away. David was a strong man in many senses, yet he gave rein to his emotions on this occasion, as he did also over the deaths of Bathsheba's child (12:19-23) and his son Absalom (18:33). We can, and should, discuss this subject on a higher level than any Old Testament character because, in Christ, we have the hope of resurrection. Other emphases important for our consideration are brought out in the outline below.

Study Aim: *To learn principles for daily living, and for the experience of bereavement, from this story of David*

STUDYING THE BIBLE

There are two accounts of King Saul's death, one in 1 Samuel 31 and the other in 2 Samuel 1. Saul was Israel's first king, chosen by God and anointed by Samuel (1 Sam. 10:1). He had excellent qualifications for rulership, but success went to his head so that he was rejected as king. A successor was found in David who, as he gained in prominence, incurred the jealousy of Saul who became his enemy. The final tragedy came in the death of Saul while he was fighting the Philistines.

I. A King's Death (1 Sam. 31)

Those constant enemies of Israel, the Philistines, got ready for a fresh campaign of attack (28:1). Saul had lost his customary courage and had nowhere to go for advice. Even the Lord remained silent (v. 6) to the inquiries of this disobedient king. So he sought counsel from a witch who professed to raise the dead Samuel, who said, "The Lord will also deliver Israel with thee into the hand of the Philistines: and tomorrow shalt thou and thy sons be with me" (v. 19). Saul had no choice but to go into battle, the result of which was that "the men of Israel fled from before the Philistines, and fell down slain in Mount Gilboa" (31:1). Saul's three sons were killed (v. 2); and when the king saw that he was about to fall into the hands of the enemy, he called on his armorbearer to kill him. When he refused, Saul took his own life by falling on his sword. "So Saul died, and his three sons, and his armorbearer, and all his men, that same day together" (v. 6).

II. A False Claim (2 Sam. 1:1-12)

David had been outlawed by Saul whom David accused of regarding him as "a dead dog" and "a flea" (1 Sam. 24:14). In despair, David took refuge with the Philistines who provided a home for him in Ziklag (27:1-7). There is clear evidence that David was playing a double game, for his attacks were on the enemies of Israel, and he carefully avoided incursions into his own tribe: Judah. Not surprisingly, some of the Philistines were suspicious of him, a circumstance that saved him from being part of the planned assault on the armies of Saul. We may assume that it was to his relief that "David and his men rose up early to depart in the morning, to return into the land of the Philistines" (29:11). There he awaited news of the battle.

1. Amalekite treachery.—News came from a man who professed to be an Amalekite. He therefore belonged to a nomadic tribe that had for a long time distressed the Israelites by raiding their lands and stealing their crops. In fact, David had only recently experienced their treachery. When he was dismissed from the Philistine army, he returned to Ziklag, only to discover that the town had been pillaged in his absence. He went after the Amalekite offenders and defeated them (1 Sam. 30).

2. The messenger.—It was a member of this group that came to David in Ziklag, doubtless hoping to curry favor with him by bringing news of Saul. His story was that he had come upon Saul in great physical distress. The king, he said, appealed to him to end his life and so put him out of his misery. This he claimed to have done and produced the king's crown and a bracelet that he wore as evidence. In light of 1 Samuel 31, this story was patently false, concocted apparently in hope of reward from David.

3. Death sentence.—Whether or not David was acquainted with the truth, we do not know. But according to his thinking, this Amalekite had accused himself out of his own mouth. During the years that David was victimized by Saul, he had several opportunities to kill the king, had he so wished (1 Sam. 24:1-6; 26:7-12). But since God had chosen to make Saul king, it was up to Him alone to end Saul's life. This was David's deep conviction, and what he would not do he could not tolerate in this Amalekite. He accordingly ordered "one of the young men" to execute the self-confessed offender (2 Sam. 1:13-16).

III. An Outpouring of Grief (2 Sam. 1:17-27)

Unfortunately, translation from Hebrew into English forfeits the special rhythm of this lament, considered by scholars to be an outstanding example of this kind of poetry. But even to read it in English is to sense its style and beauty.

> **17 And David lamented with this lamentation over Saul and over Jonathan his son:**
>
> **18 (Also he bade them teach the children of Judah the use of the bow: behold, it is written in the book of Jasher.)**

1. A lost book (v. 18).—The NRSV reads, "(He ordered that The

Song of the Bow be taught to the people of Judah; it is written in the Book of Jashar.)" Joshua 10:13 contains another reference to this book of Jasher. It appears to have been a collection of poems of national interest, a sort of patriotic songbook. Unfortunately, it has not survived. Had it done so, it may have found a place in the Old Testament.

19 The beauty of Israel is slain upon thy high places: how are the mighty fallen!
20 Tell it not in Gath, publish it not in the streets of Askelon; lest the daughters of the Philistines rejoice, lest the daughters of the uncircumcised triumph.
21 Ye mountains of Gilboa, let there be no dew, neither let there be rain, upon you, nor fields of offerings: for there the shield of the mighty is vilely cast away, the shield of Saul, as though he had not been anointed with oil.
22 From the blood of the slain, from the fat of the mighty, the bow of Jonathan turned not back, and the sword of Saul returned not empty.
23 Saul and Jonathan were lovely and pleasant in their lives, and in their death they were not divided: they were swifter than eagles, they were stronger than lions.

2. Sorrow expressed (vv. 19-23).—Although David made no attempt to hide his grief, he was anxious that it should not come to the ears of the Philistines (Gath and Askelon were Philistine cities), whose women would find in it cause for rejoicing. Rather, he called on the women of Israel to mourn with him over the death of a king who had brought them great benefits (v. 24). The mountains of Gilboa, on which Saul and Jonathan had died, were henceforth to produce no harvests. Thus nature would mourn with David over the deaths of these two leaders, father and son, who stood together on the battlefield, and died together. Probably David had in mind the loyalty of Jonathan, who, though siding with David in many matters, never rebelled against Saul.

24 Ye daughters of Israel, weep over Saul, who clothed you in scarlet, with other delights, who put on ornaments of gold upon your apparel.

3. Tribute to Saul (v. 24).—David had many negative memories of Saul, but this was not the time to recall them. He showed his own noble spirit by majoring on the better accomplishments of the dead king. By his successful campaigns against Israel's enemies, Saul had enriched the people with the spoils of war. Women particularly had benefited, though no mention was made of the losses they sustained as the consequence of war. This was a time for positive thoughts about a man who had just died facing the nation's foes.

> **25 How are the mighty fallen in the midst of the battle! O Jonathan, thou wast slain in thine high places.**
>
> **26 I am distressed for thee, my brother Jonathan: very pleasant hast thou been unto me: thy love to me was wonderful, passing the love of women.**

4. Love for Jonathan (vv. 25-26).—The deep friendship between David and Jonathan began when they were both youth (1 Sam. 19:1-4). When his father's enmity toward David became apparent, Jonathan risked his life to warn David to whom he pledged undying friendship (20:42). This pledge he renewed, at the same time acknowledging that David would be Israel's future king (23:16-18). At that time, Jonathan expressed the belief that he would be second in the kingdom, a hope that was destroyed by his untimely death on the battlefield of Gilboa. That David's death tribute to Jonathan was more than words was later evidenced by his gracious treatment of Jonathan's son, Mephibosheth. The story is told in 2 Samuel 9, a chapter that concludes, "So Mephibosheth dwelt in Jerusalem: for he did eat continually at the king's table; and was lame on both his feet." This lameness made David's action particularly generous because it was customary to keep physically afflicted persons away from the royal presence. By remaining loyal to his father, Saul, Jonathan paid the price with his life. This loss in battle of a splendid young man prepares us for the concluding phrases of David's lament.

> **27 How are the mighty fallen, and the weapons of war perished!**

5. Futility of war (v. 27).—The *Good News Bible* translates this verse, "The brave soldiers have fallen, / weapons abandoned and useless." This captures the pathos in David's words. Songs with a patriotic theme often tend to glorify war. But the greatest of soldiers, of whom David was one, have joined in condemning war as a solution to human problems. Even when there is no apparent alternative, war's consequences are worse than its cures.

APPLYING THE LESSON

Reality and relief in death.—The impact of death is impossible to calculate. Relief comes in the presence of God to comfort us and the promise of Christ to encourage us. The relief that Christ brings was beautifully expressed by F. B. Meyer, gifted English preacher (1847-1929). A few days before his death he wrote to a friend: "I have just heard, to my surprise, that I have only a few more days to live. It may be that, before this reaches you, I shall have entered the palace. Don't trouble to answer. We shall meet in the morning."

Getting even.—The doctor brought the bad news to the patient who had been bitten by a dog. Tests revealed the dog had rabies. The man had waited so long to go to the doctor that nothing could be done about his condition. After telling the sad news, the doctor left. Later, he stopped back by to check on the patient. He was writing something on a piece of paper. "Are you writing a will?" the doctor asked. "No," he said, "I'm making a list of all my enemies I want to bite!"

That desire for revenge is a typical response to our enemies. In the "eye for eye, tooth for tooth" mentality of the Old Testament, a desire for revenge inevitably followed an offense. Because of the common mentality of the day, David's refusal to seek revenge on Saul is even more remarkable. Rather than seeking revenge on Saul, David repeatedly spared him. Rather than gloating over the report of Saul's death, he put to death the man who claimed to have killed Saul.

A new note.—William Barclay recalled the experience of His mother's agonizing death from cancer. The death of someone he loved caused William Barclay to review the theological bases on which he was building his ministry. She was a godly woman, and he had just been licensed as a preacher. Yet, she had to go through a painful, agonizing death. His father said to him, "You'll have a new note in your preaching now." Barclay concluded, "And so I had—not the note of one who knew the answers and had solved the problems, but the note of one who now knew what the problems were."[1]

Could that not be the secret of the power and influence of David's psalms. The note of reality, of power, of hope in his psalms grew out of his experiences with death. They gave a new note to his songs.

A good book to have.—A certain pastor kept a book on his desk that more pastors should have. It was labeled "Complaints of Members Against Other Members." Whenever someone would come by to see the pastor to complain about another member, the pastor would say, "Here is my complaint book. I'll write down what you say, and you can sign it. Then, when I have to take up the matter officially, I'll know what testimony to expect from you." The critics would stop at the sight of the notebook and the pen. They would say, "I can't sign a book like that," and quickly exit from the pastor's office. The minister said he kept the complaint book for over forty years and opened it hundreds of times. Not once did anyone write anything down.

How easy it is to criticize! When we remember we are accountable for our words and that we have to be willing to confirm such words of complaint, we ease up on our criticism. David could have criticized Saul. Saul had many faults to which David could have pointed. However, David chose to take the positive approach.

The importance of friends.—One of the most beautiful friendships in the Bible was the one between Jonathan and David. Their friendship was not of the "fair-weather" variety. Their friendship lasted through good times and bad. A statue in Budapest has this inscription: "When the weather is fine, you have many friends. When the skies are cloudy, you will be alone." Real friendship, like that between Jonathan and David, endures even when the skies are cloudy.

TEACHING THE CLASS

Main Idea: Life's experiences are common to humans and can be used by God for growth.

Suggested Teaching Aim: Learners will regard life's experiences as each having some potential for learning about himself or herself and God.

Introduce the Bible Study

Ask: What are some life experiences that are common to all persons? Elicit response and list on the chalkboard. Response should include birth, death, limitations of the physical body, etc.

Circle the word *death.* State that death is a much-discussed subject today. Share information from the introduction to *Studying the Bible.* Use comments titled "Reality and relief in death" (*Applying the Lesson*).

State that the Scripture passage for study today is from David's poetic lament about the death of his friend Jonathan and King Saul. Invite learners to turn in their Bibles to 2 Samuel 1.

Search for Biblical Truth

Share information about the death of King Saul found in the first paragraphs of *Studying the Bible.* Share the comments titled "Getting even" (*Applying the Lesson*).

Call on a learner to read 2 Samuel 1:17-18 aloud. Share information about the "book of Jasher."

A Teaching Outline

1. Focus on the current interest in response to death and dying.
2. Discover David's response to the experience of the death of two important persons in his life.
3. Identify some useful principles for handling the death of persons important to us from David's response.
4. Discuss the potential for learning about ourselves and about God in dealing with the death of loved ones.

Invite learners to listen to the poetic beauty of David's language as another learner reads 2 Samuel 1:19-27. Ask questions similar to the following: What words indicate David's grief about these deaths? How did he pay tribute to Saul? How did he express his feelings about

Jonathan? Use information from *Studying the Bible* to supplement responses.

Give the Truth a Personal Focus

Direct learners to discuss with those sitting near them what pattern for handling the experience of death can be seen in this response from David to the death of persons important to him. After several minutes, call for learners to share their conclusions. Make some notes on the chalkboard. Responses should include conclusions like the following: acknowledgment of the personal pain associated with loss resulting from death of persons important to us, refusal to criticize the lives of those persons, focus on positive memories, and recall love shared with the deceased persons. When considering the principle of refusal to criticize, share the story titled "A good book to have" (*Applying the Lesson*). When considering love shared, use the story titled "The importance of friends" (*Applying the Lesson*).

Continue by asking: What good could possibly come from the loss of someone whom we love and who is important in our lives? Elicit response. During the discussion, recall what effect the deaths of Saul and Jonathan had on David. Ask: What does it appear that David learned from this experience about himself and about God? Elicit response.

Continue: Would you agree that each of life's experiences, including death, has some potential for our learning about ourselves or God? What might you learn about yourself in the process of handling experiences of death? How might such an experience change your life? Elicit response.

Conclude with the story titled "A new note" (*Applying the Lesson*).

---

1. William Barclay, *A Spiritual Autobiography* (Grand Rapids: William B. Eerdmans, 1975), 6.

December 22

Songs of Hannah and Mary

Basic Passage: 1 Samuel 2:1-10; Luke 1:26-56

Focal Passages: 1 Samuel 2:1-5; Luke 1:46-55

Christmas is a time for songs and singing. Most suitably, therefore, our lesson invites a study of the songs of two women: Hannah, the mother of Samuel, and Mary, mother of our Lord. Both were sung in anticipation of significant births, for Hannah's son was to be both priest and prophet in Israel, while Mary's Son came to be Savior of the world. Closely associated with Mary was another woman, Elizabeth, whose child would be John the Baptist, herald of Jesus the Christ. Three women and three boys, the circumstances of whose births had similarities and yet great differences. One purpose of this lesson must surely be to emphasize the uniqueness of the birth of Jesus and the superiority of His person and mission. The music of Christmas pays tribute to Him who is Immanuel, "God with us," long foretold in the ancient Scriptures of His people, and revealed as newborn "King," "the desired of all nations," (NIV) and "Son of God."

Study Aim: *To join with gratitude and commitment in the songs of Christmas*

STUDYING THE BIBLE

The two songs, Hannah's and Mary's, depend for meaning on their contexts. There would seem to be no alternative but to present them, therefore, in the settings in which they arose. This will mean using Bible passages outside the selections indicated for this study.

I. A Song for Samuel (1 Sam. 2:1-10)

Elkanah, father of Samuel, was probably a Levite. He may have been an official at the "temple" at Shiloh. (The use of "temple" and "post" may indicate a more permanent building than the tabernacle.) Elkanah's office would descend to Samuel, which would commit him to periodic duties at Shiloh. But his mother planned constant and life-long service for him in the Lord's house.

1. A childless wife (1 Sam. 1:1-8).—For Elkanah to have two wives was not an unusual situation in those days, probably to ensure offspring. Hannah was her husband's favorite (in itself a condemnation of bigamy), but she was barren while the other wife had children. Peninnah took out her indignation on Hannah and made her life difficult. This was specially so when the family visited the Shiloh temple on annual pilgrimages.

2. Prayer to God (1:9-18).—Hannah felt the shame of any Hebrew woman who failed to provide her husband with a son. So she took this to the Lord in prayer, promising to devote the child that God might give to His service. She was observed in her praying by Eli, the priest, who erroneously decided by her behavior that she was drunk. When Hannah told her story, Eli's attitude completely changed; and he gave her his blessing.

3. Gift of a son (1:19-28).—In due course, God gave Hannah a son whom she named Samuel ("name of God"). Elkanah had apparently obligated himself to make annual pilgrimage to Shiloh, but Hannah remained at home until Samuel was weaned, probably making him about three years old. Then the family again went together to the temple, and Hannah introduced herself to Eli and committed her young son into his care. Of him she said that "as long as he liveth he shall be lent to the Lord" (v. 28). In the spiritual exuberance of that moment, Hannah expressed herself in song.

> **1 And Hannah prayed, and said, My heart rejoiceth in the Lord, mine horn is exalted in the Lord: my mouth is enlarged over mine enemies; because I rejoice in thy salvation.**
>
> **2 There is none holy as the Lord: for there is none beside thee: neither is there any rock like our God.**
>
> **3 Talk no more so exceeding proudly; let not arrogancy come out of your mouth: for the Lord is a God of knowledge, and by him actions are weighed.**
>
> **4 The bows of the mighty men are broken, and they that stumbled are girded with strength.**
>
> **5 They that were full have hired out themselves for bread; and they that were hungry ceased: so that the barren hath born seven; and she that hath many children is waxed feeble.**

4. Words of praise to God (vv. 1-7).—Of two elements in this song, the first is praise to God for who He is and what He does. God is holy and firm as a rock, so there is none like Him. For these reasons, the proud, or arrogant (perhaps a reference to Peninnah), need to be warned since God knows everything and does His own evaluation of personal conduct. As a result, human values and conditions are reversed: the strong are humbled and the weak sustained; the affluent are reduced to hunger, and the impoverished find relief; fruitful women become enfeebled while the barren are given families. There are clear references to Hannah's own situation in these words. However, they also extend to others as God is praised for His actions of judgment and justice.

5. Relief for God's people (vv. 8-10).—This wider application becomes more evident in these concluding verses. God is sovereign and executes His will against His enemies, who are also the enemies of His people. What is true of the past will also be true of the future. References to "his king" and "his anointed" (v. 10) occasion difficulty for some, but they are understandable if we relate them to God's greatest intervention in behalf of His people in the gift of a Messiah-King, whose birth we now celebrate.

II. A Song for the Savior (Luke 1:26-56)

There are interesting parallels between Hannah's song and that of Mary, the mother of Jesus. Both were expressions of gratitude, one for a child already born, the other for a Son of promise. But Samuel came through normal human processes while Jesus' birth was supernatural, a difference that needs to be kept in mind. Luke 1:26-38 tells how God set aside the course of nature by granting Mary a child whose birth would be accounted for in this way: "The Holy Ghost shall come upon thee, and the power of the Highest shall overshadow thee: therefore also that holy thing which shall be born of thee shall be called the Son of God" (v. 35).

1. Two mothers-to-be (vv. 39-40).—Luke's opening chapters tell of the births of two boys, one to become John the Baptist and the other Jesus of Nazareth, Savior of men and women. They were related, their respective mothers being kinswomen (v. 36, RSV). John's conception took place six months before the angel's announcement to Mary (v. 36). Yet John was to say of Jesus, "This was he of whom I spake, He that cometh after me is preferred before me: for he was before me" (John 1:15). One of the purposes of Luke 1—2 is to establish the supremacy of Jesus, eternal Son of God, made flesh that He might become Savior of the world.

2. Elizabeth's tribute (vv. 41-45).—When Mary visited Elizabeth in her pregnant condition, she was greeted as "the mother of my Lord" (v. 43). We do not know all that passed between the two women, but since Elizabeth "was filled with the Holy Ghost" when she spoke (v. 41), we may believe that she helped Mary to a fuller understanding of the miracle that was happening to Mary. Out of this deep spiritual experience, Mary sang her song, known as the Magnificat from its first word in the Latin version.

46 And Mary said, My soul doth magnify the Lord,
47 And my spirit hath rejoiced in God my Savior.
48 For he hath regarded the low estate of his handmaiden: for, behold, from henceforth shall all generations call me blessed.
49 For he that is mighty hath done to me great things; and holy is his name.
50 And his mercy is on them that fear him from generation to generation.
51 He hath showed strength with his arm; he hath scattered the proud in the imagination of their hearts.
52 He hath put down the mighty from their seats, and exalted them of low degree.
53 He hath filled the hungry with good things; and the rich he hath sent empty away.
54 He hath helped his servant Israel, in remembrance of his mercy;
55 As he spake to our fathers, to Abraham, and to his seed for ever.

3. The Magnificat.—Mary's song is full of Old Testament phrases and concepts. It has strong parallels to Hannah's song, which, we may be sure, was well known to—and greatly loved by—Jewish women to whom the birth of a child was their highest aspiration. At the same time, the Magnificat has features of its own. It looks into the future as Mary declared, "All generations shall call me blessed" (v. 48). It also looks back as far as Abraham and reveals the birth of Jesus as the fulfillment of Old Testament prophecy. The two parts of the song are as follows.

***a.* Personal blessings (vv. 46-50).**—Gabriel's greeting to Mary, "Hail, thou art highly favoured, the Lord is with thee: blessed art thou among women" (1:28), and Elizabeth's greeting that followed had made deep impressions on this young woman of humble origin. In spite of legends to the contrary that make Mary the child of wealthy parents, the biblical record indicates conditions of poverty. Like Joseph, she may have been of royal descent, but her family had fallen on hard times, like many others in Israel. The man she eventually married was the village carpenter in Nazareth. She could rightly describe herself as of "low estate" (v. 48). In spite of this, God had chosen her to be the mother of His Son, in consequence of which her name would be honored through generations to come. Unfortunately, some have taken this to imply adoration and worship, an error from which it is possible to rebound so vehemently as to deprive Mary of the respect that is her due. That she was an exemplary young woman we may be sure, for would the Father have entrusted His Son to anyone less?

b. **Promises fulfilled (vv. 51-55).**—In common with all women of her race, Mary may have prayed that she might be the mother of the promised Messiah. The concluding verses would seem to indicate that she believed that this supreme honor was being conferred on her. She expressed herself in terms of the prevailing hope, namely, that the Messiah would be the deliverer and champion of His earthly people. But she also saw His mission as compassionate, anticipating that day when Jesus Himself would read from Isaiah 61:1-2, "He hath anointed me to preach the gospel to the poor; he hath sent me to heal the brokenhearted," and He added, "This day is this scripture fulfilled in your ears" (Luke 4:16-21).

APPLYING THE LESSON

Music and Christianity.—Christianity has been a singing religion from the beginning. Jesus and His disciples sang a hymn at the close of the Lord's Supper (Matt. 26:30). Paul and Silas sang in prison (Acts 16:25). James in his letter (Jas. 5:13) and Paul in his epistles (1 Cor. 14:15; Eph. 5:19) encouraged singing. The writer of Revelation mentioned singing a number of times. Writers during the first three centuries such as Pliny the Younger (about 115), Tertullian (about 160-230), and Clement of Alexandria (about 150-215) often alluded to Christian singing. Perhaps some portions of the New Testament, like 1 Timothy 3:16, were originally hymns sung by the Christian church. Music and Christianity go together.[1]

A promise kept.—An old story tells of a man on an airplane who became frightened at the rough ride. The pilot even suggested that the flight could end in disaster. This businessman cried out, "Lord, if You get me down safely I promise to give half of what I have to Your work." A preacher who was sitting on the row behind him heard this promise to the Lord. When the plane made it through the rough weather and landed safely, the preacher approached the businessman. "I heard the vow you made on the plane," he said, "and I would be happy for you to fulfill your promise by giving your money to my church because I'm involved in the work of the Lord." The businessman replied, "I made a better deal. I told the Lord if He ever got me back on another plane, I'd give Him everything!"

Most of us make promises in the heat of the moment that we do not fulfill. Sometimes we intend to but just fail to follow through. On other occasions, we never intended to fulfill the promise in the first place. In light of our usual approach, Hannah's action is remarkable. She asked the Lord for a son and promised to give him back to the Lord. God honored her request, and then Hannah honored her commitment.

Today Christ is born.—John Killinger tells of a friend who was going through a difficult time. He was professor of church history at a large university. However, problems developed, and he did not receive tenure. Consequently, he lost his job. The search for a new job led to dead-end streets. After a long time, he found a job heading up a seminary consortium. Within two years, this job ended, and he knew once more the trauma of joblessness. In despondency, the man turned again to the practice of prayer. He practiced fantasizing a relaxing scene, putting himself in it, and then allowing God to lead the action from there. He pictured himself on the rockbound coast of northern New England, walking along the coast on a beautiful, sunny day in June. The warmth and beauty of the scene made him feel good all over. In his mind, he saw a pathway leading down the cliff to the rocks below. He took it and found himself on the very edge of the water. He saw a bottle floating in the water with what looked like a message inside of it. He knew this was the word God had for him. He opened the bottle expectantly and read the message. Written on the note were these words: "Today, Christ is born." He was disappointed. He was at the lowest ebb in his life. He needed direction on where to turn for a job. His family was floundering. He needed a word from God, and all he received was a message he had known since he was a little boy. Then, suddenly the truth of the message dawned on him. He allowed Christ to be born in him again. The living Christ took the central place in his life again and all of the anxieties and fears moved to the periphery.

Christmas is not just about a baby who was born into the world two thousand years ago. It is the glad announcement of a Savior who can take up residence in human life today and give power and peace and purpose.

Never too little.—Someone once said, "You can be too big for God to use but never too little." No one illustrates that more clearly than Mary. Many in her day were more glamorous, more prosperous, more prominent, and perhaps even more beautiful. God does not choose according to those outward standards. He chooses according to what's in the heart.

TEACHING THE CLASS

Main Idea: Song was the response of two women through whom God chose to help His people and to save the world.

Suggested Teaching Aim: Learners will praise God for the beautiful response of two women used in His redemptive work.

Introduce the Bible Study

If appropriate in your class, provide each learner a small Christmas ornament. Direct learners to take a few moments for creative thinking and be ready to describe how their ornaments could be used to praise God for the birth of Jesus Christ. After a few moments, call for response. Responses may include focus on the color. Example: These colors can be used to express joy in the birth of Jesus. The focus might be on the sound the ornament makes or the form. Encourage creativeness and accept all suggestions without evaluation.

State that the study for today focuses on responses of praise from two women whom God used in special ways. Write *Hannah* and *Mary* on the chalkboard. Invite learners to find both 1 Samuel 2 and Luke 1 in their Bibles.

Search for Biblical Truth

Invite learners to share any information they might recall about Hannah.

Share background information about Hannah from *Studying the Bible.* Note that the praise she expressed in song was at the point of committing her young son into the care of Eli, the priest. Call on a learner to read Hannah's words from 1 Samuel 2:1-10.

A Teaching Outline

1. Focus on ways of praising God during celebration of the Christmas events.
2. Identify the praise and worship of the songs of two women used by God in His redemptive work.
3. Identify feelings of personal joy during this special season.
4. Praise God for the personal response of joy because of the birth of Christ and for the response of two women used by Him in those events.

Share the story titled "A promise kept" (*Applying the Lesson*). Note that while it may seem difficult to us to give up the care of a son for whom she had so earnestly prayed, Hannah considered it an act of worship and joy to keep her promise.

Share information from *Studying the Bible* about Hannah's song of worship and praise. Note the wider application of verses 8-10. Continue by asking: What did Hannah know of the Messiah-King: Jesus? Elicit response indicating that she would have known of the promise of a messiah for Israel and praised God for that assurance.

Call attention to the next woman listed on the chalkboard. Share the story titled "Never too little" (*Applying the Lesson*).

Invite learners to turn to the Luke 1 passage. Share information from *Studying the Bible* that includes the events of Luke 1:26-45. Emphasize Elizabeth's response of praise to God.

Note that Luke 1:46-55 contains Mary's song of joy and praise to God as she considered this event with her cousin Elizabeth. Call on a learner to read the verses aloud.

Note that Mary's song, like Hannah's, in verses 46-50 addresses her own blessings from God and then takes on a larger focus of the fulfillment of the promise to all persons.

Give the Truth a Personal Focus

Share the story titled "Today Christ is born" (*Applying the Lesson*). Emphasize that Jesus was not just a baby born two thousand years ago to Mary, but He is equally born in the hearts of persons as they accept them as their personal redeemer. Encourage any person without Jesus as Savior to accept Him by faith.

Note that songs have been the response of many to the events of this birth. Recall and review the carols that are common at Christmas. Note that these express the feelings of both the writer and the singer to the birth of Jesus. Point out that we too are the singers as we share in the songs of Christmas.

Lead learners in moments of praise and prayer for the beautiful responses of Elizabeth and Mary to God's redemptive work through them and for the songs of praise in their hearts that grew out of the acts of God celebrated at Christmas.

---

1. David Music, "The Earliest Christian Music," *Biblical Illustrator* (Winter 1983): 84.

December 29

A Hymn to the Creator

Basic Passage: Psalm 8

Focal Passage: Psalm 8

When written, this psalm attributed to David was referred to "the chief Musician," according to the title at the head of the psalm. This notation is to be found at the beginning of fifty-five psalms, an indication that they were to be used in the worship of the sanctuary. Though written mainly in the first person, Psalm 8 begins and concludes with an address to "our Lord," making clear that the writer intended for others to share his experience and understanding of God and so engage together in His praise. Here, then, is a selection from the hymnbook of the Hebrew people that introduces us to songs suitable for public worship. Like many other psalms, it consists of pure worship, no complaints, no requests, but undiluted praise to Almighty God. We may like to think of compositions in our own congregational hymnals that help us to give glory to God in ways that might otherwise go unexpressed.

Study Aim: *To consider reasons why we should praise God and ways in which to do it*

STUDYING THE BIBLE

In the title of Psalm 8 appears the words "upon Gittith." We cannot be sure what this means, but many scholars see in it a reference to a winepress. They accordingly associate the psalm with harvest, and more particularly with the Jewish Feast of Tabernacles when God's providing mercies during the wilderness journey were recalled. On this last Sunday of the year we should have no difficulty finding reasons for our own praise.

I. The Majesty of God (Ps. 8:1-2)

The psalmist began by thanking God for being what He is. The capitalized word "Lord" stands for the covenant name Yahweh. This was the name by which He introduced Himself to Moses and, through Moses, to the people of Israel (Ex. 3:14-15).

> **1 O Lord our Lord, how excellent is thy name in all the earth! who hast set thy glory above the heavens.**
>
> **2 Out of the mouth of babes and sucklings hast thou ordained strength because of thine enemies that thou mightest still the enemy and the avenger.**

1. "Our Lord" (v. 1).—Another favorite psalm begins, "The Lord is my shepherd" (Ps. 23:1). We cannot really praise God unless we have a personal relationship with Him. In Psalm 8, the writer was about to magnify the name of God for what he had discovered about Him. But he wanted others to know that he had no proprietary rights to this great and glorious God. He was willing to be their God too. Therefore, they could join in the praise he was offering. In Hebrew thought, the name and the person were identical and inseparable. It is, therefore, the Lord Himself whose majesty is recognized both on earth and in heaven. The latter refers to the heavenly realm where God is glorified by saints and angels, a thought that is in contrast to the next verse.

2. Children's praises (v. 2).—Kirkpatrick says that Yahweh "has ordained that even the feeblest representatives of humanity should be

His champions to confound and silence those who oppose His kingdom and deny His goodness and providential government."[1] The psalmist's statement is mentioned in Matthew 21:16 in connection with the Hosannas raised by little children as our Lord made His triumphal entry into Jerusalem, prior to His crucifixion. We shall notice other links between this psalm and the Savior.

II. A Marvel of Concern (Ps. 8:3-4)

This has been described as a psalm in praise of nature, whereas it is nature's God who is praised. The magnificence of the created universe should always lift our thoughts to the Creator. But this is not always the case. We need more than physical eyes to see beyond material things to the spiritual truths they can teach us.

> **3 When I consider thy heavens, the work of thy fingers, the moon and the stars, which thou hast ordained;**
>
> **4 What is man, that thou art mindful of him? and the son of man, that thou visitest him?**

1. The universe considered (v. 3).—Now that we know something of the vastness of the universe and have even put men on the moon, our estimate of the Creator's skill should be correspondingly enhanced. Astronauts, looking back on planet earth from their skybound vehicles, have testified to the beauty they saw. Our psalmist only knew what he could see with the naked eye, but that was enough to fill him with amazement. As the fingers of potters and others enable them to add shape and design to what they make so the fingers of God are extolled for their intricate handiwork.

2. A caring Creator (v. 4).—Turning from the wonders of creation to himself, a mere mortal, the psalmist expressed surprise that God should care for him. If we think of the word "man" as referring to Adam (we may well do so since this psalm has clear echoes of the opening chapters of Genesis), then "the son of man" describes his every descendant. The verbs used describe a constant, ongoing care, such as the Lord showed toward His wayward and often rebellious people during their wilderness wanderings.

III. Our Human Dignity (Ps. 8:5-8)

Although the Bible is strong in its condemnation of human sin and shows full awareness of our many frailties, it also affirms our dignity as creatures made, as the Lord said, "in our image, after our likeness" (Gen. 1:26). The significance of the following verses is emphasized by the Old Testament passages they recall and the New Testament statements that refer to them.

5 For thou hast made him a little lower than the angels, and hast crowned him with glory and honor.

6 Thou madest him to have dominion over the works of thy hands; thou hast put all things under his feet;

7 All sheep and oxen, yea, and the beasts of the field;

8 The fowl of the air, and the fish of the sea, and whatsoever passeth through the paths of the seas.

1. Lower than whom? (v. 5).—Commentators are largely in agreement that this verse should read "a little lower than God" (NRSV). Leupold says, "The statement is so bold that the early translators . . . have substituted the word 'angels' for 'God.' "[2] However startling, this claim is fully supported by the Genesis record that anticipates our psalmist's words as it reads, "God said, Let us make man in our image, after our likeness: and let them have dominion over the fish of the sea, and over the fowl of the air, and over the cattle, and over all the earth, and over every creeping thing that creepeth upon the earth. So God created man in his own image, in the image of God created he him; male and female created he them" (Gen. 1:26-27).

2. Creation recalled (v. 6).—When the psalmist asked, "What is man?" (v. 4), he was doubtless considering himself and his contemporaries. There was little in humanity as he saw it to merit the care and concern of God. So he looked back, before sin and corruption spoiled the human scene, to the original purposes of God when He made Adam and Eve and set them in Eden. No more noble a beginning can be imagined for our race than what is stated in the creation story. The biblical concept of humankind begins at an unimaginably high level with God alone as superior. We can contrast some of the prevailing theories of human origins.

3. Humanity's lapse.—The writer of the Epistle to the Hebrews quoted Psalm 8:5-8 almost completely, beginning, "What is man that thou art mindful of him?" (2:6-8). After repeating the psalmist's words about God-given dominion over the natural order, he added, "But now we see not yet all things put under him." The intentions of God have been frustrated by the entrance of sin which has stripped the human race of qualities with which God endowed us. This was dramatically illustrated in the banishment of Adam and Eve from the perfections of Eden. "Therefore the Lord God sent him forth from the garden of Eden, to till the ground from which he was taken" (Gen. 3:23).

4. Authority and responsibility (vv. 7-8).—Few causes have grown with greater rapidity and strength in recent years than that of the environment. Concern over pollution and the destruction of natural resources is justified and commendable. But some would-be protectors of the environment have charged that the Bible is responsible for the abuse of nature. These verses have been quoted as an example of mischievous teaching. This, of course, is to misunderstand what the Bible does say about our relationship to the world around. God did not hand His universe over to us to do what we like with it. He made us trustees, caretakers, of all that He had made. For the believer, the truth of Psalm 24:1, "The earth is the Lord's, and the fullness thereof," still remains in force (see 1 Cor. 10:26).

5. The Last Adam (vv. 4-8).—To return to the New Testament use of this passage in Hebrew 2:6-8, the acknowledgment of humanity's failure to live up to the potential and purpose that the Creator intended, is followed by the statement, "But we see Jesus . . . crowned with glory and honor." The first Adam's tragic fall from his high estate is put in contrast to the triumph of Christ, the last Adam, whose completed work of redemption has become the hope of humanity. What was lost by sin will be restored by grace, a thought developed by the apostle Paul in Romans 8:18-23.

IV. Concluding Doxology (Ps. 8:9)

The note of praise on which this psalm began brings it to a conclusion by a repetition of verse 1.

9 O Lord our Lord, how excellent is thy name in all the earth!

As we have seen, we need to turn to the New Testament use of Psalm 8 to realize that the dignity conferred by God on the human race has been blurred by sin. The psalm, therefore, should not be taken as a song of praise for humankind but of the "Lord our Lord," who by His grace and the atoning work of His Son, will one day restore that image of Himself that He stamped upon Adam. Contemplating this, Paul wrote of "the glory which shall be revealed in us" (Rom. 8:18).

APPLYING THE LESSON

A definition of worship.—Warren Wiersbe has written, "Worship is the believer's response of all that he is—mind, emotions, will, and body—to all that God is and says and does."[3] A major part of that response is praise. Because God is the sovereign Creator and Ruler of all, because God speaks the truth about life, because God redeems and forgives, the only proper response is adoration and praise. Therefore, the Psalms of the Old Testament that were worship tools are permeated with praise. Praise needs to become a more prominent part of our worship today.

A ladder of praise.—When praise is a part of our worship today, I'm afraid our understanding of praise is shallow at times. We need to contemplate

Leonard Griffith's idea of a ladder of praise. He illustrated each step of the ladder with a text.

The first step on the ladder is thanking God for our good fortune when we compare ourselves to others. This kind of praise is illustrated by the Pharisee in the temple who looked at the tax gatherer and said, "God, I thank Thee that I am not like other people: swindlers, unjust, adulterers, or even like this tax-gatherer" (Luke 18:11, NASB).

The second step on the ladder of praise is thanking God for His goodness to us, apart from what others might be experiencing. We see this in the leper Jesus healed. Upon realizing he had been healed, "he fell on his face at His [Jesus'] feet, giving thanks to Him" (Luke 17:16, NASB).

The third step of praise is to thank God for who He is. The psalmist said, "Let them give thanks to the Lord for His lovingkindness, / And for His wonders to the sons of men!" (107:8, NASB).

The final step on the ladder of praise is to be able to thank God in the midst of suffering. Paul approached this level in 2 Corinthians 12:8-10. Jesus most clearly expressed this kind of praise. Paul said that Jesus "in the night in which He was betrayed took bread; and when He had given thanks, He broke it" (1 Cor. 11:23-24, NASB).[4]

The psalmist lived on all four of these levels. The psalm that is our text fits most closely into steps two and three.

The value of humanity.—Only in the biblical witness do we read about the true value of human beings. Secular evolution teaches that we come from nothing. Secular philosophy today suggests that we are headed nowhere. According to secular evolution and philosophy, we have zeroes for both our origin and destiny. How different from the picture painted in the Bible. According to the biblical witness, human beings were created by God in God's very image. According to the biblical witness, humanity is headed for a destiny determined and directed by God. Our text focuses on the special value God gives to human beings.

The shape of the world.—A little boy was asked in class if the world is flat or round. The boy answered, "My grandpa says it's crooked!" That's how the Bible describes the world. Created by God with a special purpose and a distinct destiny, humanity turned from obedience to God. Instead of living in fellowship with God, humanity chose to walk in disobedience. Humankind turned what God intended to be a rose garden into a jungle.

What we are doing to God's earth.—The challenge to take dominion over the earth has led to the kind of irresponsibility that is wreaking havoc on our earth. One writer said, "If the American people and their solid wastes were spread evenly over the United States there would be in each square mile of the nation 56 people surrounded by 54 tons of rubbish which would include: 3 junked cars, 25 discarded tires, 8,500 bottles, 17,000 cans, one ton of plastics, and 8½ tons of paper." Americans are producing a total of 340 million tons of solid wastes per year.

We are not only polluting the earth around us, but also we are polluting the atmosphere. We are dumping into the atmosphere toxic pollutants which fall back onto the earth as "acid rain." One study has revealed that acid rain has reduced cotton yields by 33 percent and tomato harvests by 21 percent. A United States Department of Agriculture employee called acid rain "the most serious environmental dilemma of this century."[5]

TEACHING THE CLASS

Main Idea: God is above all others and worthy of our praise.

Suggested Teaching Aim: Learners will design ways to offer undiluted praise to God.

Introduce the Bible Study

If appropriate for your group, call on two learners who have previously prepared to role-play a situation in which one is giving profusive praise for another. One learner should offer to the other praise for who he is, the kind of life the person leads, his family, the way he looks, and any other comments she can make about the other. The one being praised will play the role of one who is simply receiving the praise without response.

The role-playing will probably elicit uncomfortable laughing from the learners. When the comments have been concluded, ask questions like the following and elicit response. Why do we feel slightly uncomfortable in a situation like this? Why do we feel uncomfortable when it happens in real life? Does it appear to be genuine praise? Why? Why is praise hard to receive? Why is it hard to give? Is it important or can it be abandoned since it is difficult to give and receive appropriately?

Write the *Main Idea* on the chalkboard. Ask: Is it easy to praise God? Why or why not? Is it necessary? Why? Do we do it enough in private worship? in public worship? Why or why not?

Note that the study for today is a psalm that offers undiluted praise to God. Invite learners to turn to Psalm 8 in their Bibles. State that the purpose of our study is to help us determine ways we can offer appropriate praise to God and that when the study is finished, learners will be asked to design suggestions.

Search for Biblical Truth

State that because this is a familiar and especially beautiful psalm of praise, it will be read aloud before learners study its content. Call on a learner who has previously agreed to read the psalm aloud.

A Teaching Outline

1. Role-play a praise situation.
2. Discuss the points of an outline of Psalm 8.
3. Consider yourself on a "ladder of praise."
4. Design ways to praise God.

When the reading is finished, share information from *Studying the Bible* about the writer, David. Share the comments titled "A definition of worship" (*Applying the Lesson*).

Display this outline.

Psalm 8

1. The Majesty of God (vv. 1-2)
2. A Marvel of Concern (vv. 3-4)
3. Our Human Dignity (vv. 5-8)
4. Concluding Doxology (v. 9)

Share information from *Studying the Bible* as each of these points is individually discussed. When discussing point 2, share the comments titled "What we are doing to God's earth" (*Applying the Lesson*). When discussing point 3, share the comments titled "The value of humanity" (*Applying the Lesson*). Conclude this section with a dramatic proclamation of verse 9.

Give the Truth a Personal Focus

Share the comments titled "A ladder of praise" (*Applying the Lesson*). Ask: Where would you fit yourself on that ladder of praise to God? Are you satisfied with your ability to praise God in worship of Him? These questions may need to be rhetorical.

Remind learners that our purpose for the study was to design ways to offer undiluted praise to God. Suggest that they work with the persons sitting around them to consider suggestions for ways to praise and worship Him more completely.

After a period of discussion, invite learners to share their responses. Encourage learners to choose ways they will personally use to give greater praise to God.

---

1. A. F. Kirkpatrick, *The Book of Psalms* (Cambridge: University Press, 1902), 38.
2. H. C. Leupold, *Exposition of the Psalms* (Columbus: Wartburg, 1959), 104.
3. Warren Wiersbe, *Real Worship* (Nashville: Oliver Nelson, 1986), 27.
4. Leonard Griffith, "A Ladder of Praise," *Pulpit Digest* (November-December 1977), 3-8.
5. Richard J. Foster, *Freedom from Simplicity* (San Francisco: Harper and Row, 1981), 176.

January 5

A Song for Temple Visitors

Basic Passage: Psalm 84

Focal Passage: Psalm 84

Do we look forward to Sunday and the assembly of God's people for worship? The Book of Psalms contains not only spiritual songs to be used in the actual worship of the Lord but also a number of songs sung in anticipation of that privilege. Some of these have been put into a collection found toward the end of the Psalter (Pss. 120—134), each of them described as "A Song of degrees," or, "of goings up," and they were sung by pilgrims on their way to Jerusalem for one or other of the great feasts. Other similar songs are scattered throughout the book, and of these Psalm 84 is an outstanding example. Its beauty has appealed to believers of all centuries. When set to appropriate music, it is still sung by choirs around the world. This study should stimulate us to evaluate our own attitudes toward the house of God and the worship of the sanctuary. Can we employ the ecstatic language of the psalmist, and, if not, why not?

Study Aim: *To consider the privilege of worshiping God in His house and renew our devotion to both*

STUDYING THE BIBLE

Again in this psalm we notice a mixture of pronouns, some single, others plural. Though the writer is expressing his own thoughts and desires, "My soul . . . my heart and my flesh" (v. 2), he makes these applicable to others by his use of "they," "our," and "them." Like many contributors to our church hymnals, the writer is not claiming an exclusive personal experience. On the contrary, he recognizes that others feel as he does, and he offers his lines for their use. We will surely acknowledge that the sacred songs we sing often express our thoughts better than we could possibly do.

I. Matters of Interest

No book of the Bible has stimulated more thoughtful inquiry than the Psalms. A steady stream of books has been written and published, answering questions on difficult points, expounding the meaning of these glorious poems, and exploring their devotional value. Following are three points of interest.

1. The title.—As in Psalm 8, the word "Gittith" appears in the title. This could refer to a musical instrument, but a preferred meaning relates to a winepress (see previous lesson). The ascription, "for the sons of Korah," can have "by" or "of" as substitutes for "for." It refers to a guild of temple singers (2 Chron. 20:19) who had their own collection of psalms that they used to lead public worship.

2. Author and circumstances.—The psalm is anonymous, and it is not possible to establish an author. Mention of "courts of the Lord" and persons "that dwell in thy house" (vv. 2,4) seem to indicate a period after David when there was a standing temple. The psalmist was prevented from attending its services by some unstated cause.

3. Selah.—The psalm is divided into three sections by the use of this obscure word. Though the subject of much study, *selah* has not positively revealed its meaning. In spite of its popularity, "Think of that!" is the most unlikely. It could have indicated a musical rest, or with the meaning of "forever," have marked the place for singing a doxology, for example, "And blessed be his glorious name forever" (Ps. 72:19). We just do not know.

II. Longing for God's House (Ps. 84:1-4)

Many things can prevent attendance at our church's worship services. For older people, physical handicaps are often the reason. The worst malady of all, however, is a lack of desire. Our psalmist set an example of fervent appreciation for the opportunity of worship in the sanctuary. He had the temple in mind, but we should remember the words of Jesus to the Samaritan woman, "The hour cometh, when ye shall neither in this mountain, not yet at Jerusalem, worship the Father. . . . the true worshipers shall worship the Father in spirit and in truth" (John 4:21,23). Not location, but attitude and purpose are what matter.

> **1 How amiable are thy tabernacles, O Lord of hosts!**
>
> **2 My soul longeth, yea, even fainteth for the courts of the Lord: my heart and my flesh crieth out for the living God.**
>
> **3 Yea, the sparrow hath found an house, and the swallow a nest for herself, where she may lay her young, even thine altars, O Lord of hosts, my King, and my God.**
>
> **4 Blessed are they that dwell in thy house: they will be still praising thee. Selah.**

1. Deep desire (vv. 1-2).—The word "amiable" carries the sense of "worthy to be loved." That God is addressed as "Lord of hosts" is acknowledgment of His majesty. He is the supreme God, the sovereign over all. The verb tense in verse 2 indicates that the psalmist was looking back to a time when he was cut off from God's house. His entire being was affected, "soul . . . heart . . . flesh," by his sense of spiritual deprivation. With churches on almost every street corner, we may find it difficult to imagine what it was like to have no place of worship. But see the earlier quote from John 4 that opens up the opportunity for worship wherever we are and whatever the circumstances.

2. More privileged (vv. 3-4).—Our psalmist recalled seeing birds flying around and roosting in the temple precincts. They were to be envied. There is also a tender tone in this observation. Birds are highly nervous creatures, easily scared away by anything that appears to threaten. But the temple courts were friendly to them, even protective of them. They could build their nests and raise their young there. There were persons, however, who were even more fortunate. The temple area provided accommodation for priests, Levites, and others while they discharged their official duties. Naturally, these would be constantly praising God. However, though the psalm does not say so, there would be danger that these would come to take their privileges for granted so that their worship activities would become mechanical.

III. Happiness of Pilgrims (Ps. 84:5-9)

As with most poetry, this psalm has passages that need explanation and understanding. The next few verses are in this category. We will follow the rendering that reads, "How happy are those whose strength comes from you, / who are eager to make the pilgrimage to Mount Zion" (v. 5, GNB).

> **5 Blessed is the man whose strength is in thee; in whose heart are the ways of them.**
>
> **6 Who passing through the valley of Baca make it a well; the rain also filleth the pools.**
>
> **7 They go from strength to strength, everyone of them in Zion appeareth before God.**
>
> **8 O Lord God of hosts, hear my prayer: give ear, O God of Jacob. Selah.**
>
> **9 Behold, O God our shield, and look upon the face of thine anointed.**

1. Strength through hope (vv. 5-6).—In Bible times, the journey to Jerusalem, from any direction, was arduous, even risky. Faint hearts might be tempted to turn back. But the prospect of seeing the temple and worshiping there gave strength to the weary and courage to the afraid. The second part of verse 5 may best read, "In whose heart are the highways to Zion" (NRSV). The mention of Zion (Jerusalem) two verses later may justify the assumption that the psalmist was acclaiming the happiness of people who set their hearts on treading the road that leads to the holy city and the temple, even though it takes them through "the valley of Baca," that is, tears.

2. Glad arrival (vv. 7-8).—"They grow stronger as they go; / they will see the God of gods on Zion" (v. 7, GNB). These are triumphant words. In spite of the hazards of the way, the travelers reach their destination, gaining strength as they go. There they appear before their God in worship. Verses 8-9 form a prayer that focuses on the King, "thine anointed." Jerusalem had both spiritual and patriotic meaning for these Hebrews. So, when they met there for worship, they made petition for their reigning monarch. Who this was, we do not know. But we are reminded of the apostle Paul's injunction, "I exhort therefore, that, first of all, supplications, prayers, intercessions, and giving of thanks, be made for all men; for kings, and for all that are in authority" (1 Tim. 2:1-2). We can substitute president and governors here as we include national leaders in our prayers, both private and public.

IV. Joy in Arrival (Ps. 84:10-12)

Whether this final section of the psalm should begin with verse 9 or 10 is a moot question. The placing of "Selah" after verse 8 would suggest the former. This would indicate prayer for the king as a priority in worship, not an unreasonable thing for a pious Jew who regarded the king as the descendant of David and therefore in line for the messianic promises. "Bless our king, O God, / the king you have chosen" (v. 9, GNB).

> **10 For a day in thy courts is better than a thousand. I had rather be a doorkeeper in the house of my God, than to dwell in the tents of wickedness.**
>
> **11 For the Lord God is a sun and shield: the Lord will give grace and glory: no good thing will he withhold from them that walk uprightly.**
>
> **12 O Lord of hosts, blessed is the man that trusteth in thee.**

1. Considered alternatives (vv. 10-11).—We do not know the circumstances that kept this psalmist from attending God's house. But it seems likely that he had been forced into close association with people who "dwell in the tents of wickedness," perhaps idolaters, or, in any case, transgressors of God's laws. Once he had tasted the satisfactions of the temple, so that he had decided that one day there was to be preferred to a thousand days elsewhere, he then affirmed that he would sooner perform the lowliest of tasks in God's house than to have to live among the indifferent and scornful. Our daily associations may scarcely merit such strong language, but is it not a relief to step out of our everyday world into the blessedness of God's house and the company of His people?

2. An invitation (v. 12).—On this, the first Sunday of a new year, the invitation is given to "taste and see that the Lord is good" (Ps. 34:8). This invitation is followed, in this earlier psalm, by the words printed above, "Blessed is the man that trusteth in thee." Why not put God to the test?

APPLYING THE LESSON

The importance of attitude.—Paul Powell tells of a young woman from the East Coast who accompanied her husband to the army camp where he was stationed. The camp was located in the Mojave Desert in California. The conditions were deplorable. The heat was unbearable. She had to live in a rundown shack, and her only neighbors were Indians, none of whom spoke English. In great despair, she wrote her mother and told her she was coming home. Her mother responded with a two-line quotation from a well-known poem: "Two men look out through the same bars: / One sees mud, and one the stars." The young woman was convicted by the poem and decided she needed to change her attitude. She made friends with the Indians and began to learn their language. As she learned to make some of their crafts, she began to make friends with them. She noticed for the first time the beauty of the sunrises and sunsets on the desert. She learned about the area, its terrain, and its vegetation. She grew to love the land, and, later, she even wrote a book about it. The land had not changed. Instead, the woman changed. With a new attitude, she was able to see what she had not seen otherwise. Attitude made the difference.[1]

Attitude also makes the difference when a person comes to worship. Two people can be in the same place, during the same worship service. One can have a deeply moving experience with God. The other one can go away unmoved. The difference is attitude. The expectant attitude of worship is clearly expressed in the Psalms.

The place where love met.—An ancient legend of the rabbis tells a story about why a certain location was selected for a temple. Two brothers lived on adjoining farms. One was married and had several children. The other was single. After the harvest, the married brother said to his wife, "We have so much, and God has blessed so richly. In addition, we have our family. My poor brother is all alone. Tonight I will load up a portion of my harvest and take it to my brother. Maybe it will help him in his loneliness." At the same time the single brother was sitting alone by his fire, thinking of his good crop and of the manifold blessings of God on his life. He said to himself, "My brother has no larger harvest than I do. Yet, he must not only feed himself but his family as well. Tonight I will load up a portion of my harvest and take it to my brother. Maybe it will help him in his need." As each headed toward his brother's farm with a wagon load of harvest, they met. The temple was built there, on the spot where love met.

Goals and persistence.—A clergyman once said, "I have studied leaders and organizations. I have devoured biographies and autobiographies. I have immersed myself in history. I have carefully observed the contemporary leadership of my day. I've come to the conclusion that one factor distinguishes the organization that wins. It's staying power."[2] Worthy goals provide the staying power necessary to reach those goals.

In a similar way, the Hebrew believers whose goal was to worship in the temple in Jerusalem were provided staying power to enable them to arrive at their destination.

A small church.—Have you heard about the church with two members? The pastor was one, and the layman was the other. Committee meetings could be held over a cup of coffee. Business meetings could be taken care of over lunch. Such meetings would also take care of the pastoral visitation. Since the one layperson could serve in any position he wanted, no one's feelings would be hurt. In such a church there would be no need for enlisting teachers and developing a training program. However, there is also a down side to the two-member church. If the layman decided he was too busy to come to church or if he wanted to sleep late or if he was going to the lake, the preacher would not have a congregation. If he decided to "let George do it," then the preacher would have to fill the role of George. Also, if George got mad at the preacher, the fellowship of the church would be seriously affected.

Despite the problems and the possibilities of the two-member church, this fact remains. When the two came together to worship, they could experience the presence of God, for Jesus said, "For where two or three have gathered together in My name, there I am in their midst" (Matt. 18:20, NASB).

TEACHING THE CLASS

Main Idea: Worship of God and renewing devotion to Him is a privilege.

Suggested Teaching Aim: Learners will renew commitment to worship God with others because of renewed awareness of its privilege.

Introduce the Bible Study

Note that the study of Psalm 8 on last Sunday was the first lesson of Unit II titled "Songs From Festive Occasions." Note that the psalm for today celebrates the occasion of public group worship.

A Teaching Outline

1. Focus on personal attitudes about public worship.
2. Identify the attitude of the psalmist about public worship.
3. Lead learners to evaluate their own attitudes in view of these teachings.
4. Invite learners to renew their commitment to worship God with others because of renewed awareness of the privilege that it is.

Direct learners to rate their attitude about public worship on a scale of 1-10 using response to these questions. Direct them to privately write their responses.

1. Sunday is a festive day in my home and in my heart.
2. Nothing can take away my commitment to be in God's house for worship.
3. Nothing can take away my joy in the experience of public worship.
4. I believe God blesses those who engage in public worship.
5. I am blessed because of my commitment to public worship.
6. I consider public worship a privilege—not a duty.
7. When I take part in public worship, I renew my devotion to God.

When the attitude scale has been completed, review each statement inquiring whether they think the statement is true of most church members. Discuss the problems interfering with responding as the statements indicate.

State that the Scripture for today extols the privilege of public worship and the desire in the heart of the psalmist for that kind of worship. Invite learners to open their Bibles to Psalm 84.

Search for Biblical Truth

Share background information from *Studying the Bible* to increase understanding of this psalm. Display the following outline:

Psalm 84

1. Longing for God's House	(vv. 1-4)
2. Happiness of Pilgrims	(vv. 5-9)
3. Joy in Arrival	(vv. 10-12)

Share information from *Studying the Bible* as each group of verses is read aloud and discussed. When point 1 is discussed, share the comments titled "Goals and persistence" (*Applying the Lesson*). When point 3 is discussed, share the comments titled "The place where love met" and "A small church" (*Applying the Lesson*).

Give the Truth a Personal Focus

Write the main idea on the chalkboard. Ask rhetorically: Do you believe this is the teaching of the Scripture? Is it also a teaching that you personally accept? Does your attitude about public worship with your church reflect that you believe it is a privilege to worship God with others and to renew your devotion to Him?

Recall that the earlier discussion identified many things which make these positive attitudes about public worship difficult. Share the comments titled "The importance of attitude" (*Applying the Lesson*). Invite learners to renew their commitment to worship God with others.

---

1. Paul Powell, *A Faith that Sings* (Nashville: Broadman Press, 1989), 145-46.
2. John Haggai, *Lead On!* (Waco: Word Books, 1986), 38-39.

January 12

A Hymn to the Redeemer

Basic Passage: Psalm 103

Focal Passage: Psalm 103:1-17

One of the attractions of the Book of Psalms is the appropriateness of its contents for every circumstance of life. Among many writers who have sought to demonstrate this was Rowland E. Prothero whose book, *The Psalms in Human Life*, abounds in illustrations from life and literature. In his opening chapter Prothero wrote of the Hebrew Psalter, "In it are gathered the lyrical burst of [man's] tenderness, the moan of his penitence, the pathos of his sorrow, the triumph of his victory, the despair of his defeat, the firmness of his confidence, the rapture of his assured hope."[1] An example of this is furnished by comparing Psalms 102 and 103. The former is introduced by this statement, "A Prayer of the afflicted, when he is overwhelmed, and poureth out his complaint before the Lord." The opening verses that follow this title reveal a person in deep trouble who prays, "Hear my prayer,

O Lord, and let my cry come unto thee." What a contrast with the way Psalm 103 begins, "Bless the Lord, O my soul," words of heartfelt praise and gratitude that have been adopted by God's people down the centuries!

Study Aim: *To find in this psalm words to express our own praise and gratitude to our Heavenly Father*

STUDYING THE BIBLE

"Let us repeat together the words of Psalm 103:1-2." How often congregations are invited to join in this act of praise! The words of this psalm are especially appropriate in times of rejoicing for mercies received. But they also express truths that are always valid, in the gloom as well as the sunshine, and can warm the believing heart with renewed confidence and trust, even on the darkest day.

I. Praise for Personal Blessing (Ps. 103:1-5)

The psalms are anonymous. No claims to authorship appear in the psalms themselves, only clues. Traditional opinion has ascribed many psalms to David, and although this opinion is often challenged, much can be said for its antiquity. In the absence of any strong evidence to the contrary, we are inclined to accept the Davidic authorship of Psalm 103. But let it be said that those who differ are entitled to respect.

> **1 Bless the Lord, O my soul: and all that is within me, bless his holy name.**
>
> **2 Bless the Lord, O my soul, and forget not all his benefits:**
>
> **3 Who forgiveth all thine iniquities; who healeth all thy diseases;**
>
> **4 Who redeemeth thy life from destruction; who crowneth thee with loving-kindness and tender mercies;**
>
> **5 Who satisfieth thy mouth with good things; so that thy youth is renewed like the eagle's.**

1. Forgiveness (v. 3).—If this is the thanksgiving of a king, we may be impressed by the things for which he did not thank God: his wealth, his palace, his extensive realm, his victories, and so on. He spoke for everybody in giving thanks for what might be considered life's common mercies, and he began with forgiveness. This was the first of his "forget not's" (v. 2), a reminder to us all of the debt we owe to God for His pardoning grace. David had once exclaimed, "Blessed is he whose transgression is forgiven, whose sin is covered" (Ps. 32:1). We know the cost of our forgiveness, even the death of the Son of God, and our thanksgiving should be the greater.

2. Healing (v. 3).—Good health is one of life's greatest boons, not enjoyed by all but when possessed, always a reason for saying thank you to God. Old Testament believers were specially aware of His healing activities, for they had little hope for help from any other source. Today's progress in medical science can well be a reason for us to give thanks. Behind every miraculous recovery we need to see the activity of God who has given us bodies that have amazing potential for resisting disease and overcoming its consequences.

3. Preservation (v. 4).—Many things threatened the lives of people in the psalmist's day. Many threaten our lives today. The truth is, we live in a dangerous world and engage in various dangerous activities. The perils of today's highways are constantly brought to our attention. To thank God that we are still alive and in one piece should have a place in our daily prayers.

4. Sustenance (v. 5).—Daily supply for our needs is suggested here, for God gives us "good things," in tune with the truth that, "Every good and every perfect gift is from above" (Jas. 1:17). So we survive into old age, like eagles that are reputed to enjoy perpetual youth.

II. Thanksgiving as a Nation (Ps. 103:6-18)

The psalmist's field of vision enlarged as he thought of God's dealings with the nation of which he was a part. To review God's dealings with us as individuals stimulates praise. But even greater evidence of His justice and mercy is to be found in history, in which He is still at work.

6 The Lord executeth righteousness and judgment for all that are oppressed.

7 He made known his ways unto Moses, his acts unto the children of Israel.

8 The Lord is merciful and gracious, slow to anger, and plenteous in mercy.

9 He will not always chide: neither will he keep his anger forever.

10 He hath not dealt with us after our sins; nor rewarded us according to our iniquities.

11 For as the heaven is high above the earth, so great is his mercy toward them that fear him.

12 As far as the east is from the west, so far hath he removed our transgressions from us.

13 Like as a father pitieth his children, so the Lord pitieth them that fear him.

14 For he knoweth our frame; he remembereth that we are dust.

15 As for man, his days are as grass: as a flower of the field, so he flourisheth.

16 For the wind passeth over it, and it is gone; and the place thereof shall know it no more.

17 But the mercy of the Lord is from everlasting to everlasting upon them that fear him, and his righteousness unto children's children.

1. History in a nutshell (vv. 6-7).—Israel had no identity as a nation before the exodus. The promise to Abraham stood, "I will make of thee a great nation" (Gen. 12:2), but four hundred years of slavery in Egypt prevented its fulfillment. Then God gave deliverance through Moses, to whom, our psalmist wrote, the Lord "made known his ways." Those revealed ways brought not only liberation but also laws, not intended as restraints and restrictions but as guideposts to the kind of life that was pleasing to God and beneficial to all who observed them. Under the leadership of Moses, an emancipated crowd of slaves was brought safely through the Red Sea, given a covenant relationship with the Lord at Sinai, and after prolonged desert wanderings, brought to the borders of the promised land.

2. Goodness and mercy (vv. 8-12).—Those desert wanderings were the result of disobedience to the guidelines provided at Sinai. In one of the books attributed to Moses, the revealing statement occurs, "There are eleven days' journey from Horeb by the way of mount Seir unto Kadesh-barnea" (Deut. 1:2). Horeb is another name for Sinai. Kadesh-barnea was the gateway town into Canaan. Israel had the possibility of entering Canaan only eleven days after the events at Sinai. But a tragic failure of faith shut the door on them and turned them back into the wilderness where they wandered until a whole generation died. Those wasted years were filled with acts of disobedience and rebellion bringing occasional punishment but also providing evidence of the truth of verses 8-12. So it was through Israel's continuing history illustrated in the Book of Judges in repeated cycles of sin, repentance, pleas for mercy, and the provision of deliverers. In fact, the Old Testament as a whole contains historic witness to the patient dealings of God with sinful people.

3. Fatherly concern (vv. 13-16).—Mark the contrast between the description of humanity in Psalm 8 (lesson for December 29) and these verses. In the earlier psalm, emphasis is on human dignity and potential, in which the grace of God is magnified. Here our frailty is the theme, "We are dust. . . . as grass . . . a flower of the field . . . gone." Yet once again tribute was paid to the Lord, who because of His knowledge of our weaknesses, looks with pity on us, "as a father pitieth his children." This is not a display of condescending pity but of heartfelt compassion that reaches out to help.

4. Covenant keepers (vv. 17-18).—There is a current phrase, "cheap grace," that rebukes the idea of God as an indulgent Father ready to overlook human guilt and issue pardons on a wholesale basis. The psalmist knew nothing of this. He saw the mercy that endures "from everlasting to everlasting" to be for those who take God seriously and order their lives according to His will. The New Testament has truth to add to this, for its forgiveness is offered on the ground of Christ's atoning work that is available to all who believe in Him.

III. Call for Universal Praise (Ps. 103:19-22)

The psalmist began with personal praise: "Bless the Lord, O my soul" (v. 1). But he was not satisfied with a solo. God is too great for that. He realized that God was the universal Sovereign, Lord over all. This being so, nothing less than universal praise would suffice. So the psalmist enlisted a mighty choir. He began with "his angels" and called on them to praise God's glory with heavenly obedience. But angels know nothing of God's forgiveness, so we should be able to outsing them. Then the psalmist called on "his hosts. Omitting no created thing, the final call was to "all his works in all places of his dominion." That must include you and me.

APPLYING THE LESSON

What forgiveness means.—The root word for forgiveness in both the Old and the New Testament means "to send away." What is sent away is not just the feeling of guilt about what was done but the wrong act or fault itself. This act of God was illustrated in the action of the high priest on the day of atonement (Lev. 16). The high priest would take two goats. One of these goats would be sacrificed as a sin offering to God. After sacrificing the one goat, the high priest would lay his hands on the head of the live goat and confess over it all the sins of the people of Israel. Then, he would send it away into the wilderness. The Bible concludes, "The goat shall bear on itself all their iniquities to a solitary land" (Lev. 16:22, NASB). That's what God does for our sin, He sends it away from us.

The death of a health nut.—Euell Gibbons became famous in the United States in the seventies as a health fanatic. He wrote on health food and ate health food and promoted health food all his life. During one period of his life, he fed his family for a month with puffball mushrooms, pinon nuts, and other wild foods he found in the mountains. However, his commercials for Grape Nuts spread his fame on a much broader basis. He also became a best-selling author writing about his health foods. Paradoxically, Gibbons developed an ulcer and eventually died of an undisclosed stomach ailment. His lifelong commitment to health food did not bring health. This is simply another reminder that health and wholeness come from God.[2]

God will provide.—Years ago, a poor widow had no money to buy food. With complete trust in God, she knelt and prayed, "Dear Lord, please send me a side of bacon and a sack of corn meal." Over and over again she prayed the same prayer in a loud voice. One of the town's scoundrels happened to be walking by her house one day. Because her window was open, he heard her prayer. He decided to have some fun at her expense. He went to the local store and bought a side of bacon and a sack of corn meal. He climbed up on her house and dropped the sack down through the chimney. It landed right in front of the hungry woman. When she saw what it was, she jumped to her feet and cried out, "Oh, Lord, thank you for answering my prayer!" At that point the scoundrel knocked on the door and informed her that he was the one who had dropped the food down the chimney, not God. She responded, "Well, it came from the Lord even if he used the devil to deliver it!" God does provide for our needs, and He uses a multitude of ways in which to do it.

Wasted lives.—History is full of men and women of great potential who wasted their lives. Samuel Taylor Coleridge is a good example. Someone said of him, "Never did so great a mind produce so little." He left Cambridge for the army, then left the army to go to Oxford, and then left Oxford without a degree. He had the poetic gift, but he did not have the sustained and concentrated effort necessary to turn potential into production. He had in his mind all kinds of books, and on occasion Coleridge would boast that soon he would send to the press his manuscripts. Few manuscripts were ever completed. His was the tragedy of a wasted life.

Like Coleridge, the Hebrews wasted their lives in the wilderness wandering. Their problem was not the lack of sustained and concentrated effort. Their problem was the lack of trust in a God who promised to provide all they needed to take possession of the promised land. Their lack of trust kept them from entering Canaan.

The steadfast love of God.—Have you ever wondered what song Jesus and His disciples sang at the close of that first Lord's Supper? We sing songs like "We are one in the bond of love" or "Blest be the tie that binds." Scholars suggest that they probably sang Psalm 136, which is known as the great Hallel. This was more of a chant than a song. The leader or rabbi would chant the first part of the verse, and the group would respond with the second part of the verse. If you will study Psalm 136, you will discover that the last half of each verse is the same in every verse: "For His lovingkindness is everlasting" (NASB).

The disciples needed to be reminded of the everlasting quality of God's love, for they were about to endure the trauma of the cross. Likewise, the people of Israel constantly needed to be reminded of God's steadfast love for them.

TEACHING THE CLASS

Main Idea: God's love and mercies bring forth praise and gratitude from those who acknowledge Him.

Suggested Teaching Aim: Learners will express their own praise and gratitude to God for His love and mercies.

Introduce the Bible Study

Ask: What are some ways we express gratitude and appreciation to someone whom we admire in our society? Elicit response. Possible responses are dinners honoring them, plaques, statues, gifts, and words, etc.

Continue by asking: How do you personally show your gratitude and appreciation to persons such as parents, mentors, and others who are important in your life? Elicit response.

State that the Scripture study for today is Psalm 103, an expression of praise and gratitude to the Heavenly Father. Invite learners to turn to the psalm in their Bible.

Search for Biblical Truth

Display the following outline.

Psalm 103

1. Praise for Personal Blessings (vv. 1-5)
    a. Forgiveness (v. 3)
    b. Healing (v. 3)
    c. Preservation (v. 4)
    d. Sustenance (v. 5)
2. Thanksgiving as a Nation (vv. 6-18)
    a. For revelation (vv. 6-7)
    b. For goodness and mercy (vv. 8-12)
    c. For fatherly concern (vv. 13-16)
    d. For continuing love (vv. 17-18)
3. Universal Praise Due (vv. 19-22)
    a. From angels and heavenly hosts (vv. 19-21)
    b. From all creation (v. 22)

Call on a learner who has previously agreed to read the entire psalm aloud. Share information from *Studying the Bible* about the author of this psalm.

Direct learners to review verses 3-5 as you share comments about these personal blessings that are found in *Studying the Bible.* When discussing offering praise for forgiveness, share comments titled "What forgiveness means" (*Applying the Lesson*). When discussing praise for preservation, share comments titled "The death of a health nut" (*Applying the Lesson*). When discussing praise for sustenance, share the comments titled "God will provide" (*Applying the Lesson*).

A Teaching Outline

1. Discuss responses that express gratitude.
2. Identify reasons gratitude was expressed to God in Psalm 103.
3. List reasons for expressing gratitude and praise to God today.
4. Plan to express gratitude and praise to God this week.

Direct learners to review verses 6-18 as you share information from *Studying the Bible* concerning the things for which the nation of Israel expressed thanks to God. When discussing God's leading and revelation to the nation, share the comments titled "Wasted lives" (*Applying the Lesson*). Share the comments titled "The steadfast love of God" (*Applying the Lesson*) when discussing thanksgiving for continuing love.

Note that the psalm closes with a call for universal praise. Review verses 19-22.

Give the Truth a Personal Focus

Write the words *gratitude* and *praise* vertically on the chalkboard. Provide paper and pencil for learners.

Direct learners to spend several minutes listing reasons they have for expressing praise and gratitude to God that begin with each letter of the two words. After a short work period, invite learners to share their conclusions. Write examples on the chalkboard. Encourage learners to complete their lists if they had omissions for a letter.

Recall the discussion that began the study about ways gratitude and praise are expressed. Ask: What are ways we might express our gratitude and praise to God for our blessings? Note that our ways need not be as eloquent as the words of the psalmist, but they are equally valid. Elicit response.

Invite each learner to choose ways that they will plan to express gratitude and praise to God this week.

---

1. Rowland E. Prothero, *The Psalms in Human Life* (London: Nelson, 1903), 7.
2. Malcolm Forbes, *They Went That-a-way* (New York: Ballantine Books, 1988), 122-23.

If you prefer a "Sanctity of Life" lesson, you will find it in the back of this book.

January 19

Lyrics of Love

Basic Passage: Song of Solomon 2:8-17

Focal Passage: Song of Solomon 2:8-17

For many people, the most unlikely book for a Sunday School lesson would be the Song of Solomon. This raises an important question: Should any portion of Holy Scripture be off limits to the Christian? Though it is true that there was much objection among some Jews to its inclusion in the Old Testament, since the early years of the Christian era it has obtained recognition as part of the inspired record. Those who were in favor of its inclusion were enthusiastic in their praise. To them it was the "Song of Songs," an alternative title that means "greatest among songs." A third title is "Canticle of Canticles," found in Roman Catholic versions. Whatever interpretation imposed on it, this book is basically a poem, or series of poems, in praise of human love. This is not out of place in an inspired volume that begins its story with a man and a woman, made by the hands of the Creator. Adam, seeing Eve for the first time, exclaimed ecstatically, "At last, here is one of my own kind" (Gen. 2:23, GNB). Read Genesis 2:21-25.

Study Aim: *To establish acquaintance with an unfamiliar book of the Bible and seek its lessons*

STUDYING THE BIBLE

More songs have been written about love than any other subject. Approaches to the subject vary from period to period and culture to culture. In this study, we need to keep in mind that we are dealing with literary material "embellished by rich Oriental imagery."[1]

I. Varied Interpretations

There is a real sense in which the Song of Solomon will be made to mean what the reader wants it to mean. The Christian will, of course, seek the Holy Spirit's help in its interpretation. This does not mean that we will all understand it the same way. Its message may vary according to a person's background, circumstances, and concept of Scripture. In this sense, this lesson offers a challenge to all of us to seek a meaning that serves our situation and meets our needs. Following are the three major views about the book.

1. Allegorical.—Most Jews regard the story that unfolds in the book as an allegory of the relationship between Yahweh and the nation Israel. Did not the Lord say, through Hosea, "I will betroth thee unto me forever"? (See Hos. 2:19.) Particularly in the early centuries of the Christian era, the relationships in this song were interpreted as those between Christ and the church. The concepts of Christ as bridegroom and the church as bride are strong in the New Testament.

2. Typical.—A modification of the previous viewpoint prevails in many quarters today. The book is accepted as a love story of Solomon and the Shulamite (6:13), but these are regarded as types of Christ and His church. This idea expresses itself in many of the hymns we sing.

3. Literal.—The third viewpoint, and probably the most popular today (though not necessarily right for that reason), is that "The song of songs, which is Solomon's" (1:1) testifies to the beauty of human love, with this conclusion, "Many waters cannot quench love, neither can the floods drown it" (8:7).

II. Characters Introduced

If we are dealing with a biblical type of drama, how many characters appear on its stage? Here again there is disagreement, but a case can be made for the following:

1. Solomon.—This book is probably to be regarded as "about" Solomon rather than "by" him. The preposition used may mean "to," "for," "about," or "concerning."

2. The maiden.—Described, as we have previously noted, as the Shulamite (6:13), probably indicated that she was from the village of Shulem, or Shunem, near Jezreel, in the north of Palestine.

3. A shepherd.—Some of the songs appear to be addressed to a third person. The maiden asks, "Tell me, O thou whom my soul loveth, where thou feedest, where thou makest thy flock to rest at noon?" (1:7), presumably, a shepherd.

III. The Song of Songs (2:8-17)

Coming now to our assigned passage, difficulty must be acknowledged in determining who the speakers are and who they are addressing. The story line is at points obscure. But an acceptable outline is that the maiden fell in love with a shepherd. Her beauty, however, captured the attention of Solomon who wanted her for his household. An arrangement was made, presumably with the consent of her family, for this to happen. But the girl's longings for her shepherd lover continued. Whether these longings were finally satisfied is open to question. Chapter 2 begins, "I am the rose of Sharon, and the lily of the valleys," descriptions that are referred to Christ in devotional materials, an example of how the Song of Songs has been adapted to Christian use. We pick up a few verses later:

> **8 The voice of my beloved! behold, he cometh leaping upon the mountains, skipping upon the hills.**
>
> **9 My beloved is like a roe or a young hart: behold, he standeth behind our wall, he looketh forth at the windows, showing himself through the lattice.**

Another rendering supports the suggestion that the maiden is speaking of her beloved shepherd: "Look, there he stands behind our wall, / gazing in at the windows, looking through the lattice" (NRSV). Are we to think of the beautiful Shulamite as virtually a prisoner in Solomon's palace? If so, she sees, either in reality or wishful imagination, her true love coming to find her. She hears his voice and sees him coming toward her, moving swiftly through the countryside like an agile deer or gazelle. He reaches the place of her confinement and looks through windows and lattices, searching for her. Then he calls to her in words that follow:

> **10 My beloved spake, and said unto me, Rise up, my love, my fair one, and come away.**
>
> **11 For, lo, the winter is past, the rain is over and gone;**
>
> **12 The flowers appear on the earth; the time of the singing of birds is come, and the voice of the turtle is heard in our land;**
>
> **13 The fig tree putteth forth her green figs, and the vines with the tender grape give a good smell. Arise, my love, my fair one, and come away.**

Tennyson wrote, "In the spring a young man's fancy lightly turns to thoughts of love." It was springtime for our lovers. Through the long winter, the shepherd had been prevented from seeking reunion with his sweetheart. But improvements in the weather and the beauty of awakening nature provided opportunity to make the journey. His description of springtime conditions is hailed as some of the most beautiful poetry of its sort ever composed. In Palestine, the arrival of March brings a transformation in the countryside. Flowers burst forth. Birds return from their winter migrations. Trees and shrubs, figs and vines, begin to produce their fruit. These verses have frequently been used to describe revival seasons in the church. The renewal of nature's beauty, after the barrenness of winter, is a fitting parallel to the awakening of the soul to the warmth of God's love. For the Christian, the spring brings an annual reminder of resurrection and of Him, the greatest expression of divine love, who, as Paul wrote, "was delivered for our offenses, and was raised again for our justification" (Rom. 4:25). We are studying a great love song. But the greatest of all is the song of the redeemed, "Thou art worthy . . . for thou wast slain, and hast redeemed us to God by thy blood out of every kindred, and tongue, and people, and nation" (Rev. 5:9). Of these heavenly singers, however, it is written that they "came out of great tribulation" (7:14), for love's fulfillment usually follows love's testing. It was so for the Shulamite and her shepherd.

14 O my dove, thou art in the clefts of the rock, in the secret places of the stairs, let me see thy countenance, let me hear thy voice; for sweet is thy voice, and thy countenance is comely.
15 Take us the foxes, the little foxes, that spoil the vines: for our vines have tender grapes.

As already stated, the absence of indication as to the identity of speakers makes it difficult to assign words, with any degree of certainty, to individuals. We will assume that the shepherd is still speaking in verse 14; and, if so, his are words of frustration. He compared his ladylove to a "dove . . . in the clefts of the rock." He was referring to rock pigeons that build their nests on inaccessible cliffs, beyond human reach. The next phrase is rendered "in the covert of the cliff" (NRSV), repeating the previous idea. He had traveled far, only to be prevented from access to his beloved. If only he could catch a glimpse of her or hear her voice! Verse 15 is problematical, and some think that it has been misplaced. However, it appears to say that little things can do great mischief. This is sadly true in human relationships. It is also true of our relationship to the Lord. The chapter concludes with the voice of the Shulamite as she expresses her feelings about the lover who cannot reach her.

16 My beloved is mine, and I am his: he feedeth among the lilies.
17 Until the day break, and the shadow flee away, turn, my beloved, and be thou like a roe or a young hart upon the mountains of Bether.

These are words of confidence and enduring love. Perhaps the unhappy circumstances caused some to say that the Shulamite might as well forget her shepherd because he would soon forget her. She would have none of this. "My beloved is mine," she affirmed, "and I am his," words that lend themselves easily to the relationship between the Lord and His people. The shepherd would not change in his feelings toward his beloved, even though forced to return to his flock. The concluding words of verse 16 can read, "he pastures his flock among the lilies" (NRSV). There would be an end to separation, for it was only "Until the day break." Christians know this to be true for them and their Lord.

APPLYING THE LESSON

Too much calculation.—The professor of mathematics and his fiancee were out roaming in the fields when she plucked a daisy and began to pull off the petals one by one, saying, "He loves me, he loves me not . . . " The professor interrupted her by saying, "You are giving yourself a lot of unnecessary trouble. You should count up the petals. Then, if the total is an even number, the answer will be in the negative. If the total is an uneven number, the answer will be in the affirmative."

Some people do make of love a very cold and calculating thing. In contrast, our text highlights the warmth and spontaneity of love.

This is love.—Love is one of the more difficult items in life to define. What is love? One man said, "Love is a four letter word with two vowels, *o* and *e*, two consonants, *l* and *v*, and two fools, you and me!" Another has suggested, "If life is one crazy thing after another, then love must be two crazy things after another." Someone else said that while love is not what makes the world go round, it is what makes the ride worthwhile. Along a more serious line, someone has said that love is "an unconditional commitment to an imperfect person." True love is more than physical attraction, and it is more than just feeling. True love involves commitment, faithfulness, and self-giving.

The renewal of life.—They thought Max Hoffman was dead. This five-year old-boy had contracted cholera. The time was 1865. The place was a small town in Wisconsin. Three days after Max became sick, the doctor pronounced him dead. That night Max was buried in the village cemetery. During the night the mother had a terrible nightmare. She dreamed that Max was still alive. When she repeated the dream the following night, the father reluctantly went with a friend to exhume the coffin. When they opened the coffin, they found Max on his side. They took the boy back to the house where the doctor tried to revive him. After an hour, Max's eyelids fluttered, and he began to stir around. After a week, he was out playing again. This boy who died at five lived for almost eighty more years. He enjoyed showing his friends in Clinton, Iowa, the metal handles which were taken from his own coffin![2]

This remarkable story is a parable of what God does in the lives of those who turn to Him. He brings spiritual renewal and new life. Like the opening of blossoms in spring, God blossoms forth into new life within us.

Where did love go?—Seated in front of the family counselor were a husband and wife whose marriage was obviously in trouble. The distance between them on the couch testified to the estrangement that marked their relationship. Once they stood before a pastor with stars in their eyes and a hope of a bright future. Now, the stars were gone, and they had lost their hope. After some introductory remarks, the counselor asked them to describe the problem. The husband said, "Oh, what's-her-name says I don't love her anymore!"

How different from the love of the Shulamite woman. Hers was a love that would not die.

The loss of hope.—An ancient story tells of a woman named Pandora to whom was given every charm. These charms were in a box which she was forbidden to open. However, her curiosity overcame her, and she opened the box to see what was in it. When she did, everything in the box escaped. By the time Pandora replaced the lid, only one thing remained: hope.

Sometimes hope is all that we have left, but as long as we have hope we can keep going. The well-known saying "As long as there is life, there is hope" might be rephrased to say, "As long as there is hope, there is life."

In our text, hope that she would eventually be restored to the one she loved kept the Shulamite woman going in an unpleasant situation.

Likewise, hope keeps us going today. Hope for the second coming of Christ keeps a Christian going during difficult times. Hope for our resurrection body enables an older person to keep going in the midst of physical deterioration. Hope for a return to his family keeps a salesman going during the days away from home. Hope for a precious child keeps an expectant mother going during the days of her pregnancy.

TEACHING THE CLASS

Main Idea: Human love is celebrated in the Song of Solomon.

Suggested Teaching Aim: Learners will be able to state information they did not previously know about the Song of Solomon.

Introduce the Bible Study

Write *Song of Solomon* on the chalkboard. Invite learners to share with the group any information they already know about this book of the Old Testament. When learners have exhausted their supply of information, ask rhetorically: Do you think there is more to the Song of Solomon than most of us know?

State that the purpose of the study today is that, when it is finished, learners will be able to state information that they did not previously know about the Song of Solomon. Invite learners to open their Bibles to Song of Solomon 2.

Search for Biblical Truth

Share information about the book and varied interpretations found in *Studying the Bible.*

Write *Solomon, the maiden,* and *a shepherd* on the chalkboard. Provide information about these three characters from *Studying the Bible.*

Call on a learner who has previously agreed to read Song of Solomon 2:8-17 aloud. Invite learners to listen to get a feeling for the style and story of the passage.

When the reading is finished, direct learners to review verses 8 and 9. Share information from *Studying the Bible* related to these verses.

A Teaching Outline

1. Identify known information about Song of Solomon.
2. Discover new information about Song of Solomon.
3. Identify attitudes toward human love reflected in Song of Solomon.
4. State new facts learned in this study.

Share the quote from Tennyson found in *Studying the Bible.* Describe springtime in Palestine from information in *Studying the Bible.* Share the comments titled "The renewal of life" (*Applying the Lesson*).

Direct learners to read verses 10-13 again to themselves. Ask: What part of these verses is familiar? Had you heard any of them before? In what circumstances?

Point out the difficulty of determining the speaker in verses 14-15. Share information from *Studying the Bible* about the possibilities. Direct the learners to read these verses to themselves. Share the comments titled "This is love" (*Applying the Lesson*).

Note that verses 16-17 are the words of the Shulamite woman as she expresses her feelings about the lover who cannot reach her. Direct learners to read the verses silently. Share additional comments from *Studying the Bible.* Share the comments titled "Where did love go?" (*Applying the Lesson*).

Give the Truth a Personal Focus

Write the main idea on the chalkboard. Ask: Would you agree that this is the main idea of the study? Do you have a more appropriate suggestion?

Share the comments titled "Too much calculation" (*Applying the Lesson*). Ask: What attitudes about human love have you seen reflected in this passage from Song of Solomon. Wait for their response.

Share the comments titled "The loss of hope" (*Applying the Lesson*). Ask: Would you agree that there is always an element of hope in love? Is so, what part does it play? Elicit response.

Recall that the purpose of the study was to be able to state some information about the Song of Solomon that learners did not previously know. Ask: What new information have you learned this morning? Write their responses on the chalkboard, as appropriate.

---

1. *New Bible Commentary* (Grand Rapids: Eerdmans, 1953), 547.
2. Richard B. Manchester, *Incredible Facts* (New York: Galahad Books, 1985), 51.

January 26

Song of the Vineyard

Basic Passage: Isaiah 5:1-7

Focal Passage: Isaiah 5:1-7

Israel's prophets used a variety of means to get attention. Sometimes their dress made them objects of remark and inquiry. Reference to recent translations of the Bible will reveal that their utterances were mainly in poetic form. Isaiah's "Song of the Vineyard" illustrates how this literary form could be employed to capture interest and convey a message. It was a teaching tool. The same could be said of Moses' song (lesson for December 1), which, by its review of history, helped to stamp the memory of events on the minds of the people Israel. Our church hymnals contain many modern examples, such as the children's simple song, "Jesus loves me! this I know, / For the Bible tells me so." Here, in few words, is teaching about Jesus and the Bible, readily implanted in young minds. The concern of many people about the character of some contemporary lyrics arises from the knowledge that rhyming words and catchy tunes may make indelible impressions on hearers.

Study Aim: *To understand that privilege brings responsibility, and that Christians, as privileged persons, are accountable for their actions*

STUDYING THE BIBLE

To end our study at verse 7 would be to miss the reasons for Isaiah's song. The song was a tool to get the attention of the prophet's audience. It could be compared to a parable in that, through a familiar situation, it conveyed solemn truth about God, the nation Israel, their serious transgressions, and the consequences that must follow.

I. The Prophet as Minstrel (Isa. 5:1-6)

Isaiah appears to have been a man of Jerusalem. Perhaps he was born there. Certainly his ministry was exercised in and around the holy city. We can suppose that this song was sung to crowds that gathered there for one of the religious feasts. It did not disclose its purpose immediately but briefly told the experience of a friend of the prophet, who owned a vineyard. We learn later that he was speaking of God, but this is not revealed in the song itself.

1 Now will I sing to my well-beloved a song of my beloved touching his vineyard. My well-beloved hath a vineyard in a very fruitful hill:

2 And he fenced it, and gathered out the stones thereof, and planted it with the choicest vine, and built a tower in the midst of it, and also made a winepress therein: and he looked that it should bring forth grapes, and it brought forth wild grapes.

3 And now, O inhabitants of Jerusalem, and men of Judah, judge, I pray you, betwixt me and my vineyard.

4 What could have been done more to my vineyard, that I have not done in it? wherefore, when I looked that it should bring forth grapes, brought it forth wild grapes?

5 And now go to; I will tell you what I will do to my vineyard: I will take away the hedge thereof, and it shall be eaten up; and break down the wall thereof, and it shall be trodden down:

6 And I will lay it waste: it shall not be pruned, nor digged; but there shall come up briers and thorns: I will also command the clouds that they rain no rain upon it.

1. Care and expectation (vv. 1-2).—The prophet's "well-beloved," or friend, had a hillside vineyard with very fertile soil. He cultivated it, removed the rocks that abound in Palestine, and surrounded it with a protective fence, or ditch. Then he planted it with "the choicest vine," a term for a vine that bore high quality fruit. As a final measure, he built a watchtower in the vineyard from which constant guard could be maintained against any who might try to harm or steal his grapes. Now, in anticipation of a rich harvest, he constructed a winepress, probably the most expensive part of his undertaking. Winepresses consisted of a pair of pits hewn out of rocky ground, one higher than the other, so that the juice from the trodden grapes would flow through a channel into the lower reservoir.

2. Audience addressed (vv. 3-4).—His brief song ended, Isaiah involved his audience by asking questions. What more could the owner of the vineyard have done to ensure a good harvest? Why had it produced "wild grapes," literally, "stinking fruit"? The prophet gave no answer, neither did his listeners, for there was no answer. The questions, however, like the song, were teaching tools. They were intended to provoke thought, and they should be part of the method of every teacher.

3. Vineyard abandoned (vv. 5-6).—Up till now, no mention had been made of God, although Isaiah's use of the first person pronoun, "I," should have aroused his listeners to realize that it was of God he was speaking. The owner's total disappointment with his vineyard would cause him to abandon it so that it would become desolate.

II. The Meaning of the Song (Isa. 5:7)

It was time to speak plainly by identifying the owner and the true nature of the vine, that "choicest vine" that was given every opportunity to produce a bountiful harvest but miserably failed.

> **7 For the vineyard of the Lord of hosts is the house of Israel, and the men of Judah his pleasant plant: and he looked for judgment, but behold oppression; for righteousness, but behold a cry.**

1. The vine was a symbol.—Perceptive listeners to Isaiah's song could have understood its meaning from the beginning. The vine was a national emblem of Israel. One psalmist had written, "Thou hast brought a vine out of Egypt: thou hast cast out the heathen, and planted it. Thou preparedst room before it, and didst cause it to take deep root, and it filled the land" (80:8-9). During the Maccabean period of Jewish history, coins were minted with a grape vine depicted on them. George Adam Smith tells us in Herod's temple on beams before the entrance to the holy place "trailed the Golden Vine, of the size of a man, to which liberal worshipers contributed leaves and clusters."[1] Some expositors suggest that our Lord was in sight of that golden vine when He said, "I am the true vine, . . . ye are the branches" (John 15:1,5).

2. Bitter fruit.—That there might be no failure to understand, Isaiah came right out and named Israel as God's vineyard and Judah as "his pleasant plant," or, "what he planted with such delight." In a few words the prophet condensed the Lord's more detailed indictment (vv. 9-25). Where He had expected to find justice, He had seen oppression of people unable to protect themselves. Where right actions (righteousness) were looked for, there was "a cry," that is, an appeal for help from persons being abused. Our English translations obscure the play on words used here, the Hebrew words for "justice" and "oppression" having a similar sound, as also do the words "righteousness" and "a cry." Here was another device for capturing and holding attention, and for thrusting home the intended message. Isaiah used it frequently and probably proved its effectiveness. An important message deserves to be presented with all the skill available.

III. The Lord's Indictment (Isa. 5:8-25)

In all, God delivered six charges against His people: covetousness (vv. 8-10), debauchery (vv. 11-17), unbelief (vv. 18-19), self-opinion (v. 21), and injustice (vv. 22-23). Each is introduced by the word

"Woe," which can be understood as a pronouncement of judgment, an expression of shame or of sorrow over the fate Israel had brought on itself. It is not necessary to make a choice between these for they are all included in Isaiah's purpose. He delivered God's message of judgment with tears in his eyes and a sob in his voice, as should be the case with all who speak of sin and its consequences.

1. Social abuses (vv. 8-10).—The decade of the eighties has been described as the decade of greed. Will the nineties prove any different? It seems that the human spirit is seldom satisfied with what it has but must always be reaching out to grasp more. This was the case in Isaiah's time. Then, as now, the appetite for more power, more money, and more recognition found its satisfaction at the expense of others. The particular offense named here was the acquisition of real estate without regard for the rights of others. The prophet Micah, who was Isaiah's contemporary, was specific about this: "They covet fields, and take them by violence; and houses, and take them away: so they oppress a man and his house, even a man and his heritage" (Mic. 2:2). Justice required that property thus obtained would be taken away from the greedy owners. The story of King Ahab and Naboth's vineyard may be cited (1 Kings 21).

2. Indulgent life-styles (vv. 11-17).—The abuse of strong drink has been with us since the days of Noah (Gen. 9:18-21). In Isaiah's time, those who could afford it engaged in all-day carousing, from "early in the morning . . . until night." This reckless partying was carried on to the accompaniment of "lyre and harp, tambourine and flute" (NRSV). Alcohol and music dulled their senses so that they "do not regard the deeds of the Lord, / or see the work of his hands" (v. 12, NRSV). They made themselves unaware of, and indifferent to, God's activity in judgment. To bring the picture up-to-date, we could add drug addiction to this wanton behavior. The situation was so grave that the prophet spoke of the coming consequences in terms of captivity (v. 13) and death (v. 14), one for the nation, the other for the individual.

3. Moral blindness (vv. 20-21).—To "call evil good, and good evil" is a devilish activity. It perpetuates Satan's question in Eden: "Yea, hath God said" (Gen. 3:1). It repudiates every divine commandment by saying, "Does God tell me this is wrong? I say it is good, and I intend to go on doing it." This is the root of all sinfulness, crime, and perversion. For Israel, its darkest expression was the replacement of the worship of the true God with the abominations of idolatry.

4. Disastrous consequences (vv. 24-25).—In a few vivid phrases, Isaiah described the disasters that would overtake Israel as a result of their failure to be God's fruitful vine. We know how history brought these things to pass. For further description, read on to the end of the chapter. God would use a foreign invader, first Assyria and then Babylon, to inflict judgment on His rebellious people.

APPLYING THE LESSON

Elements of communication.—Someone once said that communication involves three things: ethos, pathos, and logos. Ethos refers to the character of the speaker. The integrity or lack of integrity of the one speaking can determine whether or not he or she communicates to a listening audience. Pathos has to do with the emotion of the audience. Persons with integrity can express themselves clearly but still not communicate if the emotion of the audience puts barriers in the way. Logos has to do with the reason of the speech. Even people without integrity can sometimes communicate with an audience which is emotionally opposed to the speaker if the right words are used. Communication can occur with only one of these three elements. When all three are involved, however, is when communication is done effectively. Music aids in communication because it affects the emotion of the audience.

Are you a Southerner?—A male quartet was singing plantation melodies at a concert. As the melodies went on, a man in the front seat wiped his eyes furtively and after a few more minutes burst into tears. The manager of the quartet slipped around and touched him on the shoulder. "My dear sir," he said, "our quartet deeply appreciates the compliment you have paid it by this display of emotion. You are a Southerner, no doubt?" "No," the man sobbed, "I'm a musician."

What constitutes good music is not always the content but also the music itself. We do not know exactly the style of the music of the Bible. All we can do is to evaluate the content of the songs. Every song in the Bible communicates a truth about God and His redemptive activity.

The purpose of a teacher.—The word *educator* comes from the Latin *educare,* which means "to lead" or "to guide." That's what a teacher is, one who leads or guides someone to the discovery of truth. The prophet Isaiah was motivated by this purpose as he shared the song of the vineyard. He was not just entertaining. He was educating, leading his listeners to an important truth about God.

Responsible.—Two little boys were talking one day about the things little boys talk about. One said to the other, "Why do doctors wear masks over their faces when they operate on somebody?" The other boy thought about it for a minute. Then he made this suggestion: "They wear masks so in case they mess up no one will know who did it!"

Isaiah stripped off the masks the Israelites were wearing and revealed to them that they were the ones who had done it! They were the keepers of the vineyard who had failed their owner. Instead of displaying the kind of justice God demanded of them, they related to their fellow human beings with oppression.

I'd give it back.—A school teacher was trying to impress her students with the importance of being honest in all things. She said, "Suppose you were walking down Main Street and you found a briefcase containing two million dollars in cash. What would you do?" Little Johnny on the back row raised his hand, and she called on him. Johnny said, "Well, teacher, if it belonged to a poor family I would return it. Otherwise, I would keep it all for myself."

Shining through the boy's answer is the greed that has captured our age. The theme song of many today is: "I want more." Of course, this is no new thing. Such greed was the target of Isaiah's stinging attack.

The number one drug problem.—What is the number one drug problem in America today? It is not crack or cocaine or heroin. The number one drug problem today is alcohol. Alcohol is related to most of the social disasters of our day: suicide, murder, family violence, automobile accidents, and absenteeism at work.

TEACHING THE CLASS

Main Idea: God holds persons to whom He gives privilege responsible for their actions.

Suggested Teaching Aim: Learners will review their actions to determine whether they are consistent with their privilege and responsibility.

Introduce the Bible Study

Divide the chalkboard into two columns. Label one column *privilege.* Label the other *responsibility.* Invite learners to name a privilege they enjoy. List it on the chalkboard. Ask: What responsibility goes along with the privilege? List it on the chalkboard. Continue the activity for several minutes. Examples are:

PRIVILEGE	RESPONSIBILITY
freedom of speech	abstinence from liable
family love	demonstration of loving behavior to family
work at joy	fair effort for pay

Conclude with the summary statement that privilege brings responsibility is equally true in the Christian life.

Note that the study for today is from Isaiah and is titled "Song of the Vineyard." State that this song points out that God holds His followers to whom He has given great privilege highly responsible for their actions. Invite learners to open their Bibles to Isaiah 5.

Search for Biblical Truth

Share the comments titled "Are you a Southerner?" (*Applying the Lesson*). Note that our purpose in trying to evaluate this song is to discover a truth about God and His redemptive activity. Share the comments titled "The purpose of a teacher" (*Applying the Lesson*). Provide information about Isaiah and his ministry from *Studying the Bible.*

Display this outline to guide the study of the Bible passage:

The Vineyard: Care and Expectation	(vv. 1-2)
Hearers Asked Questions	(vv. 3-4)
The Vineyard: Abandoned	(vv. 5-6)
The Song's Meaning Explained	(v. 7)

Call on a learner to read Isaiah 5:1-2 aloud while others listen to learn of the care provided the vineyard and the expectations of the owner. When the reading is finished, call for response. Share informa tion about these verses from *Studying the Bible.*

A Teaching Outline

1. Focus on things that accompany privilege.
2. Learn how Isaiah's song demonstrates that Israel accepted privilege but abandoned responsibility.
3. Review personal actions to determine whether they reflect acceptance of privilege and abandonment of responsibility.

Call on a learner to read verses 5-6 aloud while other learners listen for the results of lack of care of the vineyard. Call for response. Share information about these verses from *Studying the Bible.*

Call on a learner to read verse 7 aloud. Share information from *Studying the Bible* about this verse. Share the comment titled "Re sponsible" (*Applying the Lesson*).

Note that the song of the vineyard continues. Share information from *Studying the Bible* about verses 8-25.

Give the Truth a Personal Focus

Share the comments titled "I'd give it back" (*Applying the Lesson*). Recall that Christian privilege also carries with it responsibility. Make two additional columns on the chalkboard. Label one *Christian Privi lege.* Label the other *Responsibility.* Follow the procedure used earlier to list privileges and corresponding responsibilities of the Christian. The following is an example.

CHRISTIAN PRIVILEGE	RESPONSIBILITY
Salvation	Life lived for the Lord
Worship	Regular practice of worship
Access to God	Prayer

Conclude by asking: Does your behavior reflect responsibility con sistent with your Christian privilege?

1. George Adam Smith, *Jerusalem* (London: Hodder and Stoughton, 1908), 503.

February 2

The Model Prayer

Basic Passages: 1 Chronicles 29:10-13; Matthew 6:7-15

Focal Passage: Matthew 6:7-15

Perhaps no spiritual activity is more written about, and less well practiced, than prayer. Christian book stores abound in books on the subject of prayer, and more are added to them every year. Is this evidence of a widespread desire on the part of believers expressed in the disciple's words, "Lord, teach us to pray" (Luke 11:1)? There are few, even among mature Christians, who would declare themselves satisfied with their prayer lives. We all need help, as the first disciples realized when they listened to Jesus at prayer. This was the more remarkable since, as Jews, they had been raised in a religious culture that gave high prominence to prayer. But the methods and contents of prayer the rabbis taught them fell short of the practice of their Lord. They turned to Him for help, as we do at this time, seeking both inspiration and instruction in the Model Prayer that He provided.

Study Aim: *To find answers for ourselves to the disciple's petition, "Lord, teach us to pray"* (Luke 11:1)

STUDYING THE BIBLE

We have the New Testament as our best textbook on prayer. The disciples had the Old, from which has been taken for our study material one of the greatest of its prayers, offered by King David shortly before his death. To read 1 Chronicles 29:10-13, and following verses, is to realize that David understood the basic principles of prayer. Parallels with the Lord's Prayer are interesting. David spoke first in terms of worship. He made mention of God's kingdom. He acknowledged God as the Source of all good things. He showed a spirit of humility.

I. How Not to Pray (Matt. 6:5-8)

Matthew's version of the pattern prayer has its place in the Sermon on the Mount. Counsel from our Lord on how not to pray precedes it. He warned against hypocrisy in prayer, describing those who turned prayer into a performance by going through their devotions at street corners and in public places such as synagogues. Of these He said that they are "paid in full," that is they get human praise and nothing more. The more appropriate place for prayer is in the privacy of the home where the words uttered are for the ears of God alone. This does not discount the value of congregational prayers offered by the church at worship.

7 But when ye pray, use not vain repetitions, as the heathen do: for they think that they shall be heard for their much speaking.
8 Be not ye therefore like unto them: for your Father knoweth what things ye have need of, before ye ask him.

This rebuke of "vain repetitions" may be appropriately referred to prevailing synagogue prayers that abounded in repeated phrases, such as "do it for the sake of." One prayer repeated these words forty times and suggested twisting the arm of God to do something He was unwilling to do. Jesus said this is not the way to pray, for to do so is to copy the heathen. He was about to give an example of conciseness and simplicity in prayer.

II. "Teach Us to Pray" (Luke 11:1)

The Gospels clearly indicate that Jesus repeated His teaching. Matthew included the pattern prayer in the Sermon on the Mount. Luke related it to a time when Jesus "was praying in a certain place" (11:1). This writer furnishes other information concerning the circumstances in which the pattern prayer was given.

1. Jesus at prayer.—Following custom, Jesus prayed aloud, and the disciples were privileged to hear His words. They heard none of the "vain repetitions" to which they were accustomed, but a directness and intimacy that arrested their attention. The disciples were ready to learn to pray as Jesus prayed.

2. Disciple's request.—Several of the disciples had been followers of John the Baptist who, following the practice of the rabbis, gave his loyal group a brief prayer formula for use on busy days. Such were known as fountain prayers, and it was reasonable that Jesus would provide one for the twelve. So the request was made, "Lord, teach us to pray, as John also taught his disciples."

III. A Pattern Provided (Matt. 6:9-15)

In David's prayer, he addressed the Almighty as, "Lord God of Israel our father" (1 Chron. 29:10), conveying the concept of God as Father of the nation. The disciples, listening to their Master at prayer, heard Him use the intimate, personal term *Abba* (see Mark 14:36), the word a child might use in speaking to an earthly father. Doubtless to their amazement, He authorized them to address God in the same way, "Our Father." The prayer that followed breaks down into six petitions, three for God's glory and three for our needs.

> **9 After this manner therefore pray ye: Our Father which art in heaven, Hallowed be thy name.**
>
> **10 Thy kingdom come. Thy will be done in earth, as it is in heaven.**

1. Reverence for God (v. 9b).—The phrase, "which art in heaven," is not meant to describe God's location but to affirm His majesty, particularly His holiness. His fatherhood is unique, because He is above all. For this reason, His name should be hallowed, or held in reverence. The abuse of His name, in everyday speech, is indicative of contempt for His person, and a shameful commentary on present-day attitudes toward that which is holy.

2. God's kingdom (v. 10a).—To return to David's prayer, it contains the words, "thine is the kingdom," an acknowledgment by an earthly king that God in heaven was supreme. When Jesus talked about the kingdom (Matt. 4:17), He was referring to the rule of God, partly realized in those who submit to His authority in loving obedience and ultimately to be manifested in His eternal reign. To pray, "Thy kingdom come," is to express desire for more and more people to place themselves under God's rule. It is, therefore, a missionary prayer. Also this prayer expresses longing for the time when the "kingdom of the world has become the kingdom of our Lord and of his Messiah" (Rev. 11:15, NRSV).

3. His will on earth (v. 10b).—Even a casual survey of conditions today reveals major areas in which God's will is not being done on earth. We could point to immorality and crime, but we must not overlook oppression, starvation, and conflict. To pray for a change in this worldly scene is surely to obligate ourselves to do something about it. Once again, the petition becomes a missionary challenge. In what ways can we line up with those of whom it was said, "These that have turned the world upside down are come hither" (Acts 17:6)? We must make a beginning in our own lives and conduct.

> **11 Give us this day our daily bread.**
>
> **12 And forgive us our debts, as we forgive our debtors.**
>
> **13 And lead us not into temptation, but deliver us from evil: For thine is the kingdom, and the power, and the glory, forever. Amen.**

1. Our physical needs (v. 11).—The head of a household is frequently referred to as the breadwinner. But behind every human agency is God, the great Provider. Although a lot of scholarly argument rages around the word translated "daily," the purpose of the prayer is clear. It is a reminder of a constant dependence on God for the necessities of life and an opportunity for acknowledging Him as the Source of supply. The prayer provides encouragement for the practice of giving thanks before eating. To a child, the source of supply may be the local supermarket. Therefore the need for a reminder that, like Israel in the wilderness, we are the beneficiaries of divine concern and provision.

2. Our need for forgiveness (v. 12).—A debt is something that is owed but remains unpaid. Luke used the word "sins" (11:4) but followed this by reference to "every one that is indebted to us." Our debts to God are our failures in showing obedience to His commandments to which we should pay heed. Such debts pile up until they become unpayable. We have no alternative but to throw ourselves on the mercy of God and plead for His forgiveness. The message of the gospel is that forgiveness is always available to those who repent.

3. Plea for protection (v. 13a).—Here, as elsewhere in the New Testament, "temptation" should be understood as "trial." This is an appeal to be saved from trying, testing experiences to which, in our human weaknesses, we might be vulnerable. The teaching of Scripture is that "God cannot be tempted with evil, neither tempteth he any man" (Jas. 1:13). So we are to pray that God will not permit us to be put under pressures "above that [we] are able; but will . . . make a way to escape" (1 Cor. 10:13).

4. Doxology (v. 13b).—The concluding doxology is not in the best manuscripts, neither does it occur in Luke. Most agree that it was added early in Christian history to furnish a conclusion similar to the beginning of the prayer. There should always be room for praise to God in our prayers, so the addition is most appropriate.

> **14 For if ye forgive men their trespasses, your heavenly Father will also forgive you:**
> **15 But if ye forgive not men their trespasses, neither will your Father forgive your trespasses.**

Do these two final verses, which emphasize the second part of verse 12, state a legalistic position on forgiveness? Are we forgiven by God because we forgive others? This is not what the two verses say. Forgiveness is not granted as a reward for forgiving others, or withheld because we fail to forgive. To quote Dr. Martyn Lloyd-Jones, "The proof that you and I are forgiven is that we forgive others. If we think that our sins are forgiven by God and we refuse to forgive somebody else, we are making a mistake; we have never been forgiven. The man who knows he has been forgiven, only in and through the shed blood of Christ, is a man who must forgive others."[1] So Jesus taught His disciples to pray and furnished a Model Prayer for us to be used as given or to provide a pattern of praise and petition for all our praying.

APPLYING THE LESSON

The importance of prayer.—Warren Wiersbe has written, "Prayer is both the thermometer and the thermostat of the local church; for the 'spiritual temperature' either goes up or down, depending on how God's people pray."[2]

That has always been true, in every generation. The New Testament church was on fire for the Lord because they gave prayer a priority. The early disciples were powerful and effective because they were committed to the practice of prayer. Even though they had prayed all their lives, they desired to experience a deeper level of prayer. So they approached Jesus asking Him to instruct them. Why? Because they were convinced of the importance of prayer.

How not to do it.—A certain Christian who wanted to do right but who was always taking the easy way out applied that same approach to his prayers. He wrote out a prayer and tacked it on the ceiling over his bed. When he fell in bed at night, he would just point to the ceiling and then fall asleep!

That could fit into the list in our text of how not to go about praying. Prayer demands our personal involvement and our passionate concern. Simply pointing to a prayer pinned on the ceiling will not do!

The power of this simple prayer.—Karl Marx's daughter was raised without religion, but she eventually became a Christian. How did it happen? She explained, "I found this old German prayer and I thought, 'If there's a God like that, I could believe in Him.' " What was this "German" prayer that led to her conversion? She answered, "The prayer started like this, 'Our Father which art in heaven . . .' "[3] The Lord's Prayer is simple in its expression but overwhelming in its spiritual power.

The one to whom we pray.—A little boy shouted at his family, "I'm getting ready to pray. Does anyone need anything?" Another little boy was asked by his mother if he had said his prayers the night before. "No," the little boy responded, "I didn't need anything." The first priority of prayer, however, is not to get something from God but to meet God. The purpose of prayer is not to obtain from God what we want but to open ourselves to God so that we will desire what He wants. The higher level of prayer is to meet the One to whom we pray—that must be first.

The focus of the Lord's Prayer.—An anonymous poem expresses well the focus of the Lord's Prayer.

You cannot pray the Lord's Prayer
In the first person, "I"—
You cannot say the Lord's Prayer
And even once say, "My."
Nor can you pray the Lord's Prayer
And not pray for another,
For as you ask for "daily bread,"
You must include your brother.
Yes, others are included
In each and every plea;
From the beginning to the end of it,
It doesn't once say, "Me."

Going to church.—A little boy asked his parents why the family went to church every Sunday. They answered, "We go to church to worship." That was a word the boy did not know, so he came as close to it as he could. He explained to his friends that they went to church every week to "wash up!" The boy was closer to the truth than he knew. Part of the purpose of worship is to confess our sins to the Father and to experience the cleansing of His forgiving love. Part of the purpose of prayer is to confess our sins to the Father and to ask His forgiveness. So the little boy was right. We go to church, and we pray, to "wash up" spiritually.

Praise and thanksgiving.—Someone has distinguished between praise and thanksgiving. Praise is thanking God for who He is, and thanksgiving is thanking God for what He does. I'm not sure such a distinction can be made. However you define them, praise and thanksgiving are a part of prayer. The doxology with which Jesus ended the Model Prayer includes praise for who God is and thanksgiving for what God has done.

TEACHING THE CLASS

Main Idea: Prayer is a behavior of believers for which Jesus gave specific instructions.

Suggested Teaching Aim: Learners will determine to engage in prayer after the model taught by Jesus.

Introduce the Bible Study

State that today's study begins the final unit of the quarter's study and is concerned with selected prayers from the Scriptures. Share the comments titled "The importance of prayer" (*Applying the Lesson*).

Ask: How has your praying changed during your lifetime? Elicit response. Note that most of us start with prayers taught to us as children. Some of us grow in our understanding and practice of prayer. However, some of us still approach prayer as we did when we were children. Ask: Why is this so? Elicit response.

State that the study for today uses a passage of Scripture that shows the disciples asking Jesus to teach them how to pray. Note that the purpose of the study is that we would also learn how to pray in a manner that is pleasing to God.

Search for Biblical Truth

Invite learners to open their Bibles to Matthew 6. Share information from *Studying the Bible* to provide background for the Scripture study. Share the comments titled "How not to do it" (*Applying the Lesson*).

A Teaching Outline

1. Focus on learner's prayer habits.
2. Discover how Jesus taught His disciples to pray.
3. Identify the components of the Model Prayer.
4. Determine to engage in regular prayer following the model that Jesus gave His disciples.

Call on a learner to read Matthew 6:7-8 aloud. Ask questions like the following: What were the vain repetitions used by the heathen? What vain repetitions are common in prayer today? Elicit response.

Note that when Jesus had told the disciples how not to pray, He then showed them a pattern for how to do it. Share information from *Studying the Bible* about the content of this pattern. Call on a learner who has previously agreed to read Matthew 6:9-15 aloud.

Write these phrases on the chalkboard to show the content of this prayer pattern.

Reverence for God
Concern about the kingdom
Concern about God's will
Concern for physical need
Concern about forgiveness
Convern for protection
Doxology of praise

Direct learners to review the Scripture passage to locate verses where the particular event is illustrated. Allow a few minutes for review. Call for response. Note responses on the chalkboard. Share information from *Studying the Bible* as each point is noted.

Share the comments titled "The power of this simple prayer" (*Applying the Lesson*) when "Reverence for God" is discussed. Share the comments titled "The one to whom we pray" (*Applying the Lesson*) when "Concern about God's will" is discussed. Share the comments titled "Going to church" (*Applying the Lesson*) when "Concern about forgiveness" is discussed. Share the comments titled "Praise and thanksgiving" (*Applying the Lesson*) when the "Doxology of praise" is discussed.

Give the Truth a Personal Focus

Ask rhetorically: If we did a detailed analysis of your prayers, do you think the content of this prayer pattern would be reflected? Continue by asking: Which parts would most frequently be present? Which parts would most frequently be missing? Elicit response.

Direct learners to write down the content guide of this Model Prayer. Encourage them to use it as a guide for their personal prayer during this week.

---

1. D. Martyn Lloyd-Jones, *Studies in the Sermon on the Mount,* vol. 2 (Grand Rapids: Wm. B. Eerdmans, 1960), 75.
2. Warren Wiersbe, *Be Dynamic* (Wheaton: Victor Books, 1987), 18.
3. Bruce Larson, *Wind and Fire* (Waco: Word Books, 1984), 84.

February 9

Jesus' High Priestly Prayer

Basic Passage: John 17

Focal Passages: John 17:1-11,20-21

We have just studied the prayer Jesus gave to His disciples. Now we consider the prayer He prayed for His disciples after He had first prayed for Himself. We at once notice a difference between the two prayers, for in the former He taught that prayer should begin with praise. The difference, however, is not so acute as might first appear. In John 17 our Lord's ultimate purpose was to glorify God; "glorify thy Son," He prayed, "that thy Son also may glorify thee" (v. 1). Nevertheless, we should not minimize the differences between the two prayers, for the one is a prayer we should pray, and the other a prayer we cannot. It was uniquely Christ's prayer, only possible to God's Son, our Savior, who glorified Himself and His Father by His redemptive offering at Calvary. We are privileged to eavesdrop on Him as, shortly before He was crucified, He opened His heart to His Father in deep desire for Himself and His people. We may be sure that He still prays in these terms, for "he ever liveth to make intercession" (Heb. 7:25).

Study Aim: *To realize from our Lord's high priestly prayer what are His chief concerns and share them with Him*

STUDYING THE BIBLE

We are about to enter the holy of holies of the New Testament Gospels. The fact that an entire chapter is devoted by John to this prayer is indication of its importance. It is idle to ask how it was remembered and recorded in such detail, for the very question ignores the activity of the Holy Spirit whose function, as Jesus Himself said, was to "bring all things to your remembrance" (John 14:26). Such a prayer as this would surely be stamped indelibly on the memories of those who heard it, and repeated again and again among themselves.

I. Jesus and His Father (John 17:1-5)

The threefold division of the prayer needs no argument. Jesus had just finished talking to His disciples about His departure, an event that would cause them to "weep and lament" (16:20) because of their inability at that time to understand it. He turned from them and "lifted up his eyes to heaven" (17:1) as He talked to His Father who had perfect understanding of all that had happened and was yet to happen.

1 These words spake Jesus, and lifted up his eyes to heaven, and said, Father, the hour is come; glorify thy Son, that thy Son also may glorify thee:

2 As thou hast given him power over all flesh, that he should give eternal life to as many as thou hast given him.

3 And this is life eternal, that they might know thee the only true God, and Jesus Christ, whom thou hast sent.

4 I have glorified thee on the earth: I have finished the work which thou gavest me to do.

5 And now, O Father, glorify thou me with thine own self with the glory which I had with thee before the world was.

1. The glory of redemption (vv. 1-3).—Our Lord had no need to explain to the Father what He meant by "the hour is come" (v. 1) and "I have finished the work" (v. 4). There had been an eternal contract between them concerning what was about to happen, for "God was in Christ, reconciling the world unto himself" (2 Cor. 5:19). The price of human redemption had been agreed upon and was now about to be paid. The cross would glorify both the Father and the Son as it manifested the full measure of divine love, mercy, and grace. So committed was our Lord to redemption's task that He could speak as though it was already accomplished.

2. The glory to come (vv. 4-5).—Nothing was said about suffering and death, but only about glory. Speaking as though the cross was already behind Him, our Lord prayed to be reinstated in the heavenly glory He had forfeited by His incarnation. The great theological emphasis here is on His eternal Sonship, for the glory that would be restored was His "before the world was."

II. Jesus and His Disciples (John 17:6-19)

Judas Iscariot was going about his traitorous business when Jesus uttered this prayer. Eleven men were left, called for two purposes: "that they should be with him"—that is, to learn from Him—and "that he might send them forth"—that is, to be His messengers to others (Mark 3:14). Before He left them through death, resurrection, and ascension, He prayed for them.

> **6 I have manifested thy name unto the men which thou gavest me out of the world: thine they were, and thou gavest them me; and they have kept thy word.**
>
> **7 Now they have known that all things whatsoever thou hast given me are of thee.**
>
> **8 For I have given unto them the words which thou gavest me; and they have received them, and have known surely that I came out from thee, and they have believed that thou didst send me.**
>
> **9 I pray for them: I pray not for the world, but for them which thou hast given me; for they are thine.**
>
> **10 And all mine are thine, and thine are mine; and I am glorified in them.**
>
> **11 And now I am no more in the world, but these are in the world, and I come to thee. Holy Father, keep through thine own name those whom thou hast given me, that they may be one, as we are.**

1. A mission completed (vv. 6-8).—Jesus had come into the world as revealer of the Father. No Gospel more strongly affirms this than the Fourth. This had been His special mission to the twelve. "I have manifested thy name" means that He had made known the nature of God to His disciples. He did not come to start a new religion; He came to amplify the understanding and knowledge of God imparted by the Old Testament. Not a new revelation, but a fuller, is ours in the gospel. "God . . . hath shined in our hearts, to give the light of the knowledge of the glory of God in the face of Jesus Christ" (2 Cor. 4:6).

2. Unity maintained (vv. 9-12).—"I pray not for the world" means that at that moment Jesus was focusing His prayer on the disciples. By

His presence with them, they had been held together as a group, growing in love and loyalty. This had not always been easily maintained, for they were but human. With the exception of Judas (v. 12), they had been brought to this moment when they would soon be parted from the Master. So Jesus committed them to the care of His Father that, no matter what happened, their unity might be preserved.

3. Joy experienced (v. 13).—Jesus prayed in full knowledge that others were listening. That we have this chapter is proof of His knowledge. Because it was heard and recorded, we can share the joy of the disciples. In the near future, they would have much to make them sad. But the prayer of their Lord would impart comfort and confidence, ingredients of what He called "my joy," a sense of total well-being in the knowledge that they were in the Father's care.

4. Security and sanctification (vv. 14-19).—Jesus founded no monastic order. His will for His followers was that they remain part of society, in the world but not of it. He recognized the dangers involved, so He prayed for the sanctification, or separation, of His followers, to be brought about by the word of truth. "Let the word of Christ dwell in you richly" (Col. 3:16) Paul admonished, indicating that this was necessary to live a consecrated life. Continuing His prayer, our Lord spoke of His own sanctification, or consecration, referring to His redemptive work which was "for their sakes," and ours. In life and death, our Lord furnished the perfect example of what it means to be set apart for doing the will of God for the benefit of others.

III. Jesus and His Church (John 17:20-26)

Looking into the future, our Lord saw an unnumbered host of people who would believe in Him as the result of the witness of disciples. He saw His church, already existing in a small group of followers (1 Cor. 15:6), growing and extending until it became an influence in the world. His prayer was in behalf of every future believer, including ourselves. And it is a prayer continued in heaven.

> **20 Neither pray I for these alone, but for them also which shall believe on me through their word;**
>
> **21 That they all may be one; as thou, Father, art in me, and I in thee, that they also may be one in us: that the world may believe that thou hast sent me.**

1. Oneness in Christ (vv. 20-23).—It is often pointed out that Jesus did not pray for uniformity among His followers but for unity, a spiritual quality similar to that found in the relationship of the Father to the Son. We deplore the denominational differences that keep us apart from other Christians. Yet on the mission fields of the world, representatives of various denominations work together in the common purpose of carrying the message of God's love to those they serve. In the task of evangelism, churches wearing different labels often unite to bear witness to a shared faith in Christ as Savior. In such circumstances, a basic unity is discovered and demonstrated. Disputes within Christian fellowships that impede the progress of the gospel and frustrate the desire of our Lord "that the world may believe" are most regrettable.

2. Glorified with Christ (v. 24).—However wavering the love of Christ's followers, toward Him or one another, His love remains firm and constant. He prayed that eventually we all might be with Him to behold and share His glory. To His immediate disciples He had already promised to "go and prepare a place for you . . . that where I am, there ye may be also" (14:3). Now He sealed that promise with a prayer to the Father of whom He said, "Thou lovedst me before the foundation of the world." Could such a love refuse this request?

3. Summation (vv. 25-26).—Into a world that knew not God came the Son as revealer of the Father. Though the process was slow, His disciples were convinced that in the person of their Master, God was making Himself known. They therefore listened and paid heed as He declared to them the name and nature of the Father. They became partakers of the love of God, and as they shared this love with others, they gave evidence of the indwelling Christ, "I in them." This is the true Christian experience.

APPLYING THE LESSON

Intercession.—In his book on prayer, Tom Elliff has given this purpose of intercession: "The proper purpose of intercession is seeking to secure the grace of God for an individual, or individuals, so that fellowship with God and usefulness for God will be established or maintained."[1] We see that purpose clearly illustrated in Jesus' prayer of intercession for His disciples.

The power of intercession.—We cannot pray the prayer Jesus prayed in our text. However, we can follow His example of intercession. Although we do not completely understand how it works, we know that our prayers for others make a difference. I remember seeing this beautifully illustrated a number of years ago. I was visiting in the First Baptist Church of Jackson, Mississippi. Dr. Frank Pollard, the pastor, shared an experience of the previous week. Chester Swor, from Jackson, Mississippi, was in Norfolk, Virginia, preparing for a message to be delivered to the Southern Baptist Convention. He was struggling to bring it all together. Finally, on Wednesday night, everything became clear, and the message fell into place. Later, Chester Swor discovered that at the very moment the message fell into place, a group of people at First

Baptist Church in Jackson were praying specifically for him. How do the prayers of a group of Christians in Jackson, Mississippi, bring clarity and understanding to a man in Norfolk, Virginia, as he prepared a message for the Convention? I don't know how it works. I simply know that it does. Our prayers of intercession for others do make a difference.

The importance of unity.—Jesus prayed for unity for His disciples. Paul Powell explained the importance of such unity: "Soldiers together make an army. Trees together make a forest. Shingles together make a roof. Bricks make a wall. Drops of water make a river. Links make a chain. Flowers make a bouquet. And players make a team. A snowflake is not much, but when enough of them cooperate, they can shut down whole cities. Togetherness is the benchmark of any successful organization, team, club, business, or church."[2]

Lack of joy.—Jim and his wife, Janice, were at a football game. The temperature was below freezing. A drizzling sleet had been falling during the entire game. Janice was feeling nauseous from the hot dog she ate. The men behind them in the stands were using abusive language and spilling their drinks on Jim and Janice. In addition, the team Jim and Janice were pulling for was behind 40 to nothing. Janice turned to Jim and said, "Honey, tell me again how much fun we're supposed to be having."

I see a lot of people like that in church every week. Somehow they have lost the joy which should be ours in Jesus Christ. Why is that? Perhaps, we misunderstand the source of true joy. We think joy is found in circumstances or happenings. Real joy is found in a vital relationship with Jesus Christ, which provides assurance that our past sins are forgiven, gives confidence that our future destiny is secure, and provides power for the challenges of today. In Jesus we have an answer for our past, an adequacy for our present, and an assurance about our future. Remembering that, we should experience true joy.

TEACHING THE CLASS

Main Idea: Jesus' prayer for us expressed concerns that we can share.

Suggested Teaching Aim: Learners will identify the concerns of Jesus expressed in His high priestly prayer and commit to aligning themselves with those concerns.

Introduce the Bible Study

Recall the study on last Sunday of the Model Prayer. Ask any learners who are willing to do so to comment about the use of the content guide in their personal prayer during this week.

Continue by asking: What are the most common concerns expressed in personal and public prayer? Elicit response. Examples are need for the forgiveness of sins, personal needs, and thanksgiving.

Note that John 17 gives us an example of a prayer of intercession from Jesus' prayer life. Ask: How much of most people's prayer life is spent in intercession for persons outside their own families? State that the purpose of the study is to give us a pattern for intercessory prayer that we can use in our own prayer lives.

Search for Biblical Truth

Share the comments titled "Intercession" (*Applying the Lesson*). Invite learners to open their Bibles to John 17:1. Call on a learner who has previously agreed to read verses 1-21 aloud. Invite other learners to listen to compare this prayer with the Model Prayer Jesus gave to His disciples at an earlier time. When the reading is finished, call for response.

Use the following outline to guide the study of this prayer:

Jesus and His Father (vv. 1-5)
Jesus and His disciples (vv. 6-19)
Jesus and His church (vv. 20-26)

Call attention to the first topic in verses 1-5. Ask: What was Jesus discussing with His Father? Elicit response. (The end of His work and the immediacy of His crucifixion.)

A Teaching Outline

1. Identify common concerns expressed in personal prayer.
2. Identify concern expressed by Jesus in His high priestly prayer.
3. Identify persons and their needs for whom learners want to offer intercessory prayer.
4. Commit to intercessory prayer during this week.

Call attention to the next section of the passage. Note that here Jesus begins His prayer of intercession for His disciples. Share the comments titled "The power of intercession" (*Applying the Lesson*).

Note that Jesus said to His Father that He had completed His work with the disciples. Ask: what was Jesus' special mission with the twelve? Elicit response. (He had made known the true nature of God. He had amplified their understanding and knowledge from the Old Testament.)

Note that Jesus prayed for the unity of the disciples (v. 11). Share the comments titled "The importance of unity" (*Applying the Lesson*).

Note that Jesus prayed for joy for the disciples (v. 13). Ask: Why would joy be important for them in the work they were to do? Share the comments titled "Lack of joy" (*Applying the Lesson*).

Note that Jesus prayed for those who would believe at some time in the future (vv. 20-26).

Give the Truth a Personal Focus

Direct learners to think of persons for whom they would like to become intercessors with God. Suggest that they privately list the names of those persons. Allow a few minutes for consideration.

Continue by directing learners to make a list of what they might talk with God about on behalf of these persons. Encourage learners to think more broadly than just physical needs. Perhaps there is a need for unity and joy and the keeping power of God just as Jesus prayed for His disciples.

Challenge learners to spend time this week in intercessory prayer for those close to them.

---

1. Thomas Elliff, *Praying for Others* (Nashville: Broadman Press, 1979), 51.
2. Paul Powell, *A Faith that Sings*, 191.

February 16

Praise for Christ, God's Servant

Basic Passage: Philippians 2:1-11

Focal Passage: Philippians 2:1-11

The inclusion of this lesson in a series entitled "Songs and Prayers of the Bible" raises an interesting question. Is our passage a song or a prayer, or both? A case can be made for it being both. The apostle Paul was expressing his desires for his Philippian friends, particularly that they might live together in harmony. In doing so, he echoed the high priestly prayer of our Lord, "Holy Father, keep through thine own name those whom thou hast given me, that they may be one, as we are" (John 17:11). What Paul wrote to the Philippians, he undoubtedly prayed for them. He gave splendor to his appeal by including verses 5-11, as beautiful a passage as can be found anywhere in

Scripture. His epistles were letters and had the expected qualities of letters: informality, variety of content, and intimacy. Philippians as a whole is no exception. It does not use polished language, except in this one passage that has all the beauty of poetry. Some consider it an early Christian hymn. Its word will sing in the heart of every Christian.

Study Aim: *To seek to apply the example of our Lord to our attitudes and relationships*

STUDYING THE BIBLE

The relationship between Paul and the Philippian church was unique. He never lost an opportunity to express gratitude to them and commendation of them. But no church is perfect, and in Philippi there were seeds of dissension. See what Paul wrote about two women in 4:2. Things must have been pretty serious between them for the apostle to call their names. His call to harmony is impressive in every way.

I. Plea for Christian Harmony (Phil. 2:1-4)

The church in Philippi was born in an atmosphere of strife. Paul and Silas were imprisoned as men who "do exceedingly trouble our city" (Acts 16:20). An early convert was their jailer. This condition continued so that, in his letter, the apostle referred to "your adversaries" (Phil. 1:28). To effectively withstand enemy assaults, the believers of Philippi needed to present a united front, "stand fast in one spirit, with one mind striving together for the faith of the gospel" (v. 27). This exhortation precedes and reinforces the powerful plea of the following verses.

> **1 If there be therefore any consolation in Christ, if any comfort of love, if any fellowship of the Spirit, if any bowels and mercies.**
> **2 Fulfil ye my joy, that ye be likeminded, having the same love, being of one accord, of one mind.**
> **3 Let nothing be done through strife or vainglory; but in lowliness of mind let each esteem other better than themselves.**
> **4 Look not every man on his own things, but every man also on the things of others.**

1. Fourfold appeal (vv. 1-2).—The NRSV reads, "If then there is any encouragement in Christ, any consolation from love, any sharing in the Spirit, any compassion and sympathy, make my joy complete." The repetition of "if" (KJV) justifies making this verse a series of penetrating questions. Does your relationship to Christ influence you? Do you allow your actions to be motivated by love? Is the Holy Spirit's presence a compelling force? Are you possessed by feelings of affection and sympathy toward others? If the answers are yes (and they should be), then Christians should live in harmony with one another.

2. Need for self-effacement (vv. 3-4).—This cannot be as long as we see ourselves as the big "I." No New Testament teaching is more contrary to the prevailing spirit of the times than this. But the teaching is in complete harmony with the Sermon on the Mount. Persons with material success as their one objective in life believe this can only be achieved by the promotion of self and self-interest. The result is the "dog-eat-dog" syndrome that prevails in so much business. Among Christians, this spirit is not allowable. A mutual regard and respect for one another is necessary. Other people's interests ("things," v. 4) are to be as important to us as our own. Our great example is the Lord Jesus Himself.

II. The Example of Our Lord (Phil. 2:5-11)

Our Lord's self-effacement for the purpose of our redemption loomed large in the thinking of Paul. He wrote in another letter, "For ye know the grace of our Lord Jesus Christ, that, though he was rich, yet for your sakes he became poor, that ye through his poverty might be rich" (2 Cor. 8:9). Writing to the Philippians from Roman imprisonment, Paul enlarged on this theme in words and phrases, as Greek scholars tell, that were carefully chosen and beautifully expressed.

5 Let this mind be in you, which was also in Christ Jesus:

6 Who, being in the form of God, thought it not robbery to be equal with God:

7 But made himself of no reputation, and took upon him the form of a servant, and was made in the likeness of men:

8 And being found in fashion as a man, be humbled himself, and became obedient unto death, even the death of the cross.

9 Wherefore God also hath highly exalted him, and given him a name which is above every name:

10 That at the name of Jesus every knee should bow, of things in heaven, and things in earth, and things under the earth;

11 And that every tongue should confess that Jesus Christ is Lord, to the glory of God the Father.

J. B. Lightfoot translated the opening statement, "Reflect in your own minds the mind of Christ Jesus."[1] Christians are to display the same attitudes that they see in their Lord as He denied Himself, to the point of sacrificing His life, for the sake of others. In His case, this self-effacement was the more remarkable because of who He was and what He forfeited to be our Savior.

1. His preexistence (vv. 5-6).—Before His coming in mortal flesh,

Jesus Christ existed "in the form of God," that is, He possessed the essential attributes of Deity. "In the beginning was the Word, and the Word was with God, and the Word was God" (John 1:1). However, He did not consider this equality with God a thing to be held on to when faced with the task of becoming Redeemer of human beings. Today some still teach that Jesus was adopted as God's Son at the beginning of His ministry (Matt. 3:17) but was not in a relationship of eternal sonship. This is contrary to the consistent message of the New Testament that "he is before all things, and by him all things consist" (Col. 1:17).

2. His incarnation (v. 7).—He who was "in the form of God" assumed "the form of a servant" as He "emptied himself" (NRSV). He did not appear on earth as a divine being but "in the likeness of men." This meant divesting Himself of His Godlike majesty, though nothing changes His relationship to His Father. As A. T. Robertson said, "No son can change the fact of His sonship." Controversies have raged around the meaning of "emptied himself," or, "made himself of no reputation" (KJV). Paul's statement is clear. He changed His role by becoming "a servant . . . in the likeness of men." We have no way to measure what He forfeited for our sakes, but we can only imagine the contrast between His heavenly glory and His earthly state. What was in His mind to persuade Him to make so great a sacrifice should be in our minds also as His humble followers.

3. His ultimate sacrifice (v. 8).—This dramatic verse ably describes the descending road of humiliation, suffering, and death that our Lord accepted in our behalf. He could have made a royal entry upon this earthly scene, but He came as a baby in the charge of a peasant couple. He accepted poverty and hardship so that He had no place to lay His head. He experienced opposition and rejection that led eventually to a demand for His death. Betrayed by His own people and condemned by the representative of a foreign occupying power, He died a cruel death, "even the death of the cross."

4. His exaltation (vv. 9-11).—Verse 9 begins with "Wherefore" as does verse 12. The first occurrence of the word marks the Father's response to the self-sacrifice of the Son, and the second the believer's response to His sublime example of selflessness. We will come back to this latter response. What is the "name . . . above every name" bestowed by the Father on the Son? It is possible to regard "name" as meaning "reputation," as we may say, "So-and-so won a name for himself by what he did." The statement of verse 10, "That at the name of Jesus every knee should bow," suggests that His human name and nature were given eternal significance, for it was in the body of His incarnation that He returned to the Father. Again, verse 11 contains the ringing phrase, "Jesus Christ is Lord." Early Christians used the phrase to defy death when they refused to say, "Caesar is Lord." To us who owe everything to Him, He is our "Lord and Savior Jesus Christ," surely a name "above every name."

III. The Apostle's Application (Phil. 2:12-16)

Verse 11 carries us to such heights of glory that we may be content to end our study there. To do so would be to miss the practical application that touches every believer in the ascended and glorified Lord. Paul's second "Wherefore" is a summons to us to respond to Him who "became obedient unto death" for our salvation.

1. Earnest endeavor (vv. 12-13).—Such is human nature, even in the case of the believer, that we do better and try harder when under observation. Paul exhorted the Philippians to work out their salvation as heartily in his absence as in his presence. Salvation is a present possession as well as a future expectation. It is to be highly prized, carefully preserved, and energetically expressed. Only because God is at work within us can we do these things.

2. Cheerful spirit (vv. 14-15).—The apostle showed continued concern for good attitudes to prevail among his readers. Only so could they "shine as lights in the world."

3. Ultimate attainment (v. 16).—The apostle looked ahead to "the day of Christ," when the ransomed will be gathered home and the Savior enthroned. He wanted to give thanks then for those who would stand around him, saved out of paganism and made complete in Christ who was "obedient unto death."

APPLYING THE LESSON

If she's not welcome.—Fred Craddock tells of an experience he had in Winnipeg, Canada, where he had gone for a preaching conference. A blizzard came in overnight, and the next morning the town was immobilized. Craddock's host called him to say the conference had been canceled, and he could not even pick up Fred for breakfast. He told Fred to walk around the corner to a bus station. He could get some breakfast in a coffee shop there at the bus station. The place was packed, but Fred found a seat. The owner offered him soup. Fred took it since that's all that was available. He was eating his "breakfast" soup when a lady walked in out of the cold. Everyone squeezed over so she could sit down. The owner asked her what she wanted, and she responded, "A glass of water." He said, "Order something." She said, "I just want a glass of water." He said again, "Order something or get out. We've got paying customers who will be coming in here. We can't have someone just taking up space not ordering anything." The woman got up to leave. When she did, everyone else got up to leave. The owner said, "Oh, all right. Just sit down."

And he brought her a glass of water. Fred, intrigued by the response of the people, turned to the person next to him and asked, "Who is she?" The man said, "I don't know her from Adam. But if she isn't welcome here, nobody's welcome here." Craddock concluded the story with this comment: "I wish that would happen in my church."

Wouldn't it be great if we cared so much about other people that we would make sure everyone felt welcome? That's the kind of openness of spirit Paul desired for the Philippians.

The plague of pride.—One of the plaguing problems in church life today is the pervasiveness of pride. How do you know if you have pride? Apply these three tests. First, apply the test of *precedence*. How do you react when someone else is selected for an assignment that you expected or desired? How do you feel when someone else is given precedence over you? Second, apply the test of *sincerity*. In moments of honest self-criticism, a person often says things about his or her faults and weaknesses and shortcomings. But how do you feel when other people, especially those you don't like, say the very same things about you? How sincere are you in your own self-criticisms? Third, apply the test of *criticism*. Does criticism from others arouse hostility in you and lead you to attempts at self-justification? How do you react to criticism? If you are deeply hurt when others are given precedence over you, if you are insincere in your self-criticism, or if you react to criticism with hostility, then pride is at work in your life. All of us need to pray for a true spirit of humility.

An overrated man.—When President Grant was on the way to a reception in his honor, he was caught in a shower and shared his umbrella with a stranger. The stranger, it turned out, was going to the reception too. This was before the days of television and media exposure. The stranger said, "I have never seen Grant, and I merely go to satisfy a personal curiosity. Between us, I have always thought that Grant was a very much overrated man." Grant replied, "That's my view also."

That is the spirit of humility, demonstrated in the life of Christ, that should also be apparent in the lives of Christians today. Instead of thinking more highly of ourselves than we ought, we should recognize our own limitations.

I did this for you.—In 1858, Frances Ridley Havergal visited Germany with her father who was being treated for his eye affliction. She stayed in a pastor's home. While there, she saw a picture of the crucifixion on the wall. Under the picture were the words: "I did this for thee. What has thou done for Me?" The picture inspired Frances Havergal to write a poem based on that motto. She was not satisfied with the poem, however, so she wadded up the piece of paper and threw it in the fire. Miraculously, the paper was not burned. Later her father encouraged her to publish it. The song has survived through the years as a great hymn about the cross. We know it as "I Gave My Life for Thee." The cross is the ultimate example of the sacrificial spirit of our Lord.

TEACHING THE CLASS

Main Idea: Becoming like Jesus in attitude and behavior will help others to confess that He is Lord.

Suggested Teaching Aim: Learners will identify the qualities of Jesus mentioned to the Philippians and determine to make them a part of their lives so that others will come to confess Him as Lord.

Introduce the Bible Study

Use information from *Studying the Bible* to introduce the study of the passage in Philippians.

Write the main idea of the passage on the chalkboard. State that the purpose of our study is to identify the qualities of Jesus that we want to have in our lives and to determine to develop them so that others will come to accept Him.

Search for Biblical Truth

Invite learners to open their Bibles to Philippians 2. Display this outline to guide the study of the passage.

Philippians 2

1. Plea for harmony (vv. 1-4)
2. Example of Jesus (vv. 5-11)
3. What to do (vv. 12-16)

Call on a learner to read verses 1-4 aloud. Note the caption on the outline for these verses. Share the comments titled "If she's not welcome" (*Applying the Lesson*).

Continue: Why do you think believers have such great difficulty living in harmony with one another? Elicit response. Share the comments titled "The plague of pride" (*Applying the Lesson*).

Call on a learner to read verses 5-11 aloud as other learners listen to discover some of the qualities of Christ that provide an example for us to emulate. When the reading is finished, call for response. Responses should include the attitude of humility and behaviors like refusal to promote Himself, obedience, and a servant role.

Ask: Why do most of us have trouble with the attitude of humility? Elicit response. Share the comments titled "An overrated man" (*Applying the Lesson*). Note that most of us are not able to identify with President Grant.

A Teaching Outline

1. Introduce the Philippians passage and the purpose for the study.
2. Discover the attitudes and behaviors of Jesus which Paul was imploring the Philippians to emulate.
3. Determine what attitudes and behaviors should be a part of learners' lives so that others will come to Jesus.
4. Decide to make these a part of learners' lives out of response to what Jesus has done for them.

Call on a learner to read verses 12-16, noting that this is the practical application for the Philippians. Direct learners to listen for Paul's instructions to them. When the reading is finished, call for response. Response should include being concerned about one's own salvation, refusal to grumble, and sticking to the Word of God.

Give the Truth a Personal Focus

Recall that the purpose of the study was to identify the qualities of Jesus that we should imitate as a witness to those around us. Ask: What behaviors and attitudes does this study suggest for us? Wait for their response.

Ask: How difficult is it to live in this way? After they have responded, share the comments titled "I did this for you" (*Applying the Lesson*). Call on your group to personally commit themselves to live following the example of Jesus, because of what He has done for us.

1. J. B. Lightfoot, *Epistle to the Philippians* (London: Macmillan, 1869), 108.

February 23

The Hallelujah Chorus

Basic Passages: Revelation 15:2-4; 19:1-8

Focal Passages: Revelation 15:2-4; 19:4-8

The songs of God's people will be projected into eternity. The Bible's portrayal of the heavenly state abounds in references to music and singing. We had better get our voices in tune down here to be ready for our part in the heavenly choirs, and if not our voices, then our spirits. For the praise of God will be the continuing activity of the redeemed. We may have difficulty understanding some features in the last book of the New Testament, but there can be no failure to understand its depiction of multitudes of "all nations, and kindreds, and people, and tongues" who "stood before the throne, and before the Lamb, clothed with white robes, and palms in their hands," and who "cried with a loud voice, saying, Salvation to our God which sitteth upon the throne, and unto the Lamb" (Rev. 7:9-10). Their identity is made clear, "These are they which came out of great tribulation, and have washed their robes, and made them white in the blood of the Lamb" (v. 14). Read the entire passage as preparation for this lesson.

Study Aim: *To establish our relationship with Jesus Christ, the Lamb of God, and so make sure our place in the heavenly choirs*

STUDYING THE BIBLE

We will make no attempt to schedule the order of final events as depicted in the Book of Revelation. Two brief passages from the concluding chapters of the book afford neither reason nor opportunity to do this. What seems clear is that we shall be dealing with closing scenes of time as eternity is ushered in, if it has not already begun. As they stand on this amazing threshold, God's people, who have worshiped Him on earth, continue their worship in praise for His righteous acts and redeeming grace. Two of their songs form our lesson material.

I. A Song of Deliverance (Rev. 15:2-4)

Chapter 15 is introduced by John the apostle, writer of the book (1:4), saying, "I saw another sign in heaven, great and marvelous, seven angels having the seven last plagues; for in them is filled up the wrath of God." The Scriptures are consistent in stating that this world age will end with divine judgment. Israel of old was warned against thinking of the coming of God's kingdom in terms only of advantage. "Woe unto you that desire the day of the Lord! to what end is it for you? the day of the Lord is darkness, and not light" (Amos 5:18). Only to those who are reconciled to God through Christ will the day of the Lord bring joy everlasting. For others it will mean judgment and condemnation. The singers of the following song were among the former.

> **2 And I saw as it were a sea of glass mingled with fire: and them that had gotten the victory over the beast, and over his image, and over his mark, and over the number of his name, stand on the sea of glass, having the harps of God.**
>
> **3 And they sing the song of Moses the servant of God, and the song of the Lamb, saying, Great and marvelous are thy works, Lord God Almighty; just and true are thy ways, thou King of saints.**
>
> **4 Who shall not fear thee, O Lord, and glorify thy name? for thou only art holy: for all nations shall come and worship before thee; for thy judgments are made manifest.**

1. Victors over "the beast" (v. 2).—Revelation was written for the comfort and assurance of believers who were persecuted by the Roman Empire. Its message is one of ultimate victory over every evil power; and as such, it continues to be a source of confidence to present-day Christians, especially those who are oppressed because of their faith. There is an early reference to a sea of glass in 4:6 where it is part of the majestic environment of the throne of God. That this crystal sea is here "mingled with fire" could signify divine judgment; but on the other hand, it could be another symbol of Deity as elsewhere in Scripture. The victors have "harps of God," the harp being a recognized instrument of worship.

2. Two songs in one (v. 3).—Only in the writings of John the apostle is Jesus called the Lamb though the figure had its origin in Isaiah 53:7. Though basically associated with sacrifice, the Lamb of Revelation is a triumphant figure (see 5:6-14). The song that is sung in chapter 15 is about two deliverances, that under Moses at the Red Sea and that accomplished by Christ as the Lamb of God (John 1:29). The song of Moses, recorded in Exodus 15:1-19 celebrated deliverance from the power of the Egyptians, an event that anticipated the greater deliverance wrought by Jesus at Calvary. The theme throughout is victory, granted to Moses over Pharaoh and his hosts, accomplished by the Lord Jesus against sin and death and by His people over "the beast."

3. Universal worship (v. 4).—The reference to "all nations" raises the question as to the identity of these. Are they the redeemed of all nations? The greater probability is that in the light of the final triumph of divine justice all criticism is silenced and people everywhere bow before God in subjection. His victory is complete in the expression of universal homage.

II. A Song of Praise (Rev. 19:1-8)

Following the passage just studied comes a series of judgments referred to in 15:1 as "the seven last plagues" and "seven golden vials full of the wrath of God" (15:7). Chapters 17 and 18 are occupied with the destruction of "the great whore," also described as "that great city" (17:18) and "Babylon the great" (17:5; 18:2). To first-century Christians, this would be imperial Rome where Paul and Peter died for the faith, together with thousands of others who refused to say, "Caesar is Lord." In 18:24 it is said of this infamous Babylon that "in her was found the blood of prophets, and of saints, and of all that were slain upon the earth." No wonder that the news of her destruction was greeted by shouts of praise by "much people in heaven" (19:1).

4 And the four and twenty elders and the four beasts fell down and worshiped God that sat on the throne saying, Amen; Alleluia.
5 And a voice came out of the throne, saying, Praise our God, all ye his servants, and ye that fear him, both small and great.
6 And I heard as it were the voice of a great multitude, and as the voice of many waters, and as the voice of mighty thunderings, saying, Alleluia; for the Lord God omnipotent reigneth.
7 Let us be glad and rejoice, and give honor to him: for the marriage of the Lamb is come, and his wife hath made herself ready.
8 And to her was granted that she should be arrayed in fine linen, clean and white: for the fine linen is the righteousness of saints.

1. The church triumphant (v. 1).—The Book of Revelation uses many symbols, characters, and phrases without clear definition of what they represent. We are dependent on other Scriptures, and on context, for our conclusions; but even so we must exercise caution. Who are the "great multitude" of verse 1 (NRSV)? The mention of salvation in the same verse and the address, "all ye his servants" (v. 5), point to the redeemed people of God who, in heaven, engage in His praise. They respond to the call to thanksgiving for the fall of "Babylon, that mighty city!" (18:10), which may well represent to us all that resists the purposes of God. "Rejoice over her, thou heaven, and ye holy apostles and prophets; for God hath avenged you on her" (18:20). This heavenly praise begins with a word derived from two Hebrew words, "Alleluia," or, "Hallelujah," meaning "Praise the

Lord." In our previous passage, 15:2-4, praise was offered for deliverance. An alternative word, "Salvation," is used here as tribute is paid to God as the source of salvation.

2. Evil overcome (vv. 2-3).—History itself furnishes many examples of the fall of oppressive and corrupt regimes, some in our own times. Unfortunately, new tyrannies replace the old, and new dictators arise as others disappear. The second "Alleluia" from the heavenly multitude is followed by the statement, "her smoke rose up forever and ever," implying finality. This goes beyond the fall of Rome, and any other subsequent ungodly power, to affirm the ultimate victory of divine righteousness over every evil. These acts of judgment are "true and righteous," for they are the work Him who has been previously addressed, "Great and marvelous are thy works, Lord God Almighty; just and true are thy ways, thou King of saints" (15:3).

3. Worship offered (v. 4).—The "four and twenty elders and the four beasts" are first mentioned in 4:4,6. Commentators are in sharp disagreement as to what these represent, one writer listing twenty-one explanations. Acceptable to many is the suggestion that the twenty-four are made up of representatives of the twelve tribes of Israel plus the twelve apostles. This would imply the totality of God's people, in both Old and New Testaments, all engaged in heaven in the worship of God. They express approval of God's righteous judgments by the use of "Amen" (so let it be), and to this add their "Alleluia."

4. Mysterious voice (v. 5).—The fact that the voice says, "Praise our God" indicates that this was not the voice of God Himself. We must regard it as an undisclosed voice calling on all the servants of God, "both small and great," to join in His praise. For all who reach His heavenly courts, whatever their station in this life, have reason to return thanks. This is the pattern of many of the psalms (104—150) that conclude, "Praise ye the Lord."

5. Marriage of the Lamb (vv. 6-8).—The climax to all this praise is a wedding, "the marriage of the Lamb." Throughout the Bible the concept of God's people as His bride prevails. "For thy Maker is thine husband" (Isa. 54:5) and "as the bridegroom rejoiceth over the bride, so shall thy God rejoice over thee" (62:5). This idea carries over into the teaching of the New Testament in the teaching of our Lord (Matt. 25:1-13) and of the apostle Paul, particularly in Ephesians 5:25-32 where Christ's bride, the church, is described as "a glorious church, not having spot, or wrinkle, or any such thing; but that it should be holy and without blemish." In the Revelation passage, we see a sharp contrast between Christ's bride and the gaudy attire of "the great whore," who was "arrayed in purple and scarlet color, and decked with gold and precious stones and pearls" (Rev. 17:4). Christ's bride is seen "arrayed in fine linen, . . . the righteousness of saints."

APPLYING THE LESSON

Amazing grace.—John Newton not only wrote the great hymn "Amazing Grace," he also lived his life under the blessings of grace. He said on one occasion that he expected to find three wonders in heaven. "First, to meet some I had not thought to find there. Second, to miss some I had thought to find there. Third, the greatest wonder of all, to find myself there."[1]

This was not an expression of uncertainty about the assurance of Newton's salvation. Rather, this was an expression of the unworthiness of any of us to experience the wonders of heaven apart from the grace of God. This overwhelming sense of unworthiness resulted in the spontaneous praise the apostle John wrote about in the Revelation.

Our hope in Christ.—The New Testament is permeated with the idea of hope. A close study of the New Testament passages on this subject reveals some interesting insights. Our hope is a gift from God (2 Thess. 2:16). Hope comes through the Scriptures (Rom. 15:4). Our hope is based on the resurrection of Jesus Christ from the dead (1 Pet. 1:3). Hope is confirmed in us through the Holy Spirit (Rom. 15:13). Our hope not only helps us to face the challenges of life, but it also removes our fear of death (Col. 1:5). Our hope is secure and nothing can take it away from us (Heb. 6:17-18). Our hope will be fulfilled in the second coming of Christ (Titus 2:13).

What did he say?—When someone mentions the name Yogi Berra, one will not only think of a Hall of Fame baseball player, but one will also think of someone who says things that don't make sense. They have been referred to as "Berraisms." On golf, Yogi says, "Ninety percent of putts that are short don't go in." About a baseball game, Yogi says, "It ain't over till its over." About success in baseball, Yogi says, "Baseball is 90 percent mental; the other half is physical." About decisions, Yogi says, "If you come to a fork in the road, take it." About playing baseball on the East coast, Yogi says, "It gets late early out there." When Johnny Bench broke Yogi's record for most home runs by a catcher, Yogi said, "I knew the record would stand until it was broken." About a well-known restaurant, Yogi says, "No one goes there anymore—it's too crowded." And on and on it goes. In his autobiography, Yogi explained what he meant by most of those sayings; and with his explanation, they suddenly made sense.[2]

One of the most difficult challenges in New Testament study is to make sense of the symbols and images of the Book of Revelation. Understanding the context of the time in which the book was written brings clarification to many of these symbols.

You oughta been there.—A man from the country made his first trip to the big city. A part of his weekend venture was a trip to a large church downtown. He was in awe from the moment he entered the building. He had never seen such a magnificent edifice. More people were in the service than lived in his town. The choir was magnificent, and the preacher displayed a skill and an intellect he had never been exposed to. When he arrived at home that night, he got down on his knees and said, "Oh, Lord, what a day I've had. I went to the greatest church I've ever seen. The choir was fantastic, and the preacher was wonderful. I was moved beyond words. Oh, Lord, you oughta been there!"

As overwhelming as our experiences of worship are here on earth, they are nothing when compared to the experience of worshiping in the very presence of God as we will do in heaven. No wonder the songs of the saints recorded in the Revelation are full of praise.

We have Jesus.—In the days of the depression, Clarence Darrow, the brilliant lawyer, was addressing the members of a black church in Chicago. Most of these people were desperately poor. They didn't have jobs and had little in which to place their hope. Darrow recounted their troubles and then noted how joyfully they had sung. Then he asked this pointed question: "What do you have to sing about?" A lady in the congregation jumped to her feet and said, "We've got Jesus to sing about!"

In the end, that's what all of us must say. The things of this world will be gone, and we will have only Jesus to sing about.

TEACHING THE CLASS

Main Idea: The praise of God will be the continuing activity of heaven.

Suggested Teaching Aim: Learners will review the songs of the redeemed in heaven and make sure of their place in that group.

Introduce the Bible Study

Recall that the study for the quarter has included songs from the Old Testament and prayers from the New Testament. State that this final lesson focuses on the activity of singing in heaven.

Share information from the introductory paragraph of *Studying the Bible.* Note that during this study learners will review the songs of the redeemed in heaven. State that a secondary purpose is to consider whether we will be among those who will be singing those songs in that day.

Search for Biblical Truth

Share the comments titled "What did he say" (*Applying the Lesson*). Note that despite common reluctance to understand the Book of Revelation, much is to be gained from its study. Invite learners to open their Bibles to Revelation 15.

Display the following outline to guide the review of two songs of the redeemed in heaven:

A Song of Deliverance: Revelation 15:2-4
Victors over the beast (v. 2)
Song of Moses; Song of the Lamb (v. 3)
Universal worship (v. 4)
A Song of Praise: Revelation 19:1-8
The church triumphant (v. 1)
Evil overcome (vv. 2-3)
Worship offered (v. 4)
Mysterious voice (v. 5)
Marriage of the Lamb (vv. 6-8)

Proceed through the outline for the purpose of reviewing the content of the two songs of the redeemed in heaven. Call on learners to read the verses as indicated. Call attention to the outline caption. Share comments from *Studying the Bible.*

A Teaching Outline

1. Focus on the songs of heaven found in Revelation.
2. Learn the elements of the praise songs sung by the redeemed in heaven.
3. Determine how one becomes a part of that singing group.
4. Examine personal experience of learners with Christ to determine whether they know they will be a part of the redeemed of heaven.

When the experience of worship is discussed, share the comments titled "You oughta been there" (*Applying the Lesson*).

Give the Truth a Personal Focus

Note that being there in great experiences of worship is a special experience. Note further that learners will want to be there for the ultimate worship experience in heaven when worship is offered at the feet of Jesus. Ask: How do you get to be a part of those singers in heaven?

After listening to their responses, take as much time as seems appropriate to explain that the way persons become a part of that heavenly choir is to accept Jesus as their Savior. Even if class members are all members of the church, spend some time discussing accepting Jesus Christ as Savior. Emphasize that He is the only way of salvation.

Invite any persons who are not sure that they would be a part of that heavenly choir who will sing praise to God to speak with you privately. Be prepared to lead them into a saving knowledge of Jesus Christ.

Note that when we know Jesus, singing doesn't have to wait until we get to heaven. Share the comments titled "We have Jesus" (*Applying the Lesson*). Close the study with a prayer of praise and rejoicing for the song of Jesus in the hearts of believers.

---

1. Paul Powell, *The Saint Peter Principle* (Nashville: Broadman Press, 1982), 89.
2. Yogi Berra with Tom Horton, *Yogi: It Ain't Over*. . . (New York: Harper and Row, 1989), 6-22.

March, April, May 1992

The Strong Son of God

Aids from BROADMAN for Studying and Teaching

Books:
A Guide for New Testament Study, William Stevens
The Broadman Bible Commentary, Volumes 2,8
Layman's Bible Book Commentary, Volumes 3,16

The first part of this quarter will focus on peak incidents in the Gospel of Mark, leading up to Easter. Throughout the study, our Lord will be presented in the strength of His character and actions. In Unit I, "Mission and Message," we will begin with His salute from heaven at His baptism, His temptation in the wilderness, the mounting hostility that He faced, and the ministry of compassion that He pursued and enjoined on His disciples. This will come to conclusion in the offering of Himself on the cross followed by His resurrection, Unit II, "Confession and Crucifixion."

March 1

Identification and Testing

Basic Passage: Mark 1:1-15

Focal Passage: Mark 1:1-15

There are four Gospels. They all relate to the person and ministry of the Lord Jesus Christ. But each of the four writers had his own viewpoint. Matthew wrote of God's kingdom and Jesus as the Messiah-King. Mark saw and presented our Lord as the strong Son of God (our theme for this series of eight lessons). To Luke, the only Gentile writer, He was the Savior of the world. John's Gospel distinctively features Jesus as the incarnate Son of God. Each Gospel, again, had different audiences. Matthew had in mind a Jewish readership, though not exclusively. Mark wrote for the Roman world, and Luke for Jew and Gentile alike. John addressed himself to the developing church of Jesus Christ, beset by error without and within. Together these four Gospels provide a many-sided portrait of our Savior and complement one another in describing His life and message. For today's readers, Mark has special appeal with its crisp style and focus on the prevailing Christ.

Study Aim: *To reaffirm the call of Jesus Christ, the Son of God, to repent and believe the gospel*

STUDYING THE BIBLE

Mark's Gospel is believed to be the first to be written, somewhere between A.D. 60 and 70. Argument for an earlier date continues. We should be impressed by the realization that in Mark's Gospel we are reading a record of our Lord written within thirty to forty years of His death, less time than the interval between the end of World War II and today.

I. The Second Gospel

All four Gospels are anonymous. The people who wrote them were not aspiring to personal fame, but they wrote to magnify the name of Jesus. There may be a personal reference to the author in 14:51-52, but if so no name is given to the "certain young man." By ascribing the

Gospel to Mark we are depending on early Christian tradition that is unanimous in naming him.

1. John Mark.—His mother played a prominent part in the life of the New Testament church (Acts 12:12). Generous Barnabas of Acts 4:36-37 was his cousin (Col. 4:10, NRSV). In spite of early failure (Acts 13:13), which made Mark the cause of dissension between Barnabas and Paul (15:36-40), Mark later became the trusted companion of Paul (Philem. 24). He is also named as companion to Peter (1 Pet. 5:13). These and other contacts gave him remarkable opportunity to gather information about our Lord.

2. His material.—Several second-century writers described Mark as "the interpreter of Peter" and stated that he prepared his Gospel primarily for Christians in Rome and Italy. That he wrote with non-Jewish readers in mind is supported by the few Old Testament quotations, the explanation of Jewish customs (7:2-4), detailed geographical information about Palestine (13:3), and the use of Latin words. Noticeable also is his use of energetic words such as "immediately" and "straightway."

II. Herald of the Christ (Mark 1:1-8)

Why did Mark begin his Gospel with the ministry of John the Baptist? One answer may be that this was the point at which Peter first made contact with our Lord. Along with his brother Andrew, Peter was probably a disciple of the Baptist (John 1:35-42). That he was in the same locality as Andrew when this event occurred supports this.

1 The beginning of the gospel of Jesus Christ, the Son of God;

2 As it is written in the prophets, Behold, I send my messenger before thy face, which shall prepare thy way before thee.

3 The voice of one crying in the wilderness, Prepare ye the way of the Lord, make his paths straight.

4 John did baptize in the wilderness, and preach the baptism of repentance for the remission of sins.

5 And there went out unto him all the land of Judea, and they of Jerusalem, and were all baptized of him in the river of Jordan, confessing their sins.

6 And John was clothed with camel's hair, and with a girdle of a skin about his loins; and he did eat locusts and wild honey;

7 And preached, saying, There cometh one mightier than I after me, the latchet of whose shoes I am not worthy to stoop down and unloose.

8 I indeed have baptized you with water: but he shall baptize you with the Holy Ghost.

1. Old Testament roots (vv. 1-3).—Departing from his later practice, Mark provided Old Testament roots for the "good tidings" (Luke 2:10) that came with Jesus Christ. He quoted Isaiah 40:3 and Malachi 3:1. When dealing with Romans, it was important to present Christianity in an Old Testament context. New religions were not tolerated, and, as a historic fact, the church became more and more endangered as the rift with Judaism became evident. For Christians, however, it also was important to know that their faith was not a novelty but the outgrowth and consummation of beliefs many centuries old, born, in fact, in the mind and heart of God.

2. John's witness (vv. 4-8).—The ancient prophecy described one "crying in the wilderness," so it is as a wilderness character that John is presented in verse 6. The emphasis of these verses is on the contrast between the persons of John and Jesus and their baptisms. John, though intensely popular (v. 5), declared himself unworthy to untie our Lord's shoes. The baptism he administered, though accepted by many, was unto repentance and forgiveness. The baptism Jesus would introduce would be "with the Holy Ghost," that is, it would bring the possibility of renewal, new beginnings by spiritually transformed people. Romans 6:1-11 associates baptism with resurrection to newness of life.

III. Divine Endorsement of Jesus (Mark 1:9-11)

The meeting between John and Jesus was momentous. The two were related (Luke 1:36), and both were children of promise. But John had spent his years "in the deserts" (v. 80), while Jesus grew into manhood in Nazareth. The news of John's activities, preaching and baptizing, must have been the signal to Jesus that His public ministry was due to begin. He stepped out of thirty years of obscurity and silence and made His way to the place where John was baptizing.

> **9 And it came to pass in those days, that Jesus came from Nazareth of Galilee, and was baptized of John in Jordan.**
>
> **10 And straightway coming up out of the water, he saw the heavens opened, and the Spirit like a dove descending upon him:**
>
> **11 And there came a voice from heaven, saying, Thou art my beloved Son, in whom I am well-pleased.**

1. His baptism (v. 9).—Since baptism involved acknowledgment of sin, why did Jesus present Himself for baptism? He was the Sinless One, yet He was the world's sin-bearer. Others came to John confessing their sin and expressing repentance for it. Jesus assumed our guilt, though Himself free from it, that He might ultimately bear it to the cross where its penalty was paid in His death. May we not also believe that our Lord's action was intended as an endorsement of the Baptist's ministry? For of him He would later say, "Among them that are born of women there hath not risen a greater than John the Baptist" (Matt. 11:11).

2. Vision and voice (vv. 10-11).—In John 1:32-34 it is stated that the Baptist had been told, presumably by God, that he would recognize Jesus as the Messiah by the descent of the Holy Spirit upon Him in the form of a dove. What happened, therefore, as described in these verses, was of importance to John as well as to Jesus. For John, the message was that his mission had been completed. For our Lord, He had received the endorsement of His Heavenly Father for the mission on which He was about to embark. For Mark's readers, the significance was that He who identified with sinful humankind in baptism had been acknowledged from heaven as the divine Son of God. This term was applied to Mark's readers by some Roman emperors whose false claim was challenged every time a courageous Christian declared his or her faith by saying, "Jesus is Lord."

IV. Confrontation with Satan (Mark 1:12-13)

In his "straightway" style, Mark moved quickly through the events that marked the beginning of our Lord's public ministry. It was the divine Spirit that "driveth him into the wilderness." This does not imply any unwillingness on our Lord's part but emphasizes the controlling force of the Spirit throughout His earthly life.

> **12 And immediately the spirit driveth him into the wilderness.**
> **13 And he was there in the wilderness forty days, tempted of Satan; and was with the wild beasts; and the angels ministered unto him.**

This record is strikingly short, compared to Matthew 4:1-11. But even in its brevity, it apparently served Mark's purpose. The praise of the Baptist (Mark 1:7-8) and the acclaim from heaven (vv. 10-11) did not insulate Jesus from trial and testing. For Christians exposed to opposition amounting to persecution, this was important to know. Mark alone mentions "wild beasts," apparently to emphasize the intensity of the attacks. But there was divine aid available and freely given as angels came to help Jesus. Every pressured believer has supernatural allies.

V. Christ's Ministry Begins (Mark 1:14-15)

The arrest and imprisonment of John seems recorded to emphasize that the Baptist's task was completed as he announced the coming of the Messiah and the task of Jesus was beginning. "The time is fulfilled," He said, indicating that ancient prophecies and John's preaching were about to become history.

> **14 Now after that John was put in prison, Jesus came into Galilee, preaching the gospel and the kingdom of God,**
> **15 And saying, The time is fulfilled, and the kingdom of God is at hand: repent ye, and believe the gospel.**

All the hopes of the past concerning a new and better age, and all the needs of the present, were satisfied in the announcement that God's kingdom (rule or reign) was beginning. The response to this dramatic news should be repentance and faith, then and now.

APPLYING THE LESSON

Different perspectives.—The boss watched the men carrying the lumber from the truck to the bin at the lumberyard. One man carried only a single board while others carried two boards. The boss called him over and said, "Why are you carrying only one board when the other men are carrying two? Are you lazy?" "No," responded the quick-thinking worker. "They are the ones who are lazy. They are too lazy to make a second trip."

This story illustrates a simple truth: different people can see the same thing in different ways. It is a matter of perspective. Two people describing an accident will tell slightly different stories about the same facts because of their perspective. Two children will recount the same incident at school in a different way because of their perspective. Members of a congregation can listen to the same sermon and then suggest different lessons they learned from the sermon because of their perspective.

Likewise, the Gospel writers told the same story about Jesus. But the stories are somewhat different because of their perspective.

A man of action.—The church member was deeply moved by his pastor's sermon. The pastor's call to commitment took root in his heart. Before the sermon was over, this convinced church member leaped to his feet and cried out, "Oh, Lord, Use me! Use me!" But then he added this restriction: "Use me in an advisory capacity!" Many church members have that kind of commitment—a commitment that talks and promises but never works and serves.

The relation of the Old Testament to the New Testament.—A young man lived in a city built upon tall hills. He had an old jalopy that had largely lost its power. Therefore, in order to get up some of the steepest hills, the car had to get a running start. He would start at the top of the preceding hill and gun the car all he could. Only then would he be able to make it to the top of the next hill. On one such occasion, he approached the bottom of the hill and noticed that two cars were coming from his right on the road he had to cross. In a split second, he decided he would try to go between them. So he slowed the car down just enough to let the first car go by, and then he gunned his car to make it between the two cars. However, he had a problem. He had not noticed that the first car was towing the second car! He learned the hard way that one cannot divide two things that are integrally connected.

Likewise, we cannot divide the Old Testament from the New Testament, for the two are integrally connected. The Old Testament is prediction; the New Testament is fulfillment. The Old Testament begins; the New Testament completes. Thus, when Mark began the story of Jesus, he quoted two Old Testament prophets whose message pointed to Jesus.

The meaning of baptism.—The little boy was impressed by the baptismal service he had observed at church, so he decided he would try his hand at it. He chose the cat to baptize. The baptismal was the bathtub. As you may imagine, when the boy tried to dunk the cat into the water, the cat let out a screech and jumped out of his hands. In disgust, the boy said, "You will never be a Baptist cat!"

Baptism has been practiced over the centuries. Baptism was practiced before Baptists emphasized it, before John came on the scene, and before Jesus was baptized. The Jews baptized those who came over into Judaism. Yet the baptism of the Jews had a different meaning from the baptism of John, and the baptism of John had a different meaning from the baptism of Jesus.

The reality of Satan.—In Wartburg Castle, Germany, a large, dark stain marks one of the walls. According to tradition, this was the spot where Martin Luther found the devil so real that he hurled an inkwell at him in defense and frustration.

Don't feel bad when you are tempted and when Satan works on your life. From Martin Luther to the Master Himself, every person faces the reality of temptation.

TEACHING THE CLASS

Main Idea: Introduction of others to the Son of God is a high calling of believers.

Suggested Teaching Aim: Learners will plan to introduce others to Jesus as John the Baptist did.

Introduce the Bible Study

Introduce the study for this quarter using information from the introductory comments under *Studying the Bible.* After noting that the first eight lessons are from the Book of Mark, share comments titled "Different perspectives" from *Applying the Lesson.*

Use the comments titled "A man of action" (*Applying the Lesson*) to introduce the study for today. Write the main idea for this lesson on the chalkboard. Ask rhetorically: Do you believe this statement? Do you take action on this truth?

Note that the study for today focuses on a man who did take action, John the Baptist. Invite learners to open their Bibles to Mark 1.

Search for Biblical Truth

Note that John the Baptist is a familiar figure who is spoken of in both the Old Testament and the New Testament. Share the comment titled "The relation of the Old Testament to the New Testament" (*Applying the Lesson*).

Call on a learner to read Mark 1:1-3 aloud. Call on other learners to read Isaiah 40:3 and Malachi 3:1 aloud. Note that John the Baptist was the fulfillment of the Old Testament prophecy. Ask: Why might Mark have begun his Gospel with this reference to the Old Testament? Elicit response. Use information from *Studying the Bible* to supplement the responses.

A Teaching Outline

1. Introduce the study for the quarter and the first unit.
2. Introduce the lesson for today.
3. Identify ways John the Baptist used to introduce Jesus to his hearers.
4. Determine who the learners' hearers might be and how to introduce Jesus to them.
5. Plan to introduce Jesus to someone this week.

Invite learners to read verses 4 and 5 to learn the results of John's "crying in the wilderness." Share the comments titled "The meaning of baptism" (*Applying the Lesson*).

Call on a learner to read Mark 1:6-8 aloud while other learners listen to how John the Baptist explained the difference in his baptism and a baptism that was to come. Call for response. Continue: In what way was John's presentation of Jesus, the Messiah, unique? (Include the appearance of John and the message that he preached.)

Note that the importance of baptism is emphasized by the next recorded event in verses 9-11. Call on a learner to read them aloud. Ask: Why did Jesus submit to baptism? See "1. His baptism v. 9" (Studying the Bible).

Note that most believers accept baptism as a part of public commitment to following Jesus. However, the next event of Jesus' life is resisted by most. Call on a learner to read verses 12-13 aloud. Share the comments titled "The reality of Satan" from *Applying the Lesson.*

Note that verses 14-15 provide the outcome of this witness of John the Baptist. Invite learners to read them to themselves to identify that outcome. Call for response.

Give the Truth a Personal Focus

Note that John the Baptist is a valid example of the main idea of the lesson. Direct learners to review the Scripture to identify ways John the Baptist used to introduce others to Jesus Christ. Suggest that learners discuss conclusions with those sitting near them. Call for response.

Ask: Would John's approach be useful today? Why or why not? Emphasize that John's style was designed to fit his hearers. Ask: Who might "hear" your witness of Jesus Christ today? Give time for response. Note that it is important to know who we might influence so that the message can be presented in a way that will make the greatest impact.

Ask: How can the message that Jesus Christ is the Messiah and Savior best be presented to those who will hear you? Ask for response that will generate ideas that learners may use during the coming week.

Conclude by inviting learners to plan today to introduce others to Jesus during this week. Share in a prayer of commitment to that high calling.

March 8

The Clash of Ideas

Basic Passage: Mark 2:23—3:6

Focal Passage: Mark 2:23—3:6

The Gospels were written for people known to the writers, people with specific needs to be met. This was made specially clear by Luke who addressed himself to "most excellent Theophilus" (Luke 1:3), perhaps a personal name, perhaps a group made up of people who could be described as a "friend of God," for that is what Theophilus means. As already suggested, Mark wrote for Roman Christians whose circumstances were well known to him. They were living in a situation of worsening oppression. Nero was the emperor who, in

A.D. 64 to escape responsibility himself, blamed Christians for a fire that destroyed much of Rome. Widespread persecution resulted. "If Christians were to be strengthened and the gospel effectively proclaimed it would be necessary to exhibit the similarity of situation faced by Jesus and the Christians of Rome."[1] Throughout his Gospel, Mark described Jesus in conflict with critics and foes. In the section 2:1—3:6 particularly, he assembled incidents to remind readers of the constant struggle in which their Master engaged.

Study Aim: *To see Jesus as the strong Son of God who endured opposition without lessening His dedication to His redemptive task*

STUDYING THE BIBLE

We must not reduce Mark's Gospel to any single purpose. If our Lord presented an example of endurance, He also impressed those who knew him as "The Strong Son of God." In fact, it was His very strength of character and purpose that brought Him into conflict with others. Both traits are clearly seen in the incidents we will study.

I. Jesus Facing Conflict (Mark 2:1-22)

Events that led up to the confrontation in the grainfields (vv. 23-28, NIV) merit attention. They inform us on the wide range of issues raised by our Lord's critics and the persistence of their attacks on Him.

1. Blasphemy charged (vv. 1-12).—The idea prevailed that physical affliction was punishment for sin committed. The palsied man probably believed this; he may, in fact, have had reason to attribute his condition to past misbehavior. So Jesus dealt first with the man's spiritual malady and brought condemnation on Himself from "certain of the scribes." In their eyes, He was claiming powers that belonged to God alone. They refused to consider the possibility that He was God in the flesh, Immanuel, "God with us" (Matt. 1:23).

2. Socializing with "sinners" (vv. 13-17).—Anyone who failed to conform to the ritual laws of the Old Testament was classified a sinner. Table fellowship with such was unthinkable and defiling. But it was to save such that Jesus came into the world.

3. Question of fasting (vv. 18-22).—Since our Lord died by crucifixion, it was widely believed that He committed some criminal act. Romans needed to know the charges brought against Him concerned the practices of religion, such as fasting. The Mosaic law stipulated only one fast ("afflict your souls," Lev. 16:31) in the year. The Pharisees observed two fasts a week, man-made ordinances.

II. Jesus and the Sabbath (Mark 2:23-28)

We know that the observance, or nonobservance, of special days was a divisive issue among the Christians of Rome (Rom. 14:5-6). This would include the Sabbath, Jewish believers, for the most part, adhering to the seventh day of the week and Gentile believers preferring, again for the most part, the first. What was our Lord's position as one raised in the Jewish tradition with no available alternative? How did He regard the Sabbath?

> **23 And it came to pass, that he went through the corn fields on the sabbath day; and his disciples began, as they went, to pluck the ears of corn.**
>
> **24 And the Pharisees said unto him, Behold, why do they on the sabbath day that which is not lawful?**
>
> **25 And he said unto them, Have ye never read what David did, when he had need, and was an hungered, he, and they that were with him?**
>
> **26 How he went into the house of God in the days of Abiathar the high priest, and did eat the showbread, which is not lawful to eat but for the priests, and gave also to them which were with him?**
>
> **27 And he said unto them, The sabbath was made for man, and not man for the sabbath:**
>
> **28 Therefore the Son of man is Lord also of the sabbath.**

1. Gleaning (v. 23).—In the King James Version, the word *corn* stands for any small grain such as wheat or barley. The disciples were taking advantage of an ancient Old Testament provision that allowed persons crossing vineyards or corn fields to sample fruit or grain, but not to gather either in quantity (Deut. 23:24-25).

2. Sabbath laws (vv. 24-26).—The charge of "not lawful," then, referred to the occasion and not to the gleaning. The disciples were breaking a law of the Sabbath that the Pharisees themselves had made burdensome by petty restrictions they had added to the basic law of Exodus 20:9-11. In their eyes, plucking grain was the equivalent of reaping and husking: it was threshing. Our Lord defended the action of His disciples by quoting an Old Testament incident involving David (1 Sam. 21:1-6). He and his men, in an emergency, had eaten showbread, which was reserved for the use of priests alone. Human need was thus made a reason for setting aside a requirement of the law. The Pharisees, who were not critical of David for this incident, were judging the disciples for a minor infraction of their elaboration of the Sabbath law.

3. Our Lord's claim (vv. 27-28).—In the order of creation, human beings appeared before mention of the Sabbath concept (Gen. 1:27;

2:2-3). Although intended for the worship of God, the Sabbath also provided a rest day for toiling humanity (Ex. 20:10-11). It was designed for our good. As the divinely appointed Representative of our human race, the Son of man, Jesus claimed authority over the Sabbath as to its purpose and observance. In acceptance of this principle, the Christian church would later shift from the Jewish Sabbath to the Lord's Day to be observed on the first day of the week when He arose from the dead and was thus "declared to be the Son of God with power" (Acts 20:7; 1 Cor. 16:2; Rom. 1:4).

III. Jesus and His Enemies (Mark 3:1-6)

That our Lord did not question the importance of the Sabbath as a God-given institution is made plain by repeated references to His attendance at synagogue services on that day. Chapter 3 begins with such a reference. The apostle Paul, after Him, showed similar regard for both Sabbath and synagogue (Acts 9:20; 13:14). The break came gradually as the churches became increasingly Gentile and opposition to the gospel and its messengers became more and more intense (Acts 18:6-7).

1 And he entered again into the synagogue; and there was a man there which had a withered hand.

2 And they watched him, whether he would heal him on the sabbath day; that they might accuse him.

3 And he saith unto the man which had the withered hand, Stand forth.

4 And he saith unto them, Is it lawful to do good on the sabbath days, or to do evil? to save life, or to kill? But they held their peace.

5 And when he had looked round about on them with anger, being grieved for the hardness of their hearts, he saith unto the man, Stretch forth thine hand. And he stretched it out: and his hand was restored whole as the other.

6 And the Pharisees went forth, and straightway took counsel with the Herodians against him, how they might destroy him.

1. Healing (v. 1).—The Pharisees followed, and sought to enforce, their own rules for healing on the Sabbath. It should only be performed in cases where life was threatened. Less serious cases must wait until the Sabbath was over. But our Lord, confronted by a situation of human need, responded immediately. Notice that His critics did not question His ability to heal. This had been amply demonstrated. But they wanted to confine His healing activities to certain days and so protect their narrow Sabbath laws. While Pharisees on this occasion acted viciously against Jesus, we should recognize that their movement began, after the Babylonian exile, as an effort to recall their compatriots to a full observance of Old Testament laws. The problem was that this crusade of laypeople drifted into fanaticism and so away from the spirit of the Mosaic law.

2. Objection (vv. 2-4).—Whether the man with the withered hand had been "planted" in the synagogue that Sabbath we cannot say. But the developments pointed to this. Our Lord, perceiving His critics' intentions, questioned them on their own regulations for Sabbath healings (v. 4). But they would not respond, probably recognizing that they would be the losers in any public debate.

3. Reaction (v. 5).—The marks of an eyewitness (Peter?) are clearly seen throughout this Gospel with repeated references to Christ's looks, here of compassion, there of indignation, or even anger. The "Lord also of the sabbath" (2:28) was reacting in judgment against persons who showed more regard for their brand of prohibitions than they did for human tragedy. Unmoved by their antagonism, Jesus healed the maimed worshiper.

4. Conspiracy (v. 6).—More unlikely bedfellows than Pharisees and Herodians are hard to imagine. They were united in their determination to destroy Jesus Christ, but for very different reasons. For the Pharisees, the reason was religious; for the Herodians it was political. We now see why Mark brought together five incidents of controversy between Jesus and His critics. The crisis of hatred described in 3:6 did not take place only because of the healing of the man with the withered hand. There had been a series of confrontations in which our Lord had rejected interpretations of the law held by Pharisees. They, therefore, saw Him as a threat to their teaching and to their prestige. The Herodians, on the other hand, were Jews who had allied themselves with Herod Antipas, who held office under the appointment and authority of Rome. They saw Jesus as a danger to the peace and stability of the empire. For Mark's readers, these companions in conspiracy supplied the answer to Pilate's question about Jesus, "Why, what evil hath he done?" (15:14). The answer was none. He died the victim of prejudice and passion.

APPLYING THE LESSON

Two kinds of people.—Someone has suggested two kinds of people are in the world. One group is made up of those who get pleasure out of everything. With optimism and enthusiasm, they find the best in even the worst situations. The other group is made up of those who take pleasure out of everything. With criticism and complaining, they find the worst in even the best situations. Jesus often had to confront members of the second group.

Social gospel.—The term *social gospel* has fallen into disrepute in our day, but it is rooted in the example of Jesus Himself. Jesus did not isolate Himself from the world; He involved Himself in the world. He did not focus simply on spiritual needs; He provided assistance in the physical realm as well, healing the sick and feeding the hungry. The Salvation Army's motto, "Soap, soup, and salvation" beautifully encompasses the full dimensions of Christian concern. Like Jesus, we must be willing to associate with the sinners and the outcasts, so we can put them in touch with a God who can meet their needs.

A barn burner.—Especially close basketball games are often referred to as "barn burners." The phrase developed in an interesting way. In the early part of this century, basketball was just beginning to spread in popularity. Indiana became a seedbed for the developing interest in basketball. As early as 1911, the first official state high school tournament was held in Indiana with 12 teams competing. Basketball games were being staged everywhere: at skating rinks, in the driveways of a lumberyard, and even in a barn. That's where the term *barn burner* developed. The barns had wood-burning stoves to keep everyone warm. On certain occasions, when the game was especially close, the person responsible for tending the stove would forget. Consequently, a stray ember would fall to the floor, and often the barn would catch on fire.

The term *barn burner* has to do with priorities. The person responsible for the fire became more interested in watching the game than in tending the fire. Priorities became confused.

The religious leaders of Jesus' day had a problem with confused priorities. They were more concerned with "the letter of the law" than with human need. Consequently, they often clashed with Jesus to whom people were priority number one.

The importance of the Sabbath.—James Stewart illustrated the importance of the Sabbath with a reference to an ancient wall built across the north part of England. The Romans built the wall. At one mile intervals, they built towers that rose above the ordinary level of the wall. Sentinels, placed in the towers, were able to stand watch. Stewart applies this picture to the Sabbath. He said, "And when God built the battlements of our human life He placed at every seventh day a tower, a day thrust up above life's common levels, for the safeguarding of our souls."[2]

Compassion within the law.—Fiorello La Guardia was one of the most famous New York mayors. He gave strong leadership to the city, but he did so with compassion. On one occasion, he chose to preside in night court on a cold New York evening. An old lady was brought before the court and charged with stealing a loaf of bread. When asked why she did it, the poor lady responded, "My family is starving to death." The mayor replied, "I have to punish you because you broke the law, and the law makes no exceptions. I fine you $10." At that point, he pulled out of his own pocket $10 to cover the fine. In addition, he gave this challenge to the court: "I'm going to fine everybody in this courtroom fifty cents for living in a town where a person has to steal bread in order to eat." Then he ordered the bailiff to collect the fines and give them to the defendant." The hat was passed, and a total of $47.50 was given to the lady.

That's the spirit Jesus displayed. He did not wink at those who broke the law. Yet he found a way to affirm them and give them a chance to make a new beginning.

TEACHING THE CLASS

Main Idea: Opposition may follow presenting truth and doing good.

Suggested Teaching Aim: Learners will determine to deal constructively with opposition that may accompany presenting the truth of Jesus.

Introduce the Bible Study

Invite any learner who would like to do so to share an experience of introducing Jesus to someone during last week. Encourage learners to share witnessing testimonies for the purpose of encouraging one another. Note that the results of the witness is not the primary point in this discussion. Emphasize that it is the privilege and responsibility of learners to introduce others to Jesus. The results are between the hearer and God.

Share the story titled "Two kinds of people" (*Applying the Lesson*). Note that it may be expected that there would be opposition when the truth is presented. Ask: Did any of you experience opposition as you tried to introduce Jesus to others last week? Wait for their response.

State that the study for today shows how Jesus dealt with opposition that followed His doing good. Note that the purpose of the study is to enable us to identify some guidelines that will help us deal with opposition. Invite learners to open their Bibles to Mark 2.

Search for Biblical Truth

Note that the Scripture passage for today presents two incidents in which Jesus did something to help others and was soundly criticized for it. Assign a group to study Mark 2:23-28 to learn what the criticism was and discover how Jesus responded. Assign another group Mark 3:1-6 with the same instructions. Allow a time for study and discussion among the groups. When the group study is finished, call for response. Use questions like the following to guide the discussion:

What were Jesus and His disciples doing that received criticism in Mark 2:23-28? What was the custom about taking "corn" from a field that you did not own? Why were Jesus and His disciples criticized for this?

How did Jesus handle this criticism? (He used Scripture and the experience of His critics.) What claim did Jesus make for Himself?

What does the claim mean? Use the comments titled "Social gospel" (*Applying the Lesson*) during the discussion.

Continue with the second group using questions similar to the following to guide the discussion:

For what was Jesus criticized in the second incident? By whom was He criticized? Note that they did not question the ability or authority of Jesus to heal. How did Jesus handle the criticism? (He used logic, v. 4; He displayed anger and grief; He continued with His work.) What was the outcome of Jesus continuing to present truth in the face of such opposition?

A Teaching Outline

1. Consider the experience of facing opposition.
2. Discover the opposition Jesus faced.
3. Identify principles for dealing constructively with opposition.
4. Determine to accept and deal with opposition in constructive ways.

Share the comments titled "A barn burner" (*Applying the Lesson*). Emphasize the misplaced priorities of the Pharisees. Share comments titled "The importance of the Sabbath" (Applying the Lesson). Conclude this section with comments titled "Compassion within the law" from *Applying the Lesson.*

Give the Truth a Personal Focus

Direct learners to review the Scripture and recall the discussion to identify some principles that they may use to deal constructively with opposition. After a few minutes for review, call for response. Note responses on the chalkboard. Include the following. To deal with opposition,

1. be sure of your position in light of the Scripture.
2. share scriptural insight with those who criticize you.
3. be angry and sin not! Jesus felt anger but did not act on it.
4. understand the misguided position of those who criticize and feel grief for them.
5. continue to do what you know is right to do.

Conclude the study with a challenge to learners to determine to accept and deal with opposition in the way that Jesus did.

---

1. William L. Lane, *The Gospel of Mark* (Grand Rapids: Wm. B. Eerdmans Publishing Co., 1974), 15.
2. James Stewart, *The Strong Name* (Grand Rapids: Baker Book House, 1972), 241.

March 15

Without Honor in His Own Country

Basic Passage: Mark 6:1-13

Focal Passage: Mark 6:1-13

Official persecution from the emperor downward was not the only form of opposition that Christians in Rome had to bear. They were subjected to a good deal of misrepresentation and abuse from the citizenry in general. Scurrilous rumors were circulated about their observance of the Lord's Supper, which was seen as cannibalistic. Christian love feasts were distorted into orgies. Refusal to join in the salute "Caesar is Lord," substituting the words *Christ is Lord*, made Christians rebels against society. Mark, who—as seen in our previous lesson—described Jesus as the subject of attack from religious leaders, proceeded in 6:1-6 to tell how Jesus was rejected in His home territory. Had God's Son come into this world to live a protected life, He would have had little comfort or encouragement to offer to those who endure suffering. Because He "was in all points tempted [tested] like as we are" (Heb. 4:15), He is able to sympathize and help in every distress befalling His people.

Study Aim: *To add new dimensions to our understanding of "What a Friend we have in Jesus"*

STUDYING THE BIBLE

Mark clearly intended the contrast between the contents of chapter 5 and chapter 6. In the former, our Lord was in "the country of the Gadarenes" (v. 1), territory on the eastern shore of the Sea of Galilee that was predominantly Gentile. There He healed a demoniac, the daughter of a synagogue official, and an afflicted woman. In the heart of this record is the statement that "all men did marvel" (v. 20) followed by the information that "much people gathered unto him" (v. 21). Jesus enjoyed occasions and periods of popularity. But there also were times when those to whom He could reasonably look for support turned against Him.

I. Rejected in Nazareth (Mark 6:1-6)

Because of His frequent visits to Capernaum it is referred to as "his own city" (Matt. 9:1). Mark's reference to "his own country," however, indicates the place where He was raised: Nazareth (Mark 6:1). A small and unimportant town ("Can there any good thing come out of Nazareth?" John 1:46), it furnished residence and income for our Lord until the beginning of His public ministry, a period approaching thirty years.

1 And he went out from thence, and came into his own country; and his disciples follow him.

2 And when the sabbath day was come, he began to teach in the synagogue: and many hearing him were astonished, saying, From whence hath this man these things? and what wisdom is this which is given unto him, that even such mighty works are wrought by his hands?

3 Is not this the carpenter, the son of Mary, the brother of James, and Joses, and of Juda, and Simon? and are not his sisters here with us? And they were offended at him.

4 But Jesus said unto them, A prophet is not without honor, but in his own country, and among his own kin, and in his own house.

5 And he could there do no mighty work, save that he laid his hands upon a few sick folk, and healed them.

6 And he marveled because of their unbelief. And he went round about the villages, teaching.

1. Synagogue teaching (vv. 1-2a).—That was an interesting congregation in Nazareth's synagogue that Sabbath morning. Jesus was there with His disciples, and presumably His mother and her family, plus a variety of friends and neighbors. Jesus was of sufficient repute to be asked to expound the reading from the Old Testament. But what He said, and the way He said it, served only to arouse hostility.

2. Critical questions (vv. 2b-3).—Here is the only place in Scripture where Jesus is called "the carpenter." We are left to assume that Joseph was dead and Jesus had followed his trade. But on the lips of His critics, the statement was derogatory: He is not an educated person but only a manual worker. Probably "the son of Mary" was also said in spite, perpetuating the rumor that Jesus was her illegitimate child. Of the brothers named, James became a leader in the Jerusalem church (Acts 12:17) and author of the epistle that bears his name, while Juda, or Jude, also has an epistle to his credit. Of His half-sisters we are told nothing, not even their names. Apparently, the family as a whole did not rate very high in the estimate of the critics.

3. Proverb quoted (v. 4).—Our Lord reacted with a proverbial saying that He elaborated to include "his own kin" and "his own house."

Prophets had been notoriously rejected by the people to whom they were sent, some even being put to death, as would happen in Jesus' own case. Mark had already told us of the attitude of His family and friends (3:21,31-35). Mary's part is not clearly spelled out, but Luke 2:52 and John 19:25 encourage the belief that she remained loyal and loving.

4. Limited ministry (v. 5).—Mark did not intend to suggest any loss of healing power on the part of our Lord. This is why he recorded the miraculous healing of a "few sick folk." But the majority of the people of Nazareth placed themselves beyond the possibility of healing by their unbelief. While our Lord did not always respond to demonstrated faith in His works of healing, blatant unbelief was and is a barrier to blessing.

5. Other fields (v. 6).—Should the second half of this verse be considered as the conclusion to the previous verses, or as introductory to what follows? Opinions differ. If the former, then it says that our Lord entered other areas because of the unbelief in Nazareth. If the latter, it tells us that after a tour of teaching in Galilee, in which He saw the need, Jesus commissioned His disciples to a missionary journey of their own. The text does not help toward a decision, but we can make our own. We could conclude that the statement, "And he went round about the villages, teaching," looks both backward and forward.

II. Commissioning the Twelve (Mark 6:7-13)

Parallel accounts of the commissioning of the disciples are found in Matthew 10:5-15 and Luke 9:1-6. In the former it is expressly stated that the disciples were not to enter Samaritan cities, but they were to "go rather to the lost sheep of the house of Israel" (vv. 5-6). This contrasts with our Lord's farewell instructions, "Go ye therefore, and teach all nations" (28:19) and indicates that Mark's verses concern a temporary approach and do not provide instructions for all missionary endeavors.

7 And he called unto him the twelve, and began to send them forth by two and two; and gave them power over unclean spirits;

8 And commanded them that they should take nothing for their journey, save a staff only; no scrip, no bread, no money in their purse:

9 But be shod with sandals; and not put on two coats.

10 And he said unto them, In what place soever ye enter into an house, there abide till ye depart from that place.

11 And whosoever shall not receive you, nor hear you, when ye depart thence, shake off the dust under your feet for a testimony

against them. Verily I say unto you, It shall be more tolerable for Sodom and Gomorrah in the day of judgment, than for that city.
12 And they went out, and preached that men should repent.
13 And they cast out many devils, and anointed with oil many that were sick, and healed them.

1. Two by two (v. 7).—There was more than provision of companionship in sending the disciples in pairs. In the Old Testament, truth was established in the mouths of two witnesses (Deut. 17:6). Since the mission of the disciples was to Jews, their message was more impressive coming from two people. The dual witness also made rejection the more serious.

2. Minimum baggage (vv. 8-9).—The mission was to be brief and urgent. Time was of the essence. So the disciples were to take no excess baggage; they were to depend on the hospitality of others. Two essentials were permitted, staff and sandals. The staff would serve as a walking aid, for they must walk wherever they went. It also might be necessary for protection against unfriendly animals. Other prohibitions were "no bread, no bag, no money in their belts," and "two tunics" (NRSV). For food they were to depend on those to whom they ministered. The bag was that carried by beggars, and this role was forbidden. The word used for money defined the copper coins that were least in value, as we might say, "no small change." A second tunic, or shirt, would be carried as protection against night chills. Again, the intention was that the twelve should learn to depend on God for all supplies, and they might expect needed provision from people whom He moved to generosity.

3. Lodging instructions (v. 10).—Accommodations first offered were to be stayed with for the duration of a visit to a community. Temptation to exchange inadequate or uncomfortable lodging for something better would be strong. But to yield would be to insult well-intentioned hosts and would violate the spirit of humility Christ's followers were supposed to display.

4. Rejection response (v. 11).—Clear warning was given the disciples that they would suffer rejection as had their Master. This message would have special meaning for many first-century Christians who read Mark's Gospel. An established custom among Jews was to shake dust from the feet on leaving Gentile territory, a gesture of dissociation from unbelievers. For the disciples to do this was "a testimony against" people who rejected their message, a warning of judgment to come. For it would not be the disciples who were rejected, but He who sent them, of whom it was written that "He came unto his own, and his own received him not" (John 1:11). Rejection of the gospel is more serious in God's sight than the sins of Sodom and Gomorrah, cities that were destroyed in Abraham's time (Gen. 18—19).

5. Message and ministry (vv. 12-13).—The mission of the twelve was an extension of their Lord's. They preached repentance, healed the sick, and cast out demons. Illness and demonic possession are distinguished here, as elsewhere in the New Testament. The two should not be confused. By words and works the twelve were heralds of God's kingdom, setting a pattern that is followed in missionary service today.

APPLYING THE LESSON

Misjudging the value.—Just before the Civil War, a young man named Jim was in search of work. He approached Worthy Taylor's prosperous Ohio farm. The farmer decided to give the boy a job. Jim spent the summer cutting wood for the stove, bringing in the cows, and making himself generally useful. He ate in the kitchen and slept in the barn. Worthy Taylor liked the boy's work, but he became concerned when he learned that Jim had fallen in love with his daughter. Mr. Taylor refused to let Jim marry his daughter. He reminded him that he had no money, no name, and few prospects for the future. In great disappointment, Jim packed his few things and left.

Twenty-five years passed. One day Taylor pulled down his barn to build a new one. On one of the rafters just above the place where young Jim had slept, Taylor saw a name carved on the wood. Only then did he learn that Jim had a full name—James A. Garfield. By that time, Jim had a name and great prospects for the future, for James A. Garfield, the boy whom Taylor had refused to let his daughter marry, was president of the United States.

Sometimes we overlook the value of someone because we measure them on the basis of external factors. Such was the approach of the citizens of Nazareth. They judged Jesus on the basis of their knowledge of His past and His family. They did not realize that this Jesus who seemed to have no name and few prospects for the future was actually the long-awaited Messiah.

You wouldn't have believed it.—When Billy came home from Sunday School, his mother asked him what he had learned. Billy said, "The teacher told the story about Moses and the Hebrews escaping from Egypt." Trying to draw her son out a little, Billy's mother asked, "And how did it happen?" "Well," Billy said, "the Hebrews were trying to get away from the Egyptians when all of a sudden they came up to this big body of water. So Moses called his engineers, and they constructed a pontoon bridge across that sea. The Hebrews crossed over to the other side. But then here came the Egyptians. They were crossing over the pontoon bridge when Moses called his explosion experts; they set some dynamite and blew up that pontoon bridge. And all the Egyptians were killed!"

The mother said, "Now, Billy, are you sure that's the way your teacher told the story?" Billy hung his head and replied, "No, but Mom, you wouldn't have believed it the way she told it!"

We have difficulty at times accepting the miraculous. We're no different than the people of the first century. They too had difficulty accepting the fact of Jesus' miraculous power. Their lack of faith limited what Jesus did in their midst.

The urgency of evangelism.—A friend of mine named Ken once pastored a small church in Mississippi. He planned a revival, and part of the promotion was a "pack-the-pew" night. He asked for volunteers. One man said, "Preacher, I haven't ever done it before, but I want to try. Do you mean we are to get people who have never been to church and pack them in the pew?" Ken replied in the affirmative. On the first night of the revival, this man brought 44 people to the revival service. On the second night he brought 69. Then, on the third night, he brought 26 more. He just dropped off a load, and then went back after another load. During the invitation on the third night, this man who had packed several pews during the revival walked forward to rededicate his life. He told Ken, "I just don't think I've been doing enough for the Lord." That's the kind of urgency Jesus encouraged His disciples to have as they went out with His message.

Living your witness.—At the age of 79, Malcolm Muggeridge, a British atheist, found the Lord. Asked to explain his conversion, he said, "I could resist all the great books and sermons. But when I saw Mother Teresa in Calcutta with the poor, I said to myself, 'If this is it, I've got to have it.' " Mother Teresa's life confirmed her faith, and together they made a tremendous impact for Christ on the life of Malcolm Muggeridge.[1]

TEACHING THE CLASS

Main Idea: The gift of God to humanity, Jesus Christ, is sometimes refused.

Suggested Teaching Aim: Learners will determine to present the gift of God to humanity, Jesus Christ, and leave the acceptance of the gift between the hearer and God.

Introduce the Bible Study

Remind learners that the unit of study focuses on highlights in the life of Jesus from the Book of Mark. State that the passage for today presents a strange but not uncommon phenomenon.

Share the comments titled "Misjudging the value" (*Applying the Lesson*). State that the Scripture for today illustrates how easy it is to misjudge the value of a gift. Invite learners to turn to Mark 6.

Search for Biblical Truth

Call on a learner to read Mark 6:1-6 aloud. When the reading is finished, ask: What gift was offered? What was the response? Why was its value misjudged? What was the result of the refusal of the gift?

A Teaching Outline

1. Focus on refusing a gift.
2. Discover how Jesus was refused by those who first knew Him.
3. Discover how the disciples were to handle refusal from their hearers.
4. Determine how to offer the gift of eternal life through Jesus to people.
5. Decide to leave the acceptance of the gift between the hearer and God.

Call on another learner to read Mark 6:7-13 aloud. When the reading is finished, ask: Who were the twelve? What assignment were they given? What were the specific instructions for carrying out the assignment? What was the result of their work?

Continue by focusing on the fact that the gift both Jesus and His disciples offered in these situations was rejected by some. Ask: Do you find that hard to believe? What would seem to have made the value of the gift unmistakable? (The miracles done both by Jesus and the disciples.) Share the comments titled "You wouldn't have believed it" from *Applying the Lesson.*

Give the Truth a Personal Focus

Share the comments titled "The urgency of evangelism" (*Applying the Lesson*). Note that this is the kind of urgency Jesus encouraged His disciples to have as they went out with His message, and it continues to be the kind of urgency that disciples today need in taking the message to others.

Recall the comment from last Sunday that the results of sharing the message of Jesus Christ is not the issue. Ask: What is a follower of Jesus to do when the gift of Jesus Christ is refused? Note Jesus' example and His instructions to the disciples in verse 11. Emphasize to learners that their task is to offer the gift, Jesus Christ, to other persons. Whether those persons receive that gift is to be left between those persons and God.

Share the comments titled "Living your witness" (*Applying the Lesson*). Point out that when Jesus instructed His disciples to go out, He told them how they were to live as they went. Ask: Why is the way you live your witness today important in the process of offering the gift of Jesus to others? Elicit response.

Invite learners to decide today to follow the instructions of Jesus about how to live their witness and to determine to leave acceptance of the gift of eternal life through Jesus Christ between the hearer and God.

1. Bruce Larson, *Wind and Fire* (Waco: Word Books, 1984), 89.

March 22

Restoration to Wholeness

Basic Passage: Mark 7:24-37

Focal Passage: Mark 7:24-37

Although the mission of the twelve—as we saw last week—was to Jewish communities with a restriction, "Go not into the way of the Gentiles" (Matt. 10:5), this was not to be the pattern for their future work. The principle, "to the Jew first," was embodied in our Lord's ministry but not to the exclusion of others. He created opportunities for a wider ministry as part of His introduction to the disciples, although they proved slow to learn that the good news entrusted to them was for all people. In the chapter from which this lesson is taken, a discussion about food is recorded, growing out of criticism of the disciples for not washing their hands before eating. The conclusion of those who heard, concerning the position taken by Jesus, was this: "Thus he declared all foods clean" (v. 19, NRSV). Yet later, when the question of clean and unclean foods was raised in a rooftop vision, Peter appeared to have forgotten this important lesson (Acts 10). Prejudices, particularly religious and racial, die hard. We all need the lesson of our Lord's Gentile ministries.

Study Aim: *To take as our example the compassion of our Lord who responded to human need wherever found*

STUDYING THE BIBLE

The two miracles of healing recorded in our lesson passage took place in non-Jewish territories. Tyre and Sidon were seaports in the Roman province of Syria, along the northern Mediterranean coast. They have survived as part of modern Lebanon. The Decapolis (Ten

Cities) was an area to the east and south of the Sea of Galilee with a predominantly Gentile population.

I. Jesus in Gentile Territory (Mark 7:24-30)

Mark's swiftly moving story recorded the execution of John the Baptist (6:17-29), the feeding of the five thousand (vv. 35-44), a summary of our Lord's healing activity (v. 56), and conflict with a delegation of Pharisees from Jerusalem over ritual practices (7:1-13). If Mark's intention was to present an energetic Christ, he certainly succeeded. But this intense activity was not without cost. Jesus sought relief in "a desert place" (6:32) and in mountaintop prayer (v. 46). Our lesson passage opens with a third effort to obtain peace and quiet.

24 And from thence he arose, and went into the borders of Tyre and Sidon, and entered into an house, and would have no man know it: but he could not be hid.

25 For a certain woman, whose young daughter had an unclean spirit, heard of him, and came and fell at his feet:

26 The woman was a Greek, a Syrophenician by nation; and she besought him that he would cast forth the devil out of her daughter.

27 But Jesus said unto her, Let the children first be filled: for it is not meet to take the children's bread, and to cast it unto the dogs.

28 And she answered and said unto him, Yes, Lord: yet the dogs under the table eat of the children's crumbs.

29 And he said unto her, For this saying go thy way; the devil is gone out of thy daughter.

30 And when she was come to her house, she found the devil gone out, and her daughter laid upon the bed.

1. Quest for rest (v. 24).—In His search for rest, it was reasonable that our Lord should get out of the territory ruled by Herod Antipas, the man who had put John the Baptist to death. But by so doing, He gave emphasis to His teaching in the earlier verses of the chapter. The legalism that required hand washing and the avoidance of certain foods had also been made to apply to association with foreigners. Though having a major mission to His own people, our Lord had the world in His heart.

2. A mother's faith (vv. 25-26).—She is described as Greek, or Gentile, and a native of the area. Although Jesus was in "an house" (v. 24), this mother sought Him out. Mark's comment, "he could not be hid," reflects the growing fame of Jesus, which penetrated into Gentile territory. The woman evidently had heard of His miracles of healing and boldly requested that He should heal her daughter.

3. A test passed (vv. 27-28).—The racial slur that referred to Gentiles as "dogs" would be generally known. Our Lord used the diminutive of the word and thus softened the implication. Had we heard His tones, or seen His eyes, we would doubtless have recognized that He was probing the woman's faith. She rose splendidly to the occasion, and echoing His phrase, "little dogs," or puppies, she claimed His help for her afflicted child. Puppies, she said, eat the crumbs that fall from the children's table. The disciples were witnesses to this witty exchange and hopefully benefited from it.

4. Request granted (vv. 29-30).—There was pleasure and commendation in our Lord's reaction, "For this saying go thy way." The Gentile woman had shown remarkable faith and confidence in Him, and for this her wish was granted. No contact was made with the daughter, only an instruction to the mother to return home where she found the miracle had taken place.

II. Jesus Praised by Gentiles (Mark 7:31-37)

The miracle performed ended the possibility of further rest for our Lord in that place. So He left "the region of Tyre" (v. 31, NRSV), made His way northward toward Sidon, and then made a broad sweep east and south into what was known as the Decapolis. He remained, therefore, in Gentile territory, skirting Galilee but not entering it. No reason for this is given, but the journey would have been long and arduous, testing the physical condition of Jesus and His disciples. It would certainly have provided a lot of solitude, which we may believe Jesus used for the instruction of the twelve.

31 And again, departing from the coasts of Tyre and Sidon, he came unto the sea of Galilee, through the midst of the coasts of Decapolis.

32 And they bring unto him one that was deaf, and had an impediment in his speech; and they beseech him to put his hand upon him.

33 And he took him aside from the multitude, and put his fingers into his ears, and he spit, and touched his tongue;

34 And looking up to heaven, he sighed, and saith unto him, Ephphatha, that is, Be opened.

35 And straightway his ears were opened, and the string of his tongue was loosed, and he spake plain.

36 And he charged them that they should tell no man: but the more he charged them, so much the more a great deal they published it;

37 And were beyond measure astonished, saying, He hath done all things well: he maketh both the deaf to hear, and the dumb to speak.

1. Man in distress (vv. 31-32).—Who brought this deaf-mute to Jesus, identified only by the pronoun "they," we cannot tell, but we must presume it refers to friends of the man. They had learned of our Lord's healing powers and sought His help for this afflicted man. The history of his disease is not disclosed, but deaf people frequently have distorted speech, described in this case as "an impediment." A somewhat rare Greek word is used here, also found in the Greek translation of Isaiah 35:5, "Then the eyes of the blind shall be opened, and the ears of the deaf shall be unstopped," a verse that must have been in Mark's mind as he wrote. There is no specific statement as to the race of the deaf-mute, but the strong possibility is that he was a Gentile. Edersheim wrote of the Decapolis that "the district and all the surroundings were essentially heathen, although in close proximity to, and intermingling with, that which was purely Jewish. . . . Remembering, that alike the subject of the miracle and they who brought him were heathens, but in constant and close contact with Jews, what follows is vividly true to life."[1]

2. Faith stimulated (vv. 33-35).—Clearly our Lord wanted to concentrate the attention of the man upon Himself and what He would do. He drew him away from the crowd before He began a process of healing that was appropriate to the sufferer. First, He put His fingers in the man's ears to make him aware that attention was being paid to his defective hearing. Probably until this point, the man was totally unaware of what was going on and why he had been brought to Jesus. Then He applied saliva to the man's tongue, indicating that both his hearing and speech were matters of concern. Saliva was regarded as a remedy for some conditions. Familiar words from our childhood may perpetuate this idea: "Let mother kiss it and make it better." Then Jesus looked up to heaven, perhaps a hint to a person of limited understanding that the desired help would come from above, from God. Then He sighed, or groaned; either word applies. Was He expressing His own deep desire to help this stranger? Or was He releasing the power within Him that was available to all persons in distress? The sigh was followed by one spoken word, *Ephphatha*, in the language of everyday Palestinian speech, Aramaic. This was a command, "Be opened!" that was immediately obeyed by the man's normally unresponsive ears and tongue.

3. Popularity gained (v. 36).—Our Lord consistently sought to avoid the kind of popularity that centered in works of healing. He had an important ministry of teaching to discharge, and curious crowds could hinder this. At this particular time He was seeking solitude with His disciples for they all needed rest before engaging in other activities. But efforts to restrain the enthusiasm of the crowds were in vain.

The healing they had witnessed made them ardent publicity agents so that "the more he ordered them, the more zealously they proclaimed it" (NRSV). Though this zeal frustrated the immediate purpose of our Lord, its irrepressible nature was to the credit of these inhabitants of Decapolis.

4. High tribute (v. 37).—In a real sense, the miracle of that day was not only for the benefit of one individual, but also for all who witnessed it. Many ears were opened to hear the voice of God in the words of Jesus, and many tongues were loosed to sing praises to God because of the works of the Son. This was a Gentile doxology, "He hath done all things well," destined to become a worldwide chorus so that in Rome itself Father and Son would be glorified in the grateful tributes of the church.

APPLYING THE LESSON

The packaging of the gospel.—John Killinger has concluded that how the gospel is packaged makes a great difference in how it is perceived. Then he explained: "If the gospel is located in the sacraments, as it was for the medieval church, it is endowed with a magical effect. If it is disguised in sophisticated theology, it becomes gnostic. Encased in mysticism, it appears devotional. Couched in morality, it issues in legalism. And if it is displayed in 'celebrities,' as it often is in TV religion, it simply becomes cheap and tawdry."[2]

At the beginning, the gospel was couched in "Jewish" terms, and the Jews were the first to respond. From that Jewish base, the gospel message began to spread. As it was presented to different audiences, the gospel was couched in a way that Gentiles also began to respond.

The way of health.—Jonathan Swift once wrote, "The best doctors in the world are Dr. Diet, Dr. Quiet, and Dr. Merryman."[3] That's a unique way of saying we need to eat right, rest right, and learn to laugh if we are to experience true health today. What is true today was also true in Jesus' day. Jesus recognized the need for rest; thus, on numerous occasions He tried to withdraw from the crowds for a time of solitude and prayer. Such retreats became increasingly difficult for Jesus as His popularity increased.

Confidence.—The sergeant put the binoculars to his eyes and surveyed the situation. He spotted some enemy troops to the west. He turned to the north and spotted more of the enemy. Again, to the east and south he saw the same thing. He gathered his men together and said, "All right, we are completely surrounded by the enemy. Let's not let a single one of them escape."

The Greek woman with a sick daughter had a similar attitude. Undaunted by Jesus' reference to the Gentiles as dogs, she persevered in her confidence that Jesus could and would heal her daughter. Confronted by seemingly unsurmountable obstacles, she nevertheless persisted in her faith.

The purpose of Jesus' miracles.—Warren Wiersbe suggests that Jesus had three purposes in mind when He performed His miracles: "(1) to show compassion and meet human need; (2) to present His credentials as the Son of God; and (3) to convey spiritual truth."[4] All three of these purposes were involved in the miraculous healing of the Greek woman's daughter.

The importance of friends.—Someone has defined a friend as a person who steps in when the whole world steps out. When adversity comes, that's the best time to count your friends. Often they will be fair-weather friends like those of the prodigal son who deserted him when he could no longer help them (Luke 15). Only rarely do we find true friends who will be there when we need them the most, like Jonathan was to David (1 Sam. 20). Evidently, the deaf man in our text had the kind of true friends who stood by him in his need and brought him to Jesus to be healed.

Unwilling to give thanks.—Two young adults were talking. One said to the other, "I'm on my way over to pick up my unemployment check. Then I'm going over to the university office to see what the delay is on this month's federal education grant. Then I'm going to pick up the food stamps while you go over to the free health clinic and check up on your tests. On the way home, I'll drop around at the Welfare Department and demand our eligibility limit again. Then I'll meet you at the Federal Building at 4:00 p.m. for another mass demonstration against this stinking, rotten, self-centered establishment!"

The image is perhaps a little overdrawn. The spirit of the story, however, is consistent with many in our day who receive benefits and encouragement and assistance from others, but then display a complete lack of gratitude. They take for granted what is given instead of taking it with gratitude.

When Jesus healed the deaf man, the observers responded with gratitude and praise. They recognized Jesus as the source of the healing, and they exalted Him as Someone special.

TEACHING THE CLASS

Main Idea: Compassion is not to be limited by prejudice.

Suggested Teaching Aim: Learners will determine special ways to communicate the gospel to persons who cannot receive it in traditional ways.

Introduce the Bible Study

Note that lessons in Mark have emphasized the need for believers to share the gospel of Jesus Christ with others. State that if believers are to be effective when they share the gospel, they must package the gospel so that it can be received. Share the comments titled "The packaging of the gospel" (*Applying the Lesson*).

Note that the study for today shows Jesus responding to people who were outside His usual hearing audience. It shows how Jesus demonstrated compassion on these outsiders and packaged the gospel so that they could receive it. Invite learners to turn to Mark 7.

Search for Biblical Truth

Use the following outline to guide the Bible study.

Compassion for Outsiders

1. Jesus in Gentile territory
   a. A mother's faith (vv. 24-26)
   b. Compassion extended (vv. 27-30)
2. Jesus praised by Gentiles
   a. A man in distress (vv. 31-32)
   b. Faith stimulated (vv. 33-36)

Call on a learner to read Mark 7:24 aloud. Note that Jesus tried to get away from the crowds that drained His energy. Share the comments titled "The way of health" (*Applying the Lesson*).

Call attention to the heading for verses 24-26. Direct learners to read the passage to themselves to discover who this mother was and the request that she made. After a brief study, call for response. Share information from *Studying the Bible* to supplement responses.

A Teaching Outline

1. Focus on need to package the gospel in different ways.
2. Explore Jesus' willingness to demonstrate who He was in special ways for hearers who could not hear the message in traditional ways.
3. Determine ways to share the gospel today with persons who cannot receive it in traditional ways.

Direct learners to read verses 27-30 to discover how Jesus answered the mother's request. When reading is finished, ask questions similar to these: Why did Jesus speak to her as He did in verse 27? What attitude is indicated by her response? Why was Jesus willing to extend Himself for this Gentile woman? Note the woman's confidence. Share the comments titled "Confidence" (*Applying the Lesson*).

Note that the possibility of rest for Jesus and His disciples had diminished. His fame spread quickly because of this miracle. Others were now brought to Him for healing.

Direct learners to read of one brought in verses 31-32. Note the heading for verses 33-37. Direct learners to read the verses for information about how the man's faith was stimulated. When the reading is finished, call for response. Ask: Why did the deaf man come to Jesus if he did not know enough about Him to have faith? Share the comments titled "The importance of friends" (*Applying the Lesson*). Continue by asking: What was the response of the friends after Jesus healed the man? Share the comments titled "Unwilling to give thanks" (*Applying the Lesson*).

Give the Truth a Personal Focus

Share the comments titled "The purpose of Jesus' miracles" (*Applying the Lesson*). Ask: What seems to be Jesus' purpose in these miracles? Elicit response. Responses should include demonstration of compassion, refusal to be limited by prejudice, and opening the way for these persons to believe that He was the Messiah.

Recall packaging of the gospel so that it can be received was discussed as the study began. Ask: In what special ways did Jesus package the message so that these two persons could receive it?

Continue: Who are some persons today who may not be able to receive the gospel in the traditional ways? Wait for response. Suggestions should include persons with no church or religious background, persons of another culture or ethnic background who now live in our communities, persons who speak another language, persons who have negative attitudes toward the church.

Ask: How can the gospel be more effectively packaged so that persons like these will be able to receive the message? Elicit response.

Conclude by asking: How much trouble are you willing to go to so that others may receive the message?

---

1. Alfred Edersheim, *Life and Times of Jesus*, vol. 2 (New York: Longmans Green, 1956), 45.
2. John Killinger, "The Packaging of the Gospel," *Pulpit Digest* (May-June, 1985): 53.
3. James E. Hightower, Jr., ed., *Caring for Folks from Birth to Death* (Nashville: Broadman Press, 1985), 84.
4. Warren Wiersbe, *Be Dynamic* (Wheaton, Ill.: Victor Books, 1984), 67.

March 29

The Messiah and Suffering

Basic Passage: Mark 8:27—9:13

Focal Passage: Mark 8:27—9:1

Determination of correct emphasis is important to the understand ing of many statements. Context must often be our guide in making this determination. There can be little reason for doubt that in His question addressed to the disciples our Lord put the emphasis on a personal pronoun, "But who do *you* say that I am?" (v. 29, NRSV, author's italics). Many opinions about Him were circulating among those who had contact with Him, and He was not indifferent to their opinions. Of greatest concern to Him was the opinion held by His disciples. Peter's answer, doubtless made in behalf of the twelve, was factually correct, but as events proved, mistakenly interpreted. He rightly saluted Jesus as the Messiah, but Peter's concept of messiahship was wrong. This raises the question: How many present disciples of our Lord hold incorrect, or inadequate, opinions about Him? Is He their Savior from sin and its consequences, or is He, to quote Peter's later words (2 Pet. 3:18), their "Lord and Savior Jesus Christ"? Our lesson affords opportunity to assess both our relationship to Him and opinion of Him.

Study Aim: *To deepen understanding of the person and mission of our Lord*

STUDYING THE BIBLE

We are at the watershed of Mark's Gospel, the point from which the true identity and mission of the Lord Jesus are made clear. For seven plus chapters, we have read of activities and sayings that led to such contradictory judgments as that of Jerusalem scribes who accused Him of being in league with "Beelzebub, . . . the prince of the devils" (3:22) and the testimony of the Gadarene demoniac that He was "Son of the most high God" (5:7). The time had come for clarification of Jesus' true identity and of the reason why He had come into the world as God's incarnate Son.

I. Question and Answer (Mark 8:27-29)

Chapter 7 concludes with the record of the healing of a man who "was deaf, and had an impediment in his speech" (7:31-37). The next chapter opens with the miraculous feeding of a multitude (8:1-9), presumably the second of such feedings (vv. 19-20). The healing of a blind man immediately follows (vv. 22-26), with this question separating the incidents, "How is it that ye do not understand?" (v. 21). With all the evidence before them, people, including the disciples, failed to understand who Jesus was.

> **27 And Jesus went out, and his disciples, into the towns of Caesarea Philippi: and by the way he asked his disciples, saying unto them, Whom do men say that I am?**
>
> **28 And they answered, John the Baptist: but some say, Elijah; and others, One of the prophets.**
>
> **29 And he saith unto them, But whom say ye that I am? And Peter answereth and saith unto him, Thou art the Christ.**

1. The location (v. 27).—Jesus took His disciples to an area near Mount Hermon and the source of the Jordan River. It contained a shrine dedicated to the pagan god Pan, giving the name Paneas to a nearby community. There Herod Philip had built his residence and renamed the community in honor of Caesar (Tiberius). Caesarea Philippi was associated first with pagan worship and then with the worship of the emperor. It was an impressive location for Jesus to seek an answer concerning His own identity.

2. Popular opinions (v. 28).—The opinions cited were all highly complimentary. John the Baptist remained a revered name among many Jews. Elijah occupied a prominent place among Israel's prophets and was expected to reappear as herald to the promised Messiah. Some, less enthusiastic in their appraisal of Jesus, nevertheless considered Him "One of the prophets."

3. Messiah acknowledged (v. 29).—Peter, presumably speaking for all the disciples, readily acknowledged Jesus as the Messiah, or Christ. This was a huge step of faith, but unfortunately it was qualified by the prevailing concept of messiahship. The question in Acts 1:6 shows how firmly even the disciples clung to the idea that Jesus would be a patriotic leader who would restore to Israel the power and prestige that had been lost.

II. Solemn Truth Revealed (Mark 8:30-33)

This misconception threatened our Lord's ministry. After the feeding of the five thousand, attempt was made to make Him king, causing Him to seek solitude in "a mountain himself alone" (John 6:15). The redemptive work, for which He came into the world, would not be achieved by self-glorification but by self-sacrifice.

30 And he charged them that they should tell no man of him.
31 And he began to teach them, that the Son of man must suffer many things, and be rejected of the elders, and of the chief priests, and scribes, and be killed, and after three days rise again.
32 And he spake that saying openly. And Peter took him, and began to rebuke him.
33 But when he had turned about and looked on his disciples, he rebuked Peter, saying, Get thee behind me, Satan: for thou savorest not the things that be of God, but the things that be of men.

1. Ban imposed (v. 30).—The disciples were forbidden to spread the news that He was the Christ, not because this was not true but because it would be erroneously interpreted. At a time when opposition to Roman rule was high, an outbreak of popular support for Jesus as the long-promised deliverer of His people could have disastrous consequences.

2. Future foretold (v. 31).—The time had come for a clear statement on the course Jesus would take to fulfil His mission. He spelled out in some detail the antagonism He faced, not public acclaim but official rejection that would lead to His violent death. However, this rejection would be countered by divine approval for He would "after three days rise again." This stupendous announcement concerning His resurrection was apparently lost on the disciples who, through Peter, reacted only to the prospect of His death.

3. Rebuke administered (vv. 32-33).—Peter's expressed confidence in Jesus as the Christ was so contrary to the picture Jesus had drawn that Peter broke out in loud protest. Before replying our Lord "looked on his disciples" indicating what He was about to say was important for all of them. To repudiate the sacrificial death of their Master was to do the devil's work, for from the beginning Satan had sought to steer Him away from the cross (see Matt. 4:1-11).

III. Like Master, Like Servant (Mark 8:34-38)

Misunderstanding of the true mission of Jesus carries over into misunderstanding what is involved in being His disciple. This was reflected in Peter's question, "Behold, we have forsaken all, and followed thee; what shall we have therefore?" (Matt. 19:27). True Christianity does not major on getting, but on giving.

34 And when he had called the people unto him with his disciples also, he said unto them, Whosoever will come after me, let him deny himself, and take up his cross, and follow me.

35 For whosoever will save his life shall lose it; but whosoever shall lose his life for my sake and the gospel's, the same shall save it.
36 For what shall it profit a man, if he shall gain the whole world, and lose his own soul?
37 Or what shall a man give in exchange for his soul?
38 Whosoever therefore shall be ashamed of me and of my words in this adulterous and sinful generation; of him also shall the Son of man be ashamed, when he cometh in the glory of his Father with the holy angels.

1. Saying no to self (v. 34).—Those who were disciples, and others who might contemplate discipleship, needed to know that following Jesus demanded self-denial, saying no to self. This means more than saying no to bad habits; self must abdicate that Christ may be enthroned. Surrender of life itself could be involved, as it was for some of the twelve and for many of the Christians in Rome who would read Mark's Gospel.

2. Grave alternatives (vv. 35-38).—Roman Christians were put to the test by being called on to say, "Caesar is Lord," whereas they should say, "Jesus is Lord." To suppress this Christian confession with the purpose of saving one's life (soul) would really result in losing it at the final reckoning. For the time is coming when the glorified Christ will either acknowledge or disown His professed followers.

IV. Prospect of Coming Glory (Mark 9:1)

Our Lord avoided the term *messiah* because of prevailing misunderstandings and substituted "Son of man" (vv. 31,38), possibly borrowed from Daniel 7:13. This Old Testament use of the phrase describes a victorious figure who reigned over "an everlasting dominion" and a "kingdom that which shall not be destroyed" (v. 14). The substitution, therefore, was not a denial of messiahship but an avoidance of a title that had become distorted in meaning. Both 8:38 and 9:1 support the prospect of future power and glory for the speaker.

1 And he said unto them, Verily I say unto you, That there be some of them that stand here, which shall not taste of death, till they have seen the kingdom of God come with power.

1. Possible meanings.—These words have been seen to have reference to our Lord's resurrection (see Rom. 1:4), to the descent of the Holy Spirit at Pentecost (Acts 2), and to the effective witness of the church, beginning at Jerusalem "and unto the uttermost part of the earth" (Acts 1:8). To regard them as referring to our Lord's second coming is to ignore His statement about "them that stand here."

2. Immediate significance.—Apparently, it was Mark's intention to associate our Lord's words with His transfiguration, which he described in verses 2-10. The impression made by this event on Peter is indicated in 2 Peter 1:16-18. The revelation of coming rejection and death, given in Mark 8:31, was shocking. But it was not the final scene, for the Victim of the cross would be vindicated in future glory in the setting up of God's eternal kingdom. A foretaste of that glory was given in the transfiguration.

APPLYING THE LESSON

What was it?—A beggar knocked on the door of a country home and asked the woman who came to the door for a donation. After chewing him out for wanting someone to take care of him, the woman provided this opportunity. She said, "If you will paint my porch, I'll give you $25." The beggar agreed to work for his money, so she handed him the paint and brush and went about her business. After a while the man knocked on the door again and asked for his $25. "Did you finish the job?" she asked. "Yes," he replied, "but I do need to tell you, it was not a Porsche, it was a Mercedes!"

How often we misunderstand the meanings of words. We should not be surprised, then, that in the New Testament period the word *messiah* was often misunderstood. This religious word was understood by different people in different ways. We see the misunderstanding in the encounter between Jesus and the disciples in our text.

The disentangled Christ.—E. Stanley Jones was one of the most effective missionaries in history. He led many in the Far East to a deep and abiding faith in Jesus Christ. When asked how he was able to have such effect, Jones pointed to a decision he made early in his ministry. He said, "The Christ I presented would be the disentangled Christ—disentangled from being bound up with Western culture and Western forms of Christianity."[1] At Caesarea Philippi, this is what Jesus tried to do for the disciples. He wanted to present to them a picture of the "disentangled Christ," disentangled from the images and distortions prevalent among the Jews of that day.

Another picture of the cross.—The Russian Orthodox tradition presents a cross a little different from the cross we are used to seeing. Instead of an upright with just one crosspiece, the Russian Orthodox cross has two other smaller crosspieces as well, one just slightly above the central one and the other one down toward the foot. The crosspiece at the top represents the sign nailed over Jesus' head upon which were the words: "Jesus of Nazareth the King of the Jews (John 19:19)," a message written in Hebrew, Latin, and Greek. The second piece toward the bottom of the cross represents the block placed beneath his feet so Jesus would not fall off the cross and prematurely end his punishment. This lower crosspiece is placed at a slant, with one end lower than the other. This is to show that when the pain was so severe Jesus pressed down hard on one foot, thus causing the crosspiece to be at a slant.

The Russian Orthodox cross brings together the paradoxical elements of Calvary—the suffering of Christ and at the same time the sovereignty of Christ. The cross symbolizes the suffering of Christ, but it also symbolizes the victory He won on our behalf. At Caesarea Philippi, Jesus began deliberately pointing to the cross where His suffering and sovereignty would come together.

Commitment.—A regiment in World War II was sluggish and lacking in discipline. Consequently, a new colonel was assigned to bring the troop into shape. Before long, it was the best regiment in its division. The members of the regiment were eager, enthusiastic, and exemplars of excellence. One day a general came to visit. As he carried out his inspection, he discovered the letters "AAA-O" written on all of the equipment as well as on the helmets of the soldiers. "What do the letters 'AAA-O' mean?" the general asked. The colonel replied, "they stand for 'Anywhere, Anytime, Anything bar Nothing.' " That is the kind of commitment Jesus demands of those who follow Him.

Did we win?—I still remember one of my first experiences as a soccer coach. The boys were all under eight years of age. Most had never played soccer before that season. The team finally came together, and we scored three goals to none by the opposing team. After the game, our boys were jumping up and down, patting each other on the back, rejoicing. I asked, "Does anybody have anything to say?" One little boy raised his hand and said, "Coach, did we win?"

As the shadow of the cross fell across the disciples in those final days with the Master, they may have wondered whether or not Jesus was going to win. Only from the perspective of the resurrection did the disciples realize the full meaning of the title He chose for Himself, Son of man. Only then did they realize the fullness of their victory in Christ.

TEACHING THE CLASS

Main Idea: Followers of Jesus are called to lose their lives for His sake.

Suggested Teaching Aim: Learners will evaluate their understanding of what is involved in being followers of Jesus.

Introduce the Bible Study

Share the story titled "What was it?"(Applying the Lesson). Ask: Do you think most church members today understand what is involved in being a follower of Jesus? Why or Why not? Is it possible that the mistake is as far reaching as the misunderstanding of the man who painted the Porsche?

Write the main idea on the chalkboard. Note that it is a nutshell statement of what followers of Jesus are to do. Ask: What does it mean? Response will probably indicate some vagueness about the meaning of the statement. Show that the study for today will help them to evaluate their understanding of what it means to be a follower of Jesus.

Search for Biblical Truth

Invite learners to open their Bibles to Mark 8. Remind learners of the miraculous events studied last Sunday found in Mark 7. Direct learners to scan chapter 8, verses 1-9, to discover another miracle. Direct them to verses 22-26 for another miracle. Call on a learner to read verse 21 aloud. Note that with all the evidence before them, people, including the disciples, were still confused. Note that Jesus turned aside to address the issue directly with His disciples. Call on a learner to read Mark 8:27-29 aloud. Ask: What was the popular opinion about who Jesus was? Why would they be confused about this? Who did the disciples think that He was? Although they knew the right words to say in response to the question, did they clearly understand who Jesus was? Why?

A Teaching Outline

1. Consider misunderstanding of the meaning of being a follower of Jesus.
2. Describe how Jesus explained the meaning of following Him.
3. Determine guidelines for evaluating understanding of following Jesus.
4. Evaluate personal understanding against the guidelines from Scripture.

State that, in the next portion of the Scripture, Jesus began to deal with their misunderstanding. Call on a learner to read verses 30-33. Ask: Why would Jesus address Peter as Satan in this incident? Point out the depth of misunderstanding reflected in this incident.

Note that Jesus now called together the disciples and the people to give some deeper explanation of what following Him means. Call on a learner to read verses 34-38 aloud.

Ask: Suppose you had been in the crowd on that day. How would you have interpreted Jesus' remarks? What would you have thought that He meant for you to do? Elicit brief response.

If appropriate in your group, provide paper and pen for each learner. Direct them to assume the role of one who was in the group that day and write a letter to someone back home about what Jesus said and what they are planning to do because of it. Allow time for learners to compose the letter. When finished, call on someone who is willing to do so to share his or her letter. Ask others to add comments from their letters to make clear what Jesus meant when He said His followers must lose their lives for His sake and the gospel.

Give the Truth a Personal Focus

Ask: Do you think you understand what it means to lay down your life for Jesus today? What are some guidelines by which you can measure your thinking? List them on the chalkboard. The following should be included:

1. Followers of Jesus will suffer and be rejected by others (v. 31).
2. Followers of Jesus will be more concerned about Jesus and His work than about themselves (v. 34).
3. Followers of Jesus will not have a life of their own but will, instead, give up their lives for the gospel (v. 35).

When guidelines have been noted on the chalkboard, ask: Is this what you understand is required if you are to be a follower of Jesus? Encourage learners to privately measure their understanding against these guidelines from the Scripture.

---

1. E. Stanley Jones, *A Song of Ascents* (Nashville: Abingdon Press, 1968), 110.

April 5

Love Says It All

Basic Passages: Deuteronomy 6:4-9; Mark 12:28-37
Focal Passage: Mark 12:28-37

We have entered April, and we are fast approaching the celebration of Easter. For us, the season is one of brightness and joy, for spring has come, and nature is putting on its summer finery. Moreover, as Christians, we have seen beyond the cross to the empty tomb, and perhaps we have allowed the glory of the resurrection to exclude from our minds the agony of the crucifixion. The full gospel is that "Christ died for our sins . . . that he was buried, and that he rose again" (1 Cor. 15:3-4). In his Gospel, Mark allows us to walk the weary road with our Lord that brought Him to Jerusalem, accusation, condemnation, and death. The motivating power that enabled Him to face the pain and suffering that lay ahead was love, love for sinners, love for you and me. Not surprisingly, He taught the duty of love to God, but what is surprising is that He did this in an atmosphere of hate. He enables us to understand that love is victorious over all that opposes it, and that love of God and for God are the most powerful forces in the universe.

Study Aim: *To recognize the compulsion of love in our Lords' life and respond in love toward Him and others for His sake*

STUDYING THE BIBLE

Jesus had named Jerusalem as the scene of His coming humiliation and death. Yet here He was in that city, to which He had been making voluntary pilgrimage for many days (Mark 11:1,15). That this had been a painful journey, both for Him and His disciples, is made clear. "They were in the way going up to Jerusalem; and Jesus went before them: and they were amazed; and as they followed, they were afraid" (10:32). There is Jesus striding toward a cruel fate and His disciples fearfully sensing His determination, yet following in His steps as Jerusalem loomed nearer by every mile they trod.

I. Traps Set for Jesus

The theme of love, which we are to develop, must be given its true setting. Arrival in Jerusalem brought Jesus into almost immediate conflict with the ruling authorities, "the chief priests, and the scribes, and the elders" (11:27). After His cleansing of the temple, these people "sought how they might destroy him" (v. 18). His teaching was as offensive to them as His deeds, for after He had told a parable "they sought to lay hold on him" (12:12).

1. Tribute money (vv. 13-17).—Our Lord's enemies were smart in their scheming. They sought to create friction between Him and the Roman authorities by asking a question about the payment of taxes. His answer so skillfully evaded the issue, while at the same time teaching an important lesson, that His very enemies "marveled at him."

2. Resurrection relationships (vv. 18-27).—The political trap having failed, another group, Sadducees this time, tried to embarrass Jesus with a theological question. These people did not believe in resurrection, and their question was intended to ridicule the idea. Again Jesus silenced them by a reply from the Old Testament, which He accused them of not understanding.

II. A Sincere Inquirer (Mark 12:28-34)

In the crowd that had been listening to these exchanges between our Lord and His enemies was a scribe who was favorably impressed with His replies. As a scribe, he was considered an expert in the law of

Moses and an interpreter of the Old Testament Scriptures in general. Though scribes had begun as copiers of the ancient holy documents, they had advanced to being trusted authorities. This man stood in refreshing contrast to the majority of his colleagues and furnishes an example of the mistake of condemning people by their associations.

28 And one of the scribes came, and having heard them reasoning together, and perceiving that he had answered them well, asked him, Which is the first commandment of all?

29 And Jesus answered him, The first of all the commandments is, Hear, O Israel; The Lord our God is one Lord:

30 And thou shalt love the Lord thy God with all thy heart, and with all thy soul, and with all thy mind, and with all thy strength: this is the first commandment.

31 And the second is like, namely this, Thou shalt love thy neighbor as thyself. There is none other commandment greater than these.

32 And the scribe said unto him, Well, Master, thou hast said the truth: for there is one God; and there is none other but he:

33 And to love him with all the heart, and with all the understanding, and with all the soul, and with all the strength, and to love his neighbor as himself, is more than all whole burnt offerings and sacrifices.

34 And when Jesus saw that he answered discreetly, he said unto him, Thou art not far from the kingdom of God. And no man after that durst ask him any question.

1. The first commandment (28-30).—Our basic passages for this lesson include Deuteronomy 6:4-9, the opening words of which Jesus quoted in verse 29. "The Jews call these verses from Deuteronomy the *Shema*, from the Hebrew of the word, 'Hear.' No passage of the Old Testament is more important to them. It is the first portion to be committed to memory by a Jewish child. Every synagogue service is opened by its recital. Jewish rabbinical law requires that it be repeated twice daily by the faithful. All Jews accept it as the supreme confession of their faith."[1] The recital of "heart, . . . understanding, . . . soul, . . . strength" indicate that the total person must be involved in love for God. No department of life can be omitted, for there can be no partial loyalties.

2. Love's necessity (v. 31).—The second commandment may be found in Leviticus 19:18. It is expounded throughout the Old Testament in the utterances of many prophets who made clear that professed devotion to God is valueless unless accompanied by just and compassionate treatment of others. Our Lord's parable of the good Samaritan (Luke 10:25-37) was given to correct prevailing narrow definitions as to who constitutes a neighbor. Anyone in need, whom we can help, is our neighbor.

3. Our Lord's commendation (v. 34a).—The scribe's reply was remarkable for its spiritual insight. He not only accepted our Lord's answer to his question, but he affirmed the superiority of love over ritual sacrifices (v. 33). He thus took his stand with the most revolutionary teaching of the prophets (Mic. 6:6-8) and anticipated such New Testament teaching as Hebrews 10:1-6. Our Lord saw this scribe as ready to enter God's kingdom since he had already accepted divinely revealed truth.

4. Critics silenced (v. 34b).—For the time being, our Lord's handling of His critics and the gracious response to this scribe ended the dialogue between Him and His enemies. These realized they could not gain any advantage in a battle of words. Unfortunately, they resorted to other means to achieve their goal of destroying Jesus (11:18).

III. Jesus Asks a Question (Mark 12:35-37)

Although we have no information on the circumstances that gave rise to our Lord's question, the occasion throws light upon it. The Passover season brought Jews from all parts of Palestine to Jerusalem where they met in great patriotic fervor. Hopes ran high that this festive season would bring with it the manifestation of the messiah, as seen in the cries of the crowd when Jesus rode into the holy city: "Blessed is he that cometh in the name of the Lord: Blessed be the kingdom of our father David, that cometh in the name of the Lord: Hosanna in the highest" (11:9-10). The expected messiah was figured as a heroic deliverer who would overcome Israel's foes and reestablish the nation in its former glory, as, for example, in David's time.

> **35 And Jesus answered and said, while he taught in the temple, How say the scribes that Christ is the son of David?**
>
> **36 For David himself said by the Holy Ghost, The Lord said to my Lord, Sit thou on my right hand, till I make thine enemies thy footstool.**
>
> **37 David therefore himself calleth him Lord; and whence is he then his son? And the common people heard him gladly.**

1. Son of David (v. 35).—Passages such as Psalm 2 and Isaiah 9:6-7 supported teaching that the coming messiah would be a descendant of David, the warrior king. This colored the supposed nature of the messiah ("the son of David") who, as David had conquered his enemies and enlarged the borders of Israel, would bear arms against the Romans and bring freedom and prestige to the nation. This, of course, was a dangerous as well as an erroneous concept. At feast time, with

Jerusalem crowded with pilgrims, it could lead to outbursts of patriotic zeal that would bring drastic reaction from the Romans who watched over proceedings in the temple from a fortress called Antonia. For this reason, and for the sake of His true mission, our Lord saw the importance of straightening out this popular idea.

2. Son of God (vv. 36-37a).—Quoting Psalm 110:1, Jesus asked why David referred to the messiah as "Lord" if he was to be David's son. Presumably, we have in these verses only the heart of our Lord's statement, but enough is here to make His purpose clear. He was repudiating the idea of the Messiah as only a human descendant of David and affirming His superior relationship and dignity. He is David's Lord, and, therefore, in the light of other New Testament teaching, Son of God as well as son of David. His mission, also, must be understood in the light of His divine sonship, for, as He said to Pilate, "My kingdom is not of this world" (John 18:36).

3. Popular reaction (v. 37b).—The "common people," ordinary folk as distinct from the religious leadership, responded enthusiastically to these dialogues between our Lord and their supposed spiritual superiors. No love was lost between the religious upper crust and the rank and file, for the Pharisees in particular imposed the rigorous rules and regulations that went far beyond the requirements of the Mosaic law. The question of 12:28 should be understood in light of the 613 commandments to which the basic law had been expanded. Those who bore the burden of these multiplied do's and don'ts rejoiced to see the humiliation of those who enforced them. But also there was admiration here for Jesus and a message to the believers of Rome, most of whom were "common people."

APPLYING THE LESSON

What to do with fear.—Fear is common to every life. What can we do about our fear? Step one is to clarify our fear. Sometimes, when we look closely at our fear we discover that the problem is not as great as we first supposed. On other occasions, we do discover a genuine problem which is the basis of our fear. In either case, clarifying our fear is the first step in dealing with it. The second step is then to confront our fear. An old English proverb suggests: "Fear knocked at the door; faith answered; and nobody was there."

With the eyes open.—A little boy had some puppies for sale. He had them in a box beside the road with a sign that said, "Puppies for sale. Only $5 each." Only one man stopped to investigate. After looking them over, he decided not to buy one. About a week later, this man passed by again and saw that the boy still had his puppies for sale. However, the price had changed. The sign now stated that the puppies cost $15 each. Curious at the change of price, the man stopped to talk to the boy. "Why do the puppies cost more now?" he asked the young entrepreneur. The young boy replied, "Look, Mister, they have their eyes open now, and that makes them worth a lot more!"

The boy spoke with more wisdom than he even knew. When we have our eyes open, we are worth more. No one was ever quite as alert and aware of what was going on as was Jesus. When His enemies attempted to trap Him, He had his eyes wide open.

True commitment.—Examples of true commitment can be found throughout Christian history. Colonial preacher Jonathan Edwards (1703-1758) was a man of commitment. Before he was nineteen, he wrote seventy resolutions in a diary that he kept religiously. Among those was the following: "Resolved: That every man should live to the glory of God. Resolved Second: That whether others do this or not, I will." Pioneer missionary William Carey (1761-1834) was another man of commitment. He expressed his faith in these words: "I am not my own, nor would I choose for myself. Let God employ me where he thinks fit." Dwight L. Moody (1837-1899), dynamic evangelist of the last century, was a man of commitment. After a sermon, one of his critics pointed out, "Mr. Moody, you made eleven mistakes in grammar in your message tonight." He responded, "That may be, but I'm using all the grammar I know in the service of Christ." F. B. Meyer (1847-1929) was another committed Christian. He said on one occasion, "If I had a hundred lives, they should be at Christ's disposal." Bobby Richardson, former baseball star for the New York Yankees, was also a man of commitment. He once prayed this prayer: "Dear Lord, Thy will, nothing more, nothing less, nothing else. Amen." All of these testimonies came from men who loved the Lord with all their minds, hearts, souls, and strength.

How much have you loved?—A reporter once asked Mother Teresa how she measured the success and failure of her work. She replied, "I don't think God uses categories like success and failure. His measurement is simply this: 'How much have you loved?' " That is the essence of what Jesus said in response to the question about the greatest commandment.

The impact of Christ.—Count Nikolaus Zinzendorf (b. 1700), born into Austrian nobility and trained for a career in the Saxony civil service, retired at the age of twenty-seven to his estate at Herrnhut and devoted himself to the Christian community he had started five years earlier for religious fugitives from Moravia. The spiritual fervor of his life was born out of a crisis when he was nineteen. He had just graduated in law, and he was sent off to complete his education by touring European cities. In Dusseldorf, he visited an art gallery, and he was captured by a masterly painting of Jesus. The eyes of Jesus seemed to penetrate Count Zinzendorf's heart. He was especially touched by the words written beneath the painting: "This I did for you; what are you doing for me?" Count Zinzendorf made a decision there and then to give his life in service for Christ. In every generation, from the first century to the present century, people of all levels of society and all kinds of backgrounds have been transformed by Christ and called into service for God.[2]

TEACHING THE CLASS

Main Idea: Love is the whole of the requirements of God.

Suggested Teaching Aim: Learners will examine their attitudes and commitment to love.

Introduce the Bible Study

Share the comments titled "How much have you loved?" (*Applying the Lesson*). Share information from the introduction to *Studying the Bible.* Write the main idea on the chalkboard.

State that the study for today uses terms with which most church members are familiar. Most know the teaching contained in the main idea. However, few are totally guided by love in living as followers of Christ. State that the purpose of the study is to help us examine our attitudes and our personal commitment to love. Invite learners to open their Bibles to Mark 12.

Search for Biblical Truth

Distribute copies of the following attitude survey and direct learners to mark their responses. If copies cannot be provided for each learner, read the statements aloud and ask each learner to write down a response.

1. Love is a feeling that you have toward God.
   Agree Disagree
2. Love for other people is a feeling for them that is similar to the feeling you have toward God.
   Agree Disagree
3. Love is something you do, not something you feel.
   Agree Disagree
4. Love for God is obeying His commandments and teachings.
   Agree Disagree
5. Love for others is doing what they want you to do.
   Agree Disagree

State that while most people know that a requirement of God is that we love, there is much disagreement on exactly what that means. Note that the attitude survey is meant to point out such disagreement.

A Teaching Outline

1. Focus on the Christian requirement to love.
2. Discover Jesus' explanation of the essential requirements of God.
3. Determine what a life of love looks like today.
4. Measure personal attitudes and commitment to determine if love is the whole of them.

Invite a learner to read Mark 12:28 aloud. Use information from *Studying the Bible* to set the scene indicated by this verse. Ask: What was the question from the scribe? See verse 28.

Call on a learner to read Jesus' response to the question in verses 30-31. Note the relationship of Jesus' words to the main idea written earlier on the chalkboard.

Call on a learner to read aloud the response of the scribe when he heard Jesus' words in verses 32-33. Ask: Does it seem strange that a scribe should think in this way? Why?

Note how Jesus responded to the scribe in verse 34. Ask: What do you think Jesus meant when He said the scribe was not far from the kingdom of God? (Consider this explanation: The scribe was open to truth.)

Note that the critics were now silenced and Jesus took the occasion to challenge them further. Call on a learner to read verses 35-37 aloud. Use information from *Studying the Bible* to explain His comments.

Give the Truth a Personal Focus

Share the comments titled "With the eyes open" (*Applying the Lesson*). Note that believers are more valuable with their eyes open to the truth about their attitudes and commitment to love. Ask: What does a life of love for God and others look like? Allow learners to ponder the question momentarily. Share comments from "True commitment" in *Applying the Lesson.*

Ask again: What does a life of love for God and others look like? Elicit response from learners.

Ask rhetorically: How does your day-to-day life measure up against that description? After a few moments for self-evaluation, share the comments titled "The impact of Christ" from *Applying the Lesson.*

---

1. Donald F. Ackland, *Studies in Deuteronomy* (Nashville, Convention Press, 1964), 54.
2. John R. W. Stott, *Focus on Christ* (Cleveland: William Collins Publishers, 1979), 136-38.

April 12

The Crucified Son of God

Basic Passage: Mark 15:1-41

Focal Passage: Mark 15:22-39

Suffering and death are not popular subjects. The majority of people try to banish them from their minds. As Christians, we have elected to make a cross the symbol of our faith, but for non-Catholics it is an empty cross, for we prefer to think about Easter morning rather than what happened at noonday three days before. Yet we dare not ignore the harsh realities of Good Friday, for the events of that day are at the very heart of gospel truth. Israel of old tried to explain away a portrait of the Messiah as "despised and rejected of men; a man of sorrows, and acquainted with grief" (Isa. 53:3). New Testament disciples closed their minds against their Master's own prediction of His approaching death in Jerusalem. However, the story of the crucified and risen Savior was to prove the message that would change human hearts and transform the world. Christ's disciples everywhere proclaimed that "God commendeth his love toward us, in that, while we were yet sinners, Christ died for us" (Rom. 5:8).

Study Aim: *To think about the price Jesus paid for our redemption and respond with faith, gratitude, and love*

STUDYING THE BIBLE

In order to match this lesson with the calendar, Good Friday and Easter being immediately ahead, we leap over several chapters of Mark's Gospel, all concerned with our Lord's activities in and around Jerusalem. Chapter 14 begins with mention of the approaching Feast of Passover and the grim information attached that "the chief priests and the scribes sought how they might take him by craft, and put him to death" (v. 1). They found a ready tool in one of the disciples, Judas, who plotted with them to betray his Master (vv. 10-11). In the garden of Gethsemane, their scheme was put into action by the identification and arrest of Jesus (vv. 32-52). This passage contains reference to "a certain young man" (vv. 51-52) whom some relate to Mark himself.

I. Jesus on Trial

Events moved swiftly, for our Lord's enemies were determined to complete their plan before news of what was happening reached the people. There were two trials, one ecclesiastical and the other civic, each of which can be broken down into three stages. It would be necessary to make a comparative study of all the Gospels to get the complete story.

1. Before the Sanhedrin (14:53-65; 15:1).—John's Gospel tells of a preliminary hearing before Annas, a former high priest (18:13). This was followed by an appearance before "the chief priests and all the council," that is, the Sanhedrin, the high court of the Jews (Mark 14:55). This body reached its predetermined verdict, declaring Jesus to be "guilty of death" (v. 64). Because its proceedings had been irregular, the law forbidding night meetings of the Sanhedrin, a hurried session was held the next morning (15:1) to confirm the action of the night.

2. Before Pilate (15:2-15).—The question addressed by the high priest to Jesus was, "Art thou the Christ, the Son of the Blessed?" (14:61). Pilate, the Roman governor, asked, "Art thou the King of the Jews?" (15:2). The charges brought before the two tribunals differed: the first was religious, the second, political. To gain Pilate's support for their murderous scheme, the Jewish leaders had presented Jesus as an insurrectionist, a threat to the authority of Rome. They took advantage of the moral weakness of Pilate who, though clearly wishing to release Jesus, yielded to their demands.

II. The Place of Execution (Mark 15:22-28)

Most sacred art shows our Lord carrying a complete cross along the road to Calvary. But it is now largely agreed that those condemned to death by crucifixion carried only the cross beam, the upright being already in place. The weight of this beam, however, was too much for Jesus who had been physically weakened by mistreatment. Mark added to information given by Matthew and Luke that "Simon a Cyrenian," who was enlisted to carry the cross beam, was "father of Alexander and Rufus" (v. 21), men who were apparently well known to Mark's readers. Paul, writing to the Christians of Rome, sent greetings to "Rufus chosen in the Lord" (Rom. 16:13), possibly one of these two sons.

22 And they bring him unto the place Golgotha, which is, being interpreted, The place of a skull.

23 And they gave him to drink wine mingled with myrrh: but he received it not.

24 And when they had crucified him, they parted his garments, casting lots upon them, what every man should take.
25 And it was the third hour, and they crucified him.
26 And the superscription of his accusation was written over, THE KING OF THE JEWS.
27 And with him they crucify two thieves; the one on his right hand, and the other on his left.
28 And the scripture was fulfilled, which saith, And he was numbered with the transgressors.

1. Conscious humiliation (vv. 22-25).—Two offers of drink are mentioned in our verses, and their difference needs to be recognized. In verse 23 Jesus was offered "wine mingled with myrrh," intended to relieve pain, and often provided by compassionate women to persons about to be crucified. This our Lord refused, choosing rather to be in full command of His senses. The other reference is to "a sponge full of vinegar" (v. 36), a cheap wine to assuage thirst. In full awareness therefore of the cruel proceedings, Jesus endured crucifixion, the agonizing details of which are played down by the inspired writer. The only reference is to the humiliation of being stripped as His garments were divided by the casting of lots among the executing squad of Roman soldiers. Mark recorded the time of day, 9:00 a.m.

2. King on a cross (vv. 26-28).—As verse 2 indicates, the charge made to Pilate against Jesus was that He had claimed kingship. It was customary for the charge to be displayed on the cross, largely as a warning to others against committing the same offense. But we may assume that Pilate took pleasure in the wording, "The King of the Jews," because of the embarrassment it would cause to our Lord's accusers. Only brief mention is made of the two men crucified with Jesus, here described as thieves. For a more detailed account, see Luke 23:39-43 where the two men are termed "malefactors," or evil doers. They may have engaged in violent revolt against Rome.

III. Mockery and Darkness (Mark 15:29-33)

This tragic scene is stated to have taken place at Golgotha, interpreted as "The place of a skull" (v. 22). This could have been a rocky prominence that had semblance to a skull. The word is Aramaic, and the Latin counterpart is Calvary. Its exact location is not known, although several sites have been suggested. Evidently it was near a highway as indicated by verse 29.

29 And they that passed by railed on him, wagging their heads, and saying, Ah, thou that destroyest the temple, and buildest it in three days,
30 Save thyself, and come down from the cross.

31 Likewise also the chief priests mocking said among themselves with the scribes, He saved others; himself he cannot save.

32 Let Christ the King of Israel descend now from the cross, that we may see and believe. And they that were crucified with him reviled him.

33 And when the sixth hour was come, there was darkness over the whole land until the ninth hour.

1. Unintended truth (vv. 29-32).—One of the accusations made against Jesus in the Sanhedrin trial was that He had said, "I am able to destroy the temple of God, and to build it in three days" (Matt. 26:61). An explanation of this is furnished in John 2:18-21, with its concluding words, "But he spake of the temple of his body." By perverse distortion of His meaning, His enemies turned this prophecy of His death and resurrection into an attack on the temple, the centuries-long shrine of the Jewish people, and a symbol of their national survival. By "He saved others" (v. 31), the chief priests and scribes referred to our Lord's miracles of healing, even raising the dead. But we are justified in seeing here a reference to spiritual salvation, which Jesus purchased for all who believe by the sacrifice of His life. He had to die that we might live.

2. The sixth hour (v. 33).—This would be noon when a three-hour period of darkness began. What forces of nature God employed to cast this dense shadow over the scene of His Son's death, we do not know. It lasted until Jesus surrendered Himself to death, a fitting response of creation to the darkest deed in history.

IV. A Roman's Testimony (Mark 15:34-39)

The solemn depths of our Lord's cry, "My God, my God, why hast thou forsaken me?" (v. 34) are difficult for us to plumb. In the physical darkness that enveloped Him, our Lord was plunged into a deeper spiritual darkness in which He realized momentarily the awful consequences of bearing humanity's load of sin. This was the price He paid as the world's Redeemer.

34 And at the ninth hour Jesus cried with a loud voice, saying, Eloi, Eloi, lama sabachthani? which is, being interpreted, My God, my God, why hast thou forsaken me?

35 And some of them that stood by, when they heard it, said, Behold, he calleth Elijah.

36 And one ran and filled a sponge full of vinegar, and put it on a reed, and gave him to drink, saying, Let alone; let us see whether Elijah will come to take him down.

37 And Jesus cried with a loud voice, and gave up the ghost.

38 And the veil of the temple was rent in twain from the top to the bottom.

39 And when the centurion, which stood over against him, saw that he so cried out, and gave up the ghost, he said, Truly this man was the Son of God.

Jesus spoke in Aramaic, which presumably accounted for the misunderstanding of those who thought He addressed Elijah. The rent veil is usually understood in light of Hebrews 9:2-12 and 10:19-20 as symbolic of the opening up of a way to God through Christ. Some see it, however, as a forecast of the coming destruction of the temple. The centurion's affirmation was desired by Mark from all who read his Gospel.

APPLYING THE LESSON

Death doesn't take a holiday.—A movie of 1930 vintage was called *Death Takes a Holiday.* In the movie, the angel of death spent a weekend on earth to see what it's like to be human. During this brief visit by the angel of death, the world was thrown into a panic. Without his help, people suffering from lingering illnesses couldn't die. The old and tired, who were begging for rest, could find no relief. Eventually, the angel of death went back to work, and the world returned to normal. The truth is: death does not take a holiday, not even when the Son of God lived on the earth. Jesus, too, faced the reality of death.

Turned the headlights on.—In a newspaper several years ago, this poignant letter from a family appeared on the obituary page: "Billy, you know it was just a year ago today that you left us, and the sunshine went out of our lives. But we turned on the headlights and are going on, and, Billy, we shall keep on doing the best we can until that glorious day when we'll see you again."[1]

That is the testimony of faith every Christian can voice. Why? Because when Jesus went into death, He did not stay there. When He faced death, He defeated death. Because He lives, we can live also.

Quick thinking.—The professor was aggravated at the young man who continually glanced at his watch during the professor's lecture. Deciding to embarrass the young man, he stopped his lecture and said, "Johnny, can you tell me why you look at your watch so often?" "Yes," Johnny replied, "because I was afraid you wouldn't have time to finish your interesting lecture!" He had to think quick to cover up his indiscretion.

The religious leaders who arrested Jesus in the night and brought Him to trial also had to do some quick thinking. Their actions were illegal, so they had to take additional steps to cover up their indiscretions.

Not when but what.—Someone has suggested that when suffering comes, the key question to ask is not When? but What? Instead of asking, "When am I going to get out of this?" we need to ask the question, "What am I going to get out of this?" Jesus' suffering on the cross went on for hours. However, the motivation that kept Him there was not the assumption it would soon be over but that through His sacrificial death on the cross He purchased eternal life for humankind.

Unable to write about the cross.—John Milton tried to write a poem on the cross but was unable to do so. He testified, "I will try no more. It is a never-ebbing sea in which our thoughts are drowned."[2] Henry Ward Beecher preached sermons on every aspect of Christ's life and many on the cross. But in no sermon did he describe the crucifixion. His biographer suggested that the cross was so sacred to Beecher that he never ventured to attempt a portrayal of it.[3]

Even though we cannot describe the cross, we must nevertheless declare the cross, for it is the heart of our gospel. Paul's beautiful statement to the Corinthians describes the impact of the cross: "He made Him who knew no sin to be sin on our behalf, that we might become the righteousness of God in Him" (2 Cor. 5:21, NASB).

How do you respond?—The cross demands a response in our lives. We see that response in the centurion who concluded Jesus was "the Son of God." We have seen that response in various other forms through the ages. A beautiful example is a simple man in a country church.

Many decades ago, a well-known preacher led a service in a country church one Sunday. He returned to his home on Monday. The next Saturday a man whom the preacher did not know knocked on his door. The man identified himself as the cook at the home where the preacher had eaten Sunday dinner. He said, "I heard you pray last Sunday noon that God would bless the hands that prepared the food. I looked down at these old hands, and tears came to my eyes. I decided to dedicate my hands to the Lord. All week long I have been working for the Lord, and I've never had so much fun in all my life. Now, I want you to pray that I may dedicate, not just my hands, but my whole life to Jesus."

TEACHING THE CLASS

Main Idea: Jesus' death requires a response of faith, gratitude, and love.

Suggested Teaching Aim: Learners will consider anew Jesus' death for them and respond with faith, gratitude, and love.

Introduce the Bible Study

Share the comments titled "Death doesn't take a holiday" from *Applying the Lesson.* Share information from the introduction to *Studying the Bible.*

If appropriate in your class, provide paper and markers for learners. Direct them to draw a representation of death. Give no further directions. Allow several minutes for learners to complete the assignment with some thought. When finished, invite them to share the pictures and their thoughts with those sitting near them. Invite some learners to share their drawing with the group.

A Teaching Outline

1. Raise the issue of death.
2. Examine the circumstances and incidents surrounding the death of Jesus.
3. Determine the response demanded by the death of Jesus.
4. Respond to Jesus with renewed faith, gratitude, and love.

Note that the study for today relates to the death of Jesus. Ask: Do you think that Jesus felt differently about death than you do? Did He dread it any less? Wait for response. State that the purpose of the study is to remind us of the price that Jesus paid when He died for us and to help us consider again how we should respond to what He did for us.

Search for Biblical Truth

Invite learners to open their Bibles to Mark 14. Note that many events precede the passage to be studied today. Call attention to the following outline that has been displayed.

The Crucified Son of God

I. Jesus on trial
   A. Before the Sanhedrin (Mark 14:53-65; 15:1)
   B. Before Pilate (Mark 15:2-15)
II. The execution
   A. Conscious humiliation (Mark 15:22-25)
   B. King on a cross (Mark 15:26-28)
III. Mockery and Darkness
   A. Mocking words; unintended truth (Mark 15:29-32)
   B. Deathly darkness (Mark 15:33)
IV. Death
   A. A cry of anguish (Mark 15:34-36)
   B. Death prevails (Mark 15:37-38)
   C. A Roman soldier's testimony (Mark 15:39)

Use the outline to examine the circumstances and incidents surrounding the death of Jesus. When the trials of Jesus are reviewed, use the comments titled "Quick thinking" (*Applying the Lesson*). When Jesus' suffering on the cross is reviewed, use the comments titled "Not when but what" (*Applying the Lesson*).

Give the Truth a Personal Focus

Share the comments titled "Unable to write about the cross" (*Applying the Lesson*). Ask: What response does the death of Jesus on the cross demand from you and me? Ask for response. Faith, gratitude, and love should be included. Use the comments titled "How do you respond?" (*Applying the Lesson*). Ask rhetorically: Have you responded to the death of Jesus for you with your whole life?

1. Paul Powell, *Why Me, Lord?* (Wheaton, Ill.: Victor Books, 1981), 72.
2. James Wesberry, *Evangelistic Sermons* (Nashville: Broadman Press, 1973), 12.
3. Lyman Abbott, *Henry Ward Beecher* (Cambridge: The Riverside Press, 1903), 117.

April 19

An Empty Tomb

Basic Passage: Mark 15:42—16:8

Focal Passage: Mark 15:42—16:8

This is our final lesson from Mark's Gospel. Its theme is triumphant, for it deals with our Lord's resurrection. Our major focus will be on that event with its message of life beyond death and victory in Christ over all that opposes God's eternal purposes. But another interesting matter is forced on our attention. Did Mark's Gospel end at 16:8 as many believe? This belief is expressed in the *New* International Version by the statement "The most reliable early manuscripts and other ancient witnesses do not have Mark 16:9-20." The problem is briefly discussed later in these comments, so it will suffice to say here that probably the concluding section of the Gospel was somehow lost. Fortunately, we have three other Gospels to inform us of happenings after the resurrection. The likely loss of a few verses at the end of one Gospel serves to emphasize the marvel of the preservation of the Word of God through the centuries. The discovery of the Dead Sea Scrolls, in 1947, furnished new evidence of divine protection of the sacred books so that we may read them today with confidence in their authenticity.

Study Aim: *To share with all Christians the joy of Easter and the hope of life everlasting*

STUDYING THE BIBLE

In a brief summary of the gospel he preached, the apostle Paul wrote of our Lord, "Christ died for our sins . . . was buried, and . . . rose again the third day" (1 Cor. 15:3-4). The statement "was buried" may appear superfluous. However, Paul had heard the claims of some opponents of the gospel that Jesus did not really die, but only swooned. The three-day interment of the body corrected this falsehood. So, likewise, the Gospel writers provided details of the proceedings that led to the depositing of Jesus' lifeless body in Joseph's tomb.

I. A Tomb Provided (Mark 15:42-46)

Normally, the Romans left the bodies of the crucified to decompose, or be eaten as carrion, and to furnish shocking warnings of the kind of justice meted out to the condemned. On occasion they turned the remains over to friends or relatives for decent burial. Jewish law forbade bodies of hanged persons being left overnight (Deut. 21:22-23). In our Lord's case, the beginning of the Sabbath (6:00 p.m.) being near, there was reason for swift action.

> **42 And now when the even was come, because it was the preparation, that is, the day before the sabbath,**
>
> **43 Joseph of Arimathaea, an honorable counselor, which also waited for the kingdom of God, came, and went in boldly unto Pilate, and craved the body of Jesus.**
>
> **44 And Pilate marveled if he were already dead: and calling unto him the centurion, he asked him whether he had been any while dead.**
>
> **45 And when he knew it of the centurion, he gave the body to Joseph.**
>
> **46 And he bought fine linen, and took him down, and wrapped him in the linen, and laid him in a sepulcher which was hewn out of a rock, and rolled a stone unto the door of the sepulcher.**

1. Joseph's request (vv. 42-43).—As a respected member of the Sanhedrin, Joseph would have some standing with Pilate. He was among those who, like Simeon (Luke 2:25), lived in expectation of the coming of Messiah. Joseph is not claimed as a disciple; yet by his action, he made strong public commitment to Jesus.

2. Pilate's surprise (vv. 44-45).—Death was normally slow for victims of crucifixion, which added to the cruelty of this form of punishment. Although death was largely the result of exhaustion, verse 37 describes Jesus as crying "with a loud voice" (see John 19:30); at this point He surrendered His life in the knowledge that His redemptive work was accomplished.

3. Burial care (v. 46).—Joseph's action was premeditated, for he had bought "fine linen" in which to wrap our Lord's body. The tomb was probably intended for his own use and was in the nature of a small room hewn out of natural rock. To discourage grave robbers, a heavy stone could be rolled over the opening. This fulfilled Isaiah's prophecy, "he made his grave . . . with the rich in his death" (Isa. 53:9).

II. Women at the Tomb (Mark 15:47; 16:1)

Significant tribute is paid by Mark to the loyalty of several women to the crucified Jesus (15:40-41). He does not mention Mary, our Lord's mother, who was present at Calvary and was given, by Jesus, into the care of the apostle John (John 19:25-27). But he named three who observed His burial and came later to the tomb to render normal services to the dead.

> **47 And Mary Magdalene and Mary the mother of Joses beheld where he was laid.**
>
> **1 And when the sabbath was past, Mary Magdalene, and Mary the mother of James, and Salome, had bought sweet spices, that they might come and anoint him.**

1. Love standing watch (15:47).—Mary Magdalene, or Mary from Magdala, is later described as she from "whom he had cast seven devils" (16:9; Luke 8:2). Mary the mother of James should probably be identified with "the wife of Cleophas" (John 19:25). Salome is generally regarded as the mother of James and John, wife of Zebedee, and perhaps sister to Mary, our Lord's mother. We know nothing about the "many other women" (15:41) but salute them as faithful friends who ministered to our Lord's needs both before and after His death.

2. Ministry to the dead (16:1).—Embalming was not practiced among the Jews, but it was customary to anoint corpses with perfumed oils. Although John 19:38-40 describes Joseph and Nicodemus (unmentioned by Mark) as rendering this service, the women were not satisfied until they had added their own tribute of love, which they set out to do early in the day following the Sabbath. As events happened, their anointing was no longer needed.

III. Easter Morning at the Tomb (Mark 16:2-7)

Although the Gospel records differ in detail as to what happened at that early hour, all agree that something tremendous had occurred between the entombment on Friday evening and the women's visit the morning after the Sabbath. For when the women arrived, the tomb was empty, and the news awaiting them was that Christ had risen.

> **2 And very early in the morning the first day of the week, they came unto the sepulcher at the rising of the sun.**
> **3 And they said among themselves, Who shall roll away the stone from the door of the sepulcher?**
> **4 And when they looked, they saw that the stone was rolled away: for it was very great.**
> **5 And entering into the sepulcher, they saw a young man sitting on the right side, clothed in a long white garment; and they were affrighted.**
> **6 And he saith unto them, Be not affrighted: Ye seek Jesus of Nazareth, which was crucified: he is risen; he is not here: behold the place where they laid him.**
> **7 But go your way, tell his disciples and Peter that he goeth before you into Galilee: there shall ye see him, as he said unto you.**

1. Facing difficulty (vv. 2-4).—The problem of the heavy stone that covered the entrance to the tomb did not deter the women from their mission of love. Mark, who recorded what happened, probably heard the story again and again from the women assembled with other Christians in his mother's home (Acts 12:12); "for it was very great" sounds like a personal memory.

2. Heavenly messenger (vv. 5-6).—Who other than an angel from God could be the qualified announcer of our Lord's resurrection? He invited the women to view the empty tomb and the very place where earlier (15:47) they had seen His body laid. Also the angel told of the fulfillment of our Lord's promise (14:28) that He would meet them in Galilee. We learn from other writers that there were postresurrection visits with the disciples before the Galilee rendezvous.

3. Special to Peter (v. 7).—In view of Peter's denials (14:66-72), the personal message to this disciple was specially gracious. It brought assurance that all was not over between him and his Lord, but the future held promise of resumed fellowship and forgiveness.

IV. An Abrupt Conclusion (Mark 16:8)

Were the words, "for they were afraid," Mark's intended ending for his Gospel, or did he write more? Has his conclusion to chapter 16 been lost? Scholars are generally agreed that verses 9-20 are not original to this Gospel but a later addition, written by someone who based what he wrote on the conclusions to the other Gospels. Users of the *New Revised Standard Version* will find printed not only this longer conclusion but also a shorter one that is found in some ancient manuscripts.

8 And they went out quickly, and fled from the sepulcher; for they trembled and were amazed: neither said they anything to any man; for they were afraid.

Can we accept this as an appropriate ending to Mark's Gospel? Many competent authorities feel that they can. Others think that for Mark to end on this negative note would be out of harmony with the purpose of the author to present our Lord as "The Strong Son of God" (this quarter's theme). Accordingly, and in line with the most reliable manuscripts which end with verse 8, the following two suggestions are offered: Mark wrote more, but his final verses were lost (perhaps through accidental damage to the manuscript, which would have been in the form of a scroll); Mark did not live to finish his Gospel, but he became a martyr under Nero. Unless some great archaeological discovery comes to our aid, we will probably never know the answer to this problem. But we may be grateful that the Markan record, whether complete or not, bears witness with the other Gospels, to the reality of Christ's resurrection, "He is risen" (v. 6).

APPLYING THE LESSON

The accuracy of God's Word.—In 1947, Bedouin herdsmen discovered a cave near the Dead Sea in Palestine that was filled with scrolls. These scrolls happened to be ancient manuscripts of the Bible. Portions of all the Old Testament books except Esther were found. In addition, these caves contained commentaries on the Old Testament books, writings that set forth the ethical teachings of the group who collected the manuscripts, and writings about their hopes for the future. These manuscripts, some more than one thousand years older than any previously known biblical manuscripts, have confirmed the accuracy and dependability of the translations of the Bible we Christians use today.

An incredible opinion.—Some skeptics of the resurrection have suggested another explanation of what happened that first Easter Sunday morning, an explanation that is more incredible than the biblical message. According to this "swoon theory," Jesus did not really die but instead merely swooned on the cross. He was revived by the cool atmosphere of the tomb and the odor of the spices. Consequently, he escaped from the tomb and convinced the disciples He was alive. How incredible to believe that after Jesus had been beaten and humiliated all night, after He had been flogged, and after He had spent several hours nailed to the cross, He could still have enough physical strength to untie himself from the grave clothes that bound Him hand and foot, somehow push away the stone from the inside of the tomb, overcome the Roman guards stationed to watch the tomb, and then appear to the disciples in such a powerful way that He could convince them He had been raised up from the dead! Some people will believe anything!

We're not about success.—Clarence Jordan was a Christian with both unusual abilities and unique commitment. He had two Ph.D.'s, one in agriculture and one in biblical languages. A world of opportunities was out before him. He chose to give his life in service to the poor. He moved to Americus, Georgia, back in the 1940s, and founded a farm where poor whites and blacks could work together to provide for the needs of their families. He called it Koinonia Farm. Jordan's effort was resisted by the local citizens. They boycotted him, slashed the workers' tires when they came to town, and tried everything they could to sabotage the work. For fourteen years, Jordan continued his ministry to the poor. Finally, in 1954, the Ku Klux Klan decided to get rid of him once and for all. They came at night with guns and torches and burned every building on Koinonia Farm except Clarence Jordan's home, which they riddled with bullets. The next day, a local newspaper reporter came to see what remained of the farm. Clarence Jordan recognized the reporter's voice as one of the men who had attacked his farm the night before. Clarence Jordan was in the field, hoeing and planting. Surprised that Clarence was still around, the reporter said, "Well, Dr. Jordan, you got two of them Ph.D.'s, you've put fourteen years into this farm, and there's nothing left of it at all. Just how successful do you think you've been?" Clarence stopped hoeing, turned to the reporter, and answered, "Sir, I don't think you understand us. What we are about is not success but faithfulness."[1]

When Jesus went to the cross, some of the women were standing by. Their hopes had been dashed and their dreams shattered. Yet they remained faithful.

The use of spices.—Two spices specifically mentioned in the New Testament in anointing a body for burial are myrrh and aloes. Myrrh was a fragrant substance derived from a certain balsam tree. Apparently it was available in liquid and solid forms. Aloes was an aromatic substance derived from a sandalwood tree. It was used for perfume and for anointing bodies at death. Other spices that may have been used for anointing a body at burial were balm, gum, and nard. Ointments also were used to prepare a body for burial. In Israel, olive oil was the main ingredient in ointments. To the olive oil, various perfumes were added. The raw material then was crushed, boiled, and stirred. Ointments were smeared on the body. Spices were wrapped in a linen shroud used to cover the body. Such were the spices the women took to the tomb to anoint the body of Jesus.

TEACHING THE CLASS

Main Idea: Jesus died on the cross, was buried, and resurrected after three days.

Suggested Teaching Aim: Learners will explain the work of redemption carried out in the death and resurrection of Jesus.

Introduce the Bible Study

Write these words on the chalkboard: *Resurrection, Redemption, Salvation, Eternal Life.* Ask: What do these words have to do with Easter? Wait for their response.

Continue by asking: Do most people have accurate understanding of the meaning of these words? Do you? If you were required to explain the work of redemption through the death and resurrection of Jesus to someone who did not understand "churchy" words, could you do so?

A Teaching Outline

1. Focus on redemption and its meaning.
2. Identify the events of resurrection morning and their meaning for redemption.
3. Explain the redemptive nature of the events of Jesus' death and resurrection.
4. Recommit to faithfulness as a response of gratitude.

State that as we study the wonderful happenings of the first Easter morning, our purpose is to increase our ability to explain the work of redemption carried out in the death and resurrection of Jesus. Invite learners to open their Bibles to Mark 15.

Search for Biblical Truth

Share the comments titled "The accuracy of God's Word" (*Applying the Lesson*). Note that today's study picks up where it ended last Sunday. Review the outline displayed to guide the Scripture study last Sunday. Display this outline of the events that followed.

A Glorious, Empty Tomb

I. A tomb provided
 A. Joseph's request (Mark 15:42-43)
 B. Pilate's surprise (Mark 15:44-45)
 C. Burial care (Mark 15:46)
II. Women at the tomb
 A. Love standing watch (Mark 15:47)
 B. Ministry to the dead (Mark 16:1)
III. Easter morning at the tomb
 A. An early morning visit (Mark 16:2-4)
 B. A heavenly messenger (Mark 16:5-6)
 C. A special message to Peter (Mark 16:7)
 D. An abrupt conclusion (Mark 16:8)

Use the outline to study the Scripture that tells of Jesus' burial and resurrection. When the request to bury Jesus is discussed, use the comments titled "An incredible option" (*Applying the Lesson*). When the trip of the women to the tomb is discussed, note their faithfulness even when their hopes had been dashed. Share the comments titled "We're not about success" (*Applying the Lesson*). Also share information titled "The use of spices" (Applying the Lesson) to explain the mission of the women that Easter morning.

Give the Truth a Personal Focus

Remind the learners of the words written on the chalkboard as the study was begun. Assign each word to a small group of learners for a word study. Direct them to use the resources in their own Bibles, such as a concordance or dictionary. Provide additional resources for use during this time from your church media center. Direct the learners to write an explanation of the word assigned to them that does not use "churchy" language. When the word study is finished, invite groups to share what they have written.

Ask: If you used these kinds of explanations, would you be able to explain the redemptive nature of the death and resurrection of Jesus more clearly? Call on two learners who will role play a conversation in which one explains to the other what Jesus' death and resurrection means and invites him or her to personally accept the salvation that this provides. It may be helpful to arrange before the class meeting for two learners to do this role play.

Recall the faithfulness of the women. Note that gratitude for what Jesus did for us demands faithfulness. Invite learners to recommit themselves to this miraculously risen Savior.

---

1. Tim Hansel, *Holy Sweat* (Waco: Word Books, 1987), 188-89.

March, April, May 1992

God's People in the World

Aids from BROADMAN for Studying and Teaching

Books:
A Guide for New Testament Study, William Stevens
The Broadman Bible Commentary, Volume 12
Layman's Bible Book Commentary, Volume 23

The quarter will be brought to a close by studies in the Epistles of Peter, the first of which was addressed to a persecuted church. Our themes will vary from words of comfort and hope to exhortations to live worthily in an unfriendly world. A strong emphasis will appear on the doctrine of our Lord's return and what this means to the church and the world.

April 26

The Gift of Living Hope

Basic Passage: 1 Peter 1:1-25

Focal Passages: 1 Peter 1:3-9,13-21

After a series of lessons on the Gospel of Mark, much of whose material is believed to have been provided by Peter, it is appropriate that we conclude the quarter with studies in the writings of Peter himself. While we cannot ascribe exact dates for either writings, it seems likely that they were both authored around the same time, between A.D. 60 and 67. The two men addressed themselves to different audiences, for while Mark wrote to Christians in Rome, the apostle Peter named his readers as residents in the five Roman provinces listed in 1:1, spread out along the shores of Asia Minor and the Black Sea. Apparently, the Christians in these areas were enduring persecution, of what sort and from what source is not stated, whether general or local we cannot tell. The apostle responded to the need for encouragement and exhortation of believers under pressure, coupled with a call to consistent Christian living, whatever the circumstances. The two concluding verses of the epistle helpfully summarize its message.

Study Aim: *To learn how to stand strong in faith and loyalty in an unbelieving and unfriendly society*

STUDYING THE BIBLE

The First Epistle of Peter belongs to what is known as the "persecution literature" of the New Testament. We need to be reminded of the price early believers paid for their faithfulness, that Christians in some parts of the world are paying that price today, and that prevailing indifference in our culture could easily change to open hostility in the near future.

I. A Christian's Privileges (1 Pet. 1:1-12)

The opening verse is clear with one exception: Who are "the strangers"? The NRSV reads, "exiles of the Dispersion." "Dispersion" (*diaspora*) is usually employed to describe Jews living outside the Holy Land. There are also indications that Peter wrote to others besides Jews. Verses 14 and 18 are more readily applied to Gentiles converted from paganism than to Jews. It is possible to conclude, therefore, that Peter wrote for both Jewish and Gentiles readers and that the "Dispersion" he referred to was that of all believers who, while in this life, are exiles from their future heavenly home. He thought of them all in the exalted terms of verse 2.

3 Blessed be the God and Father of our Lord Jesus Christ, which according to his abundant mercy hath begotten us again unto a lively hope by the resurrection of Jesus Christ from the dead,

4 To an inheritance incorruptible, and undefiled, and that fadeth not away, reserved in heaven for you,

5 Who are kept by the power of God through faith unto salvation ready to be revealed in the last time.

6 Wherein ye greatly rejoice, though now for a season, if need be, ye are in heaviness through manifold temptations:

7 That the trial of your faith, being much more precious than of gold that perisheth, though it be tried with fire, might be found unto praise and honor and glory at the appearing of Jesus Christ:

8 Whom having not seen, ye love; in whom, though now ye see him not, yet believing, ye rejoice with joy unspeakable and full of glory:

9 Receiving the end of your faith, even the salvation of your souls.

1. Prospect (vv. 3-4).—Following an outburst of praise to "the God and Father of our Lord Jesus Christ," Peter wrote of the "living hope" (NRSV) of believers, the result of their having been "begotten . . . again," that is, born again. This living hope is grounded in the resurrection of our Lord, in whose rising again we have hope for life everlasting. The believer's hope will have fulfillment in heaven where he or she will enter into an inheritance that, unlike earthly bequests, will also have everlasting qualities.

2. Security (vv. 5-9).—The guarantee of this future blessing is found in "the power of God" so that those who exercise faith may be sure of attaining salvation in its fullest and ultimate sense. This will be in spite of "various trials" (v. 6, NRSV) that may cause great "heaviness," or distress, but these will come to be recognized as opportunities for demonstrating unwavering faith in God. When the Lord Jesus returns, this overcoming faith will be acknowledged with "praise and honor and glory."

3. Advantages (vv. 10-12).—The several references to salvation in these verses contemplate the completion of God's work of grace in and for the believer. We are saved when we believe in and receive the Lord Jesus as Savior. But the ultimate advantages of salvation will not be known until we enter into God's presence in our heavenly home. Then we shall experience that which even the prophets were unable to comprehend (v. 10) and angels long to understand (v. 12). Though wiser than us, angels know nothing of the joy of being redeemed by the sacrifice of God's Son.

II. A Christian's Responsibilities (1 Pet. 1:13-17)

God's work of grace in the believer, with its glorious prospect for the future, imposes certain obligations on those who are the beneficiaries. Life can no longer be lived as before, in the indulgence of "former lusts" (v. 14), but must be made to conform to the character of God Himself, whose nature is holy.

> **13 Wherefore gird up the loins of your mind, be sober, and hope to the end for the grace that is to be brought unto you at the revelation of Jesus Christ;**
>
> **14 As obedient children, not fashioning yourselves according to the former lusts in your ignorance:**
>
> **15 But as he which hath called you is holy, so be ye holy in all manner of conversation;**
>
> **16 Because it is written, Be ye holy; for I am holy.**
>
> **17 And if ye call on the Father, who without respect of persons judgeth according to every man's work, pass the time of your sojourning here in fear.**

1. Alertness (v. 13a).—The exhortation to "gird up the loins of your mind" reflected the practice in those long-robed times of tucking the skirt of a garment into the waistband in readiness for work to be done. We might say, "Pull yourselves together," in a spiritual sense, for the exhortation is linked with "the revelation of Jesus Christ," that is, His coming again. Christians are always to be in a state of readiness for the Lord's return.

2. Self-control (v. 13b).—To "be sober" suggests avoidance of intoxication, which the apostle may well have intended. But we should probably understand a wider meaning, that is, a call to self-disciplined living. If this call was necessary in those days, when believers lived in a pagan society, surely it is no less necessary today.

3. Expectancy (v. 13c).—Christian hope is to be focused on the promised return of Christ. New Testament writers constantly urged this upon their readers, and although nearly two thousand years have passed since then, the possibility of our Lord's sudden return should still influence our behavior. This was the next point made by Peter to his readers.

4. Holiness (vv. 14-17).—Obedience to Christ means the abandonment of former life-styles when these do not conform to His teaching and example; "conversation" means life-style. Holiness is being set apart from all that is evil, and it belongs to the character of God Himself. The thought of having to give account to Him (v. 17) should help us in practicing this separateness from the world and its ways.

III. A Christian's Indebtedness (1 Pet. 1:18-25)

Gratitude should inspire the believer to appropriate conduct for a follower of the crucified Son of God. Peter described Jesus' redemptive work as the payment of a ransom, money paid to secure the release of a captive. Only, in Christ's case, the payment was made, not in money, but in the surrender of His life by the shedding of His blood.

18 Forasmuch as ye know that ye were not redeemed with corruptible things, as silver and gold, from your vain conversation received by tradition from your fathers;

19 But with the precious blood of Christ, as of a lamb without blemish and without spot:

20 Who verily was foreordained before the foundation of the world, but was manifest in these last times for you,

21 Who by him do believe in God, that raised him up from the dead, and gave him glory; that your faith and hope might be in God.

1. Salvation's cost (vv. 18-19).—That Peter's readers were ransomed "from the futile ways inherited from your ancestors" (NRSV) could refer to either Jews or Gentiles. God saw value in them and paid the price of their deliverance from those futile ways by the offering of His Son. The Old Testament sacrificial system (v. 19) is in view as Jesus took the place ("once for all," Heb. 10:10) of the slain lamb whose death was accepted as atonement for sins committed.

2. Salvation's plan (vv. 20-21).—Quoting Ray Summers, "That which God had planned before the creation of the world, he brought to reality at a point in history through the death and resurrection of Jesus Christ."[1] It was *faith* in Jesus as Savior that had produced in Peter's readers the *hope* of life everlasting. Note that the salvation experience begins with God and ends with God, for it was the Father's purpose that sent the Son to live and die for our sakes.

3. Salvation's agent (vv. 22-25).—To the list of Christian responsibilities in verses 13-17, Peter added love for one another. He described this as "unfeigned love," which is genuine and not superficial. Such love results from having been "born again," and as in our Lord's discourse with Nicodemus (John 3), not in a human sense but as the result of insemination with a divine seed, none other than "the word of God." Peter had in mind the preaching of the gospel through which his readers had learned of Christ and put their faith in Him. For us there is the additional truth: through becoming acquainted with "the word of God" in written and printed form, people may receive eternal blessing.

APPLYING THE LESSON

Response to suffering.—One writer described five ways we attempt to escape the grasp of suffering. First, we plead. We ask God to be fair with us. What we are really asking is for God to deal kindly with us, regardless of how He deals with others. Second, we compare. We point out to God how much better we are than others with the implication being that God should therefore be treating us better than He is. Third, we pout. When steps one and two bring no relief, we often pout. We have a pity party and feel sorry for ourselves. Fourth, we shout. How often do we become angry at God and shake our fist in His face? Fifth, we doubt. When the other steps do not change our circumstances, we often become disenchanted with God. We begin to doubt if He is able to help us or if He cares enough about us to help us.[2]

How should we respond? Peter's message is that we should expect suffering, endure it through God's power, and emerge from it better equipped to serve Him.

God carries us through.—One of the most beautiful stories of God's provision is the story of a man who had a dream. In his dream, he pictured his whole life flashing across the sky. Below this panorama of the events of his life, he pictured God walking by his side along the beach, and as they walked along, they left footprints on the sand. But every time an experience of suffering flashed across the sky, the man noticed only one set of footprints on the sand. So he cried out to God, "Why is it that you leave me when suffering comes? Why is it that you leave me to walk alone during the tough times of my life?" God answered, "In those times when you see only one set of footprints on the sand, they are not your footprints. They are Mine. I do not leave you during those times. Those are the times when I carry you through." Peter's hope in this week's text is based on the confidence that God will carry us through the experiences of suffering in our lives.

The great teacher of life.—Life's greatest teacher is not pleasure but suffering. In our suffering, we learn lessons we could not learn otherwise. Let me give two expressions of that truth.

Helen Keller once said about her physical handicaps, "I thank God for my handicaps, for through them I have found myself, my work, and my God."

The same truth is expressed in an oft-used poem:

I walked a mile with Pleasure,
She chattered all the way,
But left me none the wiser
For all she had to say.

I walked a mile with Sorrow,
And ne'er a word said she;
But, oh, the things I learned from her
When Sorrow walked with me![3]

Letting God have your life.—George W. Truett was one of the greatest of Southern Baptist preachers, but his pilgrimage of faith began just like that of every other individual, with a willingness to give his heart to God. He explained his feelings the morning after his conversion experience. Before getting up from bed, he said these thoughts ran through his mind: "Last night you made a public profession of religion. Now, the neighborhood knows about it, or will know about it, ere the day is done. What have you to say about your public profession of Christ, as your Savior and Master, this morning?" He put himself to this test: "What if Christ should now visibly come into this room, and put to you this question, 'Are you willing for me to have my way with your life, from this time on? I will not indicate to you what that way is to be—it is enough for you to know that my way is always right and safe and best. May I have your consent, without evasion or reservation, to have my way with you now and always?' " Truett gave this answer, "To such tests, I gave my unreserved 'Yes,' and a great peace filled my heart."[4]

That kind of unreserved commitment to God is necessary for Him to do in us and through us what He wants to do.

TEACHING THE CLASS

Main Idea: Hope is based on new life in Christ.

Suggested Teaching Aim: Learners will, based on their life in Christ, renew their hope in the face of life concerns.

Introduce the Bible Study

Use information from *Studying the Bible* to introduce the new unit of study in 1 Peter. State that the quarter will be concluded with the unit titled "Confession and Crucifixion."

Write *Hope* on the chalkboard. Ask: In what ways is hope vital to the life of all men? Elicit response. Continue by asking: Why do Christians emphasize hope as a vital part of their faith? Wait for response.

State that the study for today focuses on the basis for hope in the believer's life. Invite learners to open their Bibles to 1 Peter 1.

Search for Biblical Truth

State that 1 Peter 1:3-9 reflects a strong basis for hope in the life of believers. Call on a learner to read verses 3-4 aloud. When the reading is finished, ask: What reason for hope among believers is suggested here? (everlasting life in heaven). Ask: Why can Christians be confident in this hope of heaven? (Note v. 3.)

A Teaching Outline

1. Introduce the new unit of study.
2. Focus on the function of hope in believers' lives.
3. Discover the basis for hope when there is new life in Jesus.
4. Plan ways to renew personal hope in the midst of today's concerns.
5. Praise God for the reason for hope.

Note that a second reason for hope is given in verse 5. Call on a learner to read the verse aloud. Ask: Why can believers be confident in their hope of heaven? (They are kept by the power of God.) Share the comments titled "God carries us through" (*Applying the Lesson*).

Mention that the hope of believers is not developed through ease and comfort but through difficult times. Call on someone to read verses 6-9. Share the comments titled "Response to suffering" (*Applying the Lesson*).

Write *responsibility* on the chalkboard. State that the hope provided believers through confidence in Jesus Christ also carries responsibility. Write these words on the chalkboard beneath "responsibility": *alertness, self-control, expectancy,* and *holiness.* Direct learners to read verses 13-17 silently and match the words and the verses. After a few minutes of study, call for response.

Write *indebtedness* on the chalkboard. Call on a learner to read verses 18-25 aloud. Direct others to listen to discover what the indebtedness of believers is. When the reading is finished, call for response. After their response, share the comments titled "Letting God have your life" found in *Applying the Lesson.*

Give the Truth a Personal Focus

Share the comments titled "The great teacher of life" (*Applying the Lesson*). Note that in times of adversity and suffering, hope can become the most precious. Ask: Does your hope bloom or wither when you experience difficult times in your life? Why?

Suggest that learners talk with those sitting near them to determine ways to sustain and renew hope in the midst of personal stress and difficulties. After a few minutes of discussion, invite learners to share their conclusions. Include such things as remembering their security in Christ, recalling their home in heaven, and rejoicing in their present salvation. Conclude with a time of praise to God for the reasons learners have for their hope in Christ.

---

1. Ray Summers, "1 Peter" in *The Broadman Bible Commentary,* vol. 12 (Nashville: Broadman Press, 1972), 153.

2. Patrick M. Morley, *The Man in the Mirror* (Brentwood, Tenn.: Wolgemuth and Hyatt Publishers, 1989), 240-41.

3. Robert Browning Hamilton, "Pleasure and Sorrow," *Masterpieces of Religious Verse,* ed. James D. Morrison (Nashville: Broadman Press, 1977), 436

4. Powhatan James, *George W. Truett* (New York: The MacMillan Co., 1939), 25.

May 3

Called to Be God's People

Basic Passage: 1 Peter 2:1-25

Focal Passage: 1 Peter 2:1-10

Deep spiritual truths are mingled with practical advice on Christian living in this letter by Peter. Both are needed if we are to become mature in the faith. We need to realize that at the time Peter wrote his epistle the temple in Jerusalem was still standing. Its priestly officials, ornate furnishings, and impressive style of worship made the simple assemblies of Christians look inadequate, specially to Jewish converts. Gentile believers also were faced with a similar unfavorable comparison, for the pagan temples were staffed by elegant officials and their rituals outclassed the uncomplicated ordinances of New Testament churches. Peter wanted his readers to know there was no reason for any sense of inferiority. Christians were part of a massive change from the old to the new in which the church of Jesus Christ assumed roles that belonged to others in the past. The consequent spiritual privileges with which the individual believer was invested called for a life-style worthy of the faith professed.

Study Aim: *To better understand the God-given status of believers and respond with disciplined living*

STUDYING THE BIBLE

The high spiritual tone of this epistle is remarkable with Peter as its author, causing some to deny that he wrote it. But the rash, unpredictable disciple of the Gospels became a transformed man at Pentecost.

His consequent leadership position in the Jerusalem church testified to his emotional and spiritual development. Peter is, in fact, an outstanding example of his teaching that Christians should "grow in grace" (2 Pet. 3:18).

I. Growing in Grace (1 Pet. 2:1-3)

No break is intended between chapters 1 and 2. The chapter divisions, while convenient, sometimes interrupt the flow of what the writer is saying. This is largely overcome, in this case, by the opening word of chapter 2, whether we read it as "Wherefore" (KJV) or "Therefore" (NASB, NIV). Because you have been "born again" (1:23), Peter said, there are certain consequences for life and conduct.

> **1 Wherefore laying aside all malice, and all guile, and hypocrisies, and envies, and all evil speakings,**
> **2 As newborn babes, desire the sincere milk of the word, that ye may grow thereby:**
> **3 If so be ye have tasted that the Lord is gracious.**

1. Hindrances to growth (v. 1).—All of these listed are sins of the disposition, the subtler sins that may characterize persons who would avoid physical violence and sins of the flesh. The list may read, "malice, . . . guile, . . . insincerity, . . . envy, and . . . slander" (NRSV). These are to be "put away" (RSV), indicating an act of the will, in which, of course, we need to ask God's help. The popular slogan, "Say no," applies here.

2. Means of growth (vv. 2-3).—The remedy for wrong behavior is the right nourishment, what Peter called "the pure, spiritual milk" (NRSV). That he spoke of his readers as "newborn babes" would suggest that these were new converts who so far had only "tasted that the Lord is gracious." What they had experienced, however, should give them an appetite for more. As milk nourishes a young child, and produces growth, so the Word of God feeds the believer who thereby develops into maturity.

II. Endowed with Dignity (1 Pet. 2:4-10)

In 4:14, Peter wrote of his readers that they were "reproached for the name of Christ." In their daily lives they were subjected to indignities, so the apostle reminded them of their high standing before God. His repeated use of Old Testament concepts affirmed the truth that these Christians, whether Jews or Gentiles, were God's chosen people, the new Israel. Metaphors are mixed in this passage, which begins with a call to come to Christ, in faith and fellowship, that in Him they might be built up into a spiritual house.

4 To whom coming, as unto a living stone, disallowed indeed of men, but chosen of God, and precious,

5 Ye also, as lively stones, are built up a spiritual house, an holy priesthood, to offer up spiritual sacrifices, acceptable to God by Jesus Christ.

6 Wherefore also it is contained in the scripture, Behold, I lay in Zion a chief corner stone, elect, precious: and he that believeth on him shall not be confounded.

7 Unto you therefore which believe he is precious: but unto them which be disobedient, the stone which the builders disallowed, the same is made the head of the corner,

8 And a stone of stumbling, and a rock of offense, even to them which stumble at the word, being disobedient: whereunto also they were appointed.

9 But ye are a chosen generation, a royal priesthood, an holy nation, a peculiar people; that ye should show forth the praises of him who hath called you out of darkness into his marvelous light:

10 Which in time past were not a people, but are now the people of God: which had not obtained mercy, but now have obtained mercy.

1. God's new temple (vv. 4-8).—Psalm 118:22 reads, "The stone which the builders refused is become the head stone of the corner." In his speech before Jewish leaders, Peter referred this statement to the rejection of our Lord (Acts 4:10-11), as indeed Jesus Himself had done in Matthew 21:42. However, the major emphasis is not on humanity's rejection but God's approval and acceptance of Jesus, the "living stone," who is "chosen of God, and precious." He is the foundation stone in a new spiritual temple into which believers are built as "lively stones," providing not only "a spiritual house" but also "an holy priesthood." To all who regard Him as such Jesus is "precious," that is, of incomparable worth. To those who reject Him He is a "stone of stumbling," though they will eventually be forced to recognize Him as "the head of the corner."

2. Borrowed terms (vv. 9-10).—The four descriptive phrases in verse 9 are taken from Old Testament definitions of the nation Israel (Ex. 19:5-6). The word "peculiar" should be understood as meaning "cherished," as a prized personal possession. Once again, therefore, the idea of the church as successor to Israel is in view. Verse 10 echoes Hosea 1:10 and 2:23 where unfaithful Israel is replaced by others "which were not my people," foretelling the ingathering of the Gentiles and the establishment of the church. The idea of a "royal priesthood" is of special importance because it affirms the formation of a new priesthood to succeed that of Aaron and his sons. It furnishes the basis for the doctrine of the priesthood of believers, which not only implies the abolition of former priesthoods, but also repudiates the assumption of priestly functions and authority today. Under God's new covenant, all His people are priests having direct access to Him for themselves and are privileged to perform priestly services for others, not in an ecclesiastical sense but as advocates for others before God.

3. To the glory of God (v. 9b).—These privileges are not for self-gratification or advancement, but for the glory of God. As Christ, the chief "corner stone," was chosen of God (vv. 4-6), so also are those who make up a "chosen generation," believers who constitute the church. Israel of old was God's chosen people and is described as His "elect" (*chosen* and *elect* are the same word). Divine election has never been presented as a kind of favoritism by which certain people are given privileges above others. Rather, it is an appointment to service so that, while rejoicing in the benefits conferred on us as Christians, we can see these as reasons why we should minister to the needs of others, in Christ's name, thus bringing glory to our Benefactor.

III. Fulfilling Obligations (1 Pet. 2:11-25)

This idea continues to the end of the chapter and into the next as Peter mentioned areas of life into which the spirit of humble service should be carried. These are citizenship obligations, employee conduct, and family relationships (3:1-7). The historic context for these admonitions may differ from present conditions; for example, Peter wrote to slaves, but the principles have abiding value and importance.

1. As citizens (vv. 11-17).—Christianity had its beginning during times when oppression and persecution were prevalent. Believers' neighbors could be their next-door enemies, often basing their prejudiced attitudes on misinformation and misunderstanding. All kinds of false rumors were in circulation about Christians and their worship practices; thus, they became regarded as "evildoers" (v. 12). One effective answer to this was to be good citizens, for this would "put to silence the ignorance of foolish men" (v. 15). Christ's apostles consistently urged their followers to be law-abiding, cheerfully submitting to the many rules and regulations that were imposed by the Caesars and their representatives. This was not to mean violating the Christian's conscience by giving consent to things that one knew to be morally wrong or contrary to the laws of God. Over against Peter's advice in our current passage, we should recall what he said to the Jerusalem authorities when they tried to suppress the preaching of the gospel, "We ought to obey God rather than men" (Acts 5:29).

2. As workers (vv. 18-20).—In New Testament times, the slave population was in a ratio of one to five of the overall citizenry. The

Epistles indicate clearly that there were many slaves in the membership of the churches. The word translated "servants" both here and in other places refers to slaves. Some were captives of war, others debtors unable to meet their obligations. They included both the educated and the uneducated. As Christians, a potent witness to their faith could be borne by their attitude toward those who owned them. We can legitimately apply this teaching to employer-employee relationships today. The early messengers of Christ led no open opposition to the evils of slavery, except as they proclaimed the duty of mutual love, teaching that was eventually to eliminate slavery.

3. As followers of Christ (vv. 21-25).—In all the areas of life mentioned, and all others beside, the standard for our conduct is to be that of our Savior. His total selflessness caused Him to submit to death in our behalf, and He left "us an example, that [we] should follow his steps: . . . that we, being dead to sins, should live unto righteousness" (v. 21-24).

APPLYING THE LESSON

Desire to grow.—Pliny the Elder (A.D. 23-79) was a historian and scientist whose incurable curiosity has provided important details about daily life in ancient Rome. As a Roman military officer, he traveled all over the world. Everywhere he went, he recorded the geography, physics, and botany of the world he observed. His desire to learn led to both the fullness of his life and to his death. So curious was he and so desirous of learning that Pliny could not even take a bath without having some servant read to him so he could have some new fact to record in his journals later in the day. This desire for knowledge led to growth. It also led to his death. In A.D. 79, Pliny was meditating on a ship when he observed the first stages of the eruption of the volcano Mount Vesuvius. Instead of fleeing as others did, he moved his boat closer to get a better view, and he was eventually asphyxiated from the sulphurous gas that descended from the volcano.[1]

That same kind of curiosity and desire to learn was a part of the character of Simon Peter. That is why he grew from an uneducated fisherman to the gifted Christian whose Epistles are included in the text of Scripture.

Getting serious about God's Word.—Some of us are about the Bible like this little boy was. He wrote this letter to his pastor: "Dear Pastor, I've read the Bible every day since I was a little kid. So far I am up to the first page!" Like him, we often say we read the Bible but actually spend little time in God's Word.

Others of us are about the Bible like the famous outlaw of the old west, Jesse James. A minister who had known Jesse James in his earlier years bumped into him when he was in the midst of his life of crime. The minister reminded Jesse that he used to read the Bible when he was growing up. The outlaw immediately thrust his hand into his inside coat pocket and produced a

New Testament. The minister looked through the book in astonishment. It was marked up, showing constant use and frequent reading. Like Jesse James, we often read the Bible but do not follow the life-style it prescribes.

To grow spiritually, we must read the Bible, mark it, learn it, inwardly digest it, and then live by it. To those who approach the Bible in this way, the Bible is a resource Book that is never exhausted. A. T. Robertson, brilliant New Testament scholar, said late in his life, "Even after fifty years, I never open the Bible that I don't discover something new."

Church of preference.—A man was filling out a form on which he saw the words: "Church preference." He filled in the blank with the words: "Red Brick." Many times we think of the church in terms of buildings and structures. However, the essence of the church is people. Peter told us the church is made up of "living stones," that is, people who have built their lives on the "headstone of the corner."

All of us are priests.—We mark a sharp distinction today between laity and clergy. The New Testament describes all of us Christians in common terms. We are all saints. We are all believers. And we are all priests. Perhaps one dedicated Christian captured this thought when he was asked what he did for a living. He responded, "I am an ordained plumber." We are all ordained to be priests in God's new order.

What are you doing with your life?—Psychologist William Moulton Marston asked three thousand persons the question: "What are you living for?" Various answers were given, but the thrust of 94 percent of the answers was that these individuals were simply enduring the present, waiting for the future. They were waiting for something to happen. They were waiting for their children to grow up, or waiting until they could afford a trip, or waiting to get enough money to move to a new house, or waiting for someone to die, or waiting to retire. Their focus on tomorrow prevented them from fully experiencing today.

Christians must beware of that tendency. God promises a prepared place for His prepared people (John 14:1-3). God also has specific plans for His present people. We are not simply saved to enjoy the next life. We are saved to serve Christ in this life.

TEACHING THE CLASS

Main Idea: Believers are persons set apart in position and behavior by Christ.

Suggested Teaching Aim: Learners will describe their positions in Christ and the behavior expected of persons in that position.

Introduce the Bible Study

Display a picture of a child. Ask: How old would you guess the child to be? Elicit response. Continue: How would you feel if I told you this person is 42 years old? Elicit response. (Learners will probably respond with shock, sadness, and sympathy.) Ask rhetorically:

Would you agree this situation is representative of many followers of Jesus Christ? They are "old" in the faith but have not developed beyond the child level. Continue: Do we respond with equal dismay at this situation? Why?

State that the study for today focuses on the birth position of believers and their need to grow in behaviors that demonstrate who they are. Invite learners to open their Bibles to 1 Peter 2.

Search for Biblical Truth

Share the comments titled "Desire to grow" (*Applying the Lesson*). State that Peter placed emphasis on the reason for growth within believers. Call on a learner to read 1 Peter 2:1-3 while other learners listen to discover the reason believers should want to grow. When the reading is finished, call for response. (See v. 3.)

A Teaching Outline

1. Focus on personal growth.
2. Discover the reason for commitment to grow as Christians.
3. State some things to do that can produce Christian growth and development.
4. Commit themselves to growth in Christ.

Continue by asking: What things are cited as inhibitors of growth in the believer? (See v. 1.) List responses on the chalkboard.

Direct learners to discuss the meaning of each of the words on the chalkboard with those sitting near them. After a few minutes, discuss the words with the group.

Continue with the question: What will produce growth in believers? (See v. 2.) Elicit response. Continue: What is the meaning of the phrase "the sincere milk of the word"? Use the comments titled "Getting serious about God's Word" (*Applying the Lesson*).

Note that Peter turned to comment on the basis of believers growth in Christian qualities. Call on a learner to read 1 Peter 2:4-8 aloud from a modern translation. When finished, ask: What is the basis from which believers can grow in Christian qualities? (Their position in Christ.)

Direct learners to read verse 5 again to themselves. Share the comments titled "All of us are priests" (*Applying the Lesson*).

Note that verses 9 and 10 reiterate the special position of believers in Christ. Call on a learner to read them aloud. Write the four descriptive phrases from these verses on the chalkboard. Direct learners to discuss the meaning of each phrase with those sitting near them. After a few minutes, discuss the concepts with the larger group. Conclude by asking: What is the purpose of believers having this special position? (See v. 9b.)

Give the Truth a Personal Focus

Share the comments titled "What are you doing with your life? (*Applying the Lesson*). Ask: How many of us would choose to be a 42-year-old infant? Would we choose to be a 42-year-old spiritual infant? Allow a moment for learners to consider this choice.

Continue by asking: How can we prevent stunted growth as a believer? What are some things to do that produce Christian growth and development? Elicit response.

Challenge learners to commit themselves to growth based on their positions in Christ.

---

1. Malcolm Forbes, *They Went That a Way,* 237.

May 10

Witness in the Midst of Suffering

Basic Passage: 1 Peter 3:13—4:11

Focal Passages: 1 Peter 3:13-18; 4:1-2,7-11

Our lesson title could cause some of us to react: This is not for me, though I recognize it may have application to others. An important question, therefore, is: Was Peter referring to persecution already existing or to a looming probability? The tense of his verbs suggests the latter. The recurring word "if" also supports this. At the same time, Peter's readers were already experiencing opposition in the form of verbal abuse. We know from history that this abuse changed to violent hostility. This condition exists in some parts of the world today, so this lesson should stimulate our prayers for fellow believers who are paying a high price for their loyalty to Christ. Many feel that seeds of hostility are being sown in our own country where biblical values are under attack and those who hold to them are held up to ridicule and contempt. Therefore this study may challenge us to evaluate our relationship with a secular, sometimes godless, culture and force us to ask: If the cost of Christian discipleship should rise, where would I stand?

Study Aim: *To induce prayerful concern for all who suffer for Christ's sake and test our own willingness to pay that price*

STUDYING THE BIBLE

Peter wrote in desperate times. If some of his standards seem extreme (3:1-12), we should realize that they were matched to conditions in which it was of supreme importance for a clear line to be drawn between persons who made profession of faith in Christ and those who did not. Do present conditions require less exacting standards for those who confess Jesus as Lord?

I. Suffering for Righteousness' Sake (1 Pet. 3:13-18)

There is no chapter division between 3:12 and 13 though there might well be. Peter had been discussing the behavior of Christians, and their relationship to one another, concluding with the statement, "For the eyes of the Lord are over the righteous, . . . but the face of the Lord is against them that do evil" (v. 12). Then he abruptly changed themes, suggesting that he was responding to news that had just reached him, even as he wrote. Did that news concern a rising tide of opposition to the gospel and its adherents?

> **13 And who is he that will harm you, if ye be followers of that which is good?**
>
> **14 But and if ye suffer for righteousness' sake, happy are ye: and be not afraid of their terror, neither be troubled;**
>
> **15 But sanctify the Lord God in your hearts: and be ready always to give an answer to every man that asketh you a reason of the hope that is in you with meekness and fear:**
>
> **16 Having a good conscience; that, whereas they speak evil of you, as of evildoers, they may be ashamed that falsely accuse your good conversation in Christ.**
>
> **17 For it is better, if the will of God be so, that ye suffer for welldoing, than for evildoing.**
>
> **18 For Christ also hath once suffered for sins, the just for the unjust, that he might bring us to God, being put to death in the flesh, but quickened by the Spirit.**

1. Divine protection (vv. 13-14).—We are reminded of Paul's question, "If God be for us, who can be against us?" (Rom. 8:31). Such questions should not encourage any pollyannaish attitude toward pain and suffering. Rather, they are an assurance that if hostility should take an extreme form so that lives are forfeited, believers are only hastened thereby into the presence of their Lord, whereas their foes must face the justice of God (4:5).

2. Loyalty to Christ (v. 15).—Another reading is: "In your hearts reverence Christ as Lord" (RSV). The right answer to persecution is not retreat but fresh commitment to the lordship of Christ, which demands a loyalty that exceeds all others. Opposition should be made an opportunity for witness to one's personal faith. That witness should be borne in a humble spirit. Well-intentioned aggressiveness on the part of witnessing Christians can become an obstacle to positive response and may even deepen hostility. Thus it should be avoided.

3. Guarded behavior (vv. 16-17).—The word *conversation* means manner of life. Hatred toward Christians expressed itself in slander as they were falsely accused of unlawful and even immoral behavior. Peter's advice was, "Keep your conscience clear" (NRSV)—that is, no matter what people may say, see to it that their accusations are not true. If you have to suffer, it is better to do so for the good that you do and not the evil.

4. The supreme Sufferer (v. 18).—Our Savior suffered more than any of His followers. Though without sin ("just"), He died for sinners ("the unjust"); His purpose was to make it possible for unrighteous persons to be reconciled to God. (Verses 19-22, though in our basic material, are of uncertain meaning. One commentator records finding over thirty different interpretations. We shall serve our present purpose best by acknowledging the problem and leaving it unsolved.)

II. Following Christ's Example (1 Pet. 4:1-6)

We cannot but be impressed by the way Peter repeatedly presents our Lord as both Savior and Example. This is the man who, when Jesus broke the news of His coming death, responded with, "Be it far from thee, Lord: this shall not be unto thee" (Matt. 16:22). He had now become a fervent preacher of the crucified Christ, "Who his own self bare our sins in his own body on the tree, that we, being dead to sins, should live unto righteousness" (2:24).

> **1 Forasmuch then as Christ hath suffered for us in the flesh, arm yourselves likewise with the same mind: for he that hath suffered in the flesh hath ceased from sin;**
>
> **2 That he no longer should live the rest of his time in the flesh to the lusts of men, but to the will of God.**

1. The mind of Christ (v. 1).—Our Lord's example of vicarious suffering ("for us") is again offered as a pattern for the believer. Not that we should welcome suffering in general, but suffering that is for His sake and therefore honorable and redemptive. We are to "arm" ourselves with the mind of our Master, being willing to face the consequences of our loyalty to Him. Perhaps Peter used this military term because such an attitude has protective values against the onslaught of sin. To be fully committed to Christ will liberate us from evil influences so that it may be said of us that we have "ceased from sin," not sinless but no longer dominated by sin.

2. A vital choice (vv. 2-3).—These words suggest a Gentile readership rather than a Jewish, for they describe a pagan life-style that includes "idolatries." Dedication to a Christian manner of life, that may include suffering for Christ's sake, demands a complete separation from the past with its evil ways. The temptation to compromise is ever present, and only a firm purpose set on doing "the will of God" can keep us from faltering.

3. Weapons of words (vv. 4-5).—Former associates in sin may become a Christian's worst enemies. Their unregenerate minds are unable to understand the changes that have taken place in you. Therefore they become abusive. In the first Christian century, believers were slandered with a variety of false accusations. Those responsible would eventually have to face judgment from the Lord whom they maligned, for the "him" in verse 5 appears to refer to the Lord Jesus who will "judge the quick [living] and the dead at his appearing and his kingdom" (2 Tim. 4:1).

III. The Hope that Sustains (1 Pet. 4:7-11)

Included in the basic doctrine of New Testament believers was the coming again of the Lord Jesus. This doctrine is rooted in the Old Testament, which describes the Messiah in terms that were not fulfilled during His life on earth as God's incarnate Son. The Gospels contain many references to His return, statements made for the most part by Jesus Himself. Apostles taught their converts to be expectant of His return and encouraged the belief that this might happen during their life time. This was the hope that sustained a persecuted people even when faced by martyrdom.

> **7 But the end of all things is at hand: be ye therefore sober, and watch unto prayer.**
>
> **8 And above all things have fervent charity among yourselves: for charity shall cover the multitude of sins.**
>
> **9 Use hospitality one to another without grudging.**
>
> **10 As every man hath received the gift, even so minister the same one to another, as good stewards of the manifold grace of God.**
>
> **11 If any man speak, let him speak as the oracles of God; if any man minister, let him do it as of the ability that God giveth: that**

God in all things may be glorified through Jesus Christ, to whom be praise and dominion forever and ever. Amen.

1. The approaching end (v. 7a).—The Lord did not come in the first Christian century. Interestingly enough, it is Peter who is credited with explaining this, a subject we will take up on May 31. But when every explanation has been offered, the fact remains that believers of every century, including the present, should live expecting Christ's appearing.

2. Consequences in life (vv. 7b-9).—The effect of this hope can be disciplined ("be ye therefore sober"), prayerful behavior. Moreover, it should induce mutual love expressed in such ways as gracious hospitality. The more outside pressures increased, the more important it was for the Christian community to live and work together in harmony. The final statement of verse 8 means that when love abounds, criticism is suppressed as the faults and failings of others are forced into the background.

3. Humble sharing (vv. 10-11).—Apostolic teaching was in agreement. Paul taught that as members of one body believers should share their God-given abilities, using them humbly for the benefit of all (1 Cor. 12). Peter presented a similar idea, "Like good stewards of the manifold grace of God, serve one another with whatever gift each of you has received. . . . whoever serves must do so with the strength that God supplies, so that God may be glorified in all things through Jesus Christ" (NRSV). God's glory, not our own, is to be the objective of all Christian service.

APPLYING THE LESSON

Looking for trouble.—A wife woke up her husband in the middle of the night. "Someone is in the house," she whispered. To satisfy her, the husband went downstairs to look around. When he turned the lights on, he found himself face-to-face with a burglar. The burglar put a gun in the man's face and told him if he kept quiet he would not be hurt. The man told the burglar he had no intention of giving him trouble. But then he added, "I do have a favor to ask you. I wish you would wait here until I bring my wife down. I want you to meet her because she has been looking for you from time to time for twenty years."

Some people go through life looking for trouble. Truth is, we do not have to look very far to find trouble, for suffering of some kind is a part of the life experience of every person. Peter wrote about the kind of suffering that comes specifically because of our faith in Christ.

Quit playing around.—Dr. Morris Townsend dedicated his life to the cause of Christ as a physician and had to endure through many experiences of suffering and difficulty. Through it all, he remained faithful to the Lord. He was asked to share his experience and his faith at Keswick, a gathering for Christians, but was unable to fulfill the commitment because of poor health. Instead, he wrote this letter to Radcliffe Allen who had asked him to speak: "Dear Brother Allen: I had been looking forward to this, but I was restrained from getting in touch with you because I have something more important to look forward to. It has pleased God in His sovereignty to put cancer in both my lungs and in my liver, and it is the fast spreading type. So in all probability I will be in the presence of my Lord before next October." In the midst of this rather long letter, the key phrase was a challenge Dr. Townsend gave. He said, "Please convey to all the men this message: 'Stop playing around with Christianity.' "[1]

That is a good summary statement of the message of Peter's epistle. Great difficulties must be countered with great dedication.

What did you do about the boy?—Warren Cranford went to Africa on a missionary venture. He made slides while he was there and used these slides in his first presentation to a church when he came back home. On one of the slides was a little African boy. He had his nose and his hands pressed up tightly against the bakery window. Cranford went around inside the bakery and captured the expression of this little boy with his nose and hands against the window. Above his head was the sign: "Bakery." Cranford ended his slide presentation with the picture of this boy. When he asked for questions, someone in the congregation asked, "What did you do about the boy?" For the first time, Cranford realized that he had simply taken the picture of the boy, then walked away and done nothing.

All around us are "boys" like that one who need food and to hear a word about Christ. Our responsibility as Christians is to give a testimony to others about the faith that is within us.

A picture of the cross.—One of the great hymns of our faith is "When I Survey the Wondrous Cross." Like so many of our enduring hymns, the impact is made by the words of the text. Study the words of the hymn. Perhaps, you could even have your class sing the hymn. Then point out the theological truths that the hymn presents about Jesus. We see Jesus as a great Savior (v. 1) and as one who confronted a great sin (v. 3). In addition, we see that the only proper response to such a Savior is a great sacrifice (v. 2) and a complete surrender (v. 4).

A change demanded.—Alexander the Great was a conqueror who demanded unquestioned allegiance from his men. One day he heard of a soldier who had retreated instead of meeting the enemy. The man's name was the same as that of the great conqueror. Alexander the Great confronted the man. "Is your name Alexander?" he asked. "Yes," the soldier replied. "And did you retreat in the heat of the battle?" "Yes," the soldier answered. Alexander the Great retorted, "Then, young man, you need to either change your name or change your actions!"

To be a Christian means to be like Christ. If we are not willing to follow His example, we do not need to call ourselves by His name.

TEACHING THE CLASS

Main Idea: Believers are to live in love and prayer when suffering comes.

Suggested Teaching Aim: Learners will pray for power to live in love in the midst of suffering.

Introduce the Bible Study

Share the comments titled "Looking for trouble" (*Applying the Lesson*). State that for most of us looking for trouble, problems, hard times, and suffering is not necessary. If we live long enough, we will experience some of it. Ask: How do you handle it? Does being a believer make a difference in the way you handle life's pains? Elicit response.

Note that the study for today focuses on Peter's instructions to people who were experiencing serious suffering. Invite learners to open their Bibles to 1 Peter 3.

Search for Biblical Truth

Use information from *Studying the Bible* to describe the difficult times in which Peter wrote these words. Direct learners to scan 1 Peter 3:13-18 to locate words that indicate the level of difficulty these believers were experiencing. After a few minutes, call for response.

A Teaching Outline

1. Introduce the problem of suffering.
2. Review Peter's discussion of suffering in lives of believers.
3. Identify behavior appropriate for periods of suffering.
4. Pray for power to act in love in the midst of suffering.

Call on a learner to read 1 Peter 3:13-18 aloud while others listen to discover what believers were instructed to do in these circumstances. Call for response. Note them on the chalkboard. Responses should include the following: don't be afraid, don't be troubled, focus on the Lord, give an explanation for your behavior in humility, have a good conscience.

Refer to verse 18. Ask: What pattern do believers have to follow? Wait for response. Note that 1 Peter 4 continues this same thought. Call on someone to read 1 Peter 4:1-2. Ask: What is the good outcome of suffering?

Note that 1 Peter 4:7-11 gives some specific instructions about what believers are to do while living in difficult times. Direct learners to read the verses to themselves and be ready to state those behaviors. Call for response. Write responses on the chalkboard. They should include be prayerful, be serious about life, love fervently, be hospitable to others, give generously of what you have, speak for God, and minister in God's name. When the listing is finished, ask: What is the purpose of this behavior? After their response remark that the purpose is not to stop the suffering but to glorify God in it. Share the comments titled "Quit playing around" (*Applying the Lesson*).

Give the Truth a Personal Focus

Share the comments titled "What did you do about the boy" (*Applying the Lesson*). Explain that to know what should be done is not the point, but to decide how to do what should be done and then do it is the point.

Provide paper and pens. Direct learners to think of difficulties that they face. Perhaps the difficulties are financial problems, family problems, work problems, or spiritual problems. Help them to focus on the difficult times in their current lives. Direct them to consider the behavior listed on the chalkboard and privately complete this open-ended sentence: In this tough situation, I will ______________________ .

Allow several minutes for learners to complete this work.

Conclude the study with the comments titled "A change demanded" from *Applying the Lesson.* Spend several minutes praying together for power to act in love in the midst of suffering.

---

1. A. Dudley Dennison, *Prescription for Life: Medicinal and Spiritual Perspectives on Your Personal Needs* (Grand Rapids: Zondervan Publishing House, 1975), 71.

May 17

Humble, Steadfast, Vigilant

Basic Passage: 1 Peter 5:1-11

Focal Passage: 1 Peter 5:1-11

While opposition to Christ and His gospel increased, the churches continued to function as centers for worship, fellowship, and witness. One of the values of New Testament epistles is the light they shed on conditions in these first-century churches. We would like to think of those conditions as ideal, but human nature was the same then as it is today; and Christians are not immune to selfish interests, though when they give way to them they repudiate the high standards of personal conduct that their faith imposes. Peter wrote, with a deep sense of urgency, to correct trends that if not resisted could do serious damage to the progress of the gospel. That he addressed himself to "elders" and "ye younger," as distinct categories within the church, should remind us that first-century culture was different from ours. Leadership was then reserved for older people, whereas today youth are playing a growing part in most areas of life. Yet the principles of behavior laid down by the apostle are as valid now as they were then.

Study Aim: *To evaluate responsibilities and relationships within the church and enlist all concerned in resisting evil*

STUDYING THE BIBLE

Peter possessed qualifications to write this chapter that were superior to most. He was among the first disciples (John 1:40-42) and belonged to the small intimate group that witnessed the transfiguration and other significant events in our Lord's life (Mark 9:2; 14:33). Peter led the others in acknowledging Jesus as Messiah (8:29), and he was first to enter the open and empty sepulcher (John 20:6). He became spokesman for the infant church on the day of Pentecost (Acts 2:14), and he was one of the leaders in the Jerusalem church (Gal. 1:18-19), which recognized him as apostle to the Jews (2:8). Christian tradition holds that he suffered martyrdom in Rome.

I. Advice for Leaders (1 Pet. 5:1-4)

The office of elder has frequent mention in the New Testament. Paul and Barnabas "ordained them elders in every church" after their missionary tour of Asia Minor (Acts 14:23). On his final journey to Jerusalem, Paul summoned the elders of the church in Ephesus to whom he said, "Take heed . . . unto yourselves, and to all the flock, over the which the Holy Ghost hath made you overseers, to feed the church of God" (Acts 20:28). How these elders related to other church officials we do not know. It is possible that "elder" and "bishop" are interchangeable terms.

1 The elders which are among you I exhort, who am also an elder, and a witness of the sufferings of Christ, and also a partaker of the glory that shall be revealed:

2 Feed the flock of God which is among you, taking the oversight thereof, not by constraint, but willingly; not for filthy lucre, but of a ready mind;

3 Neither as being lords over God's heritage, but being examples to the flock.

4 And when the chief Shepherd shall appear, ye shall receive a crown of glory that fadeth not away.

Nothing in Scripture indicates Peter held office in a local church, apart from Jerusalem where he functioned as an apostle. Perhaps he considered the lesser office to be combined with the greater. In any case, he showed humility of spirit by describing himself as "also an elder," a humility that he enjoined on his readers. However, Peter claimed great privileges, namely, to have witnessed both Christ's sufferings and glory, the latter a probable reference to the transfiguration. He urged elders, "Feed the flock of God," which compares with Paul's words already quoted. Their ministry should be "not under compulsion but willingly, . . . not for sordid gain but eagerly. Do not lord it over those in your charge, but be examples to the flock" (NRSV). It would seem that these exhortations to humble, selfless service are needed today. The only reward to be sought is "a crown . . . that fadeth not away," not a royal crown but one of laurel that, unlike those bestowed on successful athletes, will prove imperishable. Those who prove themselves good undershepherds will be thus acknowledged by "the chief Shepherd."

II. Counsel for Followers (1 Pet. 5:5-7)

Whether "elder" is used in the same sense as "elders" in verse 1 is open to question. Here it may just mean older Christians, although this use would certainly include those previously described as "elders." The call to mutual subjection has a parallel in the apostle Paul's counsel to husbands and wives. While writing that "the husband is head of the wife," Paul also wrote, "Submitting yourselves one to another in the fear of God" (Eph. 5:21). Leadership is necessary in all areas of life, but it is to be compassionate and open to reasoning, so that the relationship is cordial, and not conflicting. The Greek for "be clothed with humility" literally means "put on the apron of humility" and therefore appears to relate to the incident recorded in John 13:1-17 in which Peter played a conspicuous part. As Jesus "took a towel, and girded himself," so all Christians, both young and old, are to render humble service to one another.

5 Likewise, ye younger, submit yourselves unto the elder. Yea, all of you be subject one to another, and be clothed with humility: for God resisteth the proud, and giveth grace to the humble.
6 Humble yourselves therefore under the mighty hand of God, that he may exalt you in due time:
7 Casting all your care upon him; for he careth for you.

The exhortation of verse 6 probably relates to the hardships Christians were undergoing at that time. God was not the cause of their hardships, but He was permitting them for an unstated purpose. The right attitude toward them was humble acceptance in the knowledge that God was in control, and He would bring His people out of their distresses "in due time." In the meantime, they should cast all their "anxiety" (NRSV), or worries, on Him "for he careth for you."

III. Dealing with the Adversary (1 Pet. 5:8-9)

The counsel of 4:7 is repeated as Peter called for disciplined living and vigilance, only here the vigilance is to be directed toward the activities of "your adversary the devil." More to be feared than any earthly foe, even than the imperial power of Rome, was Satan. He is compared to "a roaring lion," always on the prowl to catch and destroy the unwary. Effective protection against this enemy could be found in being "steadfast in the faith," that is, to exercise total and unwavering commitment to, and trust in, God. Others, they needed to remember, were experiencing the same pressures and offering the same resistance (v. 9b). A need for us today, if the profession and practice of our faith is not exposing us to abuse, is to have in mind those who are suffering for Christ's sake. A Christian publication has stated that in this century an average of 300,000 believers have been martyred each year.[1]

8 Be sober, be vigilant; because your adversary the devil, as a roaring lion, walketh about, seeking whom he may devour:

9 Whom resist steadfast in the faith, knowing that the same afflictions are accomplished in your brethren that are in the world.

Peter's imperatives should be noted: "Feed" (v. 2), "submit" (v. 5), "cast" (v. 7, NRSV), "Be sober, be vigilant" (v. 8), and "resist" (v. 9) are in agreement with Paul's exhortation to "work out" our salvation (Phil. 2:12). We can do nothing to earn salvation, which is God's free gift. But in the power of the Holy Spirit, our wills can (and should) cooperate with the purpose of God in our lives. To make a profession of faith, and then assume there is nothing more for us to do, is a grave misunderstanding. There are goals to be gained and battles to be won that demand the utmost of our efforts, made in the strength that God supplies.

IV. Facing the Future (1 Pet. 5:10-11)

Salvation begins and ends with God. For all Christians, there are crises along the way that occasion the question: "Will I ever make it?" Imagine what it was for these early believers who had to contend with the devil's schemes (as do we all), plus the animosity of unbelievers, and the cruel attacks of the civil authorities. Verse 10 reads like a prayer in the KJV, but in other versions it is a statement of confident hope as it affirms that God *will* do these things.

10 But the God of all grace, who hath called us unto his eternal glory by Christ Jesus, after that ye have suffered a while, make you perfect, stablish, strengthen, settle you.

11 To him be glory and dominion forever and ever. Amen.

Trouble is easier to bear when an end to it is in sight. Peter could assure his readers that there was an end, and that it would come "after . . . a while." The God who gives grace to bear tribulation is also the source, through Jesus Christ, of a call to enjoy His "eternal glory." When that time comes, said the apostle, He "will himself restore, support, strengthen, and establish you" (NRSV). No wonder he concluded with a doxology (v. 11).

V. Some Final Words (1 Pet. 5:12-14)

We would not want to leave this powerful letter without a glance at how it concludes. It was written, at Peter's dictation, by a "faithful brother" named Silvanus. This was the Silas of Acts 15:22, whom Paul, after his disagreement with Barnabas, chose as companion on his second missionary journey (v. 40). The tribute paid here indicates that Silas was a man of stature in the New Testament churches and may have contributed the high literary style that is recognizable in 1 Peter. The greeting from the "church that is at Babylon" (v. 13) raises the question of where this epistle was written. Wherever it was, a church existed there (v. 13), and this would appear to rule out the ancient city of that name in Mesopotamia. Historic sources tell that this city was abandoned by its Jewish community around the middle of the first Christian century. A later writer tells of the city being in ruins some sixty years later. A reasonable assumption is that Peter used the name Babylon for Rome, which had become the enemy of the church just as ancient Babylon was the enemy of Israel. We note with interest that Mark was another companion of Peter at that time.

APPLYING THE LESSON

The purpose of leadership.—What is a leader to do? Volumes have been written in answer to that question. Cut through the verbiage, and you can summarize the answers with two words: example and encouragement. A leader is to provide an example of what needs to be done. Then, he or she is to encourage others as they move in that direction. What a difference we would see in our churches today if leaders would do what leaders are supposed to do.

Faithfulness to the task.—One of the primary requirements of a preacher is faithfulness. No one better exemplified that than Charles Simeon. Born in 1759, he was converted as an undergraduate at Cambridge and longed to have an opportunity to preach there. When he walked by the Holy Trinity Church on the Cambridge campus, he would say to himself, "How I would rejoice if God gave me the opportunity to preach the gospel in this church." God answered his prayer, and in 1872, Simeon became the pastor of the church. The joy of the experience quickly evaporated in the face of stringent opposition from the people. The longtime members of the church who owned the seats, as was custom in those days, boycotted the services and locked the doors to their pews. For more than ten years the congregation had to stand. But Simeon persevered and gradually earned the respect of the town and the campus. For fifty-four years he remained at the church, teaching the Bible in a systematic way and giving exemplary leadership to the people.[2] Charles Simeon is a model of the kind of pastor Peter described in our text.

Two types of humility.—One writer described two kinds of humility and labeled them: Humility Type 1 and Humility Type 2. Humility Type 1 is described in Romans 12:3 and simply means not thinking more of ourselves than we ought to think, that is, having a right perspective about ourselves. Such humility does not mean to think little of ourselves. It simply means to think properly of ourselves. Humility Type 2 is a kind of self-debasement that causes us to miss completely the strengths and value that we do have. This kind of humility usually comes from comparing ourselves to others. Such self-debasement often leads to envy of spirit toward others.[3]

The kind of humility Peter recommended in our text is Humility Type 1, which comes from a proper perspective of God and a proper perspective of ourselves. When we look at God, we recognize that He is the source and strength of our lives. When we look at ourselves, we realize that we do have value, but only because of what God does for us and through us.

The devil's beatitudes.—Peter's mention of the devil, whose purpose is to undermine the work of God and to discourage the people of God, should alert us to the importance of the devil's beatitudes.

Blessed are they that are too tired and busy to go to church on Sunday, for they are my best workers. Blessed are they who are bored with the minister's mannerisms and mistakes, for they get nothing out of the sermon. Blessed is the church member who expects to be invited to his own church, for he is an important member to me. Blessed are they who do not go to church on Sunday evening, for they cause the world to say the church is failing. Blessed are they who gossip, for they cause strife and divisions that please me very much. Blessed are they who are easily offended, for they soon get angry and quit. Blessed are they who do not give their tithes and offerings to carry on God's work, for they are my helpers. Blessed are they who profess to love God but hate their brothers, for they shall be with me forever. Blessed are the troublemakers, for they shall be called the children of the devil. Blessed are they who have no time to pray, for they will be easy prey.

Hope helps us cope.—An executive took early retirement with this explanation, "For thirty years I have been coping with people, and I have run out of cope." Many of us come to situations in life when we feel like that. For the Christian, our hope in Christ helps us to cope. Our hope is rooted in what Christ did. Because He lived on this earth and faced the same things we face, we know He understands our situation. Because He won victory over the things we face, we know that He can enable us to win the victory as well.

TEACHING THE CLASS

Main Idea: Believers have leadership and "followship" responsibilities.

Suggested Teaching Aim: Learners will determine appropriate qualities and activities for leaders and followers.

Introduce the Bible Study

Write the following on the chalkboard: *lead, follow, or get out of the way.* Note that while this is not a Christian guideline, it communicates effectively.

Ask: Why do we need leaders? Why do we need followers? After their response, share the comments titled "The purpose of leadership" from *Applying the Lesson.*

Note that the Bible gives instructions about both the role of the leader and the follower and that Peter's writings comment about them. Invite learners to open their Bibles to 1 Peter 5.

Search for Biblical Truth

Share information from *Studying the Bible* to provide the setting from which these words were written. Display the following outline to guide the study of this chapter.

Leaders, Followers
1 Peter 5:1-11

1. Advice for leaders (vv. 1-4)
2. Counsel for followers (vv. 5-7)
3. Dealing with the adversary (vv. 8-9)
4. Facing the future (vv. 10-11)
5. Some final words (vv. 12-14)

Assign the five sections of the Scripture to groups of learners. Direct them to study the passage and be prepared to tell what advice or counsel on how to deal with the adversary, how to face the future, or final words Peter had to share. Allow several minutes for study and discussion.

A Teaching Outline

1. Consider the place of leaders and followers.
2. Discover biblical instructions concerning both roles.
3. Determine how to follow the biblical instructions in their lives.

When the study is finished, call on a learner to read the entire chapter aloud from a modern translation. Guide a discussion with questions like the following:

What advice does Peter have for leaders? Share the comments titled "Faithfulness to the task" (*Applying the Lesson*). Ask: What is the reward of a leader?

What counsel does Peter have for followers? Share the comments titled "Two types of humility" (*Applying the Lesson*). Ask: What is the reward of the follower?

How did Peter advise readers to deal with the devil? Share the comments titled "The devil's beatitudes" (*Applying the Lesson*).

How are believers to face the future? Share the comments titled "Hope helps us cope" (*Applying the Lesson*). Ask: What is the reward of those who face the future with hope?

What final words did Peter have in this letter? Share information from *Studying the Bible* to supplement response.

Give the Truth a Personal Focus

Ask: Would you consider yourself a leader or a follower in most areas of your life? Allow a moment for learners to consider their position. Direct learners to review the Scripture that applies to the position they most often take and consider the instructions from Peter. Allow several minutes for reflection.

Ask rhetorically: What specific behavior in your role would reflect these principles? Encourage learners to visualize themselves acting in the way Peter described. Conclude the study with a prayer of commitment to live out these principles in their lives.

---

1. *Christianity Today*, March 19, 1990, 12.
2. John R. W. Stott, *Between Two Worlds* (Grand Rapids: Wm. B. Eerdmans Publishing Co., 1982), 33.
3. Patrick Morley, *The Man in the Mirror*, 191.

May 24

Growing In Grace

Basic Passage: 2 Peter 1:1-14

Focal Passage: 2 Peter 1:1-14

The second letter that bears Peter's name was written to Christians exposed to false doctrine. It has three major themes: warning against heretical teaching, affirmation of the hope of the Lord's return, and exhortation to spiritual growth. The error pinpointed in this letter is gnosticism, from the Greek word for knowledge. Gnostics taught, among other things, that the way to salvation is through knowledge. From other New Testament books we know that early forms of gnosticism troubled the churches of the first Christian century, though true gnosticism did not develop till later. But the situation was serious enough for the apostle John to write against it, and 2 Peter contends with the same doctrinal enemy. This brief letter recommends growth in grace (2 Pet. 3:18) as protection against false teaching, and its recommendation is valid against every form of error, both then and now. Undeveloped and uninformed Christians are fair prey to purveyors of unbiblical ideas. Hence the importance of Christian education, including the Sunday School.

Study Aim: *To recognize spiritual maturity, and deepening understanding of biblical truth, as protection against error*

STUDYING THE BIBLE

The phrase, "cunningly devised fables" (v. 16), refers to another aspect of false teaching, namely, misrepresenting the person of Christ and His mission as Savior. In 2:1, charges are brought against "false teachers . . . even denying the Lord that bought them." The persistence of such teaching today makes this epistle relevant to our times so that we should take careful note of its counsel on how to resist its influence and stand strong in the faith.

I. A Believer's Privileges (2 Pet. 1:1-4)

Peter began his letter with a strong statement on the Christian's standing before God and its corresponding responsibilities. He wrote to those who shared with him "like precious faith" (v. 1). The unusual phrase, "of God and our Savior Jesus Christ," could have been directed against those who denied the unique relationship between the Father and the Son. Our shared faith is centered in One who, though being very God, laid aside His heavenly glory and assumed human flesh that He might become our Redeemer. The basis of our faith can be tested by our answer to the question, "What think ye of Christ? whose son is he?" (Matt. 22:42).

> **1 Simon Peter, a servant and an apostle of Jesus Christ, to them that have obtained like precious faith with us through the righteousness of God and our Savior Jesus Christ:**
>
> **2 Grace and peace be multiplied unto you through the knowledge of God, and of Jesus our Lord,**
>
> **3 According as his divine power hath given unto us all things that pertain unto life and godliness, through the knowledge of him that hath called us to glory and virtue:**
>
> **4 Whereby are given unto us exceeding great and precious promises: that by these ye might be partakers of the divine nature, having escaped the corruption that is in the world through lust.**

1. Knowledge available (v. 2).—Two references to knowledge in as many verses (2 and 3) are worthy of note. Persons who bragged about their superior knowledge, and the spiritual advantages it brought, caused others to feel inferior. Such reaction is unjustified since knowledge of the right sort is available to every believer, that is, "knowledge of God, and of Jesus our Lord."

2. Provision made (v. 3).—Emphasis continues on the adequacy of God's provision for those who seek this true knowledge, "all things that pertain unto life and godliness" covering every requirement for both physical and spiritual life. There was no need for Peter's readers to go seeking fuller revelations. All they needed was available to them in Christ who calls His people to "glory and goodness" (NRSV), that is, to share in His own nature.

3. Promises given (v. 4a).—God's people have always lived in reliance on divine promises. The hope of a coming Messiah inspired Old Testament saints with its prospect of better times to come. New Testament believers are also recipients of glorious promises for themselves (heaven and eternal life) and for the church (our Lord's return and the establishment of His kingdom). There are also "great and precious promises" that sustain us in times of trouble.

4. Relationship established (v. 4b).—A promise fulfilled for the believer is adoption into the family of God becomes a reality through faith in Christ. What a change this involves, for we are delivered from "the corruption that is in the world" and made recipients of the divine nature! The claim is stupendous, but it is in line with John's teaching, "Behold, what manner of love the Father hath bestowed upon us, that we should be called the sons of God" (1 John 3:1).

II. A Believer's Responsibilities (2 Pet. 1:5-7)

The phrase "beside this" obscures the true meaning, which is, "For this very reason" (NRSV). The Christian's high privileges provide the reason to "make every effort" (NRSV) to build on faith a life-style that is pleasing to God and a blessing to one's fellows. Eight qualities are named. (Eight is the number of notes in a musical octave and suggests a life in harmony with God's will.) All are essential, so we are not offered a cafeteria choice from which to pick our preferences but the essential ingredients of a well-rounded Christian character.

> **5 And beside this, giving all diligence, add to your faith virtue; and to virtue knowledge;**
>
> **6 And to knowledge temperance; and to temperance patience; and to patience godliness;**
>
> **7 And to godliness brotherly kindness; and to brotherly kindness charity.**

1. Incentive and response (v. 5a).—The opening words of this verse look back over all that precedes them and argues that because of all the blessings conferred on believers, they are obligated to play their part in developing a nature that is in accord with their high standing in Christ. As "partakers of the divine nature," we are to see to it that character and conduct reflect this amazing relationship. And we are to do it with "all diligence," directing our total effort toward attaining these goals.

2. Eight Christian qualities (vv. 5b-7).—They are founded in faith and crowned with love ("charity"). Faith is the indispensable starting point, because these are qualities impossible to attain apart from God's help. *Virtue* is a strong word suggesting courageous uprightness. *Knowledge* is not offered as a way to salvation but to living life at its best. For us, a growing understanding of God's way and will must come from study of the Scriptures. *Temperance* means "self-discipline," not a favorite subject with the gnostics or the pagans of those times who were more inclined to doing "what comes naturally." *Patience* should be understood as "endurance" or "steadfastness." Temptation to quit under pressure was strong but must be resisted. *Godliness* may be contrasted with "ungodly" (3:7). It describes a right attitude toward God so that fellowship with Him is deepened and strengthened. Prayer, Bible reading, and worship are necessary aids. *Brotherly kindness* refers to relationships within the church, while *charity* (*agape* love) is to be shown to all persons.

III. A Believer's Prospects (2 Pet. 1:8-14)

To possess faith without these qualities is to be an anemic Christian whose life will make little impression on others. Many who say, "I believe in God," or, "Yes, I have been saved," show little evidence in their lives. It is for this evidence that Peter pleads. Faith is tremendously important, but it should be regarded as the starting point for Christian living.

8 For if these things be in you, and abound, they make you that ye shall neither be barren nor unfruitful in the knowledge of our Lord Jesus Christ.

9 But he that lacketh these things is blind, and cannot see afar off, and hath forgotten that he was purged from his old sins.

10 Wherefore the rather, brethren, give diligence to make your calling and election sure: for if ye do these things, ye shall never fall:

11 For so an entrance shall be ministered unto you abundantly into the everlasting kingdom of our Lord and Saviour Jesus Christ.

12 Wherefore I will not be negligent to put you always in remembrance of these things, though ye know them, and be established in the present truth.

13 Yea, I think it meet, as long as I am in this tabernacle, to stir you up by putting you in remembrance;

14 Knowing that shortly I must put off this my tabernacle, even as our Lord Jesus Christ hath showed me.

1. Productiveness (v. 8).—For the individual believer, the consequences of practicing spiritual addition ("add to your faith," v. 5) begin with fruitful living. Verse 9 presents the alternative in terms of spiritual blindness, inability to recognize and respond to revealed truth.

2. Confidence (v. 10).—Faith that is undeveloped can become a wavering faith. On the other hand, making every endeavor to attain spiritual maturity results in increasing enjoyment of salvation's blessings. It is also a protection against stumbling into sin. The active, maturing Christian is less likely to become a victim of Satan's wiles.

3. Access (v. 11).—The word translated "add" in verse 5 is repeated here to describe God's action in introducing His people "abundantly into the everlasting kingdom." God will always outdo us in adding, and His overflowing generosity will culminate in bringing us to be with Him forever.

(Our lesson passage concludes with Peter's resolve to keep his readers in constant remembrance of these things that, though known already, cannot be too often repeated. His anticipation of approaching death, which he called putting off "this tabernacle," is related to our Lord's prophetic words in John 21:18-19.)

APPLYING THE LESSON

Some kind words.—Jerome was tired of being on the road. He was assigned a special project by his boss, and consequently, he had to be away from home for ten days in a row. On the tenth day, his discouragement overwhelmed him. As he ordered his food at the restaurant that night, the waitress said, "What do you need?" Jerome responded, "I want some of your lasagna and a few kind words." A few minutes later, the waitress delivered the dish to the table. As she turned to leave, Jerome said, "What about the kind words." The waitress leaned over and whispered in Jerome's ear, "Don't eat the lasagna!"

Sometimes we need words of warning. That was the situation in the early church. In this second epistle, Peter proclaimed a word of warning to the Christians of the first century.

Misplaced focus.—So often we misplace the focus of the Christian life. What does it mean to be a Christian? Simply put, to be a Christian means to believe in Jesus as the Son of God and to commit your life to Him. A man was seeking to lead a young woman to Christ one day. He asked her if she knew the joy of Jesus. Her response was: "No, I can't go to church. I have to work on Sundays." Church is important, but going to church does not make you a

Christian anymore than living in a garage will make you an automobile. From the first century to our century, Christians have had to continually focus on the essence of Christianity: personal faith in and commitment to Jesus Christ.

God's promises are for us.—A woman had an unusual dream. She saw a room crowded with people who were all obviously distraught. Suddenly, the door of the room opened, and Jesus Himself walked in. He moved from person to person. To each one He said, "My child, why are you crying?"

The first one answered, "I'm crying, Lord, because my husband died when we were so young, and from then on I was just lost without Him. I wanted to serve You, but I was too lonely and upset all those years to do anything." Jesus responded, "Didn't you get my letter?" "What letter, Lord?" came the reply. Jesus said, "I wrote you a letter and told you not to worry, that you believed in God, to believe also in me, and that I would not leave you comfortless." The woman looked surprised. "The minister read that letter at my husband's funeral, but I didn't know it was personal, from You to me."

Jesus stepped to the next person in the room. The man said, "Lord, I couldn't live for You because there were too many things I always had to be worrying about." Jesus said, "Did you not get a letter either?" The man responded, "Did You write me a letter?" "Yes," Jesus replied, "In it I told you about the birds of the air. They don't worry about their next meal, and yet they are fed. I told you to put Me first, for I had work for you to do, and I'd give you everything you really needed." The man said, "I remember reading about that, but I didn't know You meant it for me!"

Around the room Jesus went. For every malady He had words of healing and help from Scripture. But no one had taken the words to heart. For Christians of every century, God's provisions through Christ are personal, and they are adequate.

Two contrasting attitudes.—Notice the difference between these two attitudes.

One was the attitude of the father of D. T. Niles, a widely known Christian leader from Ceylon. Niles's father read the Bible through every year to deepen his knowledge of the Christian faith, and he read Shakespeare's writings every year to deepen his knowledge of human nature. This deepening of knowledge led in turn to a deepening of his faith.

The other attitude was the attitude revealed in an advertisement in the paper. The advertisement was for the sale of a set of encyclopedias. The ad was put into the paper by a certain woman who explained why she was selling her encyclopedias: "My husband knows everything."

One of these two attitudes is reflected in the life of every Christian. Some face each day with a hunger and thirst for more knowledge. Others face each day with the assumption they know everything. Peter's challenge to spiritual growth is in tune with the first of those two attitudes.

TEACHING THE LESSON

Main Idea: Growing in Christian qualities is a necessity for protection against spiritual error.

Suggested Teaching Aim: Learners will explain the need for, the meaning of, and the way to grow in Christian qualities.

Introduce the Bible Study

Share information from *Studying the Bible* that will introduce the study in 2 Peter. Share the comments titled "Some kind words" (*Applying the Lesson*). Note that Peter's words of warning are out of consideration for the well-being of his readers.

Write the main idea on the chalkboard. State that this is Peter's warning in the passage for study today. Ask: What does it mean to grow as a Christian? After their response, share the comments titled "Misplaced focus" (*Applying the Lesson*).

A Teaching Outline

1. Introduce the study in 2 Peter.
2. Focus on growing as a Christian.
3. Discover the need for growing, the meaning of growth, and how to grow in Christian qualities.

State that the purpose of the study today is to help us learn ways to grow in Christian qualities that will help protect us from spiritual error. Invite learners to open their Bibles to 2 Peter 1.

Search for Biblical Truth

Display this outline to guide the Bible study.

Growing in Grace
2 Peter 1:1-14

1. A believer's privileges (vv. 1-4)
   a. Knowledge of God
   b. Adequate provision
   c. Precious promises
2. A believer's responsibilities (vv. 5-7)
3. A believer's prospects (vv. 8-14)
   a. Productiveness
   b. Confidence
   c. Access

Call attention to the first section of the outline. Direct learners to study verses 1-4 to find the verse that supports each of the privileges noted in the outline. Write the verse beside the privilege when it is identified (knowledge, v. 2; provisions, v. 3; promises, v. 4a). Share the comments titled "God's promises are for us" (*Applying the Lesson*).

Note that the believer's privileges provide incentive to meet the believer's responsibilities mentioned in verses 5-7. Direct learners to find eight qualities in which Christians are to grow. After a moment of study, list the qualities on the chalkboard. Direct learners to write them down. Ask: What do these qualities look like in our lives? What do the words mean? Direct learners to discuss the words with those sitting near them to determine what they mean and how they would act if they develop that quality. After a period of study, call for conclusions to be shared.

Continue the Bible study by directing learners to read verses 8-14 and match a verse with the believer's prospect indicated on the outline. After a time of study, call for response. Write the verses on the outline (productiveness, v. 8; confidence, v. 10; access, v. 11). Share the comments titled "Two contrasting attitudes" (*Applying the Lesson*).

Give the Truth a Personal Focus

Ask: How can developing the Christian qualities listed here by Peter protect you against spiritual error? As they respond, establish that the need to grow in these Christian virtues is imperative.

Ask: How does a believer develop these characteristics? Encourage learners to commit themselves to those behaviors that will develop these qualities.

Focused on the Future

Basic Passage: 2 Peter 3:3-14

Focal Passage: 2 Peter 3:3-14

The story of Jesus is without beginning or end. We may think of His life on earth as starting in Bethlehem and ending at Calvary, or on the Mount of Olives where He ascended to His Father. The clear teaching of Scripture is in His eternal existence He shared in the creation of the universe (Col. 1:16-17), now "ever liveth to make intercession" for His people (Heb. 7:25), is coming again for the redeemed (1 Thess. 4:16), and will forever reign after the "kingdom of the world has become the kingdom of our Lord and of his Messiah" (Rev. 11:15, NRSV). The next great event in this divine biography will be His return to earth as He promised (John 14:3) and as angels foretold after His ascension (Acts 1:10-11). The hope of Jesus' return has led to much speculation and many misleading claims, in spite of His plain statement, "But of that day and hour knoweth no man, no, not the angels of heaven, but my Father only" (Matt. 24:36). Our lesson material reproves some false conclusions while it reaffirms the fact of Christ's return and exhorts to appropriate conduct.

Study Aim: *To reexamine our attitude toward our Lord's return both in belief and behavior*

STUDYING THE BIBLE

Chapter 3 opens with reference to "This second epistle," probably meaning 1 Peter, although we must acknowledge that some other document may have existed of which we are unaware. This is a friendly chapter—note the repeated use of "beloved" (vv. 1,8,14,17)—in spite of the reproof it contains, and it ends with a splendid exhortation and doxology (v. 18). May this study enable us to "grow in grace, and in the knowledge of our Lord and Savior Jesus Christ."

I. Christ's Return Repudiated (2 Pet. 3:3-7)

Earlier in this letter, Peter had acknowledged that the things he was writing about were already known to his readers (1:12-13). The same is stated in 3:1 and puts emphasis on the unfortunate fact that knowing and doing are two different things. We have the same thought in James 1:22. In spite of careful teaching, some of Peter's readers were falling into serious error. Head knowledge is not enough. Commitment of heart and will are also necessary.

3 Knowing this first, that there shall come in the last days scoffers, walking after their own lusts,

4 And saying, Where is the promise of his coming? for since the fathers fell asleep, all things continue as they were from the beginning of the creation.

5 For this they willingly are ignorant of, that by the word of God the heavens were of old, and the earth standing out of the water and in the water:

6 Whereby the world that then was, being overflowed with water, perished:

7 But the heavens and the earth, which are now, by the same word are kept in store, reserved unto fire against the day of judgment and perdition of ungodly men.

1. Scoffers described (vv. 3-4).—Among things that should have been known and remembered was that prophets and apostles spoke of a falling away from the true faith. Illustrative of this was the presence of persons, within the church, who were making ridicule of teaching about the Lord's return. These were saying that history was pursuing its course without any such event. Generations were born and died, and nothing happened; everything continued along a normal course without any divine intervention. Of these particular persons Peter said that they were "walking after their own lusts," that is, living in complete disregard of morality. We must not understand this to mean that persons with independent ideas about the Lord's coming are necessarily evil, only that this was true of those Peter described.

2. God always active (vv. 5-7).—The apostle went back to the Genesis account of creation to remind his readers of the activity of God. At creation God caused the earth to rise out of the waters (Gen. 1:9), but He later permitted the flood when the world was "overflowed with water," a divine act of judgment. At that time, He promised Noah that He would not so destroy the earth again (Gen. 9:11). The next judgment, according to Peter, would be by fire (see also v. 10). According to the latter verse, this fiery judgment would also be accompanied by "a great noise." In these days of nuclear bombs and missiles, it is easy to think of their destructive power. Peter was not saying that the earth's inhabitants would destroy themselves and their environments, but he meant that God would use these means. However we understand Peter's statement, he was describing a fiery end to conditions as they are, with God in control.

II. Christ's Return Affirmed (2 Pet. 3:8-10)

Peter had three other arguments to use against those who, because of the passing of time, doubted Christ's return and accordingly allowed themselves to slip into careless ways. Together they constitute a strong affirmation of the doctrine of the second coming, and they are important to us who, as we anticipate the twenty-first century, need to be reminded of the abiding value of biblical teaching.

8 But, beloved, be not ignorant of this one thing, that one day is with the Lord as a thousand years, and a thousand years as one day.

9 The Lord is not slack concerning his promise, as some men count slackness; but is long-suffering to us-ward, not willing that any should perish, but that all should come to repentance.

10 But the day of the Lord will come as a thief in the night; in the which the heavens shall pass away with a great noise, and the elements shall melt with fervent heat, the earth also and the works that are therein shall be burned up.

1. Time and timelessness (v. 8).—We are creatures of time. Our lives are ordered by clocks and calendars. Not so God. One of the hardest things for us to grasp is His eternity, without beginning and without end. One of Israel's psalmists, reaching for this truth, described God as "from everlasting to everlasting," and said of Him, "For a thousand years in thy sight are but as yesterday when it is past, and as a watch in the night" (Ps. 90:2,4). Peter reproduced this thought in order to help his readers understand that the activity of God cannot be measured by any human standard of time. We reckon the incidents of our Lord's life as taking place two thousand years ago. But if God were subject to any form of chronology, which He is not, this could be no more than two days ago. Even to make this statement is to attempt the impossible, for we are at a loss to comprehend God's eternal existence. It belongs to the mystery of Deity.

2. Compassionate delay (v. 9).—More readily understood is the apostle's statement that, if we think in terms of a delayed return of our Lord, we should regard this as evidence of God's compassion for sinners. In Old Testament times, persons who lived in expectation of a coming "day of the Lord" were warned that it would come as a day of judgment, "darkness, and not light" (Amos 5:18). Likewise the coming again of the Lord Jesus is described in a dual light, gain immeasurable for His people, and loss indescribable for the disobedient and unbelieving (Matt. 24:29-31). So long as Jesus does not come, opportunity is present for persons to repent and believe. During this period, it behooves God's people to be messengers of His gospel that all may hear and exercise faith, and so become part of the redeemed.

3. Sudden and unexpected (v. 10).—Our writer's emphasis is strong and powerful, "But the day of the Lord will come." Let doubters beware and the indifferent arouse themselves, for God's purposes are sure. Moreover, that day will come without warning and so catch many by surprise. Jesus had used the analogy of a thief when speaking of His return, and the apostle Paul echoed the idea when he wrote, "the day of the Lord so cometh as a thief in the night" (1 Thess. 5:2). The focus is on the unexpectedness of a thief's action. He does not announce his coming in advance but takes his victims by surprise. Yet people continue to fix dates for the second coming and add their names to a long list of false prophets who claim to know what Jesus Himself made no claim to knowing (Matt. 24:36).

III. Christ's Return Motivating (2 Pet. 3:11-14)

Our Lord gave several parables related to the need for active watchfulness on the part of those who look for His coming again. Three are grouped in Matthew 24:42—25:30. This is the theme of the following verses from 2 Peter:

> **11 Seeing then that all these things shall be dissolved, what manner of persons ought ye to be in all holy conversation and godliness,**
>
> **12 Looking for and hasting unto the coming of the day of God, wherein the heavens being on fire shall be dissolved, and the elements shall melt with fervent heat?**
>
> **13 Nevertheless we, according to his promise, look for new heavens and a new earth, wherein dwelleth righteousness.**
>
> **14 Wherefore, beloved, seeing that ye look for such things, be diligent that ye may be found of him in peace, without spot, and blameless.**

1. Expectant living (vv. 11-12).—The knowledge that our Lord may be revealed in power at any moment should have a sobering effect on His people. Are there places where we would not wish Him to find us? Activities that we would not wish Him to see? An old spiritual says, "He'll find me hoeing cotton when He comes," that is, busy about my rightful tasks and therefore unashamed to face Him. In verse 11, "conversation," as elsewhere in the *King James Version*, means "manner of life," and that, of course, includes speech, its character and content.

2. A new beginning (vv. 13-14).—In line with the Book of Revelation, this epistle looks into the future and sees "a new heaven and a new earth: for the first heaven and the first earth were passed away" (Rev. 21:1). The destruction earlier described precedes a new beginning and a cosmos "wherein dwelleth righteousness." Peter did not elaborate on this glorious prospect, but had he done so, it would surely have been in terms similar to Revelation 21:1-8 and 22:1-5. God has plans for a new creation, in which all His redeemed people will share in the joys . Meanwhile, He waits in order that the number of the redeemed may be multiplied.

APPLYING THE LESSON

Till Jesus comes.—The prediction of Jesus' return permeates the New Testament. Because of the certainty of His coming, we need to be ready. BO Baker in *The Lift of Love* makes some pertinent suggestions, here quoted, on what to do until Jesus comes:

1. Be sure that your salvation is firmly grounded in the person of Jesus Christ.
2. Deal thoroughly with any and all unconfessed sin and spiritual unfaithfulness. . . .
3. Deposit daily some acts of Christian love and service in heaven. . . .
4. Do today what the Holy Spirit impresses you to do without delay or the slightest anticipation that someone else will do it for you.
5. Feed upon the Word of God in order that you may have some understanding of the place, the plan, and the people with whom you will spend eternity.
6. Live your faith as a natural experience and not as an unnatural phenomenon.
7. Cultivate a consistent prayer life which forbids a fear of the unknown.
8. Make a serious and honest effort to so witness to the saving grace of God that others like you will be ready to meet Jesus when He comes.[1]

Prayer in a wagon.—A man who lived in the country fell and broke his leg. He was confined to his house for a long period of time. He had a large family and thus needed some help. The Christian friends at church held a prayer meeting to pray for this family. While the people were praying and asking God to help the family, there was a loud knock on the door of this needy family's home. A young boy stood at the door. He said to the needy family, "My father could not attend the prayer meeting tonight, so he just sent his prayers in a wagon." On this wagon were potatoes, meat, apples, and other things to help the needy family. Prayer is important, but allowing us to be instruments by which our prayers are fulfilled is even more important. In the

Christian life, what's most important is not what we know to do or what we want to do but what we actually do.

Today.—As creatures of time, we are aware of our past and anticipatory about our future, but the time in which we must live is *today.* Yesterday is a canceled check. Tomorrow is a promissory note. Only today is currency we can spend. Someone made three suggestions about today: today is all you have, today is all you can manage, and today is all you need. Each of those statements is true about us. The Bible says we have a God who is not limited by today, who is not confined by today, nor is He exhausted by today. He is God for whom "one day is . . . as a thousand years, and a thousand years as one day" (2 Pet. 3:8).

The queen of virtues.—Do you know what Chrysostom, the golden-tongued orator of another generation, called the "queen of virtues"? He was referring to patience.

Charles Allen, a gifted communicator of our generation, addressed the subject from the other direction. He said that the worse sin in America is staying too busy, as if by our busy-ness we can rush things according to our plans.

Most of us come closer to committing the sin of "busy-ness" than in exhibiting the virtue of "patience." Patience, like all virtues, is displayed in its perfect form in God. God's patience is rooted in His compassion for humankind and His desire that humankind will hear and heed His word.

Motivation for a productive life.—Many things motivate us to be our best. Martin Niemoeller, German patriot who opposed Hitler, said that whenever he was tempted to give up, he was motivated by a vision of the German youth of the future. Sam Rayburn, famous politician, was motivated by a challenge given to him as a young man by his father who said, "Sam, be a man." Larry Bird, one of the greatest professional basketball players of today, admits that much of his motivation came from those who doubted his ability. He wanted to prove them wrong.

The greatest motivation for the Christian is the fact that someday Jesus Christ will return, and we will have to give an account of our lives to Him. How wonderful it would be to hear Him say to us, "Well done, good and faithful servant."

TEACHING THE CLASS

Main Idea: The return of Jesus Christ is a fact that must affect how we live our lives.

Suggested Teaching Aim: Learners will evaluate their beliefs and their behavior related to the return of Jesus Christ.

Introduce the Bible Study

Share the comments titled "Motivation for a productive life" (*Applying the Lesson*). Note that this final study in 2 Peter emphasizes the return of Jesus Christ.

Ask: What do you know about the second coming of Christ? Elicit response. Encourage learners to express their thoughts even if unsure of the facts. Point out that while there may be disagreement about the sequence of events related to the return of Christ, the fact of His return is clearly taught in the Scripture.

Ask: What is the purpose of knowing that Jesus will return to earth again? What difference does that make? Responses may include the hope that the fact gives and confidence in their faith. If it is not included, point out that the fact of His return should also make a difference in the way we live our lives until His return.

State that the purpose of the study today is to help us evaluate both our beliefs about the return of Christ and our behavior in view of the fact of His return. Invite learners to open their Bibles to 2 Peter 3.

Search for Biblical Truth

Use information from *Studying the Bible* to provide background for this Scripture passage. State that in the day in which Peter wrote there were those who scoffed at the idea that Jesus would return to earth. Direct learners to read verses 3-4 to themselves to learn what the scoffers were saying. Call for response. (Everything is as it always has been. Nothing will change.)

A Teaching Outline

1. Focus on the return of Jesus.
2. Discover some facts about His return that were emphasized by Peter.
3. Evaluate personal beliefs and behavior in view of these facts.
4. Decide to pursue more appropriate behavior in view of the sure return of Jesus.

Note that Peter refuted their statement in verses 5-7. Call on a learner to read the verses aloud. Note that Peter affirmed that God is always at work. Use information from *Studying the Bible* to supplement comments.

State that Peter gave explanation of why it seems that nothing will change to the scoffer in verse 8. Call on a learner to read the verse aloud. Note that it is a commonly quoted verse. Ask learners to read verse 9 to themselves and discover the reason why God delays Jesus' coming. Call for response. Share the comments titled "The queen of virtues" (*Applying the Lesson*).

State that verse 10 begins Peter's description of the return of the Lord. Call on a learner to read the verse aloud. Compare this information with other information provided by learners as the study was begun.

Share that Peter now began to give instruction about how believers ought to respond in view of the sure return of Christ. Direct learners to read verses 11-14 silently. When the reading is finished, direct learners to work with those sitting near them to develop a list of Peter's instructions for living in view of the return of Jesus. After several minutes, invite learners to share their conclusions.

Give the Truth a Personal Focus

Share the information from *Applying the Lesson* titled "Till Jesus comes." If possible, provide learners copies of the points suggesting that these are very practical ways to live out the instructions of Peter.

Conclude the unit of study by asking learners to share their impressions of the writings of Peter, what his primary emphasis seems to be, and how it has influenced their thinking and behavior.

---

1. BO Baker, *The Lift of Love* (Nashville: Broadman Press, 1986), 122-23.

June, July, August 1992

God's Judgment and Mercy

Aids from BROADMAN for Studying and Teaching

Books:
The Broadman Bible Commentary, Volume 7
Layman's Bible Book Commentary, Volumes 13,14
Strong's Exhaustive Concordance, James Strong
The Heart of Hebrew History, H. I. Hester

Apart from a few of the Minor Prophets such as Hosea, Amos, and Jonah, these ancient pronouncements seldom find their way into Sunday School curriculum. In this series we are to make acquaintance with some of the lesser-known books that conclude the Old Testament: Obadiah, Nahum, and Zephaniah among them. There are two units of lessons, as follows:

Unit I, "Warnings and Promises from God," deals with prophecies of judgment against the people of Israel and other nations. God's universal sovereignty will be brought into sharp focus.

June 7

The Lord Will Restore Judah

Basic Passage: Obadiah

Focal Passages: Obadiah 1-4,10-11,15,17,21

Unfamiliar passages of Scripture are always a challenge. The little prophecy of Obadiah, only twenty-one verses, is probably among the least known of the books of the Bible. A strong note of condemnation prevails throughout the book as the prophet denounced the people of Edom for their treachery against Israel and pronounced their doom. The one positive note is the sovereignty of God who is active in history to bring deliverance to His people. A New Testament parallel may be found in recent lessons on Peter's Epistles in which the persecuted church was assured of judgment on its enemies and an abundant entrance "into the everlasting kingdom of our Lord and Savior Jesus Christ" (2 Pet. 1:11). Old Testament prophecies of a restored Israel were fulfilled in the return from Babylonian captivity and the rebuilding of Jerusalem. Our anticipation is not an earthly kingdom but a heavenly, again to quote Peter, "wherein dwelleth righteousness" (2 Pet. 3:13).

Study Aim: *To recognize God at work in history and trust His promises for the future*

STUDYING THE BIBLE

Edomites were descendants of Esau. The hostility evidenced at the birth of the twins, Jacob and Esau (Gen. 25:21-23), continued through many centuries. The Edomites, who occupied territory south of the Dead Sea, refused the plea of Moses to be allowed to lead the Israelites through their territory and threatened violence if they attempted this (Num. 20:14-21). Consequently, "Edom and Israel scorned and hated each other throughout their whole history. For centuries there existed between them an implacable animosity. They constantly waged a war of revenge against each other."[1] There were clashes between the two during Saul's reign, but David subdued the Edomites (2 Sam. 8:14). In later years, they repeatedly rebelled; and in Jehoram's reign, they revolted, selected a king, and attacked Judah (2 Chron. 21:8-10). This is the background against which Obadiah's prophecy must be studied.

I. Pride Leads to a Fall (Obad. 1-4)

Obadiah is among the common names of the Old Testament; and in the absence of information about the author in the book that bears this name, we are not able to identify him. Neither can any final determination be made as to the date of writing, but see comments below on verses 10-14.

1 The vision of Obadiah. Thus saith the Lord concerning Edom; We have heard a rumor from the Lord, and an ambassador is sent among the heathen, Arise, ye, and let us rise up against her in battle.
2 Behold, I have made thee small among the heathen: thou art greatly despised.
3 The pride of thine heart hath deceived thee, thou that dwellest in the clefts of the rock, whose habitation is high; that saith in his heart, Who shall bring me down to the ground?
4 Though thou exalt thyself as the eagle, and though thou set thy nest among the stars, thence will I bring thee down, saith the Lord.

1. Call to arms (v. 1).—Our understanding is helped by this translation, "We have heard a report from the Lord, / and a messenger has been sent among the nations" (NRSV). "Nations" should also be read for "heathen" in verse 2. A call to arms against Edom is issued, in God's name, to surrounding nations. People who had been acting in arrogance against others were due for a fall. Though big and important in their own estimation, they would be reduced to insignificance and accordingly despised by others.

2. False confidence (vv. 2-4).—The pride of the Edomites was expressed in the towering rocks in which they lived. Modern tourists in the Middle East are still fascinated by the rock city of Petra, successor to the Edomite stronghold. Most Bible dictionaries contain pictures of impressive structures hewn out of solid stone. These structures were the work of an Arab people known as Nabateans who drove out the Edomites somewhere around 300 B.C. Edomite ruins have been found in the area. The physical appearance of Petra and its neighborhood fits well into the description given in verses 3-4 as the territory occupied by Edom.

II. Callous Indifference Rebuked (Obad. 10-14)

Verses 5-9 anticipate the coming destruction of Edom. Their enemy would not be like a common thief who would take what he wanted and spare the rest, or a gatherer of grapes who would take all he needed and no more. Those upon whom the Edomites had relied for help would forsake them. The reference to "wise men" (v. 8) acknowledges that among these people were those highly rated as scholars. Neither mountain strongholds nor brains would suffice in the coming day of judgment. In two places in this passage, "Esau" is used for Edom. Teman (v. 9) was an Edomite city.

> **10 For thy violence against thy brother Jacob shame shall cover thee, and thou shalt be cut off forever.**
>
> **11 In the day that thou stoodest on the other side, in the day that the strangers carried away captive his forces, and foreigners entered into his gates, and cast lots upon Jerusalem, even thou wast as one of them.**

1. Aiding Israel's enemies (vv. 10-11).—By ancestry, Edomites were descended from Esau and Israelites from Jacob, hence the use of "Jacob" (v. 10). The charge made is that the Edomites took "the other side" by aiding the enemies of Jerusalem when they attacked that city. The precise occasion is not given, but the consensus of opinion favors the Babylonian assault (587 B.C.) when the city was destroyed and its people taken into exile.

2. Detailed accusations (vv. 12-14).—The Edomites did not merely stand aside in Jerusalem's hour of need, but they actively supported the Babylonians. They actually entered the city, gloated (NRSV) over the disaster that had befallen it, joined the enemy in looting its contents, cut off the escape of fleeing citizens, and delivered them into the hands of the attackers. The phrase, "You should not," (NRSV) introduces eight distinct charges made against Edom for which God would call them to account.

III. Divine Justice at Work (Obad. 15-16)

The prophetic word against Edom was, "As thou hast done, it shall be done unto thee" (v. 15). A century or more after the fall of Jerusalem, Nabatean Arabs forced the Edomites out of the rocky fortresses that are now Petra and drove them south into an area that became known as Idumea. Later, in the period of the Maccabees, they were forcibly incorporated into the Jewish community with which, of course, they already had a blood relationship. The Herods were Idumeans. When Rome subdued and destroyed Jerusalem in A.D. 70, Edomites fought alongside the inhabitants of the city. A secular source, however, accuses them of treachery. Whether or not, from this point on they disappeared as a recognizable people from the pages of history.

> **15 For the day of the Lord is near upon all the heathen: as thou hast done, it shall be done unto thee: thy reward shall return upon thine own head.**

The emphasis is on the judgments and sovereignty of God. Edom had boasted, "Who shall bring me down to the ground?" (v. 3), and the answer was, "Thence will I bring thee down, saith the Lord" (v. 4). Verse 16 goes beyond the fate of Edom and declares that "all the nations around you" (NRSV) will similarly fall if they resist the purposes of the Lord. In this verse, references to drinking do not refer to refreshment but to judgment; violators will drink of the cup of divine wrath. Of Edom it became true, "They shall be as though they had not been." A casual knowledge of history can produce other names of nations, small and great, that have disappeared: Babylon, for example; Assyria; the Greek and Roman empires, mighty in their day, oppressive in their policies, and now no more. Even the Northern Kingdom of Israel, after the destruction of Samaria its capital, passed into oblivion, its people apparently being merged into the general Jewish population of Palestine. There are modern examples, also, so that the warning is clear to all nations who oppose the purposes of and despise God's laws.

IV. God's Care for His People (Obad. 17-21)

The vision of God's prophets extended far beyond current events, or those in the near future. Their messages related to these, as when Obadiah foretold the fate of Edom. But in his concluding verse, this prophet reached into the distant future when the reign of God would prevail.

17 But upon mount Zion shall be deliverance, and there shall be holiness; and the house of Jacob shall possess their possessions.

....

21 And saviors shall come up on mount Zion to judge the mount of Esau; and the kingdom shall be the Lord's.

1. Jerusalem's security (v. 17).—Under the name of mount Zion, Jerusalem is promised deliverance from its enemies. We do not know when Obadiah's words were written, but they appear to refer to the return from exile when the walls of the city were rebuilt and the temple restored. The statement "There shall be holiness" can be variously understood. It can mean that Jerusalem would again be a sacred place and, therefore, under the protection of the Lord. Moreover, "the house of Jacob"—the Israelites as a whole—would recover lost possessions, probably lands occupied during the exile.

2. Possessions recovered (vv. 18-20).—The "house of Jacob" mentioned together with "the house of Joseph" (v. 18) indicated a coming together of the two kingdoms of Judah and Israel. The times of the divided kingdom would end. Together they would execute judgment on "the house of Esau" (Edom). Other neighboring people also took advantage of Israel's misfortunes. They too would be dispossessed of land that was not theirs by right (vv. 19-20).

3. Justice enthroned (v. 21).—All this spoke of the ultimate victory of God over His foes and the foes of His people. Looking into the distant future, the prophet wrote, "The kingdom shall be the Lord's." This note of optimistic expectations is characteristic of all Israel's prophets. No matter how dark a picture they presented, the prophets invariably concluded with a triumphant message that declared God to be in charge of history, of which He would write the ultimate chapter. Though nations rise and fall, His kingdom stands firm and will be revealed one day in all its splendor.

APPLYING THE LESSON

Sowing and reaping.—William McKinley, who later became president of the United States, was on a streetcar one night. He took the last empty seat at the rear of the car. At one of the stops, an old washer woman, carrying a heavy basket, boarded the car. With no place to sit, she stood in the aisle. A man was sitting right in front of the old lady, but he shifted his newspaper in such a way as to act like he didn't see her. McKinley walked down the aisle, picked up the basket of washing, and led the old lady back to his seat.

What seemed to be nothing more than a slight unkindness by the man who refused to help was in fact more than that. This man who displayed obvious unconcern was a politician who held public office. Many years later, McKinley was trying to decide between two men to appoint to an important diplomatic post. Suddenly, McKinley remembered the incident from the streetcar many years earlier, for the man who had refused to offer a seat to the lady was one of the candidates for the diplomatic seat. McKinley gave the position to the other candidate. The man never knew that his act of unkindness would later deprive him of what would have been the most important opportunity in his life.

This story illustrates a truth that is at the heart of the Book of Obadiah: what we sow we will eventually reap.

Watch out for your enemies.—Yogi Berra became a famous baseball player not only because of his ability but also because of some of the "tricks of the trade" that he learned over the years. For example, Ken Harrelson, who later became a great baseball player himself, came to the plate for his first time at bat in the big leagues. It was Yankee Stadium, NBC game of the week. Whitey Ford was pitching. Yogi Berra was catching. The first pitch was a strike. The second pitch was a strike. With two strikes, Harrelson tensed up. His mother was watching him play on television, and he did not want to strike out. Just before the next pitch came, Harrelson said, he felt something warm on the back of his sock. He glanced down to see what it was as the pitch swished by for strike three. Yogi had spit on the back of his leg to distract him, and while he was distracted, Whitey Ford zipped in the third strike. Harrelson was dumbfounded. Yogi grinned and said, "Welcome to the big leagues, kid!"

"All's fair in love and war" is an adage that applies to professional baseball. Unfortunately, we also apply that adage to our relationships with other people. Consequently, we do things to our enemies that we would not do in normal circumstances. That truth explains the intensity of feelings between the Israelites and the Edomites. The hatred of these two nations for each other, which was rooted in their earliest history, was reflected in the unkind actions and attitudes they manifested toward each other.

Two sides of pride.—Pride is condemned in the Bible and from the pulpit, but the word *pride* has two sides. Pride can be commendable when it expresses a healthy sense of contentment with who we are and what we have accomplished. Such pride is expressed in Paul's familiar statement, "I can do all things through Him who strengthens me" (Phil. 4:13, NASB). However, pride has another face. Pride can also be defined as "an excessively high opinion of oneself." This kind of pride can be called "conceit," and it is condemned unequivocally in the Bible. This second kind of pride characterized the Edomites.

Typo or the truth?—Sometimes typographical errors reveal more truth about us than we like. One rather cold, sophisticated church wanted to create an air of compassion and concern. So at the bottom of the bulletin each Sunday, they printed this statement, "We take interest in everyone." However, one week a typographical error produced another revealing version. The typo said, "We fake interest in everyone."

The Edomites did not even "fake" interest in the Israelites. Theirs was an obvious and intense dislike, and this feeling was revealed in their gloating over the defeat of Israel.

TEACHING THE CLASS

Main Idea: God's righteous indignation can bring human downfall.

Suggested Teaching Aim: Learners will describe the quality of God that reflects indignance and consider righteous indignation in their lives.

Introduce the Bible Study

Write *Obadiah, Nahum, Zephaniah, Jonah* on the chalkboard. Direct learners to locate the books in their Bibles. Use information from the introduction to the study for the quarter to comment about the two units from these books. Write the names of the units on the chalkboard.

A Teaching Outline

1. Introduce the study, "God's Judgment and Mercy."
2. Introduce the Book of Obadiah and today's study.
3. Discover why God expressed indignation through Obadiah's words.
4. Consider the place of indignation in the response of a believer.
5. Consider the possibility of personal arrogance that brings the indignation of God on learners.

Direct learners to turn again to Obadiah. State that the purpose of today's study is to learn of the righteous indignation of God and its result.

Search for Biblical Truth

Share information from the introduction (*Studying the Bible*) to provide background for understanding the passage. Display the following outline to guide the Bible study.

Obadiah 1-4,10-11,15,17,21

I. Pride leads to a fall (vv. 1-4)
II. Callous indifference rebuked (vv. 10-14)
III. Divine justice at work (vv. 15-16)
IV. God's care for His people (vv. 17-21)

Call on a learner to read verses 1-4 aloud after noting the outline heading for these verses. Use information from *Studying the Bible* to comment about Edom's false confidence.

Share the comments titled "Sowing and reaping"(*Applying the Lesson*). Note that the next section of Scripture for study begins the reaping. Call on a learner to read verses 10 and 11 aloud. Ask: What was the accusation against the Edomites? (They sided with the aggressors against God's people.)

Note that specific accusations are aimed at the Edomites in verses 12-14. Use information from *Studying the Bible* about these verses.

Call attention to the third heading. Call on a learner to read verse 15 aloud while other learners listen to learn the judgment pronounced. Call for response.

Note the future focus of the next verses. Call attention to the outline heading. Use information from *Studying the Bible* to clarify the meaning. Call on a learner to read verses 17 and 21 aloud.

Give the Truth a Personal Focus

Share the story titled "Typo or the truth?" (*Applying the Lesson*). Note that such arrogant behavior caused God to look on the Edomites with condemnation. Their pride created indignation in the response of God. Share the comments about pride found in the paragraph titled "Two sides of pride" (*Applying the Lesson*).

Ask rhetorically: Is God justified in expressing indignation at behavior like that of the Edomites? Continue: Are Christians ever justified in expressing indignation about the behavior of other people? If so, when and in what circumstances? Elicit response. Discuss appropriate ways of expressing indignation.

Continue by asking rhetorically: Are there behaviors and attitudes about which God might be indignant in our own lives? Do you have some of the arrogant characteristics of the Edomites? How would God deal with you in such circumstances? Allow several minutes for learners to consider their own relationship with God.

---

1. George L. Robinson, *The Twelve Minor Prophets* (Grand Rapids: Baker Book House, 1952), 67.

June 14

Fleeing From God

Basic Passage: Jonah 1—2

Focal Passages: Jonah 1:1-9,15-17

Racial prejudice is not new. In our previous lesson we saw how enmity existed, for long centuries, between Israel and Edom. Explanations for this are not difficult to find. But the fact remains that these two contestants were descended from twin brothers, Jacob and Esau, and should have learned how to live in peace with one another. There were no close blood ties between Israel and Assyria, a nation that terrorized its neighbors until its eclipse around 612 B.C. For Jonah to be sent by God as missionary to Nineveh, capital of Assyria, meant ministering to his nation's worst enemy. He was not prepared to do that and went to great lengths to escape the responsibility given to him. His story is left open-ended, with no conclusive finish. Jonah was left sitting on a bluff, waiting to "see what would become of the city" (4:5). He knew well his God-given duty but still struggled with his prejudices. Isn't this the condition of many people today in a world divided by hatred and mistrust?

Study Aim: *To face our prejudices, identify them, and resolve what we should do with them in light of the teaching of Christ*

STUDYING THE BIBLE

The Book of Jonah falls into four dramatic scenes, conveniently marked by its four chapters. It bears Jonah's name but was written by some other anonymous person, with the exception of the prayer in chapter 2. When it was written is difficult to determine, but its message suits a time, possibly after the Babylonian exile, when the Jewish people were expressing a high sense of national pride with a corresponding disdain for other nations.

I. The Man and His Book

Critical scholarship has tried to present the Book of Jonah as an allegory, with no historical basis. This ignores clear statements about the prophet, in both the Old and New Testaments. In our attempts to interpret the book we should remember that it was written after (perhaps long after) the events described. The author found in Jonah's story a much-needed message for his own times.

1. Jonah's period.—The Old Testament reference to Jonah is in 2 Kings 14:23-27 where he is said to have foretold the victories of Jeroboam II, king of Israel. His identity is confirmed by his being described as the son of Amittai (see Jonah 1:1). In spite of Jeroboam's evil reign, this was a time of national recovery for the Northern Kingdom. We may assume that Jonah was happy as messenger of good tidings to the king's court and had no desire to change his job. Our Lord compared Jonah's adventure in the big fish with His own burial and resurrection (Matt. 12:38-42; 16:4). His reference was coupled with another to the "queen of the south," that is, Sheba (12:42), an unquestioned historical figure.

2. The book's purpose.—There were other prophets to Israel around Jonah's time, namely, Amos and Hosea. Unlike Jonah, these men reproved national sin with a strong emphasis on social oppression. So we have a picture of a nation "externally strong, prosperous, and confident of the future" but "inwardly rotten and sick past curing."[1] Material prosperity and military success blinded the people to their true condition and encouraged a national pride that was their undoing. The archenemy, Assyria, was in decline, and this encouraged a sense of superiority that expressed itself in a distorted patriotism. These dangerous attitudes were to be repeated in later history, so Jonah's story was revived in order to rebuke and correct a spirit that had brought previous disaster. God's universal compassion was an idea that had been buried by a deluge of pride and prejudice.

II. Jonah's Commission (Jonah 1:1-3)

The court prophet's easygoing life was disturbed by an order from God to go preach in Nineveh, Assyria's capital. This was a very ancient city (Gen. 10:11) and, according to all reports, had become one of the more corrupt communities of the ancient East. Jonah, who seems to have closed his eyes to the evil that was going on in Israel, was being sent to a notoriously wicked city whose rulers had long been oppressors of his people.

> **1 Now the word of the Lord came unto Jonah the son of Amittai, saying,**
>
> **2 Arise, go to Nineveh, that great city, and cry against it; for their wickedness is come up before me.**
>
> **3 But Jonah rose up to flee unto Tarshish from the presence of the Lord, and went down to Joppa; and he found a ship going to Tarshish: so he paid the fare thereof and went down into it, to go with them unto Tarshish from the presence of the Lord.**

In willful disobedience toward God, Jonah decided to get as far from Nineveh as possible. He was willing to take a long, hard sea voyage to avoid carrying out the divine command. Tarshish is usually located in Spain; and if this was Jonah's destination, it was at the ends of the earth according to the limited geographical knowledge of those days. The Scripture states twice that his flight was "from the presence of the Lord." Does this reveal a misunderstanding of the nature of God? The psalmist asked, "Whither shall I go from thy spirit? or whither shall I flee from thy presence?" (Ps. 139:7). He made several suggestions only to acknowledge that there is no escaping God. This Jonah learned the hard way.

III. Flight and Its Consequences (Jonah 1:4-10)

Important to note are the opening words of verse 4, "But the Lord sent out a great wind." Similar statements are, "Now the Lord had prepared a great fish" (v. 17); "The Lord spake unto the fish" (2:10); "The Lord God prepared a gourd" (4:6); and, "But God prepared a worm" (4:7). We are not dealing with natural processes but with the activity of God in behalf of Jonah, for his instruction, and for instruction of all who read his story.

4 But the Lord sent out a great wind into the sea, and there was a mighty tempest in the sea, so that the ship was like to be broken.
5 Then the mariners were afraid, and cried every man unto his god, and cast forth the wares that were in the ship into the sea, to lighten it of them. But Jonah was gone down into the sides of the ship; and he lay, and was fast asleep.
6 So the shipmaster came to him, and said unto him, What meanest thou, O sleeper? arise, call upon thy God, if so be that God will think upon us, that we perish not.
7 And they said everyone to his fellow, Come, and let us cast lots, that we may know for whose cause this evil is upon us. So they cast lots, and the lot fell upon Jonah.
8 Then said they unto him, Tell us, we pray thee, for whose cause this evil is upon us; What is thine occupation? and whence comest thou? what is thy country? and of what people art thou?
9 And he said unto them, I am an Hebrew; and I fear the Lord, the God of heaven, which hath made the sea and the dry land.

1. Asleep in a storm (vv. 4-6).—This extraordinary storm had the crew, probably Phoenicians, scared to death. Its fury is suggested by the rendering, "But the Lord hurled a great wind" (NRSV). The seamen cried to their gods for help, and then they took practical measures to save themselves by throwing overboard everything that was not nailed down. This was a normal procedure for the purpose of lightening the ship so that it would ride higher in the rough water (see Acts 27:38). Meanwhile, Jonah was fast asleep (the Greek version of the Old Testament reads, "was asleep, and snored"). This must have been a sleep of emotional and physical exhaustion from which the ship's captain had difficulty awakening him. Here was a passenger who was not contributing to the emergency by praying for deliverance, as the crew had done.

2. Confession made (vv. 7-10).—The belief of the pagan seamen was that someone on board was responsible for this furious storm. To find out who, they cast lots, perhaps with stones, perhaps with long and short straws. This procedure pointed to Jonah as the culprit, and he was plied with questions to find out more about him and to possibly obtain explanation for what was happening. In doing this, the crew showed some hesitation in jumping to a conclusion, merely on the basis of the lot. They were giving Jonah a fair chance. In making reply, this reticent prophet did some preaching to the men who shared his danger (v. 9) and then made a surprising confession: he was running away from the Creator God whom he professed to worship ("fear").

IV. A Refuge Provided (Jonah 1:11-17)

Jonah's action in this acute situation shows that he was more of a misguided patriot than a coward. He would not go to Nineveh because its inhabitants were the enemies of his people. But, after being identified as the cause of the storm, he asked to be thrown into the sea that the rest might be saved.

15 So they took up Jonah, and cast him forth into the sea: and the sea ceased from her raging.

16 Then the men feared the Lord exceedingly, and offered a sacrifice unto the Lord, and made vows.

17 Now the Lord had prepared a great fish to swallow up Jonah. And Jonah was in the belly of the fish three days and three nights.

1. Reaction of seamen (vv. 13,14,16).—The efforts of the pagan crew to save Jonah were recorded to their credit. They first tried to row to shore. Then they prayed to Jonah's God and offered a sacrifice to Him. They became examples of the fact that the most unlikely people (Ninevites among them) are capable of responding to the true God.

2. The great fish (v. 17).—This was not necessarily a whale but a specially prepared sea creature, capable of providing a safe refuge for Jonah until lessons had been learned.

V. Prayer from the Depths (Jonah 2)

Our larger lesson includes this chapter. Above all, it illustrates the power of prayer, in this case offered in an unlikely place and by an undeserving person. Jonah acknowledged that what had happened to him was God's judgment (v. 3). In his plight, he made heavy use of the psalms, a reminder of the value of committing God's Word to memory. We never know when we may need its comfort and strength. In confidence of deliverance from his underwater prison, Jonah renewed his earlier vows, and he was cast forth "upon the dry land" (v. 10).

APPLYING THE LESSON

No prejudice.—General Chuck Yeager was a pioneer in aviation history. He was not only the first man to fly faster than the speed of sound, he has also been one of the best test pilots in American history. Accusations of racial prejudice in the air force incensed Yeager. He said, "Nowadays, it has become fashionable for some companies to advertise themselves as 'equal opportunity employers.' The Air Force practiced that with me right from the start, and I would never deny to anybody else the chance to prove his worth, no matter who or what he is. There never were black pilots or white pilots in the Air Force. There were only pilots who knew how to fly, and pilots who didn't."[2]

Yeager may claim an absence of prejudice in the air force. However, the truth is, each of us is often held captive by our prejudices. Our lesson reminds us that this has been a problem for a long time.

God's love revealed.—A play entitled *The Sign of Jonah,* written shortly after World War II, clearly depicts God's love. The setting of the play is Germany right after World War II. The point of the play is to attempt to discover who was to blame for the awful atrocities of the war. One man suggested Hitler was to blame. Another blamed the problems on the Jews. Others declared the real culprit was the apathetic "average person" who did nothing to resist the movement of Hitler. Finally, one man said, "I know whose fault it is. God is to blame. He is the one who made it happen." The crowd agreed, and they decided to take God to court. He was found guilty of the crime of creation, and the judge pronounced the sentence. For punishment of the crime of creation, God was going to have to come and live in the world like human beings do. Three archangels, Gabriel, Michael, and Raphael, were sent to execute the judgment. Gabriel mused to himself, "When God serves this sentence, I'll make sure he knows obscurity and shame. He'll be born in obscurity and will know what it is like to live in an occupied country and be the object of scorn." Then Michael mused to himself, "When God serves His sentence, I'm going to see to it that He knows frustration and insecurity. He'll have no place to lay His head. His family will desert Him. In the end, even His friends will desert Him." Raphael mused to himself, "When God serves this sentence, I'm going to see to it that He knows what it is like to suffer and to die. He will be falsely accused, illegally tried, and will then die the long slow death of a common criminal." At that point, the lights go out, and the play is over. And suddenly the truth becomes clear—God has already served that sentence. He already knows what it's like to live as a human being in this kind of world. He revealed in the incarnation His unconquerable love for the world. The Book of Jonah describes the process by which the prophet came to understand about God's love.

The power of prayer.—You've probably heard the old saying: "Nothing lies beyond the reach of prayer except that which lies outside the will of God." Nowhere is that truth illustrated more clearly than in the experience of Jonah. The Bible is filled with illustrations of those who cried out to God in their time of need and found Him sufficient. However, the danger in these examples is the tendency to think of prayer only in emergency terms.

One little boy was asked by his mother if he had said his prayers before going to bed. "No," the little boy replied, "I didn't need anything."

Another child said to her family, "Does anyone need anything? I'm getting ready to pray."

Yet another child said, "God, My sister is still not married, my mother is still sick, I still failed my history test, and my daddy still doesn't have a job. I'm tired of praying and not getting any results."

When Jonah prayed, he did get results. However, that was not the most important factor about his prayer. The most important thing about Jonah's prayer was that it put him back in touch with God. A richer relationship and not necessarily rich results is the greatest product of prayer.

TEACHING THE CLASS

Main Idea: Prejudice can separate us from God.

Suggested Teaching Aim: Learners will resolve to deal with their own prejudices.

Introduce the Bible Study

Note that the study for today is from Jonah, a book more familiar to most than Obadiah. Ask: As you recall Jonah's story, what would you say were his main problems? Elicit response. Note on chalkboard. If prejudice is not listed, suggest it to learners.

Share the comments from paragraphs titled "No prejudice" (*Applying the Lesson*). Ask: Do you recognize prejudice in yourself? What prejudices do we often have whether we are aware of them or not?

Continue by asking: What is the effect of such prejudices on our relationship with God and on His will being carried out in our lives?

A Teaching Outline

1. Focus on kinds and effects of prejudice.
2. Discover the results of prejudice in the life of Jonah.
3. Determine the effect of personal prejudices.
4. Resolve to deal with personal prejudices to prevent a breach in their personal relationship with God.

State that the purpose of the study of Jonah's experience is to encourage us to deal with our own prejudices. Invite learners to turn to Jonah 1.

Search for Biblical Truth

Share information about the background of the Book of Jonah found in the introduction of *Studying the Bible*. Display the following outline to guide the study of Jonah 1.

Fleeing from God
Jonah 1—2

I. Jonah's commission (vv. 1-3)
II. Jonah's flight and its consequences (vv. 4-10)
III. A refuge provided (vv. 11-17)
IV. Jonah's prayer from the depths (chap. 2)

Assign each of the passages in the four outline headings to different groups of learners. Direct them to study the assigned section of the Scripture to find answers to the following questions. Provide copies of the questions for the group.

Group 1: Jonah 1:1-3

1. Why was Jonah directed by God to go to Nineveh?
2. Why did Jonah buy a ticket instead to Tarshish?

Group 2: Jonah 1:4-10

1. What was the cause of the great storm?
2. What caused the seamen to question Jonah about the storm?
3. How did Jonah respond?

Group 3: Jonah 1:11-17

1. Why might Jonah be considered a misguided patriot rather than a coward?
2. What is suggested by the fear and sacrifice of the seamen?
3. How would you describe the fish that received Jonah?

Group 4: Jonah 2

1. What new viewpoint does Jonah's prayer suggest?
2. How did God provide a second chance for Jonah?

Call on learners to report their conclusions to the larger group when they have finished their group study and discussion. When Group 4 discusses Jonah's prayer, share the comments titled "The power of prayer" (*Applying the Lesson*).

Give the Truth a Personal Focus

Ask: Specifically, what was Jonah's major prejudice? (He was prejudiced against the citizens of Nineveh because they were enemies of his people.) How did that prejudice affect his relationship with God? (Note that only when Jonah recognized his prejudice and the disobedience that accompanied it did he have complete fellowship with God.)

Continue by reviewing prejudices acknowledged by learners as the study was begun. Ask: Is it possible that these prejudices are separating us from complete fellowship with God? In what ways do such prejudices keep us from doing what God wants believers to do? Elicit response.

Conclude with a time of meditation and prayer directing learners to come before God acknowledging prejudices they have and asking for wisdom in dealing with them.

---

1. John Bright, *A History of Israel* (Philadelphia: Westminster Press, 1959), 248.
2. Chuck Yeager and Leo Janos, *Yeager* (Toronto: Bantam, 1985), 272.

June 21

Jonah Sulks, and God Saves

Basic Passage: Jonah 3—4

Focal Passages: Jonah 3:1-5,10; 4:1-4,10-11

The Book of Jonah is missions in the Old Testament. Centuries later, the Lord Jesus Christ was to say, "Go ye into all the world, and preach the gospel to every creature" (Mark 16:15). The reluctance of Jonah to obey God's command has had its tragic sequel in the slowness of Christians to share their blessings with others. We are familiar with the obstacles placed in the way of young William Carey when he caught the vision of a world that needed to know of the Savior. A veteran minister rebuked Carey for his enthusiasm and stated that when God was ready to convert the heathen, He would do it Himself, without human aid. The truth is, of course, that God has always been ready, as He was in Jonah's day, but His servants held back from the task. Jonah's story ends with that prophet looking out over Nineveh, with its teeming thousands of people, still unwilling to share the compassion of the Lord for those he regarded as his nation's enemies. Only when the love of God motivates can we engage in redemptive efforts that are effective in reaching people with the gospel of forgiveness and salvation.

Study Aim: *To reexamine the missionary obligation of the church and its members, including ourselves*

STUDYING THE BIBLE

"Jonah was a man in whom piety and duty were ever in conflict; a man who feared God, but at the same time ran away from his task . . .; a man in whom the spirit of humanity had been almost killed out by patriotism; in short, a man whose religion resided in the realm of emotion, rather than in the sphere of the will. Jesus, in contrast, wept over Jerusalem!"[1]

I. Called a Second Time (Jonah 3:1-4)

Chapters 1 and 3 begin with similar wording, with the exception of one significant clause: "the second time." We might well ask ourselves whether we would have given Jonah another chance to make good. He is not depicted as a pleasant character; though, to give him his due, he does appear in a more attractive light in his witness to the pagan seamen and his willingness to accept death rather than that they all should perish (1:9,12). But this glimpse of another side to his nature only serves to emphasize the depth of his prejudice toward the Ninevites. Once people are branded as enemies it can be hard to regard them in any other light.

1 And the word of the Lord came unto Jonah the second time, saying,
2 Arise, go unto Nineveh, that great city, and preach unto it the preaching that I bid thee.
3 So Jonah arose, and went unto Nineveh, according to the word of the Lord. Now Nineveh was an exceeding great city of three days' journey.
4 And Jonah began to enter into the city a day's journey, and he cried, and said, Yet forty days, and Nineveh shall be overthrown.

1. God's patience (vv. 1-2).—Jonah had been worse than disobedient; he had tried to "flee . . . from the presence of the Lord" (1:3). There was a spirit of rebellion in his action. Yet, having preserved him from a watery death, the Lord had heeded Jonah when he "prayed unto the Lord his God out of the fish's belly" (2:1). But God's patience with this willful man did not bring release from assignment. Jonah was given a second opportunity to respond to a divine command to go to Nineveh as an appointed messenger. Should we depend on second chances when we willfully reject God's revealed will for our lives?

2. Jonah's message (vv. 3-4).—Apparently, Jonah's message was brief and to the point. He was a prophet of doom; yet, from the response of the Ninevites we must assume that what he said carried with it an implication of divine forgiveness. The reference to Nineveh as "an exceeding great city of three days' journey" is difficult to interpret. Many think that a cluster of cities gathered around the capital accounts for the description. We are left to imagine the effect produced by this Israelite prophet stalking through the streets with his message of impending doom, even if it was delivered in what, to the Ninevites, was a foreign tongue.

II. Nineveh Repents (Jonah 3:5-10)

What happened in Nineveh has been offered as an example of the power of preaching. However, the word "preach" (v. 2) can be rendered "proclaim" (NRSV). Jonah's role was more that of a town crier than a preacher. His message, however brief, was nevertheless from

God; therefore, what was unquestionably demonstrated is the effectiveness of a word from the Lord to produce great change. Just as our Lord's sharp command, "Peace, be still" (Mark 4:39), ended the fury of a storm, so Jonah's blunt statement, repeated again and again, produced a response in the Ninevites.

1. Popular response (v. 5).—This began with the people as every level of society decided to take Jonah's message seriously. The depth of their repentance is open to question; but at that time, they acknowledged their sins and, following oriental custom, fasted and dressed themselves in sackcloth.

2. Ruler's reaction (vv. 6-9).—Jonah's message even reached the ears of the ruler of the city, as did also news of the people's demonstration of repentance. The king stripped himself of his royal robes, undoubtedly garments of great splendor, and donned the sackcloth of the people while he also sat on an ash heap. These actions were symbolic of great grief. In his orders to the people, the king referred to their evil ways and "the violence that is in their hands" (v. 8). While Assyria tyrannized neighboring countries, the residents of its capital had engaged in brutalities among themselves. They had plenty for which to repent.

3. God's repentance (v. 10).—The king's call to repentance was made in the hope that it would persuade God to "turn and repent, and turn away from his fierce anger" (v. 9). This expressed hope from a heathen official could not be expected to have the depth of understanding that the idea of a repenting God is given elsewhere in Scripture. But, as the following verse indicates, the command of the king, together with the response of the people, brought about the desired results.

> **10 And God saw their works, that they turned from their evil way; and God repented of the evil, that he had said that he would do unto them; and he did it not.**

Human repentance assumes guilt. Yet, with God there is no guilt; so we must look for some other explanation of divine repentance. He does not change in nature or in purpose; but as people change their behavior, so God changes His dealings with them. He is not obligated to carry out His warnings, but He is fully committed to the fulfillment of His promises. Jonah's message of coming judgment was conditional. When Nineveh repented, that judgment was postponed. Jesus also warned of judgment on sin, but He offered forgiveness to the sinner so that this judgment might be escaped. These words of our Lord are memorable: "The men of Nineveh shall rise up in the judgment with this generation, and shall condemn it: for they repented at the preaching of Jonah; and, behold, a greater than Jonah is here" (Luke 11:32).

III. An Angry Prophet (Jonah 4:1-4)

Surely some of the most amazing words in the Bible are in verse 1. Here is a prophet "very angry" because his audience responded to his message, and God accordingly withheld His judgment. In his resentment over being sent to Nineveh, Jonah hoped—even expected—that the people of that city would disregard what he said. When the opposite happened, his indignation was vented on God who had sent him. His prejudices ran so deeply that he could not accept the divine mercy that spared a large city from disaster. The extremes to which deep-rooted prejudice can lead are vividly displayed in Jonah.

1 But it displeased Jonah exceedingly, and he was very angry.
2 And he prayed unto the Lord, and said, I pray thee, O Lord, was not this my saying, when I was yet in my country? Therefore I fled before unto Tarshish: for I knew that thou art a gracious God, and merciful, slow to anger, and of great kindness, and repentest thee of the evil.
3 Therefore now, O Lord, take, I beseech thee, my life from me; for it is better for me to die than to live.
4 Then said the Lord, Doest thou well to be angry?

1. Jonah's desperation (vv. 1-3).—We see in Jonah a man correct in his understanding of God but devoid of God's Spirit. He was orthodox in belief but erroneous in behavior. In his I-told-you-so prayer, he rightly described the nature of the Lord, which he had learned from personal experience and also from his nation's history. But he did not want these gracious attitudes to be exercised in favor of a foreign people, especially the Assyrians. He felt that he had lost face as a prophet, and he wanted to die.

2. Time for thought (v. 4).—Jonah's hasty words produced a mild rebuke from the Lord, "Is it right for you to be angry?" (NRSV). This question was really advice to Jonah to pause and think. What good reason had he for his outburst? What causes lay behind his bitterness? There is no indication that Jonah made any response but continued in his peevish mood.

IV. An Open-Ended Conclusion (Jonah 4:5-11)

Three speechless teachers were used by God in an endeavor to bring Jonah to a better frame of mind. First, God created a fast-growing plant to give Jonah shelter from the sun as he sat watching for the fate of Nineveh. For this, the prophet felt some sense of gratitude, for we read that he "was exceeding glad." Then God allowed a worm to attack the plant so that it died leaving Jonah without shelter. Next God created "a sultry east wind" (NRSV) which caused such physical discomfort that Jonah again wanted to die. Then the Lord spoke to Jonah to show him his foolishness.

> **10 Then said the Lord, Thou hast had pity on the gourd, for the which thou hast not labored, neither madest it grow; which came up in a night, and perished in a night:**
> **11 And should not I spare Nineveh, that great city, wherein are more than sixscore thousand persons that cannot discern between their right hand and their left hand; and also much cattle?**

"Jonah was concerned over a plant when it was selfishly related to his person; Yahweh was concerned for the inhabitants of a great metropolis"[2] that included 120 thousand persons (NRSV). The prophet was left thinking about this, as should we.

APPLYING THE LESSON

The making of a missionary.—Bill Borden, product of a wealthy home and graduate of Yale and Princeton, did as much for the Lord during his 25 years as many do in a lifetime. He died of meningitis before he could really get to the mission field, but he was a missionary from the moment he became a Christian. One of his Princeton classmates described Bill Borden as "a missionary, first, last and all the time." What produced such a spirit in Bill Borden? One factor was an intense love for God that had been developed through a daily disciplined life. Prayer and Bible study sharpened his insights into God's will. The other factor was a view of the world that came through a round-the-world tour. The trip deepened Bill's understanding of God's love and the need to share that love with the world. Bill Borden returned from the tour with the world on his heart. This tour confirmed his desire to be a missionary. Many of his friends chided him for throwing away his life as a missionary. He simply replied, "You have not seen heathenism." Bill Borden had seen heathenism. More important, he had experienced the love of Christ. This love motivated him to be "a missionary, first, last and all the time."[3]

Jonah was not totally captured by the love of God for the world. Consequently, he did not have the passion for "the heathen" that was demonstrated in Bill Borden's life.

When at first you don't succeed.—A preacher confronted a young man one day who was a part of the drug culture. By his appearance, the young man indicated he had dropped out of society and was on the wrong road. The preacher asked the young man why he had taken this route of radical rebellion. The young man explained he had spent "a whole summer" trying to bring about political and social change in the community he lived in and nothing had come of it. The young man concluded, "I decided that it was hopeless, so I just gave up on life."

Are we not glad that God spent more than "a whole summer" to bring about change in human life? Are we not glad that God does not give up on us the first time we reject Him? The story of Jonah reveals a truth that we see throughout Scriptures: God has infinite patience with human beings. God is the God of the second chance.

The power of God to change.—Manasseh was his name, and evil was his game. He succeeded Hezekiah as king of Judah. Manasseh "practiced witchcraft, used divination, practiced sorcery, and dealt with mediums and spiritists. He did much evil in the sight of the Lord, provoking Him to anger" (2 Chron. 33:6, NASB). Manasseh ignored God until God allowed the king of Assyria to capture him. The Bible explains the change that then came over Manasseh. "And when he was in distress, he entreated the Lord his God and humbled himself greatly before the God of his fathers. When he prayed to Him, He was moved by his entreaty and heard his supplication, and brought him again to Jerusalem to his kingdom. Then Manasseh knew that the Lord was God" (2 Chron. 33:12-13, NASB). After his conversion, Manasseh was a changed person (2 Chron. 33:14-16).

As God changed Manasseh, God also changed the Ninevites. In response to the message of Jonah, they repented and turned to God.

The danger of anger.—Someone has suggested that anger is only one letter away from danger. Winfred Moore quoted a poem that illustrates the spirit of anger:

> Whatever I said in anger,
> Whatever I said in spite;
> I'm sorry I spoke so quickly,
> I thought up some worse ones last night![4]

Jonah could have written that poem. Instead of rejoicing at the repentance of the Ninevites, he regretted it.

One at a time.—Mother Teresa was asked how she could have so much love for the teeming masses of people to whom she ministered. She responded, "I love them one at a time." That could well have been God's answer to Jonah when he questioned God's love for Nineveh. God loved them, as He does us, one at a time.

TEACHING THE CLASS

Main Idea: Our obligation is to share the good news with all persons.

Suggested Teaching Aim: Learners will explain the obligations to share God's message with all persons.

Introduce the Bible Study

Share the comments titled "The making of a missionary" (*Applying the Lesson*). Ask: Who did God intend to be a missionary? Elicit response. Explore the broader meaning of being a missionary, suggesting that all believers are responsible for mission work.

State that God showed Jonah something about who is obligated to do mission work. Note that the purpose for the study today is to help us understand our own role in mission efforts. Invite learners to turn to Jonah 3.

Search for Biblical Truth

Share the quote about Jonah found in the introduction of *Studying the Bible*. Direct learners to look for these characteristics in the Bible passage.

A Teaching Outline

1. Consider who is obligated to be a missionary.
2. Discover an answer in the experience of Jonah.
3. Identify New Testament instructions about missionary efforts.
4. Explain personal obligation and the obligation of the church to be involved in missionary effort.

Display the following outline to guide the Bible study.

A Second Chance—A Second Response
Jonah 3—4

I. Called a second time (Jonah 3:1-4)
II. Nineveh repents (Jonah 3:5-10)
III. An angry prophet (Jonah 4:1-4)
IV. An open-ended conclusion (Jonah 4:5-11)

Call on a learner to read Jonah 3:1-4 aloud while others listen to learn of the second call God extended to Jonah to do some missionary work. When the reading is finished, ask questions like these: What does the second call of God to Jonah suggest about God's patience? What did Jonah do when he finally reached Nineveh? Elicit response.

Call on a learner to read Jonah 3:5-10 aloud. Direct other learners to listen to discover how the people of Nineveh responded. Call for response. Note the information from *Studying the Bible* about the oriental customs of the day and the question about the sincerity of the response.

Direct learners to review verse 10. Ask: What is the implication of the statement that God repented? Elicit response. Supplement with information from *Studying the Bible*.

Note the outline heading for the third section. Ask: Why would a speaker be angry when his audience did exactly as he told them to do? State that this is what happened with Jonah. Call on a learner to read

Jonah 4:1-4 aloud. Establish that Jonah's deep-rooted prejudice had not been overcome even though he had been obedient to the direction of God. Note his desperate depression in verse 3. Call attention to verse 4 in which God gently prodded Jonah. Apparently, Jonah continued in his anger.

Call attention to the fourth point on the outline. Note that God continued to try to teach Jonah. He used a vine, a worm, and a sultry east wind. Ultimately, He spoke to Jonah to show him his foolishness. Call on a learner to read Jonah 4:10-11.

When discussing God's second call to Jonah, share the comments titled "When at first you don't succeed" (*Applying the Lesson*). When discussing the repentance of Nineveh, share the comments titled "The power of God to change" (*Applying the Lesson*).

Give the Truth a Personal Focus

Remind learners that the purpose of the study was to determine who is responsible for mission work, that is, for telling others about the way of salvation. Direct learners to spend several minutes discussing the issue with those sitting near them. Direct them to locate Scripture from the New Testament that supports their position. Concordances may be helpful in locating passages. Call for response. Establish through the discussion that every believer has an obligation to mission effort. Ask: In what way are our responses similar to Jonah's? Elicit response.

Share the comments titled "One at a time" (*Applying the Lesson*). Challenge learners to accept their responsibility for mission effort by sharing Jesus with others one at a time.

---

1. George L. Robinson, *The Twelve Minor Prophets* (Grand Rapids: Baker Book House, 1952), 75.
2. A. J. Glaze, Jr., "Jonah" in *The Broadman Bible Commentary*, vol. 7 (Nashville: Broadman Press, 1972), 181.
3. Mrs. Howard Taylor, *Borden of Yale* (Minneapolis: Bethany House Publishers, 1988), 153-54.
4. Winfred Moore, *Faith for the Second Mile* (Nashville: Broadman Press, 1986) 27.

June 28

Judgment and Salvation

Basic Passage: Nahum 1:1—3:19

Focal Passage: Nahum 1:2-3,6-9,12-13,15

Like the Book of Jonah, the prophecy of Nahum is concerned with the city of Nineveh, capital of the Assyrian empire. The former capital had been Assur (Asshur). Nineveh's repentance for its wickedness, as recorded in Jonah, could not have lasted long. There is a probable gap of some 125 years between the respective periods of the two prophecies. Nahum described a condition of abounding evil in what he termed "the bloody city" (3:1), causing God to say, "Behold, I am against thee" (v. 5). So, given an opportunity to renounce its evil past, the people of Nineveh threw away that opportunity and reverted to their former crimes. The severe tone of Nahum must not be allowed to obscure the merciful patience of God who restrained His judgments over a long period of time. He pleaded with Nineveh through that reluctant prophet Jonah, held back His righteous judgment when the people of the city professed repentance, and, after they had revealed a lack of sincerity in this repentance, shielded them from their deserved fate for another century and more. The city fell to the Babylonians and their allies in 612 B.C.

Study Aim: *To give equal weight to what the apostle Paul called "the goodness and severity of God" (Rom. 11:22)*

STUDYING THE BIBLE

God does not settle scores on a weekly basis. While it is ever true that "the wages of sin is death" (Rom. 6:23), those wages are not necessarily paid on Friday night. To quote the title of a famous preacher's sermon, there is a "Payday Some Day." It may be after a short interval, or after the passing of many years, but the justice of God eventually overtakes the sins of individuals and nations.

I. God the Avenger (Nahum 1:2-3)

We know nothing of Nahum beyond what is stated about him in verse 1. Elkosh was apparently his home, a place of uncertain location. His reference to Judah (1:15) encourages the belief that he was a

Judean. The word "burden" describes something "lifted up," hence a proclamation or prophecy to deliver when God's messenger would lift up his hands. The message came to Nahum as a "vision," or revelation. He lost no time in delivering that message.

> **2 God is jealous, and the Lord revengeth; the Lord revengeth, and is furious; the Lord will take vengeance on his adversaries, and he reserveth wrath for his enemies.**
>
> **3 The Lord is slow to anger, and great in power, and will not at all acquit the wicked: the Lord hath his way in the whirlwind and in the storm, and the clouds are the dust of his feet.**

1. A jealous God (v. 2).—As a human trait, jealousy is often peevish and unreasonable. The word *jealous* occurs frequently in Scripture to describe the Lord's determination to make known His nature and protect that which is His. He does not act rashly, but He acts in justice against His enemies and His people.

2. Restrained power (v. 3).—God's dealings with Nineveh, and the Assyrian empire as a whole, were an example of the truth that He "is slow to anger." God does not give way to temper, as we so often do. His acts of judgment are considered and deliberate. When the time comes for Him to punish sin, He cannot be resisted, for He is "great in power." The second part of verse 3 and following verses declare that His power at work in nature can be made to serve His judgmental purposes.

II. Justice and Mercy (Nahum 1:6-11)

No answers are forthcoming to the questions asked in verse 6, for no answers are necessary. There can be no effective resistance to the judgments of God. If we are surprised at the severity of many of the statements in Nahum, we need to realize that they were addressed to Assyria, represented by its capital: Nineveh. Secular historians have recorded the heinous crimes committed by these people against their enemies. "Woe to the bloody city!" exclaimed Nahum of Nineveh (3:1), a city that bragged of the enormities for which it was guilty, recording them on sculptures made by its own kings.

> **6 Who can stand before his indignation? and who can abide in the fierceness of his anger? his fury is poured out like fire, and the rocks are thrown down by him.**
>
> **7 The Lord is good, a stronghold in the day of trouble; and he knoweth them that trust in him.**
>
> **8 But with an overrunning flood he will make an utter end of the place thereof, and darkness shall pursue his enemies.**
>
> **9 What do ye imagine against the Lord? he will make an utter end: affliction shall not rise up the second time.**

1. A contrasted witness (v. 7).—Nahum had earlier spoken a positive word for the Lord, "The Lord is slow to anger" (v. 3). He felt the need to break into the long denunciation of evil and its consequent judgment with another tribute, born out of experience, "The Lord is good" (v. 7). The words sound like a quotation from the Psalms, borrowed by God's prophet as he bore witness to other aspects of His character: His essential goodness, evidenced by His loving care for those who put their trust in Him. Thus even in a judgmental passage of the Old Testament, a note of gospel hope is sounded.

2. Finality of judgment (vv. 8-9).—Returning to the subject of Assyria, its guilt and its doom, the prophet declared the uselessness of trying to escape God's righteous judgments. For the evil empire, the end was in sight. Its destruction would be complete and final. This happened for Nineveh in 612 B.C. All that remains of this famous city are two great mounds of earth. Think of the cities, empires, and dynasties that once dominated the earth but are no more, vanished almost without a trace. Only the record of their atrocities remains to stain the pages of history. Mighty though human forces may be, God can bring them to an "utter end" so that they shall "not rise up the second time."

3. A figure of evil (vv. 10-11).—"From you one has gone out / who plots evil against the Lord, / who counsels wickedness" (v. 11, NRSV). Special mention was reserved for one Assyrian leader whose excesses helped to bring about divine judgment. He is not named, but he might well have been Assurbanipal who boasted of the cruelties he imposed on captured enemies. Almost always when great tyrannies arise, their crimes become concentrated in a single individual, as Hitler and Stalin in our own times. Happily, the opposite is also true, for the grace of God can work through a single person for the benefit of many.

III. Hope for God's People (Nahum 1:12-13)

Destruction of a power such as Assyria was not only an exercise of justice against a tyrant, but also an act of deliverance for those Assyria oppressed, especially God's people Israel.

> **12 Thus saith the Lord; Though they be quiet, and likewise many, yet thus shall they be cut down, when he shall pass through. Though I have afflicted thee, I will afflict thee no more.**
>
> **13 For now will I break his yoke from off thee and will burst thy bonds in sunder.**

1. Strength of evil overcome (v. 12a).—We need to change the word "quiet" to "strength," as in the NRSV, to get the meaning here. The power of Assyria is not denied, for there is always danger in underestimating the potential of an enemy. Assyria had the resources and abilities to conquer and subdue surrounding nations, holding them in subjection for long periods. Yet, its military might was powerless against one adversary—namely, God. In their heyday, aggressors may appear invincible and strike terror into all whom they oppose. When confronted by God, they meet their doom.

2. God's instrument (v. 12b).—The second part of verse 12 contains the admission that this fearsome empire had been an instrument in God's hands for the chastisement of His people. "Though I have afflicted thee, I will afflict thee no more." As we will see in a future lesson, God's use of another power (Babylon) to punish His people caused perplexity to the prophet Habakkuk. Yet, in His divine wisdom, this has been a consistent method, used by God throughout history. What may appear to be passing events are the tools in God's hands for imposing penalties and teaching lessons.

3. Deliverance granted (v. 13).—Once again the people Israel were to experience a great deliverance, wrought by the intervention of God. What they could not do for themselves, God did for them, as when He led them out of Egypt. For them, these were experiences of salvation, memorialized in the Passover feast and other festive occasions when they remembered how the Lord had come to their aid. The New Testament writers did not hesitate to see these events as foreshadowings of the great gift of spiritual salvation that came in Christ and is ever available to all who will accept it.

IV. Message of Good Tidings (Nahum 1:15)

Nahum's message, though alarming for Assyria, was good news to the people of Judah who, for a hundred years, had been subjugated to their cruel neighbor in the north. So the prophet assumed a role used by others (Isa. 52:7) as he sounded forth the news of coming deliverance. In days before electronic communications were even dreamed of, runners would carry messages to communities. When they neared the end of their mission, they would mount a nearby hill where they could be seen, and the people were thus prepared to receive information for which they had long waited. The runner became "the feet of him that bringeth good tidings."

> **15 Behold upon the mountains the feet of him that bringeth good tidings, that publisheth peace! O Judah, keep thy solemn feasts, perform thy vows: for the wicked shall no more pass through thee; he is utterly cut off.**

The phrase "good news" becomes "gospel" in the New Testament.

Even so, the defeat and destruction of Assyria becomes for us a symbol of that victory Jesus gained for us over Satan and sin by His death on the cross. The eradication of Israel's enemies foreshadows the time when all that is in opposition to the kingdom of God will meet its end and that kingdom will be revealed in all its glory. For the judgments of God against all that is evil must happen before the eternal reign of Christ and His people begins.

APPLYING THE LESSON

Was it God's judgment?—Jeff Keay lived in Palm Beach Gardens, Florida. This nineteen-year-old man was sitting in his living room with a can of beer in his hand. He later explained that he was listening to a song on the radio entitled, "Your Time Is Going to Come." At that moment, a lightning bolt entered his living room window, discharged through the can of beer in his hand, and sent him to the floor with the force of the jolt. Fortunately, the jolt was not fatal, but it impressed upon him the truth of the song's message for all of us: our time is going to come.[1]

God is a God of infinite patience, but eventually, human sin will be judged by the holiness of God. Nahum's message focused on that judgment side of God.

Evidences of a hard heart.—The problem in Nahum's day, as in our day, is that too many people had hardened their hearts toward God. What are some of the marks of a hard heart? This is the answer given by Warren Wiersbe: "An unwillingness to admit and confess my own sins. A bitter spirit toward another believer. An unwillingness to forgive. A resistance to the Word of God. An inflexible attitude that cannot be taught or changed. A feeling that my way is the right way and the only way. A fear of change and an unwillingness to learn new things. A refusal to let people get 'too close.' A touchiness of spirit, a supersensitive attitude that makes it difficult for people to get along with me. Being preoccupied with my own needs and not being concerned about the needs of others."[2]

Whenever these tendencies are present in our lives, we need to hear again the word of warning from God's prophet, for they are clear evidences of a hard heart.

How the mighty are fallen.—At times, perpetrators of sin appear to be invincible. Yet, as time passes, evil people and evil nations inevitably are destroyed by the consequences of their own sins.

Al Capone is a good example. That name is familiar with most Americans, even today, for it epitomized the power evil men wielded over the lives of other people. He operated out of a suite at the Hotel Lexington on Michigan Avenue in Chicago. In his prime, he ruled over a thousand men and grossed more than $100 million a year through his gambling, prostitution rings, and bootlegging. He squelched every opponent. He controlled the crime world of his day. How invincible Capone seemed to be.

And how he eventually fell! He was indicted for income tax evasion, convicted, and sent to a federal penitentiary. His medical exam revealed that he had syphilis. After several years in prison, he was found one day in 1938, staring blankly into space. He was in the final stages of syphilis. His last eleven months in prison were spent in a hospital ward; and then when released, he retired to his Palm Island estate in Florida. There he continued to lose his mind. His speech became garbled, and his mind was confused. He died on January 25, 1947, of a brain hemorrhage. The death of this man who once controlled the city of Chicago and ruled over a thousand men was reported on page seven of the newspaper. How the mighty are fallen!

Nineveh had that same air of invincibility when Nahum pronounced his message. Yet, they too would fall, victim to the consequences of their own sins.

What was God doing?—All night long the little girl trembled in her bed at the sound of the thunder. It was the worst storm she had ever known. The next morning she asked her father, "What was God doing last night during the storm?" Before the father could respond, however, she answered her own question. She said, "I know. God was making the morning."

The Israelites may have wondered where God was during the oppression they suffered under the Assyrians. The prophet Nahum answered their question: "God was making the morning."

The lessons we learn from suffering.—Alexander Solzhenitsyn described how his suffering actually led him to God. He wrote, "It was only when I lay there on rotting prison straw that I sensed within myself the first stirrings of good. . . . So, bless you, prison, for having been in my life."[3]

In a similar way, the prophet Nahum declared to the Israelites that good things would come out of their suffering under the Assyrians.

TEACHING THE CLASS

Main Idea: Ultimately God must punish evil.

Suggested Teaching Aim: Learners will respond to the fact that ultimately God must punish evil.

Introduce the Bible Study

Write *Nahum* on the chalkboard. Ask: Do you recall what the Book of Nahum is about? Elicit response. Use information from the introductory comments to the lesson to provide information.

Write the main idea on the chalkboard. Note that while God is patient and long-suffering, there is no doubt on the basis of the Scripture that the main idea is true. State that the purpose of the study is to help us to come to grips with the fact that God must punish evil, not only in the lives of the minorities but in our own lives as well. Invite learners to open their Bibles to Nahum 1.

Search for Biblical Truth

Display the following outline to guide the Bible study.

Judgment and Salvation

I. God, the avenger (Nah. 1:2-3)
II. God, just and merciful (Nah. 1:6-11)
III. God, provider of hope for His people (Nah. 1:12-13)
IV. God, messenger with good tidings (Nah. 1:15)

Call on a learner to read Nahum 1:2-3 aloud. Call attention to section 1 of the outline. Ask: What words or phrases in this passage support the truth that God is an avenger and that He must ultimately punish evil?

A Teaching Outline

1. Focus on the inevitability of judgment.
2. Discover how God ultimately judged Nineveh.
3. Determine evidence of evil in our own lives that must ultimately be punished.
4. Respond personally to the fact that God will ultimately punish evil.

Share the comments titled "Was it God's judgment?" (*Applying the Lesson*). Ask: How is the judgment of God brought into our own lives? Establish that much of our behavior has its own negative results that is used by God to bring judgment on our lives.

Share the comments titled "Evidences of a hard heart" (*Applying the Lesson*). Suggest that God's judgment on a hard heart is severe. Encourage learners to evaluate their own hearts.

Note that while God must judge evil because of who He is, He also offers justice and mercy because of who He is. Call on a learner to read verses 6-9 aloud. When the reading is finished, ask: What is the only hope against the justice of God? (His mercy is the only hope.)

Call on a learner to read verses 12-13 while other learners listen for the statement of mercy and provision of hope for God's people. Ask again: What is the source of deliverance from the judgment of God? Note verse 13. God will break the yoke of sin and grant deliverance.

Share the comments titled "What was God doing?" (*Applying the Lesson*). Note that God is always working toward a way of bringing redemption to those who turn to Him. The final verse for study sings out the joyful news that the message of salvation is from God. Call on a learner to read Nahum 1:15 aloud.

Give the Truth a Personal Focus

Ask rhetorically: Is it possible that there is sin in our own lives that God must ultimately punish? Will He punish that sin even if we are redeemed by the blood of Jesus? Remind learners that God's nature makes it impossible for Him not to avenge evil. Continue by asking further: What response do we need to make personally in view of the fact that God must punish evil?

Share the comments titled "The lessons we learn from suffering" (*Applying the Lesson*). Invite learners to spend a few moments in prayer responding to God on the basis of the fact that He must ultimately punish evil.

---

1. *Pensacola News-Journal*, 9 July 1985, 1a.
2. Warren Wiersbe, *Real Worship* (Nashville: Oliver Nelson, 1986), 105-06.
3. Charles R. Swindoll, *Encourage Me* (Portland: Multnomah Press, 1982), 43.

July 5

A Question and an Answer

Basic Passage: Habakkuk 1:1—3:19

Focal Passage: Habakkuk 1:1-7; 2:1-4

Current events can often be bewildering. We are inclined to forget that in the outworking of divine purposes, "one day is with the Lord as a thousand years, and a thousand years as one day" (2 Pet. 3:8). The span of one human life is sometimes time enough to see the triumph of truth and justice as falsehood is exposed and tyrants deposed, but not always. The children of Israel were in Egyptian bondage for some 400 years before word came to Moses from God, "I have surely seen the affliction of my people . . . and have heard their cry . . . And I am come down to deliver them" (Ex. 3:7-8). There have been prolonged periods of history during which the apparent silence of God in regard to prevailing iniquity has perplexed His people and tested their faith. The Book of Habakkuk tells of one such experience of testing; and while it may not answer all our questions about the prosperity and survival of the wicked, it delivers a strong message on the sovereignty of God, the inevitability of judgment, and the triumph of God-centered faith.

Study Aim: *To find encouragement to believe in the ultimate victory of truth, righteousness, and justice*

STUDYING THE BIBLE

The passage of time had taken care of one oppressor of Israel, the Assyrians. The prophecies of Nahum came to fulfillment, and Nineveh was reduced to ruins. This was achieved by the joint efforts of Babylonians and Medes. To stop further conquests by these allied peoples, an Egyptian army moved against them. The battle was joined at Carchemish where the Babylonian leader, Nebuchadnezzar, won a decisive victory in 605 B.C. This opened up the Palestinian area to his conquests. Habakkuk 1 describes conditions either immediately before or after this event. This places Habakkuk in the reigns of Jehoiakim and preceding kings (2 Kings 23:31—24:7). Of the prophet himself, nothing is known beyond the information provided in this book.

I. A Time of Chaos (Hab. 1:1-4)

For Israel, one oppressor had been replaced by another. The Babylonians (or Chaldeans, 1:6) had already set out on a campaign of conquest, and Judah was threatened by their aggressions. This was a matter of deep concern to Habakkuk, who was also troubled by disorders in Judah itself. These may have been the consequence of anticipated invasion or symptoms of the moral deterioration of the times. The combined crises caused the prophet to cry out to God.

1 The burden which Habakkuk the prophet did see.

2 O Lord, how long shall I cry, and thou wilt not hear! even cry out unto thee of violence, and thou wilt not save!

3 Why dost thou show me iniquity, and cause me to behold grievance? for spoiling and violence are before me: and there are that raise up strife and contention.

4 Therefore the law is slacked, and judgment doth never go forth: for the wicked doth compass about the righteous; therefore wrong judgment proceedeth.

1. Domestic disorder (vv. 1-3).—When rulers engage in evil activities, their subjects are likely to follow suit. The verdict against king after king contemporary to Habakkuk is that "he did that which was evil in the sight of the Lord, according to all that his fathers had done" (2 Kings 23:32,37). The prophet was burdened by the conditions around him, which he had made a matter of earnest prayer. But God seemed deaf to his appeals. Habakkuk continued to see "destruction and violence . . . strife and contention" (v. 3, NRSV). Similar conditions in our own communities should drive God's people to prayer today.

2. Legal corruption (v. 4).—Action against criminal activity might be expected from local courts. But, again with tragic contemporary parallels, the judiciary dillydallied so that offenders were not brought to judgment. When trials were held, the wicked elements in society were successful in overwhelming those who sought to enforce the law. If verdicts were arrived at, the same elements were able to obtain miscarriages of justice. Habakkuk complained bitterly that the Lord seemed indifferent to his pleas. His honesty in prayer was commendable, though he was mistaken in suggesting that God was ignoring these social wrongs.

II. God's Plan Revealed (Hab. 1:6-11)

The Lord's reply added to the perplexity of the prophet. Habakkuk was told to look beyond Judah and take note of the aggressions of the Chaldeans. God was at work in the world, but in ways that would pronounce astonishment and disbelief.

> **6 For, lo, I raise up the Chaldeans, that bitter and hasty nation, which shall march through the breadth of the land, to possess the dwelling places that are not theirs.**
>
> **7 They are terrible and dreadful: their judgment and their dignity shall proceed of themselves.**

1. The Chaldeans (v. 6).—The terms *Chaldeans* and *Babylonians* are often used interchangeably. The former were warlike tribes who occupied southern Mesopotamia and who eventually were successful in creating the Babylonian Empire. Nebuchadnezzar, or, more accurately, Nebuchadrezzar, was a Chaldean who by his alliance with the Medes overcame the Assyrians. His ruthless strategies fitted his armies to be described as "bitter and hasty." But they were unwitting tools in the hands of God who said of them, "I raise up the Chaldeans." Nevertheless, as Habakkuk would learn, they were held responsible for their actions.

2. Their aggressiveness (vv. 6-11).—The ruthless conquests of the Chaldeans are described. They "carry everything before them as they occupy the territory of others (v. 6); in the violence of their aggressions they follow their own standards of justice (v. 7); their mounted troops advance like ravening beasts (v. 8); they strike terror as they take multitudes captive (v. 9); none can resist them (v. 10); they make might their god (v. 11)."[1] Verse 11 can read, "Then they sweep by like the wind; / they transgress and become guilty; / their own might is their god!" (NRSV).

III. The Prophet's Perplexity (Hab. 1:12-17)

The entire Book of Habakkuk is our background material, so we should not fail to look at these verses. The Lord's reply troubled Habakkuk deeply on three counts: (1) it appeared to contradict the very nature of God; (2) it ignored the brutal behavior of the Chaldeans; and (3) it expressed no condemnation of their prideful idolatries.

1. God's nature at risk (vv. 12-13).—Habakkuk accepted the need for punishment of his people. His prayer had been that God would act in "judgment" and impose measures of "correction" (v. 12). His problem was the means that the Lord purposed using: note the repeated "them" as he contemplated the outrages committed by the Chaldeans. Habakkuk had an exalted concept of the God he worshiped whom he addressed as "everlasting" and "mine Holy One." These characteristics persuaded him that Judah would not be allowed to perish. But the instrument of God's chastisement, the Chaldeans, seemed totally inconsistent with his understanding of the Lord. Again, the prophet is to be commended by this unrestrained outpouring of his thoughts in prayer. To be honest before God is a sure way to receive enlightenment from Him.

2. No better than fish (vv. 14-17).—In their treatment of others, the Chaldeans showed that they regarded people as no better than fish, to be caught and devoured. With weapons that Habakkuk described as "hook," "net," and "seine" (v. 15, NRSV), they captured their victims, over whose plight they rejoiced. Then, to make matters worse, they worshiped their weapons as the gods who made their conquests possible, "for by them he lives in luxury, / and his food is rich" (v. 16, RSV). In perplexity that neared despair the prophet cried out, "Is he then to keep on emptying his net, / and destroying nations without mercy?" (v. 17, NRSV).

IV. A Light in the Dark (Hab. 2:1-4)

Habakkuk had a place of seclusion, his watchtower, where he could get away from the clamor of voices and listen quietly for the voice of God. He was not alone in raising the questions expressed in chapter 1, and people were looking to him for answers. He had none, but he had faith to believe that they would come from God.

> **1 I will stand upon my watch, and set me upon the tower, and will watch to see what he will say unto me, and what I shall answer when I am reproved.**

2 And the Lord answered me, and said, Write the vision, and make it plain upon tables, that he may run that readeth it.
3 For the vision is yet for an appointed time, but at the end it shall speak, and not lie: though it tarry, wait for it; because it will surely come, it will not tarry.
4 Behold, his soul which is lifted up is not upright in him: but the just shall live by his faith.

1. A message to be shared (v. 2).—God's instructions are in line with the practice of inscribing public notices on whitewashed rocks or boards. What He would say was of such importance that it must be shared with everybody. The characters must be large enough so that a person running by may read them easily. What was involved was a predecessor of the placard which, using a few simple words, arrests attention and communicates a message.

2. Certainty of fulfillment (v. 3).—In the chaotic state of Judah, swift action might be desired, but God's purposes are not to be hurried. Events would follow His schedule, not humanity's; and although there would be what some would think of as unnecessary delays, divine plans would be carried through to fulfillment. Compare the impatience for the Lord's return as described, and corrected, in 2 Peter 3:1-10.

3. Truth in brief (v. 4).—This important verse is helpfully rendered, "Behold, he whose soul is not / upright in him shall fail, / but the righteous shall live by his faith" (RSV). The first part of the verse describes the Chaldeans who, in their pride and self-sufficiency, were "puffed up" (1 Cor. 5:2). Their might notwithstanding, they were doomed to failure. But God's people, who live in faithfulness (a more adequate word than "by his faith"), will survive. These words became the basis for the doctrine of justification by faith as propounded by the apostle Paul (Rom. 1:17).

4. Concluding psalm (ch. 3).—This only free-standing psalm in the Bible should be noted for its affirmation of confidence in God. Habakkuk faced his fears (vv. 2-16) and was delivered from them so that he could say, "Come what may, I will trust Him" (see vv. 17-19).

APPLYING THE LESSON

Defeating the powers of the world.—Richard J. Foster makes some interesting suggestions about how to confront the evil powers around us in the world today. "First, we must recognize that Christ has already defeated the powers." We fight from the position of strength, not from the position of weakness. "Second, we defeat the powers by cultivating the gift of discernment." We must recognize these powers before we can effectively confront them. "Third, we defeat the powers by forthrightly facing the 'demons' within." Within us many of the same forces are at work which we confront around us. "Fourth, we defeat the powers by an inner renunciation of all things." This detachment from the things of the world makes us untouchable. The world can do nothing to really hurt us because the only thing that is valuable to us—our relationship with God—the world cannot touch. "Fifth, we defeat the powers by rejecting the weapons of power of this world." Intimidation and manipulation and human wisdom and physical strength have no effect on these enemies. "Sixth, we defeat the powers by using the weapons of Ephesians 6." Far more effective than the weapons of the world are the weapons of the Spirit. Through the weapons of truth, righteousness, peace, faith, salvation, the Word of God, and prayer, we can defeat the powers around us.[2]

The message of Habakkuk expresses much the same thoughts as these suggestions by Richard J. Foster. What human power and strength could not do, divine strength made available through faith could do.

Mistaken identity.—Tickets to the Super Bowl were to go on sale early in the morning, and as expected, the line formed around the block. Many of the fans had spent the night on sleeping bags to be at the front of the line. As the men and women in the line stood anxiously awaiting the opening of the ticket office, a young man made his way to the front of the line and stepped in front of a burly truck driver. The big guy was so angry that he picked up the newcomer and tossed him out into the grass. The newcomer stood up and moved back to the front of the line. Again, the beefy truck driver sent him sprawling to the ground. The newcomer stood up again, walked over to the truck driver, and said, "Look, buddy, if you throw me out one more time, I'm not going to open this door and sell you a ticket!" The truck driver thought this man was trying to beat him out of getting a ticket. In reality, the employee was trying to sell the truck driver a ticket.

That story illustrates the attitude of Habakkuk toward the Babylonians. Habakkuk hated them because he thought they were going to destroy Israel. God reminded him that the Babylonians were actually being used to deliver Israel.

God's kind of doubter.—*Doubt* is a "four-letter word" in Christian circles, yet doubt has always been present in the men and women of faith. Job in the Old Testament and Thomas in the New Testament are two prime examples. When confronted by the fact that God was punishing Israel by using the even-more-wicked Babylonians, Habakkuk also experienced doubt.

I read a sermon once on doubt. In this message, the preacher described the qualities of "God's Kind of Doubter." First, "God's kind of doubter struggles honestly for his faith rather than run away." Second, "God's kind of doubter struggles honestly for faith rather than settle for gullibility." Third, God's kind of doubter struggles for his faith rather than settle for hearsay."[3] Habakkuk had some doubts, but he was God's kind of doubter, confronting God with a sincere desire to understand God's heart so he could communicate that truth to the people.

The danger of a little knowledge.—Scott Walker described his pilgrimage of faith in the book *Where the Rivers Flow*. He described a time of theological confusion in his life when he questioned his own faith in God. While he meditated about his situation, he heard the voice of his father. Words came to mind that his father had spoken to him in a luminous moment in the past. His father had said, "If you learn a little about religion, it will be enough to turn you to atheism. But if you pursue your study of God for a long time, you will inevitably find faith."[4]

A surface study of the situations of our life may raise doubts about the presence and power and purpose of God. Such was the case for Habakkuk.

TEACHING THE CLASS

Main Idea: Truth, righteousness, and justice will ultimately prevail.

Suggested Teaching Aim: Learners will explain why they believe that truth, righteousness, and justice will ultimately prevail.

Introduce the Bible Study

Display articles cut from current newspapers and magazines about bewildering events in the world today. Call attention to the display. Ask: As you look at what is happening in the world today, can you see God at work carrying out His divine purpose in these events? Note that for most of us most of the time it is difficult to see how God is working in the events of our time.

Point out that we are not the only ones who have had difficulty following God's hand in the events around them. Prolonged periods of apparent silence have perplexed God's people through the centuries. Yet a primary message of the Scripture is that God is at work and that ultimately truth, justice, and righteousness will prevail.

A Teaching Outline

1. Consider doubts caused by current situations in today's world.
2. Discover how Habakkuk came to view his world and his God.
3. Identify possible reasons for continued faith that God will be victorious.
4. Explain why learners personally believe that they can defeat the world in their own lives.

Habakkuk struggled with the question but came to some answers that will be helpful to us as we consider the events of our own day. Invite learners to turn to Habakkuk 1.

Search for Biblical Truth

State that an outline will help learners follow the study in Habakkuk. Refer to the following outline, which has been previously displayed:

Questions and Answers
Habakkuk 1—2

I. A time of chaos (Hab. 1:1-4)
   A. Domestic disorder
   B. Legal corruption
II. God's plan revealed (Hab. 1:6-11)
III. The prophet's perplexity (Hab. 1:12-17)
IV. A light in the dark (Hab. 2:1-4)
   A. A message to be shared
   B. Certainty of fulfillment

Call on a learner to read Habakkuk 1:1-4 aloud while other learners listen for evidence of chaos in Habakkuk's day. When the reading is finished, ask: What was going on in the government and in the legal system in Habakkuk's day? Elicit response. Continue by asking: Do you think Habakkuk could see the hand of God at work in these events? How do you think he felt as he considered these questions?

Note that what seemed to Habakkuk to be a worsening situation is noted in verses 6-7, but it turned out to be God's own plan for bringing truth, justice, and righteousness to this situation. Call on a learner to read verses 6-7 aloud.

Share the comments titled "Mistaken identity" (*Applying the Lesson*). Note that we, like Habakkuk, can easily mistake the hand of God in events of our own world.

Call attention to point 3 of the outline. Invite learners to scan verses 12-17 as you provide information from *Studying the Bible* about the perplexity of the prophet concerning God's use of the Chaldeans. Note the three questions that deeply troubled Habakkuk.

Share the comments titled "God's kind of doubter" (*Applying the Lesson*). Ask: Can you discuss your concerns and your doubts openly and honestly with God in your prayers?

Note that despite his doubts and questions, Habakkuk waited for answers believing they would come. He secluded himself in his special place to wait to see the hand of God at work and find answers to his questions. Call attention to point 4 on the outline.

Call on a learner to read Habakkuk 2:1-4 aloud. When the reading is finished, ask: What was the instruction of God to Habakkuk? (See v. 2.) What was the message Habakkuk was to share? (See vv. 3-4.) Summarize the message of God by writing the main idea of this lesson on the chalkboard.

Give the Truth a Personal Focus

Share the comments titled "The danger of a little knowledge" (*Applying the Lesson*). Emphasize that sometimes a surface study of God at work in our world leads us to the wrong conclusion.

Ask: Can you accept that justice, truth, and righteousness will ultimately prevail? Why are you willing to accept such a promise from God in the face of the turmoil of today? Elicit response.

Share the six points for defeating the powers of this world in our own lives from the paragraphs titled "Defeating the powers of the world" (*Applying the Lesson*).

1. H. Franklin Paschall and Herschel H. Hobbs, eds., *The Teacher's Bible Commentary* (Nashville: Broadman Press, 1972), 565.
2. Richard J. Foster, *Money, Sex, and Power* (San Francisco: Harper and Row, 1985), 189-92.
3. Robert D. Wimp, "God's Kind of Doubter," *Pulpit Digest*, (July-August 1981): 47-50.
4. Scott Walker, *Where the Rivers Flow* (Waco: Word Books, 1986), 62-63.

July 12

Threatened Destruction of Humankind

Basic Passage: Zephaniah 1—2

Focal Passage: Zephaniah 1:1-3,7,12; 2:1-3

Of some people it has been rightly said that they assign all the curses to the Jews and keep all the blessings for themselves when reading the Scriptures. The Minor Prophets, as we call them—although they are minor only in length, not in importance—contain many severe messages addressed to the speaker's own people. In fact, this is their major emphasis. But the wrath of God against sin is not confined to one race, and these messengers of God made clear that He is the Judge of all the earth. Amos did this with special skill. He pronounced judgment on Damascus, Gaza, Tyre, and other of Israel's enemies, got his listeners cheering for him, and then, without warning, turned his attention to themselves as he named first Judah and then Israel (Amos 1:1—2:8). Zephaniah was not as subtle, for he began with Judah, but before he was through, he had included neighboring nations in denunciation and condemnation. He talked about the coming "day of the Lord" in a way that will make us feel that he was looking beyond his own times to the final judgment of the nations.

Study Aim: *To respond to the call for worldwide evangelism in view of the coming "day of the Lord" for all people*

STUDYING THE BIBLE

Not many sermons are preached on Zephaniah; not many Sunday School lessons are based on it. Zephaniah is one of the less-known books of the Old Testament and, therefore, affords opportunity for breaking new ground. The prophet's ancestry is given to the fourth generation (1:1), making him the great-great-grandson of a man named Hizkiah, or Hezekiah. If this was the king of that name, Zephaniah was of royal descent. The statement in this same verse that his call to ministry came "in the days of Josiah" raises the question as to whether this was before or after the reforms were instituted by that king. Zephaniah's denunciations would seem to indicate the former.

I. Universal Judgment (Zeph. 1:1-3)

The unusual details given about Zephaniah's ancestry can be accounted for if the prophet was indeed great-great-grandson to Hezekiah, of whom it is written, "He trusted in the Lord God of Israel; so that after him was none like him among all the kings of Judah" (2 Kings 18:5). This would also make Zephaniah a kinsman to Josiah with whom he shared some of Hezekiah's zeal for righteousness.

> **1 The word of the Lord which came unto Zephaniah the son of Cushi, the son of Gedaliah, the son of Amariah, the son of Hizkiah, in the days of Josiah the son of Amon, king of Judah.**
>
> **2 I will utterly consume all things from off the land, saith the Lord.**
>
> **3 I will consume man and beast; I will consume the fowls of the heaven, and the fishes of the sea, and the stumbling blocks with the wicked; and I will cut off man from off the land, saith the Lord.**

These words read like the final judgment when all evil will be vanquished and justice and righteousness enthroned. It is not impossible that the prophet was given understanding of coming universal judgment as preparation for, what the apostle Peter called, "new heavens and a new earth" (2 Pet. 3:13). In his Roman epistle, Paul indicated that the natural realm is involved in the fallen state of the human race, so that "the whole creation groaneth and travaileth in pain together until now" (Rom. 8:22). In attempting to interpret these verses it is important to have in mind two things: (1) Zephaniah was writing at a time of tremendous political upheaval with the rise and fall of such nations as Egypt, Assyria, and Babylon; and (2) the Hebrew understanding of God placed Him in sovereign control of all events that, whether good or bad, were accordingly attributed to Him.

II. Judah Named and Warned (Zeph. 1:4-6)

These verses, though excluded from our printed passages, are important to our study. The universal tone of verses 1-3 now changes into a direct indictment of Judah and Jerusalem. Three specific charges are made.

1. Idolatry (v. 4).—Baal was a god of the Canaanites whose worship involved gross sexual activities. Before entering the land, the Israelites were warned against association with this depraved religion but failed to heed the warning. "Chemarims" were priests of Baal. When God acted in judgment, these individuals, and the false religion they promoted, would be "cut off."

2. Syncretism (v. 5).—Worship of the stars was practiced by the Assyrians. This worship had been introduced into the temple itself by Manasseh, the evil son of Hezekiah (2 Kings 21:3). (Ancient astral worship and modern astrology have a common link.) The god Malcham is better known as Molech, whose worship was associated with human sacrifices (2 Kings 23:10). Zephaniah's charge in this verse was that some of the people of Judah were attempting to worship the Lord while, at the same time, paying tribute to pagan deities. This is known as syncretism.

3. Godlessness (v. 6).—There were those in Israel who professed loyalty to no god. Who these were we cannot tell, but in any large group of people there are likely to be persons totally indifferent to the claims of religion. In Israel, these would come under divine judgment, together with the worshipers of Baal and Molech.

III. Particular Groups Indicted (Zeph. 1:7-13)

This passage begins with a summons to a sacrifice. The occasion is "the day of the Lord," a repeated phrase in Zephaniah that stands for an occasion of divine visitation in judgment. The victim, sadly enough, was Judah, and presumably its enemies were the bidden guests. Preceding verses supply reasons for this tragic development when God had to act in judgment against His own people. Other reasons follow in verses 7-13.

7 Hold thy peace at the presence of the Lord God: for the day of the Lord is at hand: for the Lord hath prepared a sacrifice, he hath bid his guests.

. . . .

12 And it shall come to pass at that time, that I will search Jerusalem with candles, and punish the men that are settled on their lees: that say in their heart, The Lord will not do good, neither will he do evil.

1. Four offenders named (vv. 7-9).—The list of the guilty begins with "the princes, and the king's children." Members of the royal court had set a bad example that the people had followed. The meaning of "all such as are clothed with strange apparel" is not clear, but since *strange* can mean "foreign," this may be a rebuke of those who had adopted pagan ways. The next phrase is also difficult, "that leap on the threshold," but it probably refers to a pagan practice. The continuing practice of carrying a bride over the doorstep perpetuates a superstitious notion that evil lurks in the threshold. Those who "fill their masters' houses with violence and deceit" are the agents of rulers who make their masters rich by the proceeds of their oppression.

2. Merchants and others (vv. 10-13).—Several references to trading in these verses ("fish gate, . . . merchant people . . . silver") indicate that this indictment was leveled at persons engaged in business. God says of these, "I will search Jerusalem with lamps, / and I will punish the men / who are thickening upon their lees" (v. 12, NRSV). The sediment produced in wine making was called "lees," so the picture is of wine that has been neglected until it has become thick with sediment. The charge, therefore, was careless indifference, illustrated by the saying, "The Lord will not do good, neither will he do evil." In other words, those wicked men thought God would remain aloof in regard to human behavior and misbehavior.

IV. Call to Seek the Lord (Zeph. 2:1-3)

The pattern of doom was broken at this point with a summons to repentance. It was addressed to a "shameless nation" (NRSV), that is, Judah, and particularly to "all you humble of the land" (v. 3, NRSV). Judah as a whole had shown no shame for the evils within it. But there was a remnant within the nation that strove for better things and could prove to be the salvation of the whole. This concept is strong in Scripture.

1 Gather yourselves together, yea, gather together, O nation not desired;

2 Before the decree bring forth, before the day pass as the chaff,

before the fierce anger of the Lord come upon you, before the day of the Lord's anger come upon you.

3 Seek ye the Lord, all ye meek of the earth, which have wrought his judgment; seek righteousness, seek meekness: it may be ye shall be hid in the day of the Lord's anger.

1. Offer of escape (vv. 1-2).—The function of God's prophets was not only to warn, but also to plead. Zephaniah was in line with other prophets in making an appeal for a change of heart. Here is the gospel in the Old Testament. God's judgments are sure, but "his mercy endureth forever" (Ps. 106:1). But for Judah there was no time to waste, for judgment could fall as suddenly and silently as wind blows away chaff.

2. A remnant (v. 3).—At this worst of times in Judah's history, there were those who could be referred to as "humble" (NRSV) and so met the demands of Micah 6:8. These were not perfect, they also needed to repent, but they were the nation's hope. Think of the small group for whom God would have spared Sodom (Gen. 18:23-33).

V. Other Nations Included (Zeph. 2:4-15)

The theme of international justice is picked up in these verses. They begin by naming the Philistine cities: Gaza, Ashkelon, Ashdod, and Ekron. "Cherethites" (v. 5) is another name for Philistines who occupied the coastal plain of Palestine and for centuries invaded and spoiled the territory of Israel. They survived until the times of Alexander the Great; after that they disappeared from the pages of history. Only their name survived in the word *Palestine.* Moab, Ammon, and Ethiopia are then mentioned only to be condemned. Finally, Nineveh (Assyria) appears, and it is described as "the rejoicing city that dwelt carelessly" (v. 15). Her doom is spelled out in vivid terms:

> Herds shall lie down in it,
> every wild animal;
> the desert owl and the screech owl
> shall lodge on its capitals;
> the owl shall hoot at the window,
> the raven croak on the threshold;
> for its cedar work will be laid bare.
> . . . .
> What a desolation it has become" (vv. 14-15, NRSV).

APPLYING THE LESSON

A second opinion.—A young man went to the doctor because of a pain in his side. The doctor diagnosed it as appendicitis. The young man wanted a second opinion, so he set up an appointment with another doctor. This doctor suggested that the problem was with his gall bladder. The young man returned to the first doctor because he said he would rather have appendicitis than gall bladder trouble!

Like him, some try to minimize sin by giving it another name. But by whatever name we call it, sin is still sin. Eventually, the sin of humankind will be confronted by the judgment of God. The prophet Zephaniah proclaimed this message of judgment.

Idolatry today.—Usually, references to idolatry in the Bible go right over our heads, for we are convinced idolatry is no longer a problem. True, we do not fashion idols out of clay and set them up in our homes as they did in the biblical days. However, idolatry is still a problem, for whatever we care most about is the god in our lives. Idolatry today wears four faces: money, possessions, fame, and power. The desire to have more money, the desire to own more things, the desire to become more famous, and the desire to have more control over other people—all of these are manifestations of idolatry today. When we bow down before these things, we are as guilty of idolatry as were Zephaniah's contemporaries when they bowed down before Baal.

Syncretism today.—A new form of syncretism has surfaced in America today under the label "new age." Although this new movement is difficult to define, it brings together the following elements: the belief that all things are one, the idea that all things partake of the one divine essence, the suggestion that we are all gods, the feeling that all religions are one, and a conviction that humans can guide the course of future events.[1] Those who are involved in the New Age movement are as guilty of syncretism as were the contemporaries of Zephaniah.

Godlessness today.—Several years ago, a man who owned a small telephone company in Petersburg, Indiana, began a feature called "Dial-an-Atheist." For that achievement, he was honored as "Atheist of the Year" at the annual convention of American Atheists. I'm not sure what message you would receive if you dialed that number. Perhaps, you would dial that number and no one would answer! Are there people today who do not believe in God? Obviously so. Even more, there are those who live as if they do not believe in God. They go to church on Sunday and then live the rest of the week as if God did not exist. Someone has called them "six-day atheists." Those who live as if there is no God are as guilty of godlessness as were the contemporaries of Zephaniah.

Everybody does it.—When Johnny was six years old, he was with his father, and they were caught speeding. Johnny's father handed the policeman a twenty dollar bill along with his driver's license, and the policeman did not give him a ticket. "It's all right, son," the father said. "Everybody does it."

When the boy was eight, he was a part of a family gathering which discussed income taxes. Johnny's uncle revealed how he had cheated the government out of a thousand dollars because he didn't report some of his earnings. He turned to Johnny and said, "It's all right, Johnny, everybody does it."

When Johnny was twelve, he broke his glasses on the way to school. Johnny's mother told him, "We'll just report to the insurance company that they were stolen. That way, they will pay for them." She added, "It's all right, Johnny, everybody does it."

When he was nineteen, a college classmate offered Johnny the answers for his upcoming test for $50. "It's all right," the upperclassman explained, "everybody does it." Johnny was caught and dismissed from the school. With great indignation, the father said, "Where did you learn to act like that?"

How we are influenced by the actions of those around us! That truth explains the actions of Zephaniah's contemporaries. Influenced by the godlessness of those around them, the Israelites displayed the same kind of wickedness in their lives.

TEACHING THE CLASS

Main Idea: Our righteous God must one day punish sin.

Suggested Teaching Aim: Learners will recommit themselves to sharing how to be saved in view of the truth that God must one day punish sin.

Introduce the Bible Study

Share the comments titled "A second opinion" (*Applying the Lesson*). State that like the young man in the story we look for ways to avoid the reality of our own sins. Note that like other prophets we have recently studied, Zephaniah proclaimed a message that said God must punish sin.

A Teaching Outline

1. Focus on the effort to avoid judgment.
2. Learn about the warning of Zephaniah to those around him about the coming judgment.
3. Determine what learners should do in view of the truth that God must punish sin.
4. Commit themselves to sharing how to be saved from judgment.

Write *Zephaniah* on the chalkboard. Share the information about Zephaniah from the introduction to *Studying the Bible.* State that while the message of Zephaniah is similar to that of other prophets, the purpose of our study today is to help us to see the urgency of warning those around us of this judgment and explaining to them the way of escape. Invite learners to turn to Zephaniah in their Bibles.

Search for Biblical Truth

Point out that an outline will again be used as an aid in grasping the message from Zephaniah. Display the following:

Judgment Is Coming to All

I. Universal judgment (Zeph. 1:1-3)
II. Judah named and warned (Zeph. 1:4-6)
 A. Idolatry
 B. Syncretism
 C. Godlessness
III. Particular groups indicted (Zeph. 1:7-13)
 A. Four offenders
 B. Merchants and others
IV. A call to seek the Lord (Zeph. 2:1-3)
 A. Offer of escape
 B. A remnant
V. Other nations included (Zeph. 2:4-15)

Call on a learner to read Zephaniah 1:1-3 aloud while other learners listen for the severity of the judgment that is to come. Share information from *Studying the Bible* about the meaning of these verses.

Direct learners to scan verses 4-6. Note the three specific charges made against Israel. Use comments from "Idolatry today" (*Applying the Lesson*) about these conditions today.

Call on a learner to read verses 7-13 aloud. Note the subtopics on the outline. Use information from *Studying the Bible* to identify the four offenders. Share comments about the merchants from *Studying the Bible.*

See item 4 on the outline. Note that there always has been a remnant that strives for better things, and these verses issue a call to be a part of the remnant. Call on a learner to read Zephaniah 2:1-3 aloud. Note that verses 1-2 offer escape to those who heed the call.

Conclude by scanning Zephaniah 2:4-15 where universal judgment is again reiterated. Use information from *Studying the Bible* to emphasize the universality of this judgment.

Give the Truth a Personal Focus

Share the comments titled "Everybody does it" (*Applying the Lesson*). Ask: If everybody lives in rebellion against God's ways, what are believers to do? Is there a personal responsibility? Is it a hopeless situation only awaiting the judgment day? As learners consider the questions, point out that the outcome is not their responsibility. Rather making the way of escape known to those around them is the work of believers.

---

1. Douglas R. Groothuis, *Unmasking the New Age* (Downers Grove: Inter-varsity Press, 1986), 18-31.

July 19

God Will Restore Israel

Basic Passage: Zephaniah 3

Focal Passage: Zephaniah 3:12,14-20

This is the last of our studies in the Minor Prophets. What values do they contain for us? Admittedly, they have proved difficult for teacher and student alike. What are our rewards for probing into these unfamiliar and largely neglected books of the Bible? Our basic satisfaction should be that we have been paying heed to "the word of the Lord" (Jonah 1:1; Zeph. 1:1), given through His prophets, in times of national and international crisis. It was during such times, in the early months of World War II, that many European Christians turned afresh to the Minor Prophets and found them surprisingly relevant to prevailing conditions. They seized upon the assurance that, behind all the confusion and conflict, God was in sovereign control and was directing events toward His chosen goal. They heard His call to repentance, observed the outworkings of His justice, and rejoiced at the prospect of His coming kingdom. These messages from the Minor Prophets are always appropriate and should be heeded today.

Study Aim: *To make personal response to God's call for repentance and find security for the future in His promises*

STUDYING THE BIBLE

The severe language with which chapter 3 opens should remind us that this was a citizen of Jerusalem speaking to his fellow citizens. It is the function of a true prophet to proclaim the truth, as revealed by God, without regard for the audience or concern for the consequences. Some say that prophetic voices are lacking in our day. If this is true, ought we not to give more careful attention to what God has already said through prophets of the past?

I. The Prophet's Accusations (Zeph. 3:1-5)

Chapter 2 concludes with a denunciation of Nineveh and pronouncement of its doom. Nineveh is addressed as "the rejoicing city that dwelt carelessly," so puffed up with pride as to say, "I am, and there is none beside me." But divine justice overtook Nineveh so that it became "a desolation," "a lair for wild animals," and a subject for scorn, for, "Everyone who passes by it hisses and shakes the fist" (v. 15, NRSV). For the people of Jerusalem, this humiliation of their enemy was cause for happiness. But Zephaniah saw in it a warning; therefore, he resumed his rebuke of Jerusalem for its sins.

1. Charges itemized (vv. 1-4).—Jerusalem is described as "filthy and polluted, . . . the oppressing city," an attempt surely by the prophet to arrest attention. Its inhabitants had learned nothing from God's discipline in the past but continued on a rebellious path. Leadership was held responsible. "Princes" were designated "roaring lions," beasts of prey who took advantage of their positions to abuse others. "Judges" appear as "evening wolves that leave nothing until the morning" (NRSV), purveyors of injustice instead of justice. "Prophets," who should be messengers of God, were faithless toward their calling. "Priests" abandoned their spiritual mission and had "polluted the sanctuary," probably through idolatrous practices, and "done violence to the law" by their personal behavior. Notice in the case of princes and judges the implication of social oppression and injustice. Zephaniah was in step with other prophets who pronounced judgment on those who oppressed and exploited others.

2. God in the midst (v. 5).—While this was going on, the temple stood as witness to God "in the midst thereof." All the trappings and symbols of religion existed side by side with the evils the prophet denounced. Though these spoke of the presence, perfections, and justice of the Lord, they were ignored by people described as "the unjust [who] knoweth no shame."

II. History's Lessons Ignored (Zeph. 3:6-7)

Using verses from our background material, we have this indictment of Judah for failing to learn the lessons of history. Speaking through the prophet, the Lord said, "I have cut off the nations," followed by a description of cities wasted by war. This was a strong claim that God is active in human affairs. According to secular historians, nations such as Egypt and Assyria, and eventually Babylon, were overthrown by opposing armies. But here the Lord says, "I made their streets waste, that none passeth by: their cities are destroyed, so that there is no man, that there is none inhabitant." If we could ascertain for sure the period in which Zephaniah prophesied, we could certainly identify the nations referred to. The lack of this information, however, does not affect the message that the rise and fall of great powers are under the control of God.

Verse 7 expresses God's hope that His own people would heed these things and change their ways so that like catastrophes might not overtake them. But the sad truth emerges that there was no such response. On the contrary, "they rose early, and corrupted all their doings." There was a spirit of evil eagerness about their rebellious behavior, as though they could not wait to engage in new forms of disobedience.

III. Preservation of a Remnant (Zeph. 3:11-13)

We have already taken note of the concept of a remnant in 2:3. Here it is more precisely mentioned. "This idea of the Remnant is found throughout the Bible, and is not confined to the teaching of the prophets. The blessing promised to Abraham and his seed was limited to one of the sons of Isaac. In the time of Elijah we read of a righteous Remnant of seven thousand, who had not bowed the knee to Baal, but remained loyal to God. Amos spoke of a Remnant who were saved as a brand plucked from the burning [Amos 4:11], or as a few scraps of a sheep saved from the lion's mouth [3:12]."[1] The following verse from Zephaniah expressed the idea.

12 I will also leave in the midst of thee an afflicted and poor people, and they shall trust in the name of the Lord.

For "afflicted and poor" we may read, "humble and lowly" (NRSV). This passage looks forward to "that day" (v. 11), apparently in the future, when God will purge the nation of the proud and haughty, those who had lived in rebellion against Him, and preserve a "remnant of Israel" (v. 13) that "shall not do iniquity, nor speak lies; neither shall a deceitful tongue be found in their mouth: . . . and none shall make them afraid." Whether this was fulfilled in history, as, for example, in the return of a chastened people from Babylonian exile, or whether it awaits fulfillment, there must always be a godly remnant in society, even in the church. As the song says, "I want to be in that number."

IV. A Future Full of Promise (Zeph. 3:14-20)

After many doleful pronouncements, the prophet drew his message to a close with a call to sing and shout, to be "glad and rejoice" (v. 14). In line with other prophets, his final words were not of judgment but of hope. He saw beyond Judah's sufferings a prospect of better times when the Lord would reign as King. He was surely looking beyond Israel's future to the day when the kingdom of God would be established in the earth.

14 Sing, O daughter of Zion; shout, O Israel; be glad and rejoice with all the heart, O daughter of Jerusalem.
15 The Lord hath taken away thy judgments, he hath cast out

thine enemy: the king of Israel, even the Lord, is in the midst of thee: thou shalt not see evil any more.

16 In that day it shall be said to Jerusalem, Fear thou not: and to Zion, Let not thine hands be slack.

17 The Lord thy God in the midst of thee is mighty; he will save, he will rejoice over thee with joy; he will rest in his love, he will joy over thee with singing.

18 I will gather them that are sorrowful for the solemn assembly, who are of thee, to whom the reproach of it was a burden.

19 Behold, at that time I will undo all that afflict thee: and I will save her that halteth, and gather her that was driven out; and I will get them praise and fame in every land where they have been put to shame.

20 At that time will I bring you again, even in the time that I gather you: for I will make you a name and a praise among all people of the earth, when I turn back your captivity before your eyes, saith the Lord.

1. Some explanations.—Our version contains obscurities that have been removed in the *New Revised Standard Version.* The following are particularly helpful. Verse 16 can read, "Do not fear, O Zion; / do not let your hands grow weak," the paralysis of fear being removed because "The Lord, your God, is in your midst," and "he will rejoice over you with gladness, / he will renew you in his love; / he will exult over you with loud singing / as on a day of festival" (vv. 17-18). The second part of verse 18 has this reading, "I will remove disaster from you, / so that you will not bear reproach for it." The last verse may read, "At that time I will bring you home, / at the time when I gather you."

2. Restoration promised.—Through His prophet, God promised a return to former relationships. The repeated use of "Israel" (vv. 14-15) suggests a reunion of the two kingdoms, north and south, which separated after the death of Solomon. Again God's people would be one nation. Relationship with the Lord would also be restored, for there would be a return to covenant conditions with God as King. This prospect is sharpened in verse 17. The promise, "I will bring you home" (v. 20, NRSV), would appear to refer to the end of the Babylonian exile.

3. Ultimate fulfillment.—Much of the language used in these verses parallels that in Revelation 21 with its prospect of "a new heaven and a new earth" (v. 1). In this connection, John the apostle saw "the holy city, new Jerusalem, coming down from God out of heaven" (v. 2). Zephaniah's glad cry, "even the Lord, is in the midst of thee" (3:15), and, "The Lord thy God in the midst of thee is mighty" (v. 17), has its counterpart in, "Behold, the tabernacle of God is with men, and he will dwell with them, and they shall be his people, and God himself shall be with them, and be their God" (Rev. 21:3). So we may believe that, beyond the limits of human history, Zephaniah saw the setting up of a holy city, a new Jerusalem, in which God's people will be made forever secure by the presence among them of the Lord Himself. And who will these be who enjoy these future blessings? In Zephaniah 3:9 appears these words, "At that time I will change the speech of the peoples / to a pure speech, / that all of them may call on the name of the Lord / and serve him with one accord" (NRSV). This suggests a reversal of the confusion of tongues at Babel (Gen. 11:1-9) enabling all people, Jew and Gentile alike, to worship God and enter into covenant relationship with Him.

APPLYING THE LESSON

Afflicting the comfortable.—Someone has said that a preacher has two responsibilities: to comfort the afflicted and to afflict the comfortable. Sometimes, preachers lean toward the first of those responsibilities and neglect the second. Truth is, we need to do both.

That was John Newton's desire as he preached. This converted slave trader, whose personal testimony is sung in some church every week in the hymn "Amazing Grace," wrote that the point of his preaching was "to break a hard heart and to heal a broken heart." A word of judgment and then a word of comfort are both a part of true prophetic preaching.

That was also John Wesley's desire as he preached. After a sermon he preached in 1761, he wrote this evaluation in his journal: "I believe many were wounded and many were comforted." Wounding our listeners with a reminder of the depth of their sins and then comforting our listeners with a reminder of the breadth of God's love are both a part of true prophetic preaching.[2]

Because the "afflicting-the-comfortable" side of preaching had been so neglected in his day, the prophet Zephaniah concentrated on that dimension. However, his prophetic word also included a word of comfort.

Now she knows.—The mother left the two children in the den and was trying to prepare dinner. A cry from the den arrested her attention. She rushed into the room to find five-year-old Billy crying. "What happened?" she asked. Billy explained, "Susie pulled my hair, and it hurt." The mother tried to soothe Billy with the explanation: "She didn't know it hurt." Quickly, the mother rushed back to the kitchen only to be disturbed by another cry from the den. This time she discovered Susie crying. "What happened?" she demanded. Billy responded, "Now she knows!"

Sometimes we learn from experience. At other times, experience merely enables us to recognize our mistake when we make it a second time. Zephaniah's contemporaries did not learn from experience, but they continued on the pathway of disobedience that would eventually lead to the judgment of God.

A picture of commitment.—Difficulties and trials come to every person.

Yet, how differently we respond to the circumstances of our lives. A man belonged to our church one time whose wife died with cancer. Consequently, he became angry with God and dropped out of the church, following a lifestyle that reversed the pathway he had previously followed. Contrast with him the response of General William Booth, founder of the Salvation Army. Near the end of his life, the general was told that he was losing his sight. How did he respond? He said, "I've done all I could for God with two eyes. Now I'll do what I can without eyes."

Some of Zephaniah's contemporaries responded to the difficulties of their time by turning from God. On the other hand, some remained faithful. With this remnant, God would carry His plans forward.

God is not through making you.—Jill had a warm and sensitive heart, but she was not physically attractive. A birth defect left her face disfigured. On her first day in her new school, her first grade classmates made fun of her appearance. When she came home that night, she crawled up into her mother's lap and, with tears streaming down her face, asked: "Mother, why did God make me this way?" With great wisdom, the mother replied, "Honey, God is not through making you yet."

That was Zephaniah's message to his contemporaries. Unpleasant conditions prevailed in the land. But Zephaniah had this good news: God was not through making them yet.

A great place.—What will heaven be like? The message of the Bible about heaven can be summarized in three words: relief, reunion, and rejoicing. Heaven will be a place of relief. In heaven, we will cry no more tears, and bear no more burdens, and feel no more pain. Heaven will also be a place of reunion. In heaven, we will renew fellowship with those loved ones who have gone before us. In addition, heaven will be a place of rejoicing. The opportunity to bask in the presence of God and fellowship with the saints will permeate our heavenly existence with undiluted joy.

TEACHING THE CLASS

Main Idea: God will provide security for those who repent and follow Him.

Suggested Teaching Aim: Learners will repent of their own rebellion against God and find security in His forgiveness.

Introduce the Bible Study

Share the comments titled "Afflicting the comfortable" (*Applying the Lesson*). State that while the study for today points to the need for repentance in Israel, the purpose of the study is to help us look at our own needs.

Ask: In what ways did Israel repeatedly rebel against God? Continue by asking: Do believers today rebel against God in the same way? What specific form does rebellion take today?

Note that it is much easier to talk about the rebellion of believers as a group than it is to talk about our own personal rebellion. Ask rhetorically: Is it possible that there is rebellion in your own life that needs to be dealt with. Invite learners to continue to ask themselves this question as they look at the passage for study today. Invite them to turn to Zephaniah 3.

Search for Biblical Truth

Use a minilecture to provide insight into the content of Zephaniah 3. Use background material from *Studying the Bible.* Display the following outline and refer to it during your comments.

Accusations and Promises

I. The prophet's accusations (vv. 1-5)
II. History's lessons ignored (vv. 6-7)
III. Preservation of a remnant (vv. 11-13)
IV. A future full of promise (vv. 14-20)
  A. Restoration promised
  B. Ultimate fulfillment

After presenting the minilecture that covers the first three points, note the caption for the fourth point. Call on a learner to read Zephaniah 3:14-20 aloud. Share information about the promised restoration and its ultimate fulfillment from material in *Studying the Bible.*

Share the comments titled "Now she knows" (*Applying the Lesson*). Note that Israel did not always learn from experience, but God remained faithful to teaching them how to repent of their rebellion and to enjoy the security that He promised.

Give the Truth a Personal Focus

Note that looking at ourselves honestly and recognizing rebellion can be very discouraging. Share the comments titled "God is not through making you" (*Applying the Lesson*). Note that we continue to be sinful and rebellious though we belong to God. However, He is not through making His children either.

A Teaching Outline

1. Consider what can be done about rebellion against God.
2. Discover God's message about the rebellious people to whom Zephaniah spoke.
3. Determine God's message to us about our own need for repentance and the promise of security.
4. Consider repentance of our own rebellion and acceptance of God's security in our lives.

Ask rhetorically: What do you do when you recognize that you have moved away from God? Are you willing to accept whatever means He uses to bring you back to Him and repent of your own rebellion? After a few minutes for thoughtful consideration, ask: What does God promise for us when we do repent and walk closely by His side? (Security in His strength.) Share the comments titled "A picture of commitment" (*Applying the Lesson*).

Invite learners to spend several minutes in meditation as they consider their own need for repentance and acceptance of the security of God in their lives. Conclude with a prayer of commitment to following after the God we have chosen and to dwell in His security.

---

1. H. H. Rowley, *The Faith of Israel* (Philadelphia: The Westminster Press, 1956), 117.
2. John R. W. Stott, *Between Two Worlds* (Grand Rapids: Wm. B. Eerdmans Publishing Co., 1982), 314.

June, July, August 1992

Guidelines for Ministry

Aids from BROADMAN for Studying and Teaching

Books:
The Broadman Bible Commentary, Volume 11
Layman's Bible Book Commentary, Volume 22
Strong's Exhaustive Concordance, James Strong
The Heart of the New Testament, H. I. Hester

For the conclusion of the quarter we will address our attention to the Pastoral Epistles as we study 1 and 2 Timothy and Titus. Two units of lessons, "Guidelines for Leading" and "Guidelines for Serving," will introduce us to conditions in New Testament churches, with special emphasis on the obligations of leadership.

July 26

Understanding What You Teach

Basic Passage: 1 Timothy 1

Focal Passage: 1 Timothy 1:3-11,18-20

We begin a new series of lessons on the Letters of Paul to Timothy and Titus under the title "Guidelines for Ministry." Although the New Testament provides a great deal of information on the formation of churches, with valuable counseling for their members, we are left uncertain as to the leadership roles in those churches. We find references to "bishop" and "elder," and in a statement on the risen Lord's gifts to His churches we read, "The gifts he gave were that some would be apostles, some prophets, some evangelists, some pastors and teachers, to equip the saints for the work of ministry, for building up the body of Christ" (Eph. 4:11-12, NRSV). The functions described were for the purpose of equipping the membership to serve so that each individual church became a ministering unit composed of active members. Thus no recognition was given to a select group known as "the ministry," for all Christians are under obligation to serve. This series of lessons, therefore, should be made to conform to this concept as Paul's counsel to his younger friends is accepted as counsel to believers as a whole.

Study Aim: *To secure commitment to both believing and communicating the truth and avoiding error*

STUDYING THE BIBLE

What is written above does not deny the fact of leadership importance and responsibility. In order that the goal of a ministering church may be realized, there must be key persons who, because of their qualifications, set the pattern and furnish the instruction for others. These were the tasks assigned to Timothy.

I. A Difficult Assignment (1 Tim. 1:3-7)

Here and elsewhere (1 Cor. 4:17) Paul addressed Timothy as his "son." Biologically, Timothy was the son of a Jewish woman named Eunice and an unnamed Gentile father (Acts 16:1). Paul's use of the term "son" would indicate the apostle was Timothy's spiritual father, since the apostle spoke of him as "my own son in the faith." Paul probably led the young man to faith in Christ during his visit to Lystra (Acts 14:1-7). By the time Paul wrote his epistle, the two had been companions in missionary service during which the bonds between them had been strengthened. The apostle began his letter with a reminder of the circumstances in which the young man had been appointed to serve in Ephesus.

> **3 As I besought thee to abide still at Ephesus, when I went into Macedonia, that thou mightest charge some that they teach no other doctrine,**
> **4 Neither give heed to fables and endless genealogies, which minister questions, rather than godly edifying which is in the faith: so do.**
> **5 Now the end of the commandment is charity out of a pure heart, and of a good conscience, and of faith unfeigned:**
> **6 From which some having swerved have turned aside unto vain jangling;**
> **7 Desiring to be teachers of the law; understanding neither what they say, nor whereof they affirm.**

1. Persuasion needed (v. 3).—Timothy had been left in Ephesus with instructions that he apparently was not eager to accept. There is reason to believe that he had asked to be relieved of a difficult job, for the apostle used firm language to persuade him to stay put. The subsequent exhortation, "Let no man despise thy youth" (4:12), suggests a sense of inferiority on Timothy's part causing him to seek release. That he finally measured up is borne witness to by such a testimonial as Paul's statement to the Philippians, "I have no man likeminded, who will naturally care for your state. . . . as a son with the father, he hath served with me in the gospel" (Phil. 2:20-22).

2. Vain discussions (vv. 4,6-7).—The "myths and endless genealogies" and "meaningless talk" (NRSV) that Paul warned against were evidently related to the teaching of the Mosaic law (v. 7). Timothy's field of service was Ephesus where, as in most other places, the church consisted of Jews and Gentiles. Unfortunately, these two elements made for clashes of opinion that were destroying the harmony of the fellowship. The continued emphasis on the law in this passage points to disruptive teaching on matters that are not specifically described but were evidently concerned with interpretations of Jewish law. Paul bluntly said that these teachers did not know what they were talking about (v. 7). Unfortunately, their kind persists. Timothy was ordered to come down heavily on the offenders who were to "teach no other doctrine" (v. 3) than that given in the true gospel.

3. Love is supreme (v. 5).—As always in these situations, disagreement was threatening the harmony of the Christian fellowship. Where love prevails, differences of opinion do not necessarily divide. So Paul urged that mutual love between believers be regarded as a commandment, as indeed Christ made it (John 15:12). This love issues from "a pure heart" (no mixed motives), and "a good conscience" (totally sincere), and "faith unfeigned" (a faith that is genuine).

II. The Function of the Law (1 Tim. 1:8-11)

Having criticized self-appointed teachers of the law, Paul felt it necessary to make clear that he was not attacking the law itself. His position on the law could have been easily misunderstood, and was. His lengthy statement in Romans 7 could be the result. The greatest discovery of his life was that the law could not save, for "by grace are ye saved through faith" (Eph. 2:8). This provided the foundation for this teaching. But he was ever anxious to maintain that salvation by faith alone does not discredit the laws of God.

> **8 But we know that the law is good, if a man use it lawfully;**
> **9 Knowing this, that the law is not made for a righteous man, but for the lawless and disobedient, for the ungodly and for sinners, for unholy and profane, for murderers of fathers and murderers of mothers, for manslayers,**
> **10 For whoremongers, for them that defile themselves with mankind, for menstealers, for liars, for perjured persons, and if there be any other thing that is contrary to sound doctrine;**
> **11 According to the glorious gospel of the blessed God, which was committed to my trust.**

1. The law is good (v. 8).—Since God was its author, no other conclusion is possible. Yet even good things can be abused, as was the case with the false teachers in Ephesus. Again, we are at a disadvantage in not knowing what exactly they said about the law. But they were engaging in fantasies that the apostle saw as "vain jangling" (v. 6).

2. Its corrective purpose (vv. 9-10).—In the beginning, God gave through Moses a set of Commandments that was intended to correct existing evils. To people who were already engaged in transgression, the Lord gave His repeated, "Thou shalt not." Paul's list of crimes and vices would seem to fit a corrupt pagan society such as existed in Ephesus. He was saying that the law is appropriate to such people to bring them to a sense of sinfulness. Elsewhere he would say that in Christ there is freedom from law, not as to its moral demands, but its power and penalties.

3. Paul's gospel (v. 11).—This was the teaching of Paul's gospel, "the glorious gospel of the blessed God." Although some falsely charged him with encouraging people to sin (Rom. 6:1), in truth he denounced sin, warned of its consequences; he also taught Christ as the end of the law, "For the law of the Spirit of life in Christ Jesus hath made me free from the law of sin and death" (Rom. 8:2).

III. Incentives to Faithfulness (1 Tim. 1:12-20)

Not departing from his subject, but in order to illustrate it from personal experience, the apostle broke into a testimony of praise for what God had done in his life. His language expresses his sense of wonder that God had chosen such as he, "putting me into the ministry," in spite of what he had been and done in his unconverted days. Paul did not spare himself in describing the kind of person he had been, "a blasphemer, and a persecutor, and injurious" (v. 13), for he had fought against Christ, His gospel, and His people, "breathing out threatenings and slaughter against the disciples of the Lord" (Acts 9:1). In his testimony to the grace that turned him around to make him a messenger of the gospel, he introduced what he termed "a faithful saying" (v. 15), perhaps a line from an ancient hymn, "Christ Jesus came into the world to save sinners," to which he added, "of whom I am chief." He concluded this grateful acknowledgment of the operation of grace in his life with a beautiful doxology (v. 17) and continued:

> **18 This charge I commit unto thee, son Timothy, according to the prophecies which went before on thee, that thou by them mightest war a good warfare;**
>
> **19 Holding faith, and a good conscience; which some having put away concerning faith have made shipwreck:**
>
> **20 Of whom is Hymenaeus and Alexander; whom I have delivered unto Satan, that they may learn not to blaspheme.**

1. Vital memories (vv. 18-19a).—In addition to his own experience, the apostle offered Timothy the stimulating memory of his appointment to the ministry on the recommendation of others. Paul had taken the younger man as a colleague because he "was well reported of by the brethren that were at Lystra and Iconium" (Acts 16:2). In the difficult times that he faced in Ephesus, Timothy needed to draw strength from the thought that others (including Paul) had put their trust and confidence in him. To look back on life is to find encouragement to face the present. Timothy had a hard task; Paul compared it to warfare (v. 18), but others believed he was equal to it, and with God's help he would prove them right.

2. When others failed (vv. 19a-20).—What was the alternative? Paul offered two examples of people who had failed in their ministries and, consequently, "made shipwreck" of their lives. Hymenaeus is mentioned again in 2 Timothy 2:17-18 where he is said to "have erred, saying that the resurrection is past already" and so had overthrown "the faith of some." His guilt was in propagating false doctrine, against which Paul had warned in the early verses of our lesson passage. Alexander was a common name so that it is precarious to attempt any precise identification. But both had caused so much damage in the Christian community that Paul said, "I have delivered [them] unto Satan," clearly a stern act of discipline that had as its purpose the recovery and restoration of the offenders.

APPLYING THE LESSON

Leadership in the church.—Warren Bennis described two kinds of leadership: corporate leadership and movement leadership. Corporate leadership is based on the position of the leaders. They are in authority over those they are trying to lead. They have the power to fire those people who do not follow their leadership or to reward them if they do follow. They set the rules, and if the others want to be a part of the team, they have to follow those rules. If they do not, they are out, and the leader replaces them. Movement leadership, on the other hand, is based on the persuasion of the leader. Movement leadership requires persuading people to follow, not giving orders. The key to corporate leadership is power. The key to movement leadership is character.[1] Christian leaders should fall into the category of movement leadership.

Thank you, John.—John A. Broadus, who served as president of a theological seminary, was a pastor in Virginia during the early part of his ministry. A young man who had some mental deficiencies was the target of Broadus's concern. Some of his friends suggested to Broadus he was wasting his time, but he just kept sharing with the young man about Jesus. Eventually, the message broke through, and the young man was converted. After that, every time he would see Broadus, the young man would greet him with the same words: "Howdy, John. Thank you, John!" Soon thereafter, the young man became seriously ill. Dr. Broadus visited him in the hospital. One of the last things he said before he died was, "Howdy, John. Thank you, John!" Dr. Broadus never tired of telling that story. He would conclude the story by declaring that one of the brightest expectations of heaven was for him to see that boy and hear him say one more time, "Howdy, John. Thank you, John."

Young Timothy probably had the same feelings toward Paul as that young man had toward Broadus, for Paul's influence and witness led Timothy into a relationship with Christ.

Young and creative.—History has been shaped, to a large degree, by men and women in the early years of their lives. Napoleon had already conquered Italy at the age of 25. Lord Byron and Edgar Allen Poe are among the world's immortals in the area of literature. Yet both died at 37. Sir Isaac Newton made some of his greatest discoveries before he was 25. Jesus lived only 33 years on the earth. Young and creative men and women have shaped history.

Thus, Paul encouraged Timothy to assert himself and use the gifts God had given him.

Working against each other.—The man was obviously having a difficult time with a box that seemed to be lodged in the door. A fellow worker recognized his plight and offered to assist. He went through another door into the office and began pushing and shoving. Finally, he said to the first man, "I don't think we'll ever get this box out of the office." "Out," the other man shouted. "I'm not trying to get it out. I'm trying to get it in!"

That's a parable of the church. Many times we find ourselves on opposite sides of an issue, with some of us trying to push out and the others trying to push in. Such conflict within the church affects our witness and work for Christ. This is obviously not a new problem. Timothy had to deal with a similar problem in the church at Ephesus.

The gospel message.—The message Paul preached was both "glorious" and "gospel." It was glorious because the world had never heard another message like it. It was gospel because it was good news. The gospel message does three things. First, it solves the riddle of life. Through Christ, an individual discovers the meaning and purpose of life. Second, it solves the mystery of death. When Christ came back from the grave, He gave notice that death is not the end but a new beginning. Third, it solves the question mark of eternity. Jesus promised to prepare a place for His people and then to return to take His prepared people to that place. Is it any wonder the Christian message was called "good news"?

The full picture.—Someone has said that conversion is the miracle of the moment, but growth is the task of a lifetime. Paul referred to both dynamics in his words to Timothy. That Christ saved him forever humbled Paul. That Christ had work for him to do forever challenged Paul.

TEACHING THE CLASS

Main Idea: Communicating unadulterated truth is the responsibility of believers.

Suggested Teaching Aim: Learners will commit themselves to seeking and communicating truth without error.

Introduce the Bible Study

Write "Guidelines for Ministry" on the chalkboard. State that today we begin a new series of lessons from the Books of Timothy and Titus. Use information from the introductory paragraphs preceding *Studying the Bible* to introduce the study.

Note that the purpose of the first unit is to look at guidelines given by Paul for a functioning body of believers and to determine how our ministry within today's church should be carried out. Share the comments titled "Leadership in the church" (*Applying the Lesson*). Note that as Christian leaders we will seek guidelines for becoming more persuasive. Invite learners to open their Bibles to 1 Timothy.

Search for Biblical Truth

Share some information from *Studying the Bible* about this lesson of Paul to his "son" in the ministry, Timothy. Call on a learner to read 1 Timothy 1:1-2.

A Teaching Outline

1. Introduce the study in Timothy and the concept of discovering guidelines of ministry.
2. Discover Paul's instruction to Timothy about what and how to teach other believers.
3. Determine ways to decide what is truth.
4. Commit themselves to seeking and communicating truth without error.

Direct learners to read 1 Timothy 1:3-7 to discover the answers to the following questions:

1. Why did Paul persuade Timothy to continue to work in Ephesus?
2. What were believers in Ephesus caught up in doing?
3. What alternative was Timothy to convince them to adopt?

Displaying the questions or providing copies for learners may be helpful. After a brief study period, direct learners to discuss their answers with those sitting near them. After a discussion period, call for response to each question. Use information from *Studying the Bible* to supplement responses.

Note that Paul now turned to comment about the value and purpose of the very law that self-appointed teachers had corrupted. Call on a learner to read 1 Timothy 1:8-11 aloud. Ask: What is the purpose of the law? How does the law contrast with the gospel mentioned in verse 11?

State that Paul continued with a personal testimony of the effect of the law in his own life. Call on a learner to read 1 Timothy 1:12-17 aloud. Share information from *Studying the Bible* about this section of Scripture.

Direct learners to read verses 18-20 to themselves for answers to the following questions. Display the questions.

1. What charge was committed to Timothy?
2. What problem had occurred with two of Paul's colleagues?
3. How was Timothy to carry out his charge?

After several minutes of study, suggest that learners discuss their conclusions with those sitting near them. Call for response to the questions. Supplement response with material from *Studying the Bible*.

Give the Truth a Personal Focus

Share the comments titled "Working against each other" (*Applying the Lesson*). Ask: In what ways do believers sometimes work against each other today? Elicit response. If it is not included in responses, suggest that believes sometimes do not teach the truth accurately.

Continue by asking: How can you know that what you might teach is accurate? Elicit response that includes diligent seeking of accurate interpretation of God's Word and prayer. Share the comments titled "The gospel message" (*Applying the Lesson*). State that all that we teach must focus learners to the gospel message.

Ask: What guideline for ministry have we considered in the Scripture for today? Elicit response that reflects the main idea of this lesson. Write the guideline on the chalkboard.

Share the comments titled "Thank you, John" (*Applying the Lesson*). Invite learners to commit themselves to seeking and sharing the truth of the gospel accurately and to know that their reward will be persons who feel grateful that the unadulterated truth has been shared.

---

1. Warren Bennis, *On Becoming a Leader* (Reading, Mass.: Addison-Wesley Publishing House, 1989), 159.

August 2

Train Yourself in Godliness

Basic Passage: 1 Timothy 4

Focal Passage: 1 Timothy 4

There is an important link between belief and behavior. Throughout the Bible, this is a consistent emphasis. In Old Testament times, worshipers were warned that their attendance at the temple and offering of sacrifices had no value in God's sight unless relations with other people were just and honorable. After all, the Ten Commandments dealt with duties toward God in the first four items and with behavior toward others in the remaining six. Our Lord spelled out the same dual responsibilities in His teaching, as in the Sermon on the Mount (Matt. 5—7). The apostle Paul gave no stronger emphasis to these twin truths than in the epistles we are studying. He exhorted Timothy, for example, to be watchful in both areas, "Holding faith, and a good conscience" (1:19), the first to do with belief and the second behavior. The younger man should observe and teach "sound doctrine" (v. 10), and at the same time be an example of disciplined living. Our chapter is concerned with both these matters.

Study Aim: *To accept the connection between belief and behavior and keep these in right relationship in our own lives.*

STUDYING THE BIBLE

The apostle Paul was very plain in stating the purpose of this letter to Timothy. "These things write I unto thee, hoping to come unto thee shortly: But if I tarry long, that thou mayest know how thou oughtest to behave thyself in the house of God" (3:14-15). In the difficult situation that confronted the younger man in Ephesus, he was responsible, not only for his own belief and conduct, but also for others who belonged to "the house of God."

I. Be Watchful against Error (1 Tim. 4:1-5)

Belief has a positive and a negative side. It accepts and commits itself to that which is true and rejects that which is false. Since Timothy had been assigned to Ephesus to deal with false teaching (1:3-7), it is understandable that Paul would return to this subject when instructing his young friend how to handle affairs in "the house of God, which is the church of the living God, the pillar and ground of the truth" (3:15).

1 Now the Spirit speaketh expressly, that in the latter times some shall depart from the faith, giving heed to seducing spirits, and doctrines of devils;

2 Speaking lies in hypocrisy; having their conscience seared with a hot iron;

3 Forbidding to marry, and commanding to abstain from meats, which God hath created to be received with thanksgiving of them which believe and know the truth.

4 For every creature of God is good, and nothing to be refused, if it be received with thanksgiving:

5 For it is sanctified by the word of God and prayer.

1. Agents of Satan (vv. 1-2).—The phrase, "the latter times," refers to the period between our Lord's ascension and His return. There were prophets in the church, and they had foretold a falling away from the true faith. This would be the result of satanic activity, as the devil sought to undo the work of the gospel. Therefore, those who followed Satan's leading were teaching "doctrines of devils." They were not only theologically wrong, however, but they were also morally astray, hypocritically teaching one thing while themselves doing another.

2. Asceticism (v. 3).—Paul focused on two of the false teachings. The first concerned marriage and may indicate a gnostic influence since gnostics regarded everything material as evil, including the marriage relationship. The second may have had a Jewish source for it concerned dietary prohibitions, although gnostic influence was also possible here. Paul's endorsement of marriage is given in 3:12 and 5:14, while his position on food restrictions is made clear in such passages as 1 Corinthians 10:25-26.

3. God's good gifts (vv. 4-5).—The statement "everything created by God is good" (NRSV) refers to the repeated words in Genesis 1, culminating in, "God saw everything that he had made, and, behold, it was very good" (v. 31). For the Christian, enjoyment of God's provision should be accompanied by thanksgiving, as in grace before meals.

II. Be Valiant for Truth (1 Tim. 4:6-11)

The matters discussed by Paul were intended to be passed on to the church as a whole. By passing them on Timothy would prove himself "a good minister of Jesus Christ" (v. 6). Thus what was written as a personal letter became a message to the fellowship. As a part of the

New Testament, that same letter affords instruction and inspiration to Christians today.

> **6 If thou put the brethren in remembrance of these things, thou shalt be a good minister of Jesus Christ, nourished up in the words of faith and of good doctrine, whereunto thou hast attained.**
>
> **7 But refuse profane and old wives' fables, and exercise thyself rather unto godliness.**
>
> **8 For bodily exercise profiteth little: but godliness is profitable unto all things, having promise of the life that now is, and of that which is to come.**
>
> **9 This is a faithful saying and worthy of all acceptation.**
>
> **10 For therefore we both labor and suffer reproach, because we trust in the living God, who is the Savior of all men, specially of those that believe.**
>
> **11 These things command and teach.**

1. A good minister (v. 6).—The Greek word translated "minister" is *diakonos,* which Paul used in 3:8-13 for the office of deacon. So he was not conferring a title on Timothy but describing his role in the church, one who serves. That role is further emphasized by the use of the word "brethren," making Timothy not a ruler but a member of a family to which he was under obligation to pass on the teaching he had received.

2. Avoiding distractions (v. 7).—A strong trend obviously existed in the Ephesian church toward what Paul had earlier called "fables and endless genealogies" (1:4). The very nature of religious discussion lends itself to speculation, which in turn, can develop into fantasy. This is to be avoided and can be by staying close to "the words of faith and of good doctrine" (v. 6) in which, since his conversion, Timothy had been raised.

3. Spiritual exercise (vv. 8-9).—Paul was not knocking physical exercise, which he acknowledged has "some value" (NRSV), but he was claiming greater value for spiritual activity and training. The care of the body is good for this life, but nourishing the soul is of eternal importance. By describing verse 8 as "a faithful saying," which the apostle was quoting from some unknown source, he was at the same time endorsing it as truth worthy of acceptance.

4. High motivation (vv. 10-11).—The sacrifice and effort required in concentrating on spiritual growth and development is worthwhile because of the Christian hope that is centered in God Himself. He is "the living God," therefore a dependable source of help. He also desires to be the Savior of all persons, for which reason the gospel needs to be preached to all. He only becomes Savior though to those who respond in belief.

5. Sharing truth (v. 11).—Again Paul reminded Timothy that he was to be the channel through whom Paul's teaching would reach others. The recurring phrase, "these things" (vv. 6,11), indicates that the total content of the epistle was to be shared with others. What was necessary for Timothy was necessary also for the membership of the Ephesian church.

III. Be a Worthy Example (1 Tim. 4:12-16)

Now Timothy's dual responsibility comes into view. He was to be a teacher of sound doctrine, communicating to others the truths he had learned from Paul and others (see 2 Tim. 1:5; 3:14-15). At the same time, he was to demonstrate those truths in daily life and so provide an example for others to follow.

> **12 Let no man despise thy youth; but be thou an example of the believers, in word, in conversation, in charity, in spirit, in faith, in purity.**
> **13 Till I come, give attendance to reading, to exhortation, to doctrine.**
> **14 Neglect not the gift that is in thee, which was given thee by prophecy, with the laying on of the hands of the presbytery.**
> **15 Meditate upon these things; give thyself wholly to them; that thy profiting may appear to all.**
> **16 Take heed unto thyself, and unto the doctrine; continue in them: for in doing this thou shalt both save thyself, and them that hear thee.**

1. Meeting criticism (v. 12).—We find more than one indication in the New Testament that Timothy was a diffident individual, perhaps possessing an inferiority complex (1 Cor. 16:10). The word "youth" covered a range of years, so that while Timothy was at this time in his thirties, its use was appropriate. In a culture that valued seniority, he could be considered young for the responsibilities he shouldered. He was not to react aggressively, however, but prove his suitability by his behavior.

2. Keeping busy (vv. 13-14).—The reference is not to private study but the conduct of public worship. Following the pattern of the Jewish synagogue, the reading of Scripture was a priority. This would mean the Old Testament and possibly Paul's Letters, which were on the way to being recognized as Scripture. Preaching and teaching were also to be paid attention. Timothy did not have a natural ability for these ministries, but he should recognize them as a divine enduement. The word "presbytery" applies to a gathering of mature men, perhaps referring to the occasion when Timothy was "well reported of by the brethren that were at Lystra and Iconium" (Acts 16:2).

3. Taking heed (vv. 15-16).—In the discharge of his duties, Timothy must pay careful heed to both his teaching and his practice. The two must agree. "In personal character and in sound doctrine he is to remain steadfast, for what he does affects his own relationship to God and that of his hearers."[1] When belief and conduct are in harmony, a person is protected ("saved") from spiritual disaster and affords the same protection to others.

APPLYING THE LESSON

When ambition obscures judgment.—Watergate is well into past history now, but the name still connotes ambition gone awry. Jeb Stuart McGruder, a promising politician from a good background, was one of the main players in the Watergate scandal. When he was sentenced to prison, someone asked him why he did it. He responded, "My ambition obscured my judgment. Somewhere between my ambition and my ideals I lost my compass."[2]

This happens in spiritual circles as well as governmental circles. That's why Paul's call to moral living is so needed in our day.

The ways of Satan.—From the garden of Eden to Main Street, U.S.A., Satan's methods have been the same. First, he questions the Word of God. When Satan whispered to Eve in the garden, "Has God said, 'You shall not eat from any tree of the garden'?" (Gen. 3:1, NASB), he was not seeking information. He was making an accusation. He was calling into question the Word of God. Second, he denies the Word of God. Satan said to Eve, "You won't really die if you eat that fruit. It is just a trick God is trying to pull on you. You can do what you want to and not ever worry about the consequences." Third, Satan substitutes for the Word of God. God had told Adam and Eve not to eat the fruit. Satan told them to go ahead and eat it. He provided an alternative route for humankind, and they chose to follow it.

In the beginning, in Paul's day, and in our day, Satan continues to use those methods to discourage the people of God, to disrupt the work of God, and to deny the Word of God.

True service.—Each of us as Christians is called to service. Richard J. Foster provides insight into what real service is by listing the characteristics of self-righteous service. Self-righteous service comes through human effort, is impressed with the big deal, demands external rewards, is overly concerned about results, is selective in its service, is determined by moods and whims, is temporary, is without sensitivity, and divides instead of building up. By contrast, true service grows out of a vital relationship with Christ, does not distinguish between large and small service, does not seek attention, is needs oriented rather than results oriented, is indiscriminate in its ministry, is consistent, is permanent, listens with tenderness before acting, and consequently builds community.[3] It is to this real service that we as Christians have been called.

That's not the point.—Two comedians gave understandably humorous responses to questions about physical exercises. Red Skelton said he got his exercise as a pall bearer carrying the caskets of his friends who had spent their lives exercising. George Burns told of a doctor who had listed all the things Burns needed to give up to enjoy long life. George, of course, explained how he had rejected that advice and had actually done all the things the doctor told him were bad for his health. The questioner asked, "What does your doctor think about the way you live?" Burns replies, "He's dead."

Such a frivolous attitude toward physical exercise is not the point Paul made in our text. His point was that of priorities. Taking care of our physical health and neglecting our spiritual health is to have confused priorities.

Eager to share.—Halford Luccock, well-known preacher of another generation, shared late in his life a picture he had carried in his mind for thirty years. It happened many years before in a New Haven hospital. He said a man came running down the corridor with a chart he had taken from the foot of a patient's bed. He grabbed Luccock by the arm and shouted, "Look! The chart says her temperature's going down." Then he ran to another person in the hall and blurted out the same good news. Luccock said he never knew who "her" was, and he never saw that man again. But he added he would never forget the picture of a man so overwhelmed with some good news that he had to grab the first person he saw and share it with him.

With that same kind of urgency, Paul instructed young Timothy to "command and teach" (v. 11) the things he had experienced in Christ Jesus.

TEACHING THE CLASS

Main Idea: Consistency between belief and behavior is to be taught and practiced.

Suggested Teaching Aim: Learners will determine what they must do to bring consistency between their beliefs and behavior.

Introduce the Bible Study

Share the comments titled "When ambition obscures judgment" (*Applying the Lesson*). Ask: What problems occur within the church because there is not consistency between the stated belief and the behavior of believers? Elicit response that moves beyond publicized discrepancies to less spectacular examples among Christians.

Use information from the introductory paragraphs preceding *Studying the Bible* to comment about the link between belief and behavior. Recall that the title of the unit of study is "Guidelines for Ministry." State that the study today will continue to seek guidelines for our lives as we serve throughout the local church. State that learners will be asked to state a specific guideline that grows out of this passage of Scripture.

Search for Biblical Truth

Invite learners to open their Bibles to 1 Timothy 4. Share information about the purpose of Paul's letter to Timothy. See *Studying the Bible*. Call on a learner to read 1 Timothy 3:14-15 aloud.

Note that in the passage for today Paul gave three basic instructions to Timothy: (1) be watchful against error in the teaching of yourself and others; (2) be courageous to speak up when it is necessary to correct error; (3) be certain that there is consistency between what you teach and the way you live. Display the three statements.

Direct learners to find the words of Paul in 1 Timothy 4:1-16 that communicates these instructions and to be prepared to cite specific verses that provide the instruction. (Verses 1-5 support 1. Verses 6-11 support 2. Verses 12-16 support 3.) Share information from *Studying the Bible* as these passages are discussed.

A Teaching Outline

1. Discuss the issues of belief and behavior.
2. Discover Paul's instructions to Timothy about consistency between his belief and his behavior.
3. Identify persons that learners teach.
4. Evaluate the consistency between learners' belief and behavior.
5. Determine what must be done to bring consistency in learners' lives.

Share "The ways of Satan" (*Applying the Lesson*) when discussing the errors that will be taught.

Note that our responsibility, like Timothy's, is to defend the truth publicly and privately. Share the comments titled "True service" (*Applying the Lesson*).

Give the Truth a Personal Focus

Share the comments titled "Eager to share" (*Applying the Lesson*). Ask rhetorically: Are you eager to share? Continue by stating that whether we intend to do so or not, we do share. We do teach others by our words and our behaviors. We teach persons with whom we have contact, particularly prolonged contact. Direct learners to consider persons in their lives whom they teach in either a direct or indirect way. Encourage them to write down the names of those persons.

Ask: What guideline for ministry has the Scripture for today given for teaching these persons? Remind learners that the task of identifying the guideline was given as the lesson was begun. Elicit response that is similar to the main idea for this study.

Ask rhetorically: On a scale of 1 to 10, how would you rate the consistency between what you say you believe (teach) and the way you live (behavior)? Allow moments for reflection.

Continue by asking rhetorically: What would you personally need to do to bring consistency between what you say you believe and your behavior? Allow moments for reflection. Conclude with a prayer of commitment to that task.

---

1. E. Glenn Hinson, "1-2 Timothy and Titus" in *The Broadman Bible Commentary,* vol. 11 (Nashville: Broadman Press, 1971), 326.
2. Paul W. Powell, *The Complete Disciple* (Wheaton: Victor Books, 1982), 54.
3. Richard J. Foster, *The Celebration of Discipline* (San Francisco: Harper and Row, 1978), 112-13.

August 9

Set Your Priorities

Basic Passage: 1 Timothy 6:2c-21

Focal Passage: 1 Timothy 6:6-14,17-21

When this epistle was written is an open question. It cannot be fitted into the record of Paul's life and ministry provided in the Book of Acts. That record ends with the apostle a prisoner in Rome where he "dwelt two whole years" (Acts 28:30). Some believe that he was executed at the end of this period, others that he was acquitted and resumed his missionary journeys for another possible two years. Traditions are strong that he visited Spain and, after a brief stay there, went to Ephesus where he was reunited with Timothy and Titus. He eventually left Timothy in charge of the work there and traveled north. When he wrote 1 Timothy, he was intending to return to Ephesus (3:14), a hope he may have realized. For it is not impossible that he was rearrested there and again taken as prisoner to Rome, where he was when he wrote 2 Timothy. Paul was executed in Rome between the years A.D. 64 and 67. In light of all this, we better understand the earnestness and urgency found in 1 Timothy, especially marked in chapter 6.

Study Aim: *To find in the Lord Jesus Christ, as Paul exhorted Timothy, the needed example and authority for Christian living*

STUDYING THE BIBLE

The opening words of 1 Timothy 6 reveal something of the social mixture in the membership of the Ephesian church. Paul addressed himself to "servants," by which he meant slaves, some of whom had unbelieving masters, others being owned by fellow church members, slaves, and masters together in the same spiritual fellowship. We may be sure there were other contrasted—and normally conflicting—circumstances within that membership, as, for example, Gentiles and Jews. The potential for disagreement was strong and added to the problem of leadership for Timothy.

I. Dangers to Avoid (1 Tim. 6:6-10)

The seriousness of the prevailing situation is indicated by Paul's return to the subject of false teachers. Using particularly strong language, he again exhorted Timothy to avoid involvement with persons who "consent not to wholesome words, even the words of our Lord Jesus Christ" (v. 3). We do not know if the teachings of Jesus were available in writing at this time, although in the introduction to his Gospel, Luke acknowledged that "many have undertaken to set down an orderly account of the events that have been fulfilled among us" (Luke 1:1, NRSV), suggesting sources of information outside the Four Gospels. The important thing to note is that the authority for belief and behavior was to be found in the Lord Jesus and His teaching.

6 But godliness with contentment is great gain.

7 For we brought nothing into this world, and it is certain we can carry nothing out.

8 And having food and raiment let us be therewith content.

9 But they that will be rich fall into temptation and a snare, and into many foolish and hurtful lusts, which drown men in destruction and perdition.

10 For the love of money is the root of all evil: which while some coveted after, they have erred from the faith, and pierced themselves through with many sorrows.

1. Godliness with contentment (vv. 6-8).—There is an unhappy modern flavor to Paul's earlier reference to persons who subscribe to the idea that "godliness is a means of gain" (v. 5, NRSV). Evidently, in those faraway days, there were within the churches individuals who saw religion as a profitable profession and used it to line their own pockets. Paul accepted no compromise with such and recommended the same position to his younger friend. On the positive side, he urged Timothy to practice "godliness with contentment," to be satisfied with what God provided, knowing that we all enter this world with nothing and will leave it in similar circumstances.

2. Love of money (vv. 9-10).—Not money itself, but love of money is condemned as the "root of all kinds of evil" (NRSV). Money can achieve good and worthy purposes, but it also can be a ruthless taskmaster to those who crave it and devote their lives to obtaining it. The truth of verse 9 is borne out in many tragic stories that reach our newspapers concerning individuals who, possessing much money and desiring more, regard themselves as above all law, both human and divine.

II. Virtues to Cultivate (1 Tim. 6:11-16)

Paul dropped the subject of money temporarily (he would return to it in verse 17) in order to address an earnest appeal to Timothy whom he called a "man of God." The term is frequently applied in the Old Testament to Israel's prophets and describes a person whom God has called into His service. In New Testament thought, it can apply to all men and women who have been called by God into fellowship with Him and have thereby entered His service. It has special application, of course, to all who have leadership responsibilities.

> **11 But thou, O man of God, flee these things; and follow after righteousness, godliness, faith, love, patience, meekness.**
>
> **12 Fight the good fight of faith, lay hold on eternal life, whereunto thou art also called, and hast professed a good profession before many witnesses.**
>
> **13 I give thee charge in the sight of God, who quickeneth all things, and before Christ Jesus, who before Pontius Pilate witnessed a good confession;**
>
> **14 That thou keep this commandment without spot, unrebukable, until the appearing of our Lord Jesus Christ.**

1. Flee and follow (v. 11).—Timothy was to flee from doctrinal errors and the lure of riches and pursue those Christian traits that were embodied in Christ Himself. Listed are *righteousness,* which means the right treatment of others; *godliness,* the development of those traits found in God; *faith,* in this case meaning unswerving loyalty to Christ and the church; *love,* the agape type that is selfless and self-giving; *patience,* better understood as endurance; and *meekness,* submission before God and gentleness toward others.

2. Discipline required (v. 12).—Whether we accept the translation,

"Fight the good fight," or "Run the great race" (Barrett), the implication is the same. The Christian life, expressed in the above qualities, is demanding and requires the utmost discipline, that of a soldier or an athlete. Eternal life, to which Timothy had been called (not as a reward but as a gift of grace) was too valuable to be marred by careless living. With such a goal in view, any sacrifice or effort was worthwhile.

3. Example of Christ (vv. 13-14).—The nature of Timothy's profession (or confession) is not described beyond the statement that it was made "before many witnesses" (v. 12). This could have been at his baptism or ordination. In Ephesus there would be other occasions when, as a Christian leader, he was compelled to make a public stand for his faith. The fact that our Lord's steadfastness before Pilate is offered as an example suggests that Timothy, too, was being tested by Roman authorities. Would he say, "Caesar is Lord," or "Jesus is Lord"? Since Timothy was under orders from Christ, he must remain loyal and obedient until Christ's return. The thought of Christ's coming again was a powerful influence in Paul's life, and he wished it to be in Timothy's.

III. The Uses of Riches (1 Tim. 6:17-19)

Mention of Christ's return caused the apostle to quote, probably from an ancient hymn, a doxology of praise to God (vv. 15-16). This he introduced by a statement, still referring to Christ's return, "This will be made manifest at the proper time by the blessed and only Sovereign" (RSV), an acknowledgment that this future event is in God's timetable and His alone. After this sublime interjection, the apostle returned to the subject of wealth, its use and abuse.

> **17 Charge them that are rich in this world, that they be not highminded, nor trust in uncertain riches, but in the living God, who giveth us richly all things to enjoy;**
>
> **18 That they do good, that they be rich in good works, ready to distribute, willing to communicate;**
>
> **19 Laying up in store for themselves a good foundation against the time to come, that they may lay hold on eternal life.**

1. "Rich in this world" (v. 17).—The very phrase suggests the temporariness of riches (v. 7). Wealth can be a snare in that it can make people "high-minded," or self-important. Of the rich young ruler's unwillingness to follow Christ, the Gospel says that "he went away sorrowful: for he had great possessions" (Matt. 19:22). His wealth was a barrier to discipleship. With all his money, the young man felt self-sufficient. Timothy, on the other hand, was to put his trust in God, not in riches, for He "giveth us richly all things to enjoy." Paul was no ascetic. We are to enjoy to the full God's many good gifts.

2. True wealth (vv. 18-19).—Possession of wealth is no sin when it is used unselfishly for the good of others. The apostle echoed the teaching of our Lord who said, "Lay not up for yourselves treasures upon earth, . . . But lay up for yourselves treasures in heaven" (Matt. 6:19-20).

IV. Concluding Counsels (1 Tim. 6:20-21)

Paul's earnestness in this letter is again expressed in his final appeal to his young friend, "O Timothy." He was aware that opportunities for service were slipping away. He was therefore anxious that Timothy should acquit himself well in the years to come.

> **20 O Timothy, keep that which is committed to thy trust, avoiding profane and vain babblings, and oppositions of science falsely so called:**
>
> **21 Which some professing have erred concerning the faith. Grace be with thee. Amen.**

Literally, Paul told Timothy to "Guard the deposit," that is, anything entrusted to a person for safe keeping. What had been entrusted to Timothy? Many things, but above them all was the gospel message. This was to be protected and preserved by the avoidance of false doctrine and foolish fads ("profane and vain babblings"). He should also shun "oppositions of science falsely so called." The reference could be to gnosticism, with its claim to superior knowledge. But any claim to intellectual enlightenment that destroys faith and questions the authority of Scripture is in conflict with the will and purpose of God.

APPLYING THE LESSON

What is happiness?—An American, an Englishman, and a Russian were discussing happiness. The American said, "For me, happiness is a beautiful autumn weekend when I can go back to my old college and watch the football team win a big game." The Englishman said, "For me, happiness is sitting with my best friends gathered around me, enjoying a spot of tea." The Russian said, "Suppose I am sitting in my one-room flat in Moscow on a cold January day. My little son, Ivan, is sitting on my knee. I am reading the lead editorial in *Pravda* aloud. All at once there is a knock on the door. I answer it. Two large men are standing there. They show me KGB cards. 'Ivan Ivanoff?' they ask in an ominous tone. Happiness is saying, 'No, he lives upstairs!' "

Happiness is different things to different people. For the Christian, happiness is living in a right relationship with God and doing what God has instructed us to do.

Misunderstanding the value of money.—A modern-day Rip Van Winkle fell asleep and woke up in the year 2076. Immediately, he rushed to a phone booth to call his brokerage firm. They found his portfolio and reported, "Your IBM stock is worth $50 million. Your General Motors stock is worth $62 million. And your AT&T stock is worth $120 million." The man was hysterical. "I'm rich! I'm rich," he shouted. About that time the operator interrupted him and said, "I'm sorry, sir, but your three minutes are up. Deposit one million dollars for another three minutes."

Like that man, we often overestimate the value of our money. That this was not a new problem is clear from Paul's reference in this week's lesson.

Like Christ.—Adoniram and Ann Judson were missionaries to Burma. Their dedication to the Lord was well known throughout the community in which they served. A newspaper article one day even compared Adoniram to one of the apostles. The article did not please him; rather, it disturbed him. He explained why, "I do not want to be like one of the apostles. I want to be like Jesus."

The model for the characteristics Paul recommended to Timothy was Jesus Himself. A Christian is to display in his life the characteristics of Jesus.

Mastering the basics.—Bob Lilly, former all-pro tackle for the Dallas Cowboys, was one of the best who ever played the game. A friend asked him one day to evaluate his career: "What is the difference between playing football on the seventh grade level and playing as a pro?" Lilly responded, "Not much really. In the seventh grade, we learn how to punt, pass, and kick. As a pro we still do the same things. The difference is as pros we learn how to master the basics."

Amateur and professional are not terms used to measure Christians. Mature and immature are probably more appropriate labels. Professional Christians—mature Christians—are those like the apostle Paul who have the discipline to master the basics of the Christian life.

Ready.—In 1914 Sir Ernest Henry Shackleton, an English explorer, led an expedition to the South Pole. As the ice began to close in on his boat, he had to leave some of his men stranded on Elephant Island as he went for help. He secured another ship on South Georgia Island and returned for his men. After several unsuccessful attempts, the weather finally permitted him to sail through to where the men were, pick them up, and then get out before the ice closed up again. Shackleford asked his crew why they had their things packed and standing by when he came back. They said, "Sir, when you left, you said you would come back for us, so we never gave up hope. Whenever the weather looked favorable, we would pack up our things and say, 'Maybe Shackleford will return for us today.' We were always ready for your coming."

Paul urged Timothy to live with that same spirit of readiness for the return of the Lord.

God's hand and my mouth.—George Mueller supported his orphanage exclusively on prayer. He never directly asked anyone for a contribution. He simply prayed to God about it. Someone observed, "It looks like a hand to mouth proposition." "Yes it is," George responded, "But it is God's hand and my mouth." God's hand is much more dependable and abundant than what we can provide ourselves through our own material resources. Therefore, like Timothy, we are to trust God to provide our needs.

TEACHING THE CLASS

Main Idea: The things of God are the greatest riches and are to be sought by believers.

Suggested Teaching Aim: Learners will assess their personal life goals and determine to follow the things of God.

Introduce the Bible Study

Ask: What do you want out of life? Don't worry if the response is lighthearted at this point.

Continue: Our goals shape our thinking and our behavior. What goals do you have in these areas: family, work, financial, spiritual, health, social relationships? Elicit response that learners are willing to share with the group. Do not comment or evaluate the responses.

A Teaching Outline

1. Identify the focus of learners' lives.
2. Discover the focus Paul commanded Timothy to pursue and teach.
3. Evaluate personal life goals by Paul's instructions.
4. Determine changes in personal life focus that need to be made.

Provide learners a sheet of paper on which each of the areas above has been written. Leave a space for learners to add their own categories. Direct learners to take several minutes to briefly note some things that are important to them in each of the areas. Suggest that these are goals for their lives.

Continue by asking: What do our goals tell about us? Share the comments titled "What is happiness?" (*Applying the Lesson*).

Note that the title for today's study is "Set Your Priorities," which is a primary function of goals. Invite learners to open their Bibles to 1 Timothy 6 where Paul discussed priorities with Timothy.

Search for Biblical Truth

Remind learners that our studies focus on guidelines of ministry in our own lives and in our church. Share information for background of this passage from *Studying the Bible.*

Call on a learner to read 1 Timothy 6:6-7 aloud while other learners listen to identify the goal that Paul recommended to Timothy. When the reading is finished, suggest that learners work with those around them to state the goal Paul suggested. After a few minutes, ask for response and write it on the chalkboard. It should be similar to the following. Goal: To be content with a life centered in God.

Call on a learner to read verses 8-10 aloud. Share the comments titled "Misunderstanding the value of money" (*Applying the Lesson*). Direct learners to work together a few minutes to suggest a life goal based on these verses. Write it on the chalkboard. It should be similar to the following. Goal: To have and use money properly and to prevent the desire or need for it from corrupting life.

Continue a similar process with verses 11-12. Share the comments titled "Mastering the basics" (*Applying the Lesson*). The goal should be similar to the following. Goal: To experience the fruits of the Spirit.

Continue the process with verses 13-14. Share the comments titled "Ready" (*Applying the Lesson*). Goal: To continue in the commands of the Lord until Jesus comes.

Continue with verses 17-19. Share the comments titled "God's hand and my mouth" (*Applying the Lesson*). Indicate that the goal implied by these verses is similar to the one suggested by verses 8-10. Learners may suggest others.

Conclude with verses 20-21 using the same process. Goal: To keep that which is committed to my trust.

Give the Truth a Personal Focus

Direct learners to look again at the list of personal goals they noted as the class was begun. Suggest that they privately compare their life goals with those identified during the Scripture study. Allow several minutes for evaluation.

Ask rhetorically: What changes in your goals would help you to seek more of the things of God? Direct learners to make notes that indicate new goals they need to adopt. Goals noted on the chalkboard will provide guidelines.

Conclude by asking: What single guideline for ministry can we state from this study of goals for our lives? Elicit a response similar to the main idea of this study.

August 16

Handle God's Word Rightly

Basic Passage: 2 Timothy 2:1-19

Focal Passage: 2 Timothy 2:1-15

Paul's circumstances had changed dramatically. Instead of writing to Timothy while on a missionary journey, the apostle addressed this second letter from a prison in Rome (1:8,17; 2:9). Visitors to that city may still see the Mamertime Prison where Paul is reported to have been detained. He had several reasons for writing. (1) He knew that Timothy would be anxious for him and desired to give him firsthand news about his circumstances. (2) Facing the prospect of execution, he felt the need to underscore advice he had previously given on Timothy's personal life and his leadership in the church. (3) Paul wanted Timothy's company because others had deserted him. (4) There were certain things the apostle needed, and these he requested Timothy to bring with him (4:9,13). All this confirms the depth of friendship between the two men, in spite of the disparity in their ages. Paul was probably around 65 years of age and Timothy 35. In another letter written while detained in Rome, Paul wrote of Timothy, "I have no man likeminded, . . . as a son with the father, he hath served with me in the gospel" (Phil. 2:20,22).

Study Aim: *To measure our performance as Christians by the standards given by Paul to Timothy*

STUDYING THE BIBLE

Our two lessons in 2 Timothy omit reference to chapter 1. But there are so many treasures in that chapter we can ill afford to miss them. Notice, in particular: Paul's description of Timothy as "my dearly beloved son" (v. 2); his appreciative reference to the younger man's mother and grandmother (v. 5); his tribute to our Lord as He "who hath abolished death, and hath brought life and immortality to light through the gospel" (v. 10); and strong affirmation of confidence in Christ and His salvation, "I know whom I have believed, and am persuaded that he is able to keep that which I have committed unto him against that day" (v. 12). All this is behind Paul's "therefore" in 2:1

where the apostle exhorts Timothy to be "strong in the grace that is in Christ Jesus."

I. Summons to Loyalty (2 Tim. 2:1-7)

The imprisoned apostle was concerned for a continuity of witness to the gospel, as we also should be. He accordingly charged Timothy to pass on the truths that he had learned from himself and others ("many witnesses"). Those so entrusted needed to be chosen with care. They must be "faithful men, . . . able to teach others" (v. 2). Elsewhere he had written to Timothy, "Lay hands suddenly on no man" (1 Tim. 5:22), that is, take time to test the qualifications of persons preparing for church leadership. Mistakes, due to hasty judgment, could be disastrous in such cases.

1 Thou therefore, my son, be strong in the grace that is in Christ Jesus.

2 And the things that thou hast heard of me among many witnesses, the same commit thou to faithful men, who shall be able to teach others also.

3 Thou therefore endure hardness, as a good soldier of Jesus Christ.

4 No man that warreth entangleth himself with the affairs of this life; that he may please him who hath chosen him to be a soldier.

5 And if a man also strive for masteries, yet is he not crowned, except he strive lawfully.

6 The husbandman that laboreth must be first partaker of the fruits.

7 Consider what I say; and the Lord give thee understanding in all things.

1. A good soldier (vv. 3-4).—Christian service is not easy, or should not be if taken seriously. Paul compared such service to that of a soldier as he exhorted Timothy to "endure hardness," or "share hardships with me" (Barrett). To satisfy his commander, the Christian soldier must have a single purpose and not be distracted by other interests. It would seem that Paul was addressing himself to those engaged in the work of the ministry as a whole-time occupation. He saw the need for this, perhaps because in his own case he had been compelled to divide his time between gospel activities and tentmaking.

2. Disciplined athlete (v. 5).—Paul frequently made use of athletic activities such as running, wrestling, and boxing. In the Olympic Games, competitors had to take an oath that they would abide by the rules. They could be disqualified for not doing so, as they can be today. The coveted crown of laurel leaves was only for those who accepted the discipline and won the competition legitimately.

3. Industrious farmer (v. 6).—The third illustration of acceptable and successful Christian service is taken from agriculture. The hard-working farmer will have first claim on the fruits of harvest as his reward. There is a concept of reward in all three of these metaphors: "Beyond warfare is victory, beyond athletic effort a prize, and beyond agricultural labor a crop. In the same way, Timothy's share of hardship will be followed by reward."[1]

II. Remember Jesus Christ (2 Tim. 2:8-13)

In Jesus Christ, the Christian worker finds both a pattern for his service and inspiration for it. Paul's entire life was motivated by his vision of the Lord received on the Damascus Road (Acts 9:1-6). The risen and ascended Christ became the driving force in his life and ministry and the subject of his preaching and teaching.

> **8 Remember that Jesus Christ of the seed of David was raised from the dead according to my gospel:**
>
> **9 Wherein I suffer trouble, as an evildoer, even unto bonds; but the word of God is not bound.**
>
> **10 Therefore I endure all things for the elect's sakes, that they may also obtain the salvation which is in Christ Jesus with eternal glory.**
>
> **11 It is a faithful saying: For if we be dead with him, we shall also live with him:**
>
> **12 If we suffer, we shall also reign with him: if we deny him, he also will deny us:**
>
> **13 If we believe not, yet he abideth faithful: he cannot deny himself.**

1. Resurrection truth (v. 8).—In great brevity Paul made reference to the gospel he preached, based on Christ Jesus, who must be the ultimate inspiration of Timothy's ministry. Jesus "raised from the dead" declared His divinity and "seed of David," His humanity. Thus our Lord's earthly ministry, from birth through death to resurrection, was summarized. Characteristic of apostolic preaching, a primary emphasis was given to His resurrection, by which, as Paul wrote elsewhere, He who in coming into this world "was made of the seed of David according to the flesh," was also "declared to be the Son of God with power, . . . by the resurrection from the dead" (Rom. 1:3-4).

2. For others' sake (vv. 9-10).—The apostle did not ask more of Timothy than he was willing to give himself. He was willing to "endure all things" for the salvation of others. Paul wrote as a prisoner whose bonds, for the time being, limited his activity. But he took comfort in the thought that "the word of God is not bound." Though he would die under the executioner's sword, the message he bore would continue on its worldwide course.

3. A faithful saying (vv. 11-13).—The quotation is probably from an early Christian hymn that dealt with achievement and failure in the Christian life. Its point is that the cause of the gospel does not depend on our efforts but on the faithfulness of God to His promises and purposes. The opening words, "For if we be dead with him," may refer to baptism by which we "were baptized into his death" (Rom. 6:3-4). Some authorities suggest that the quoted material ends with "he abideth faithful" and that the next phrase, "he cannot deny himself," was Paul's triumphant addition.

III. A Workman Approved (2 Tim. 2:14-19)

If the contents of this letter appear erratic and repetitious, we should realize that we are studying a letter written under difficult circumstances, for as a prisoner, Paul did not have control over his activities. Circumstances were different during his first Roman detainment when he "dwelt two whole years in his own hired house" (Acts 28:30). In the following verses, he returned to personal advice for Timothy together with exhortation to share with others.

> **14 Of these things put them in remembrance, charging them before the Lord that they strive not about words to no profit, but to the subverting of the hearers.**
>
> **15 Study to show thyself approved unto God, a workman that needeth not to be ashamed, rightly dividing the word of truth.**
>
> **16 But shun profane and vain babblings: for they will increase unto more ungodliness.**
>
> **17 And their word will eat as doth a canker: of whom is Hymenaeus and Philetus;**
>
> **18 Who concerning the truth have erred, saying that the resurrection is past already; and overthrow the faith of some.**
>
> **19 Nevertheless the foundation of God standeth sure, having this seal, The Lord knoweth them that are his. And, Let everyone that nameth the name of Christ depart from iniquity.**

1. Do your best (v. 15).—While others wrangled over words, Timothy must devote himself to "rightly dividing the word of truth." The meaning is "to cut straight," either ploughing land or cutting cloth or carving stone. Since Paul was a tentmaker and was used to cutting cloth (or leather), this activity may have been in his mind. His meaning was that the Word of God must be rightly handled, not twisted or distorted to serve personal ideas or purposes. Only as Timothy did his best ("Study to show") in hewing a straight line would his ministry succeed.

2. Things to shun (vv. 16-18).—Repeating former warnings, the apostle named two people who were propagating error and also defined its character. The denial related to the believer's resurrection that will take place at our Lord's return. A similar heresy existed in Corinth (1 Cor. 15:12), though perhaps with variations. Probably a future resurrection was spiritualized by these people so that the believer's final hope was undermined. Not surprisingly, this false teaching was able to "overthrow the faith of some."

3. A firm foundation (v. 19).—Notwithstanding the spread of error, there was no need for fear. God had laid a firm foundation. Paul seems to have been alluding to Numbers 16:26-27. The Lord knows those who are His, and by implication, those who are not His. The former must evidence their relationship to Him by their conduct.

APPLYING THE LESSON

The importance of friends.—Someone recently suggested that only one person in five in America has a real friend. I don't know the basis for that conclusion. Perhaps it hinges on the definition of a friend. I have observed over the years some exemplary friendships. I have experienced in my own life some enduring friendships. Paul and Timothy had that kind of friendship, a friendship that was based on their common commitment to Christ.

The best advertisement.—I met recently with our media committee to determine a plan for getting the word out into our community about our church and our Lord. We discussed different options: direct mail, television, radio, and newspaper advertisements. One of the members of the committee said, "I believe the key is getting our people excited about the church. If they will tell everybody they see, then we'll get the word out."

Individuals who love the Lord who tell everyone they see about Him—that is the plan for evangelism suggested in our text. This was beautifully illustrated by a woman in an apartment who wanted to share Christ with the other tenants. So she set up her ministry in the elevator. She would ride the elevator up and down looking for ways to serve her neighbors. For example, a lady entered the elevator with a small child and some groceries one day, so this Christian witness offered to help her. Once in the apartment, she invited the young mother to come up to her apartment and have a cup of coffee. Then, as they talked over a cup of coffee, she told her about Jesus Christ. Several coffee sessions later, this young mother received Christ. Persons sharing Christ with other persons—that is the most effective plan to spread the gospel message.

Who is he kidding?—When a man says he can't stay awake during a 20 minute sermon and instead goes to a two-hour movie, who is he kidding?

When a man says Sunday is his only day of rest, and he gets up at 4:30 a.m. to spend the day fishing, who is he kidding?

When a man says the church pews are too hard and uncomfortable, then he goes to a football game and sits on wooden seats in the rain to watch 22 men push back and forth across the mud, who is he kidding?

When a man says he cannot afford to give to the church, but he then leaves his $150,000 home to drive to work in his Mercedes with a car phone, who is he kidding?

The lack of true commitment is rampant in the church today. Paul also faced the problem in the first-century church. So he gave Timothy three illustrations that indicated the kind of commitment necessary in the Christian life. As a soldier is dedicated to winning the battle, as the athlete is dedicated to winning the race, as the farmer is dedicated to bringing in the crop, the Christian must be dedicated to serving Christ.

The power of Christ.—Charles Allen, famous Methodist preacher now retired, said that many years ago he offered through a newspaper column he wrote a small billfold-size picture of Jesus. He was overwhelmed with requests. Eventually, he sent out more than one hundred thousand copies of that little picture. For months afterwards, he received hundreds of letters from people sharing experiences they had because of those pictures. One man wrote that he lost his billfold with a large amount of money in it. A few days later, he received the billfold in the mail with all the money still in it. Included was a note that said, "When I first found this I fully intended to keep the money. But when I looked at the picture of Christ, I had to send it back."[2] Even the picture of Him does something to people. That's why Paul urged Timothy to keep his focus on Jesus.

Two kinds of horses.—When Carl Hayden was sworn in as a congressman in 1913, a fellow congressman took him aside and said, "There are two kinds of congressmen, show horses and work horses. If you want to get your name in the paper, be a show horse. If you want to gain the respect of your colleagues, keep quiet and be a work horse."[3]

Perhaps we can say there are two kinds of Christians, show horses and work horses. Show horses are those who talk the talk and catch the attention of the world. Work horses are those who walk the walk and receive the affirmation of God.

TEACHING THE CLASS

Main Idea: The truth of God must be carefully handled, carefully lived, and carefully shared with others.

Suggested Teaching Aim: Learners will commit themselves to carefully dealing with the truth of God.

Introduce the Bible Study

Write the main idea from last Sunday's lesson on the chalkboard. Beneath it write the main idea for today's lesson. State that the study for today needs two definitions to make it meaningful: the truth of God and handling the truth of God.

Direct half of the learners to discuss among themselves the meaning of the phrase "the truth of God." Direct the other half of the learners to discuss among themselves the meaning of the phrase "handling the truth of God." After several minutes, call for response.

State that in his second letter to Timothy, Paul instructed Timothy in the process of handling the truth of God carefully. Invite learners to open their Bibles to 2 Timothy 2.

Search for Biblical Truth

Share information from *Studying the Bible* about the circumstances out of which 2 Timothy was written. Read 2 Timothy 2:1 aloud. Note that "therefore" implies something has been stated on which the following comments rest. Share information from *Studying the Bible* about the contents in 2 Timothy 1.

A Teaching Outline

1. Consider the meaning of handling the truth of God.
2. Discover Paul's instruction to Timothy about handling the truth of God.
3. Determine how carefully they personally handle the truth of God.
4. Commit themselves to handling God's truth as Paul instructed.

Use the information in the paragraph titled "The importance of friends" (*Applying the Lesson*). Note that Paul and Timothy had a long-standing friendship based on commitment to Christ.

Direct learners to read 2 Timothy 2:2 silently to discover instruction given by Paul for handling the truth of God. When the reading is finished, call for response. Share the comments titled "The best advertisement" (*Applying the Lesson*). Write on the chalkboard beneath the main ideas the following instruction: Teach others.

Call on a learner to read verses 3-7 aloud while other learners listen to determine further instruction given by Paul for handling the truth of God. When the reading is finished, call for response. The conclusion should be similar to the following: Live responsibly. Write it on the chalkboard.

Note that Paul gave Timothy three illustrations of the kind of commitment required to live responsibly. Ask learners to identify them (soldier, athlete, farmer). Share the comments titled "Who is he kidding" (*Applying the Lesson*).

State that the next section of Paul's letter provides reasons for living responsibly. Direct learners to read verses 8-13 to themselves and be prepared to state the reasons. Call for response.

Direct learners to read verses 14-19 silently to discover additional directions for handling the truth of God. When the reading is finished, share information from *Studying the Bible* about the section of Scripture. Call for conclusions about instructions on handling the truth of God. Response should be similar to the following: live carefully. Elicit response that indicates what careful living involves as suggested by this passage.

Give the Truth a Personal Focus

Share the comments titled "Two kinds of horses" (*Applying the Lesson*). Ask rhetorically: Are you handling the truth of God carefully?

Direct learners to rate themselves on a scale of 1 to 10 on the following questions: Do you teach the truth of God to others? Do you live responsibly? Are you careful in your manner of living? Allow time for learners to consider each question privately and rate themselves.

Conclude the study with a prayer time inviting learners to commit themselves to careful handling of the truth of God.

---

1. C. K. Barrett, *The Pastoral Epistles* (Oxford: Clarendon Press, 1963), 102.
2. Charles Allen, *What I Have Lived By* (Old Tappan, N. J.: Fleming H. Revell, 1976), 40.
3. James C. Humes, *Speaker's Treasury of Anecdotes About the Famous* (New York: Harper and Row, 1978), 188.

August 23

Fulfill Your Ministry Faithfully

Basic Passage: 2 Timothy 3:10—4:8

Focal Passage: 2 Timothy 3:10—4:5

We are to study words of a man condemned to death and knowing that the end was near. He was happy in the knowledge that he had served his Lord faithfully. But he was saddened as he thought of the young man to whom he must now say good-by and the tremendous odds that Timothy faced in Ephesus. A second cause of sadness was the existence of heresy and inconsistency in the church and Paul's conviction that things would get worse as time passed. What, then, were the circumstances in which Paul wrote this second letter to Timothy? After his first trial, according to reliable tradition, Paul was set free and resumed his missionary activities. But on July 19, A.D. 64, Rome suffered a disastrous fire for which the emperor Nero blamed Christians, though he himself may have been responsible. Paul was arrested, possibly in Ephesus, and returned to Rome where he was again put on trial. Many friends abandoned him, but, Paul said, "the Lord stood with me, . . . and I was delivered out of the mouth of the lion" (4:17). In this circumstance he desired Timothy's company (4:9). Whether Timothy arrived in time we do not know, for Paul was executed during the winter of A.D. 64-65.

Study Aim: *To give thanks for those stalwarts of the faith who lived and died for the gospel and follow in their steps*

STUDYING THE BIBLE

The concern of the apostle over the threat of false doctrine within the church, and the collapse of moral standards in general, caused him to employ vivid language to describe what he called "perilous times" (3:1). The list of vices in verses 3-4 has an alarmingly contemporary ring to it. Are there not corresponding conditions in today's society? The mischief of it all is summed up in the indictment, "lovers of pleasures more than lovers of God." But a greater tragedy is implied in the next verse, for it fingers persons who make a profession of Christianity which they betray in their conduct. These are stated to have "a form of godliness, but denying the power thereof" (v. 5). There is an air of command in the apostle's postscript: "from such turn away."

I. Apostolic Example (2 Tim. 3:10-13)

Skipping a few verses, we come to Paul's presentation of his own life as a pattern for Timothy to follow. Notice "But they" (v. 9) followed by "But thou" (v. 10). The word "thou" is emphatic in the Greek, indicating the contrast that must exist between those condemned in the foregoing verses and Timothy as a "man of God" (1 Tim. 6:11). Though the apostle recites his own experiences and accomplishments, his statement that Timothy had "fully known" these means more than just having a knowledge of them. The language used indicates a participation by Timothy in all that is mentioned (Barrett). The recent past must be his guide for the future.

10 But thou hast fully known my doctrine, manner of life, purpose, faith, long-suffering, charity, patience,
11 Persecutions, afflictions, which came unto me at Antioch, at

Iconium, at Lystra; what persecutions I endured: but out of them all the Lord delivered me.

12 Yea, and all that will live godly in Christ Jesus shall suffer persecution.

13 But evil men and seducers shall wax worse and worse, deceiving, and being deceived.

1. Cost of loyalty (vv. 10-11).—The cities mentioned by Paul, and the afflictions that befell him, are recorded in the Book of Acts. In the first, Antioch in Pisidia, Paul preached in the synagogue, being accompanied by Barnabas. Jewish resistance to their message caused them to say, "lo, we turn to the Gentiles," after which they were expelled from the area (Acts 13:44-50). Their next stop was Iconium where, after gaining converts in the synagogue, they were subjected to "an assault made both of the Gentiles, and also of the Jews" and an attempt was made to stone them (14:1-5). The next incident was in Lystra (Timothy's home town) where Paul actually was stoned and assumed dead, though the record continues, "he rose up, and came into the city" (14:19-20). The apostle's grateful testimony was, "out of them all the Lord delivered me" (2 Tim. 3:11).

2. Good and evil (vv. 12-13).—Paul saw no escape from persecution for faithful followers of Christ. Their quest for the good, both for themselves and others, would involve them in conflict with the forces of evil. We realize that the apostle was thinking of Christians in a pagan environment and under a government that was becoming increasingly hostile toward the church. But are not these conditions being repeated at the present time? Society is becoming more and more secularly oriented. There is reason for increasing concern over the growth of anti-Christian sentiment in some sections of the media and in the world of entertainment. And while we are fortunate in having many professing Christians in the area of government, some recent legal decisions have favored official interference in religious practices, opening the way for further confrontation and control. The path of Christian consistency appears to become increasingly difficult.

II. Sufficiency of Scripture (2 Tim. 3:14-17)

Under these conditions, Christians need a firm foundation for their lives and a dependable counselor for their conduct. These are to be found in the Bible. For Timothy, this meant the Old Testament, for the New was only in process of being written. We should not suppose that Timothy had a copy, or even had access to one, for books were rare and costly. But the contents of the Scriptures were known to him having been communicated to him by Paul, by family members, and others. The ready availability of the Word of God today increases our responsibility.

> **14 But continue thou in the things which thou hast learned and hast been assured of, knowing of whom thou hast learned them:**
> **15 And that from a child thou hast known the holy scriptures, which are able to make thee wise unto salvation through faith which is in Christ Jesus.**
> **16 All scripture is given by inspiration of God, and is profitable for doctrine, for reproof, for correction, for instruction in righteousness:**
> **17 That the man of God may be perfect, thoroughly furnished unto all good works.**

1. Hold fast to truth (vv. 14-15).—In Paul's time, the truths of the gospel were conveyed orally, from person to person. To a large extent, this is still so as children learn from their parents, teachers, and others. Acceptance of these truths is influenced by these human relationships. Because parents are loved, and teachers trusted, what they say is willingly accepted. (What responsibility this imposes on parents and teachers!) Timothy, as a grown man, was urged to hold on to his beliefs as he remembered those who had imparted them to him. Their lives bore witness to the genuineness and effectiveness of their faith.

2. Source of truth (vv. 16-17).—But such faith is not just hearsay. It has its source in God's revelation, the Scriptures. For Timothy, these were the books of the Old Testament with which he had been acquainted since childhood. He would hear them read and explained in synagogue services and synagogue school. Also, his mother and grandmother (1:5) had helped to deepen his knowledge and understanding, as later did Paul. These Scriptures pointed to Christ, and were, therefore, able to make Timothy "wise unto salvation." Old Testament laws revealed the need of a Savior, and psalmists and prophets pointed to His coming.

III. Farewell Words (2 Tim. 4:1-8)

The concluding chapter to this epistle opens with a solemn charge to Timothy to "preach the word, be urgent in season and out of season, convince, rebuke, and exhort, be unfailing in patience and in teaching" (v. 2, RSV). The urgency was necessary because of the tendency of people, presumably within the church, to have "itching ears" (v. 3). Not satisfied with the gospel, these people were eager to listen to every religious fad and fancy that came their way. The same condition exists today as the propagandists of error make easy prey of disgruntled, or uninformed, members of evangelical churches.

1 I charge thee therefore before God, and the Lord Jesus Christ, who shall judge the quick and the dead at his appearing and his kingdom;

2 Preach the word; be instant in season, out of season; reprove, rebuke, exhort with all long-suffering and doctrine.

3 For the time will come when they will not endure sound doctrine; but after their own lusts shall they heap to themselves teachers, having itching ears;

4 And they shall turn away their ears from the truth, and shall be turned unto fables.

5 But watch thou in all things, endure afflictions, do the work of an evangelist, make full proof of thy ministry.

1. Accountability to God (v. 1).—While these solemn words were addressed to a church leader, they have application to all Christians. We must all give account of our service at the coming again of our Lord who will then judge both the living and the resurrected dead. This should not be regarded as a threat but as an incentive to effort that we may render a good account to the One to whom we are all accountable and to whom we owe so much.

2. Responsibility for others (v. 2).—Service for Christ is not to be rendered in a haphazard way but at all times, convenient and inconvenient. It should also take a variety of forms, according to need. Patience must be exercised, for most people are slow learners, and response may sometimes be aggravatingly slow.

3. Seductive influences (vv. 3-4).—In fact, resistance to the truth may be expected. Rather than accept biblical teaching, with its heavy demands, people within the church will seek modified forms of Christianity suited to their life-styles. They will be ready to listen to "fables" such as those described in 1 Timothy 1:4.

4. Watchfulness enjoined (v. 5).—The word "watch" calls for discipline and alertness. As a counteractive to the conditions described in verses 3-4, Timothy should apply himself diligently to the task assigned to him. Specially should he do "the work of an evangelist," that is, preach the gospel, even if this involved hardship.

5. Paul faces death (vv. 6-8).—The apostle was ready to pay the supreme penalty for faithfulness, death for Christ's sake. We do not know how long an interval there was between writing this letter and facing the Roman executioner. But with a courage that offered a splendid example to Timothy, and to us, Paul wrote his last words and said his last farewell.

APPLYING THE LESSON

Bad or good?—An ancient proverb tells of a rural family that had only one horse that was used to plow the land and thus provide for their food. One day the horse ran away. Neighbors came to sympathize with the farmer. "We've heard about what happened, and it is so bad." The farmer replied, "How do you know it is bad? It is not over yet." In a few days, the horse came back leading a herd of wild horses that could be sold for a large amount of money. Again the friends showed up. "We heard about what happened, and it is so good." The farmer responded, "How do you know it is good? It is not over yet." A few days later when the boy was trying to break one of the horses, the horse threw him, and he broke his leg. Once more the neighbors showed up and said, "We heard what happened, and it is so bad." The father retorted, "How do you know it is bad? It is not over yet." The story ends by saying a great war broke out in which many of the young men were killed. But because the farmer's son had a broken leg, he was able to stay home, and he provided for his father for the remainder of his life.

Sometimes we do not know if a thing is bad or good because we are too close to it. Our perspective is distorted. So it was with Timothy to whom Paul was writing. Circumstances were bad, but Paul explained to him that God was still at work, carrying out His divine plan.

Dangerous to be good.—Gandhi led India with a vision of what the nation could become. He did so with a spirit of love and humility unmatched in his day. As a result, he was assassinated. Upon hearing of his assassination, George Bernard Shaw remarked, "This shows how dangerous it is to be good."[1] Timothy lived in a day when it was dangerous to be good. We are approaching that kind of day again. Our challenge is not to be safe but to be good, not to be in fellowship with the world but to be faithful to our God, even if it is dangerous.

The value of the Bible.—Martin Niemoller was a German pastor who opposed Hitler during World War II and thus spent much of the war in German prison camps. They took from him everything except his Bible. After his release, Niemoller gave this testimony about the Bible: "What did this book mean to me during the long and weary years of solitary confinement and then for the last four years at Dauchau? The word of God was simply everything to me, comfort and strength, guidance and hope, master of my days and companion of my nights, the bread that kept me from starvation and the water of life that refreshed my soul."[2]

That is a modern-day version of testimony affirming the word of God given by Paul to young Timothy two thousand years ago.

Knowing how to treat our children.—A little boy in a cartoon was on his knees saying his evening prayers. Evidently, his father had just disciplined him in a way he thought unfair. He prayed, "God, please don't give my father any more children. He doesn't know how to treat the ones he has." Our children might not say those words, but they probably think them from time to time.

How are we to treat our children? How are we to communicate truth to them? One sage suggested three ways to teach a child: example, example, example. That is another way of saying our children will be more influenced by what we do than by what we say. However, when what we do reinforces what we say, that is when real teaching occurs. Timothy had the happy fortune of having a mother who taught by both word and example.

What is our problem?—I heard an interesting statement the other day. The speaker said, "The greatest indictment of Christians is not that they are falling short of the mark, but that they have quit striving to reach the mark." Throughout the Bible, the men and women God used were those who kept moving toward the mark. Moses was denied by Pharaoh, but Moses kept striving to reach the mark; eventually, he led the Hebrews out of bondage. David was stalked by King Saul, but David kept striving to reach the mark; eventually, he became king of Israel. Peter denied his Lord, but Peter kept striving to reach the mark and, eventually, he became the leader of the early church. The church today needs men and women who will keep striving to reach the mark.

TEACHING THE CLASS

Main Idea: Faithfulness in all circumstances is expected of a follower of God.

Suggested Teaching Aim: Learners will measure their faithfulness by standards given by Paul to Timothy.

Introduce the Bible Study

Distribute sheets of paper. Direct learners to draw a picture that provides a definition of faithfulness. Encourage learners to participate with any kind of drawing response. Direct them to show their drawing to persons sitting near them and explain why they believe it defines or illustrates faithfulness.

Write *faithfulness* on the chalkboard. State that the study for today focuses on being faithful to God regardless of the circumstances. Share the comments titled "Bad or good?" (*Applying the Lesson*). Invite learners to open their Bibles to 2 Timothy 3.

Search for Biblical Truth

Share information from *Studying the Bible* about the circumstances out of which Paul wrote these words to Timothy. Ask: Was this situation good or bad? Refer to comments just shared from *Applying the Lesson.*

Note that the first section of Scripture for study, 2 Timothy 3:10-13, states the specifics of some of Paul's circumstances. Direct learners to read the verses to themselves. When the reading is finished, share some information from *Studying the Bible* about these circumstances.

Share the comments titled "Dangerous to be good" (*Applying the Lesson*).

Ask: Using these verses for consideration, by what standard is faithfulness to be judged? Allow a moment for learners to consider the question. Call for response. Note it on the chalkboard. Responses should be similar to the following:

Loyalty to Christ during persecution.

Patience and endurance during persecution.

Love for others during persecution.

A Teaching Outline

1. Define and illustrate the meaning of faithfulness.
2. Determine Paul's standard for measuring faithfulness.
3. Consider indicators of learners own faithfulness.
4. Measure personal faithfulness by standards given by Paul.

Share the comments titled "The value of the Bible" (*Applying the Lesson*). State that the next section of Scripture, verses 14-17, states another standard of faithfulness related to the Scriptures. Direct learners to read the passage to themselves and be prepared to state that standard. When the reading is finished, share information from *Studying the Bible*. Call for the standard for measuring faithfulness that this passage suggests. Write the response on the chalkboard. It should be similar to the following: holding firmly to the teachings of the Scriptures.

Share the comments titled "What is our problem?" (*Applying the Lesson*). Direct learners to read silently the final section of Scripture, 2 Timothy 4:1-8, to discover Paul's words to Timothy about continuing to strive to reach the mark. Share information from *Studying the Bible* about this passage.

Ask: What additional standard do these verses suggest for measuring faithfulness to Christ? Allow a moment for learners to consider the question. Call for response. Write it on the chalkboard. Response should be similar to the following: Don't give up. Keep on doing what God has given you to do.

Give the Truth a Personal Focus

Direct learners to review the standards suggested by Paul for measuring faithfulness. Direct them to continue by privately listing words that are indicators of their own faithfulness. The standards should provide some clues. Certainly invite learners to privately list others. Encourage them to carefully evaluate their own lives for evidence of their own faithfulness to God.

1. Robert McCracken, "Religion: Escape or Involvement," in *20 Centuries of Great Preaching*, ed. Clyde Fant and William Pinson (Waco: Word, 1971), 77.
2. Harold E. Buell, "Is Your Bag Packed for Eternity?" *Pulpit Digest* (January-February 1978): 53.

August 30

Be a Model in Deeds and Word

Basic Passage: Titus 1:1—3:15

Focal Passages: Titus 2:7-8,11-14; 3:1-8

In addressing our attention to the Epistle to Titus we take a brief step back in time. Paul was a free man (3:12), so we must place the time of writing before his imprisonment, perhaps between First and Second Timothy, or possibly before both. The message is similar to that Paul wrote to Timothy, dealing mainly with three issues: the personal life of Titus; his responsibilities of leadership in Crete; and the threat to sound doctrine from heretics (3:10) within the church. Crete is an island in the Mediterranean to the south of Greece. It is believed to have been the home of the Philistines who invaded the coastal plain of Palestine about the time that the Israelites fled captivity in Egypt. Jews settled in the island before the second century B.C., and they were numbered among those who heard Peter's sermon, in Jerusalem, on the day of Pentecost (Acts 2:11). These may have been responsible for introducing Christianity into Crete. Acts does not mention Paul visiting the island, although he sailed along its coast on his voyage to Rome (Acts 27:7).

Study Aim: *To learn conditions in a difficult church field, the island of Crete*

STUDYING THE BIBLE

Titus is not mentioned in the Acts narrative, but information about him is found in Paul's Epistles. He is mentioned in Galatians 2:1-3 when, with Barnabas, he accompanied Paul to Jerusalem. Titus was a

Gentile convert and became a test case in the issue of circumcision which some Jews were attempting to impose on Gentiles who became Christians. The leadership in Jerusalem imposed no such condition on Titus, thus strengthening Paul's resistance to this legalistic demand. Titus became Paul's "partner and fellow helper" (2 Cor. 8:23) and was sent by him to Corinth after Timothy had failed to settle problems there (v. 6). Crete seems to have provided the major setting for Titus' ministry. Tradition claims him as bishop in that island, where he is reported to have died.

I. Words for Church Members (Titus 2:1-10)

Briefly reviewing chapter 1, Paul stated his reasons for leaving Titus in Crete: to set things in order in a comparatively new church and to ordain elders (v. 5). The qualifications for an elder (or bishop), as given in verses 6-9, are similar to those for bishops and deacons in 1 Timothy 3:1-13. We do not have a clear understanding of the functions involved, or of the differences between these offices. The need for care in making these appointments arose from the existence in the church of "unruly and vain talkers and deceivers, especially they of the circumcision: . . . teaching things which they ought not, for filthy lucre's sake" (vv. 10-11). These are serious indictments, obviously directed against some Jewish converts who were seeking to impose Old Testament legalism on Gentiles, and these were more interested in financial gain than in spiritual service. A basic problem for Titus was the reputation of Cretans as "liars, vicious brutes, lazy gluttons" (v. 12, NRSV). These were not Paul's words but borrowed from one of Crete's own poets. Altogether, the situation was brimming over with problems. Paul offered advice, based on a long and varied experience, for a solution. Chapter 2 begins with counsel to Titus on how to deal with various age groups within the membership.

1. All ages considered (vv.1-6).—As remedy for the conditions just described, rank and file church members should be exemplary in behavior. The requirements made of older men again echo those in 1 Timothy 3, there applied to bishops and deacons, and indicating that there should not be two standards in the church, but that both leaders and followers should maintain high standards. Instructions for older women reflect conditions prevailing in Crete where overindulgence in wine was common. Their conduct should be an example to the younger women of the fellowship. For younger men there is one pointed piece of advice. They are "to control themselves" (v. 6, RSV), the first clause in verse 7, "in all things," being part of Paul's message for younger men.

2. Titus himself (vv. 7-8).—As to Timothy, so here to Titus, the apostle lays heavy responsibility on a leader to set the right example.

> **7 In all things showing thyself a pattern of good works: in doctrine showing uncorruptness, gravity, sincerity,**
> **8 Sound speech, that cannot be condemned; that he that is of the contrary part may be ashamed, having no evil thing to say of you.**

II. The Gospel in Brief (Titus 2:11-14)

The fifth group recognized in the church were "servants," more correctly, slaves (vv. 9-10). We have recognized, earlier in this series, the existence of this social class within the churches, sometimes together with their masters. Slavery was an acceptable situation in the prevailing culture, and the danger was that converted slaves might translate their newfound freedom into opposition to their owners, thus creating a serious community problem. Without endorsing slavery as an institution, Paul consistently counseled slaves to remain in good relationship to their masters while he also asked for fair treatment from owners (Col. 4:1). Here the mention of slaves prompted the apostle to enlarge on the indiscriminate grace of the Lord.

> **11 For the grace of God that bringeth salvation hath appeared to all men,**
> **12 Teaching us that, denying ungodliness and worldly lusts, we should live soberly, righteously, and godly, in this present world;**
> **13 Looking for that blessed hope, and the glorious appearing of the great God and our Savior Jesus Christ;**
> **14 Who gave himself for us, that he might redeem us from all iniquity, and purify unto himself a peculiar people, zealous of good works.**

1. Divine grace (vv. 11-12).—God's grace was a favorite subject with Paul. By grace, he had been delivered from bondage to the law into freedom in Christ. When he wrote here of grace that hath "appeared to all men" he could have been thinking of slaves or of himself or of all persons, Jew and Gentile alike, who had experienced salvation by the grace of God. Again, in saying "hath appeared to all men," he made reference to the incarnation by which God's grace was embodied in a person, His Son, the Lord Jesus Christ. The purpose was to make salvation available to all in that "*whosoever* believeth in him should not perish, but have everlasting life" (John 3:16).

2. Christian response (vv. 13-14).—God's grace is free and unconditional, but by its very existence it becomes our teacher. Those who are the beneficiaries of this grace become obligated to regulate their lives so as to free them from all evil and commit them to righteous behavior. This same sanctifying influence also flows from Christ's sacrificial death by which we are called to forsake sin and become "a peculiar people," an Old Testament phrase there meaning a people who are God's personal property. The church, as the new Israel, stands in this same relationship to God (1 Pet. 2:9). A powerful incentive to sanctified living is the "blessed hope" of the coming again of our Lord who is here named "the great God and our Savior Jesus Christ" (v. 13), a clear testimony to His deity. What we are here is preparation for what we shall be when God's eternal kingdom is inaugurated.

III. Christian Relationships (Titus 3:1-8)

The Christian's "blessed hope" lies in the future. For now, we are citizens of this world where we have obligations and duties to fulfill. Otherworldliness may have value when it is expressed in separation from evil, but it must be tempered by the prayer of our Lord for His people, "I pray not that thou shouldest take them out of the world, but that thou shouldest keep them from the evil" (John 17:15).

1 Put them in mind to be subject to principalities and powers, to obey magistrates, to be ready to every good work,

2 To speak evil of no man, to be no brawlers, but gentle, showing all meekness unto all men.

3 For we ourselves also were sometimes foolish, disobedient, deceived, serving divers lusts and pleasures, living in malice and envy, hateful, and hating one another.

4 But after that the kindness and love of God our Savior toward man appeared,

5 Not by works of righteousness which we have done, but according to his mercy he saved us, by the washing of regeneration, and renewing of the Holy Ghost;

6 Which he shed on us abundantly through Jesus Christ our Savior;

7 That being justified by his grace, we should be made heirs according to the hope of eternal life.

8 This is a faithful saying, and these things I will that thou affirm constantly, that they which have believed in God might be careful to maintain good works. These things are good and profitable unto men.

1. With authorities (v. 1).—Cretans had a reputation for resisting authority. Nevertheless, the admonition to "be subject to rulers and authorities" (NRSV) is in agreement with other apostolic counsel, as, "Let every soul be subject unto the higher powers" (Rom. 13:1). It would have been destructive of the cause of Christ if believers had gained the reputation of being rebels and lawbreakers. As Paul made clear elsewhere, submission had its limits at the point where the laws of God were in conflict with the laws of people.

2. With other people (vv. 2-3).—Since the gospel would be commended to others by the conduct of those who professed it, it behooves Christians to watch what they say and do. Gossip and quarrelsomeness are to be avoided and kindness cultivated toward all. This will not be easy, for there was a time when hateful attitudes toward others controlled the behavior of Christians. But God's grace has changed all that and continues to be available as a life-transforming power.

3. With the Lord (vv. 5-8).—In these verses, the apostle summarized the gospel that he preached, not of reformation, but of regeneration. The absence of human contribution to salvation is affirmed in that "according to his mercy he saved us" (v. 5). But he also laid on the saved the obligation to "be careful to maintain good works" (v. 8). These are the believer's grateful and loving response to the grace of God expressed in the gift of the Lord Jesus Christ.

APPLYING THE LESSON

The one I love the most.—A penitent husband was trying to pacify his wife. He said, "And what little gift can I get for the one I love the most?" Unmoved, she responded, "How about some cuff links for your shirt?" Like this husband, some in the church today love themselves more than they do others. Titus had the same problem in the church at Crete.

Qualities of leaders.—A research organization polled 500 executives, asking them what traits they thought were most important in dealing with others. Five characteristics headed the list. First, a good leader is supportive, giving people the credit that is rightfully theirs. Second, a good leader is courteous, showing consideration for other people's feelings and situations. Third, a good leader is truthful, never allowing rationalization to lend support to a lie. Fourth, a good leader is clear, being careful to communicate concisely. Fifth, a good leader is generous, recognizing it is better to give than to receive.[1]

Those qualities are essential for leadership in the church as well as for leadership in the secular world. Paul urged Titus to find such persons and give them the responsibility to lead the church.

The powerful influence of a godly life.—Dick Sheppard became one of the most popular and powerful preachers in England, but as a young minister just out of seminary his arrogance at times became a roadblock to his influence. He told of a special project he took on in his first pastorate in East London. He noticed an aged man whose days often ended in drunkenness. He became aware of the suffering this man was causing his family, so Dick Sheppard decided he would convert this fellow. He talked with him over and over again. The result was nil. The man seemed bored by Dick's attempt to change him. After a few months, Dick Sheppard heard that this man had changed. He gave up the bottle, reconciled with his family, and was making a good life again. When Dick investigated the situation, he discovered that an elderly clergyman named Strickland of Bethnal Green had been visiting the alcoholic man. This old preacher was not very attractive, uneducated, and seemed to have only an insignificant ministry. Sheppard could not figure out how that old minister had been able to help the alcoholic when he with all his gifts and ability had not been able to help the man. So Sheppard visited the changed man and asked why things were so markedly improved. The only answer the man gave was to say, "Mr. Strickland used to come round day after day." Sheppard responded, "Mr. Strickland doesn't have much to say for himself, does he?" "No," was the reply, "he is a quiet man and does not always say much. But when he is gone, it seems as if Jesus of Nazareth had passed by."

Paul urged the older men in the congregation at Crete to live in such a way that when they touched someone's life, it would be as if Jesus of Nazareth had passed by.

Worth saving.—James Carter told of a young boy who was rescued from drowning by a stranger. After artificial respiration, the boy revived. As he looked into the face of the man who had saved him from the water, he responded, "Thank you, sir, for saving my life!" The man replied, "That's all right, son, glad to do it. But see to it that you're worth saving!"[2]

Paul said something similar to Titus. After we are saved, we need to live saved lives. The way for us to show our gratitude to Jesus for being our Savior is to live for Him daily as our Lord.

Responsibility of Christian citizens.—When we shun our responsibility as Christian citizens, we endanger the future of our nation. Martin Niemoller's words about what happened in pre-World War II Germany are insightful. He said, "In Germany they came first for the Communists, and I didn't speak up because I wasn't a Communist. Then they came for the Jews, and I didn't speak up because I wasn't a Jew. Then they came for the trade unionists, and I didn't speak up because I wasn't a trade unionist. Then they came for the Catholics, and I didn't speak up because I was a Protestant. Then they came for me, and by that time no one was left to speak up."[3]

TEACHING THE CLASS

Main Idea: Difficult situations demand witness through exemplary faithfulness to Christ.

Suggested Teaching Aim: Learners will determine how they can witness about the things of God in difficult situations.

Introduce the Bible Study

Use information from *Studying the Bible* to introduce Titus and this writing to him from Paul. Describe the adverse conditions under which Titus ministered and witnessed.

Ask: Are there any places today where it is equally difficult to witness and minister? Continue by asking: Where and in what circumstances is it particularly difficult for you personally to witness or minister to others? Why? Elicit response and discussion.

Invite learners to turn in their Bibles to Titus 2 to begin to learn some suggestions and instructions Paul offered for witnessing in difficult situations.

Search for Biblical Truth

Share the comments titled "The one I love the most" (*Applying the Lesson*). Note that these were the kind of people to whom Titus had a ministry. Share information from *Studying the Bible* about verses 1-10 of Titus 2. Use the comments titled "Qualities of leaders" (*Applying the Lesson*).

A Teaching Outline

1. Identify situations in which it is difficult to witness and minister.
2. Discover Paul's instruction to Titus for ministry in difficult situations.
3. Determine more effective ways to witness and minister in learners' own difficult situations.
4. Determine to continue their effort to witness and minister even when situations are very difficult.

Note that Paul included words of instructions to Titus himself. Invite a learner to read verses 7-8 aloud. Ask: What was Paul's instruction? Continue by asking: How does a godly life such as that described by Paul for Titus to model provide a witness? Elicit response. Call attention to verse 8b. Share comments titled "The powerful influence of a godly life" (*Applying the Lesson*).

Share comments titled "Worth saving" (*Applying the Lesson*). Note that Paul said similar words to Titus in verses 11-14 of chapter two. Call on a learner to read the words aloud. Continue by asking: How does this kind of response to the gift of salvation provide witness even in difficult situations?

Note that in the final section of Scripture for our study, Titus 3:1-8, Paul gave instructions for behavior with authorities, with other people, and with the Lord. Direct learners to read the verses to themselves and be prepared to report Paul's instructions in these areas. Call for response when the reading is finished. Share information from *Studying the Bible* about these verses. Share the comments titled "Responsibility of Christian citizens" (*Applying the Lesson*).

Give the Truth a Personal Focus

Ask learners to recall the situations in their own lives in which they find it difficult to witness and minister. Ask further: What ideas do Paul's words to Titus give you for increasing your effectiveness in witnessing in these situations? Elicit response. (Make certain that the conclusions are practical and can be used in the everyday lives of learners.)

Conclude with prayer inviting learners to commit to continued witness and ministry in the difficult situations in their lives because of their love for and commitment to their Lord.

---

1. *Bits and Pieces,* vol. D/2A, 6.
2. James E. Carter, *Help for the Evangelistic Preacher* (Nashville: Broadman Press, 1985), 136.
3. C. Welton Gaddy, *Profile of a Christian Citizen* (Nashville: Broadman Press, 1974), 40.

Index

The following index gives the lesson date on which a particular passage of Scripture has been treated in BROADMAN COMMENTS from September 1986 through August 1992. Since the International Bible Lessons, Uniform Series, are planned in six-year cycles, the lessons during any six consecutive years include the better-known books and passages on central teachings. Thus, anyone who has access to the 1985-91 volumes of COMMENTS can use this index to find a discussion of almost any part of the Bible he or she may be interested in studying.

January 19

Protecting the Helpless

Basic Passages: Genesis 1:28a; Exodus 1:15—2:10; Deuteronomy 18:10a; Psalm 139:13-15; Matthew 18:10,14; 19:14-15

Focal Passages: Genesis 1:28a; Deuteronomy 18:10a; Psalm 139:13-15; Matthew 18:10,14; 19:14-15

According to the teaching of Scripture, children are a gift from God to be cherished, protected, and raised to walk in His ways. In God's original purpose, this solemn responsibility was assigned to parents, and it remains so though often neglected. Serious threats to family life have come with the abandonment of moral and spiritual values that prevails so much today. One of these threats is that responsibility for children has been assumed by others. For a long time, this responsibility was seen to extend from birth to approaching adulthood. The conviction is growing, especially among Christian people, that concern for the child should predate birth and relate to the unborn child when life is most vulnerable. Unfortunately, the widespread decline in ethical standards has resulted in a growing resort to the practice of abortion whereby the life of an unborn child is violently ended before it has opportunity for fulfillment. Society has divided itself into pro-life and pro-choice groups imposing on Christians the duty of determining where they stand on a vitally important issue.

Study Aim: *To determine, in the light of the teaching of God's Word, where we stand as individuals on the question of abortion*

STUDYING THE BIBLE

The Bible is the Christian's authority for determining the difference between right and wrong. We should not expect to find in its pages explicit prohibitions and condemnations on every issue we face, but we do find there great and far-reaching principles that enable us to know the will of God in every eventuality. Thus we are enabled to resolve our own attitudes and behavior as persons committed to love and obey God. Moreover, we also have in the Bible the example and teaching of our Lord and Savior Jesus Christ.

I. God the Creator of Life (Gen. 1:28a; Ps. 139:13-15)

Biblical faith requires the acknowledgment that God is the Creator of all things. Every living creature owes its existence to Him. After the original work of creation was completed, God ordained that the man and woman He had made should cooperate with Him in the perpetuation of the human race. He placed His blessing on them as He charged them, "Be fruitful, and multiply," a charge that resulted in the births of Cain and Abel (Gen. 4:1-2), and later Seth (v. 25) who, in turn, became the father of Enos (v. 26). Thus the future of the race was ensured. The following is from Genesis 1.

> **28 And God blessed them, and God said unto them, Be fruitful, and multiply, and replenish the earth, and subdue it.**

The processes of birth, whether in humans or animals, are mysterious and wonderful. Israel's great psalmist, David, contemplated this in Psalm 139. He wrote:

> **13 For thou hast possessed my reins: thou hast covered me in my mother's womb.**
> **14 I will praise thee; for I am fearfully and wonderfully made: marvellous are thy works; and that my soul knoweth right well.**
> **15 My substance was not hid from thee, when I was made in secret, and curiously wrought in the lowest parts of the earth.**

The psalmist acknowledged that God had formed ("possessed") his vital organs ("reins") and that like a complicated piece of tapestry He had "knit me together in my mother's womb" (NRSV). This was a staggering thought that caused the inspired writer to break forth in praise to God (v. 14). The development of the unborn child goes on unseen by human eyes, but not unseen by the Creator who marks its progress within the mother, hidden from sight as though "in the lowest parts of the earth." Earlier in this same psalm, the writer had exclaimed, "Such knowledge is too wonderful for me; it is high, I cannot attain unto it" (v. 6). Contemplation of the wonders of procreation should induce in all of us a sense of the sacredness of life and a realization that any arbitrary interference with God's creative work is wrong.

II. God's Concern for Children (Matt. 18:10,14)

The background material from Exodus 1:15—2:10 covers the story of the escape from death of the infant Moses. When Pharaoh plotted the death of every male Hebrew child, Moses' mother hid him in the bulrushes where his sister watched over him. He was found by Pharaoh's daughter who adopted him as her son, thus preparing him for the leadership role he was to assume in behalf of his people. In his review of Israel's history, in which He traced the outworking of divine purpose, Stephen included this incident in which a young life was spared for a future purpose (Acts 7:20-21). God used persons, family members, and an Egyptian princess to protect young Moses for a future mission. Surely God expects us to do what we can to protect and nurture today's children. Our Lord spoke to this subject in the following verses:

10 Take heed that ye despise not one of these little ones; for I say unto you, That in heaven their angels do always behold the face of my Father which is in heaven.

....

14 Even so it is not the will of your Father which is in heaven, that one of these little ones should perish.

Matthew 18 begins by telling how our Lord "called a little child unto him" (v. 2) and then spoke (vv. 7-14) of the tragic possibility of mistreating "one of these little ones" (v. 10). The record of what He said was released to a world where, in many places, the rights of children were ignored. Jesus affirmed His Father's concern for children who have their advocates (angels) in heaven itself. But He knew that the interests of children need protecting in this world, and so He charged His disciples to do nothing detrimental to a child. More positively He said, "Whoso shall receive one such little child in my name receiveth me" (v. 5). Young children are defenseless and should have the protective care of parents and others. But more defenseless still are the unborn who call for the protection of those who share God's estimate of the value of child life. Abortion is surely a grievous violation of His will and a frustration of His purpose.

III. God's Concern, Our Responsibility (Deut. 18:10a; Matt. 19:14-15)

The Book of Deuteronomy contains three messages given by Moses to the people of Israel prior to their entry into Canaan. There they would be exposed to pagan practices including things as depraved and devilish as the sacrifice of young children. So, as a warning against being entrapped by this horrendous practice, Moses said, in 18:10:

10 There shall not be found among you any one that maketh his son or his daughter to pass through the fire.

This repeated a similar prohibition, given in 12:31, where P. C. Craigie made this comment, "To assume the right to sacrifice a child was to assume a prerogative that was God's alone, the prerogative over human life."[1] This comment also applies to the current evil of abortion. In spite of Moses' warning, there were cases of child sacrifice in Israel's history leading to the defeat and extinction of the Northern Kingdom. "They caused their sons and their daughters to pass through the fire, . . . Therefore the Lord was very angry with Israel, and removed them out of his sight" (2 Kings 17:17-18). God will not tolerate attitudes toward children that cause people to treat them as of no value and expose them to cruelty and even death. Part of the mission of His Son was to alert us to the importance of children to whom He extended His tender loving care, as in Matthew 19:14-15:

14 But Jesus said, Suffer little children, and forbid them not, to come unto me: for of such is the kingdom of heaven.
15 And he laid his hands on them, and departed thence.

In the midst of His busy ministry, children had been brought to Jesus for His blessing. The disciples, doubtless thinking that they were protecting their Master from needless interference, rebuked those who brought the children. Aware of what had happened, Jesus in turn rebuked the disciples whom He told to allow the children to come to Him and put no hindrance in their way, for, He said, "of such is the kingdom of heaven." Here He picked up a thought already expressed in 18:1-6 where He said that childlikeness (humility, simplicity, teachability) is a necessary quality in all, of whatever age, who would enter God's kingdom. His high tributes to childhood place an obligation of caring and protectiveness on all who are His followers. Sunday Schools came into existence as a response to this obligation, as did orphanages and other institutions that minister to the needs of children, especially when they are in circumstances of acute helplessness.

IV. Concern Calls for Action

Throughout the world today there is a wave of concern for children of the Third World, multitudes of whom are starving and dying. Secular agencies and entertainment personalities are active in providing food and medical care for these afflicted boys and girls. But what of children who are being denied the right to live? Our study has provided evidence of the concern of the Creator for the welfare of all children. It has also confronted us with the teaching and example of the Lord Jesus who set high value on every life. It is incumbent on those who acknowledge Him as Savior and Lord not only to serve the needs of afflicted little ones now living, though sometimes threatened with death, but also to lend their influence against a practice that denies life to the unborn.

APPLYING THE LESSON

A child's question.—"On another occasion Luther came upon Anathasia, his four-year-old, prattling away about Christ, angels, and heaven. Whereupon the noted churchman said, 'My dear child, if only one could hold fast to this faith.' Quickly she replied, 'Why, Papa, don't you believe it?' Luther was shocked and later wrote, 'Christ has made the children our teachers.' "[2]

A speck of dust.—"A university physics professor testified that he came to the university believing he had all the answers. 'An avowed evolutionist, I knew all about *cause* and *effect*. I could begin with the present and work back. Behind every natural effect I found a natural cause.

'One day I was studying a specimen under a microscope. Suddenly I noticed a particle of dust on the lens. I asked whence came that dust. That dust was an effect for which I could find no natural cause. I had to admit that behind the dust was not a cause but the *Cause*. A speck of dust led me to God!' "[3]

God knows how.—"God has placed every part of the body so that it may function properly. Just suppose that He had placed the nose upside down. You could drown in a rainstorm. Aren't you glad God knows down to the smallest detail what He's doing?"[4]

Not enough time.—"In her syndicated column for November 11, 1971, Erma Bombeck reminded us that time hangs heavy over the heads of bored people, eludes the busy, flies by for the young, and runs out for the old. Perhaps we should view it, she counseled, through a child's eyes.

" 'When I was young, Daddy was going to throw me in the air and catch me and I would giggle until I couldn't giggle anymore; but he had to change the furnace filter, and there wasn't time.'

There is always something else to do!"[5]

Do God's will.—"In the *Sound of Music*, at the close of a frustrating day, the Reverend Mother asks Maria why she has come to the convent. Hesitating, the distraught girl replies, 'To discover and do the will of God.' "[6]

TEACHING THE CLASS

Main Idea: Christians should examine the Scripture to determine where they stand on abortion.

Suggested Teaching Aim: Learners will examine several Scriptures and decide where they stand on abortion.

Introduce the Bible Study

Many times children exercise more faith than adults. Use "A child's question" (*Applying the Lesson*) to gain the learners' attention. Then use the introduction from *Studying the Bible* to introduce the Bible study.

Ask the class to find Genesis 1:28 and Psalm 139 in their Bibles.

Search for Biblical Truth

Acknowledging that God is Creator of all is to admit He is worthy of our reverence and worship. Use "A speck of dust" (*Applying the Lesson*) to show how God can use the smallest thing to bring about saving faith.

Use the following outline to guide the Bible study. Put the outline on the chalkboard or give them a copy on a piece of paper.

I. God the Creator of life (Gen. 1:28a; Ps. 139:13-15)
II. God's concern for children (Matt. 18:10,14)
III. God's concern, our responsibility
(Deut. 18:10a; Matt. 19:14-15)
IV. Concern calls for action

Read point 1 of the outline. Have one person read Genesis 1:28a and another to read Psalm 139:13-15. Ask: How does God being Creator of life affect the way we look at life? (We should see life as God sees it.) Share the information from *Studying the Bible* on this point. When discussing Psalm 139:13-15, use "God knows how" (*Applying the Lesson*).

Call attention to point 2 of the outline. Ask each person to turn to Matthew 18 and read verses 10 and 14. Ask: How does the story of God's saving of the infant Moses illustrate Matthew 18:14? (God saved Moses to become a great leader.) Ask: Would God want to save a baby who would never be a leader? (Point them to v. 14 again.) Use the material in *Studying the Bible* to show how children are helpless and need adult care. Show that the unborn are more helpless than the born.

A Teaching Outline

1. Introduce the subject of abortion.
2. Use an outline to lead a Scripture search.
3. Decide about abortion after a Scripture search.

Move right into point 3. Read the Scripture while learners follow in their Bibles. Use material in *Studying the Bible* to be sure what "to be burned in the fire" means. Show how child sacrifice can be compared to the results of abortion. (The child is killed.)

Jesus had time for children. He knew their potential. Ask: Why do we often approach children as if they were not important? After time for discussion, share "Not enough time" (*Applying the Lesson*). Then use information from *Studying the Bible* to speak to this question.

At this point move to number 4 in the study outline. Ask: What can we do to slow down the number of abortions in America? (Answers may range from prayer to active protest.) After a time of sharing, use "Concern calls for action" (*Studying the Bible*) to finish the lecture.

Give the Truth a Personal Focus

Ask each learner to read all the focal passages again. Ask them to answer the following questions: (1) What does God's being Creator say about abortion? (2) How does Jesus' relationship with children speak to the abortion issue? (3) Where do you stand on abortion?

Close by using "Do God's will" (*Applying the Lesson*). Urge the learners to do God's will as they understand it.

---

1. P. C. Craigie, *The Book of Deuteronomy* (Grand Rapids: Wm. B. Eerdmans Publishing Co., 1976), 220.
2. G. Curtis Jones, *1000 Illustrations for Preaching and Teaching* (Nashville: Broadman Press, 1986), 130.
3. Herschel H. Hobbs, *My Favorite Illustrations,* comp. Ronald K. Brown (Nashville: Broadman Press, 1990), 118-19.
4. Hobbs, 116.
5. Jones, 346.
6. Jones, 382.